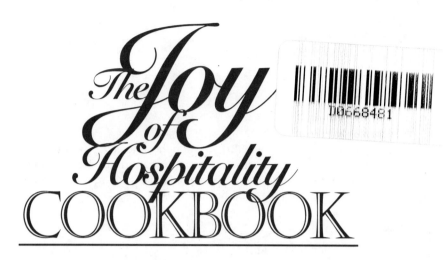

The Joy of Hospitality COOKBOOK

COMPILED AND EDITED BY

BARBARA BALL
& VONETTE BRIGHT

NewLife
PUBLICATIONS
A MINISTRY OF CAMPUS CRUSADE FOR CHRIST

The Joy of Hospitality Cookbook

Published by
NewLife Publications
A ministry of Campus Crusade for Christ
100 Sunport Lane
Orlando, FL 32809

Editing by Joette Whims.

Copyediting by Lynn Copeland.

Design and typesetting by Genesis Publications.

Cover by David Marty Design.

Printed in the United States of America.

Distributed in Canada by Campus Crusade for Christ of Canada, Surrey, B.C.

ISBN: 1-56399-077-6

Scripture quotations are from the *New International Version*, © 1973, 1984 by the International Bible Society, published by Zondervan Bible Publishers, Grand Rapids, Michigan; and from *The Living Bible*, © 1971 by Tyndale House Publishers, Wheaton, Illinois.

For more information, write:
Life Ministries—P.O. Box 40, Flemington Markets, N5W 2129, Australia
Campus Crusade for Christ of Canada—Box 300, Vancouver, B.C., V6C 2X3, Canada
Campus Crusade for Christ—Fairgate House, King's Road, Tyseley, Birmingham, B11 2AA, England
Campus Crusade for Christ—P.O. Box 8786, Auckland, New Zealand
Campus Crusade for Christ—Alexandra, P.O. Box 0205, Singapore, 9115, Singapore
Great Commission Movement of Nigeria—P.O. Box 500, Jos, Plateau State Nigeria, West Africa
Campus Crusade for Christ International—100 Sunport Lane, Orlando, FL 32809, USA

Contents

A Word From
Barbara and Vonette

Have you ever wondered, *What is hospitality? Is it entertaining with gourmet meals? Or hosting extravagant parties? Perhaps it is using a professionally decorated home to serve hors d'oeuvres and other elegant dishes.*

These are only a few of the ways we can be hospitable. True hospitality is simply treating others with Christ-like love.

The Bible describes how we should treat others through our hospitality. In the Greek language in which the New Testament was written, hospitality is defined as *love for strangers*. Romans 12:10–13 describes this kind of love:

> Be devoted to one another in brotherly love. Honor one another above yourselves. Never be lacking in zeal, but keep your spiritual fervor, serving the Lord. Be joyful in hope, patient in affliction, faithful in prayer. Share with God's people who are in need. Practice hospitality.

We like to give hospitality a broader meaning—showing love to everyone. Hospitality is more than entertaining. It is expecting God to do great things through you as you reach out to touch the lives of others. It is focusing on relationships, especially the greatest relationship of all—walking and talking with the Lord Jesus. Hospitality is a natural outflow of Christ's love for us and in us. Our response is to prayerfully consider how we can "love [our] neighbor as [ourselves]" (Matthew 22:39) through our daily lives.

Hospitality is best displayed through our homes. The home is the most important institution in the world—it is the center and builder of the family. In turn, the Christian family is the builder of the church, the foundation God established as His plan to reach the world for Christ. In the same way, the family builds the school and our government. If the home is weak, the other fundamental institutions are directly affected. No democracy can survive without biblical standards and a strong family unit.

One of the greatest contributors to the strength of the family is time together. And one of the most important times for family togetherness is over a meal. It's then that children learn basic lessons of life. Communication and bonding take place in discussions around the table as we get to know each other, work through relationships, and develop family loyalty.

The home is also one of the greatest places to share the Christian message. Many families today have no idea what a Christian home is or how satisfying a godly atmosphere can be. Christians can invite other believers into their homes for fellowship or invite nonbelievers to experience Christian family life in action. Using your home as a witness trains children for a lifestyle of evangelism that is a part of everyday life, not an occasional event.

The home is no less essential for singles. Their homes are a place for expressing their creative abilities and personality. They too have a great opportunity for showing love to others through their hospitality.

Hospitality includes all kinds of entertaining, from inviting one person in for a casual cup of tea or planning a family night, to getting together with several singles or hosting an elaborate holiday dinner. In *The Joy of Hospitality Cookbook*, we have tried to include recipes to serve almost any type of event. The recipes were contributed by Campus Crusade for Christ staff members and volunteers from all over the world. We also selected favorite recipes from two previous cookbooks published by Campus Crusade that are now out of print. Together with the best recipes from staff and volunteers, you will find just what you need to host the event you have in mind.

We encourage you to use our companion book, *The Joy of Hospitality: Fun Ideas for Evangelistic Entertaining*, to help you plan, prepare, and host many kinds of events. Included are ideas for women's, men's, children's, and youth get-togethers. You will also learn how to share your faith through entertaining and how to encourage Christians to grow in their faith.

As you begin using these recipes and inviting others into your home, we are sure you will get excited about what you are doing. This happened to both of us once we started using our homes for evangelism.

We believe the purpose for every Christian life is to bring honor and glory to our heavenly Father. Practicing hospitality does just that and brings such great rewards. As we invite others into our homes, we are delighted to see how God uses the creativity, talents, and energy that He gives us to bring honor to Him.

We hope this cookbook will enable you to make the very best use of all that God gives to you, in ability as well as material resources. We wish you well and trust that you truly will find the joy of hospitality.

KEY TO RECIPES	
◐ Easy	✪ International
♡ Healthy	📕 From *Delectable Collectibles*

Appetizers &
Beverages

Appetizers

Alice's Chili Dip

1 pound ground beef
1 onion, chopped
dash garlic salt
dash Worcestershire sauce

½ cup tomato juice
½ package chili seasoning mix
1 pound Velveeta cheese, cubed

Brown ground beef with onions; drain. Add remaining ingredients in order while cooking on low heat until cheese is melted. Serve with tortilla chips or King-size Fritos chips.

Maggie Bruehl
Special Representative, FL

Artichoke Dip

1 can artichoke hearts
8 ounces cream cheese

1 cup mayonnaise
1 cup grated Parmesan cheese

Preheat oven to 350 degrees. Thoroughly drain artichokes (squeeze out juice by hand), then cut up. Mix all ingredients and bake for 30 minutes. Serve hot with crackers.

Rita Ruzzi
Executive Ministry, FL

Artichoke Nibbles

2 6-ounce jars marinated artichoke
   hearts
1 small onion, finely chopped
1 clove garlic, minced
4 eggs, beaten
¼ cup fine bread crumbs

¼ teaspoon salt
⅛ teaspoon pepper
⅛ teaspoon oregano
⅛ teaspoon Tabasco
2 cups shredded sharp cheddar cheese
2 tablespoons minced parsley

Preheat oven to 325 degrees. Drain marinade from 1 jar of artichoke hearts
into a medium skillet. Drain and discard marinade from the second jar (or
reserve for use in salads). Chop artichokes and set aside. Add onion and
garlic to drained marinade; sauté until onion is limp, about 5 minutes. In
a bowl, combine eggs, bread crumbs, and seasonings. Fold in cheese and
parsley. Add artichokes and sautéed onion mixture; blend well.

Pour into a 9-inch square glass baking dish. Bake for about 30 minutes.
Allow to cool briefly before cutting into 1-inch squares. Serve warm or cold.
May be prepared a day or two ahead and reheated for 10–12 minutes.

Debra Brady
Staff & Ministry Opportunity, FL

Barbecue Pita Bites

1 cup shredded mozzarella cheese
½ cup chopped pepperoni
¼ cup pizza sauce
¼ cup barbecue sauce

2 packages (10 each) refrigerated
   biscuits
1 tablespoon milk
¼ cup grated Parmesan cheese

Preheat oven to 350 degrees. To prepare filling: combine mozzarella, pepperoni, pizza sauce, and barbecue sauce in small bowl. Set aside. Separate
biscuits and place on greased baking sheets. Flatten biscuits, and spoon
1 tablespoon filling into center of each biscuit. Fold biscuit in half and pinch
seams together. (Biscuits will look like half moons.) Brush with milk; sprinkle with Parmesan cheese. Bake for 12–15 minutes or until golden brown.
Serve warm.

Angela Rosa
Sunport Ministry Office, FL

Blue Cheese Ball

1 8-ounce package cream cheese
4 ounces blue cheese
1 teaspoon Worcestershire sauce
1 teaspoon garlic salt

1 large chopped sweet pickle or
  1 tablespoon sweet pickle relish
1 cup chopped parsley
¾ cup chopped pecans

Mix all ingredients except parsley and pecans. Shape into a log or ball. Roll in parsley and pecans. Wrap and refrigerate. Keeps well.

Ann Abel
Military Ministry, VA

Bruschetta

4 tomatoes
¼ onion (red or white)
1 teaspoon lemon juice
1½ teaspoons olive oil
2 tablespoons celery seed
1–2 cloves garlic, minced

parsley flakes
fresh cilantro
onion salt (optional)
1 loaf French bread
butter
garlic powder

Chop tomatoes and onions into chunks, and place in a bowl. In a separate bowl, combine lemon juice, olive oil, celery seed, and garlic. Pour over tomato mixture and stir. Add parsley, cilantro, and onion salt to taste. Refrigerate about an hour. When ready to serve, prepare the French bread with butter and garlic powder, and heat in the oven. Allow guests to spoon bruschetta mixture onto bread according to their tastes. Serves 6–8.
Optional: Melt mozzarella cheese onto the garlic bread.

Anita Evans
Campus Ministry, FL

Confess — 1 John 1:9
Receive — Ephesians 5:18
Believe — 1 John 5:14,15
Put these verses on a card in the kitchen, and ask God daily
for His infilling of the Holy Spirit. — Barbara Ball

Caviar Crown

6 hard-boiled eggs, diced
3 tablespoons mayonnaise
1–1½ cups chopped green onions
salt and pepper to taste
8 ounces cream cheese
½ cup sour cream
2 tablespoons mayonnaise

1 teaspoon horseradish
1 teaspoon Worchestershire sauce
1 teaspoon lemon juice
3½ ounces black caviar, drained
parsley for garnish
1 lemon, cut into wedges

Mix eggs with mayonnaise and spread over the bottom of a 9-inch spring-form pan. Sprinkle with onions, salt, and pepper. Mix cream cheese with the next five ingredients. Spread over egg and onion mixture and chill overnight. Before serving, remove rim of springform pan, leaving egg mixture in pan bottom. Set the bottom on a serving plate. Cover with caviar and parsley. Garnish with lemon wedges around the outside edge. Serve with crackers or a sourdough baguette.

Barbara Ball
ChurchLIFE, FL

Cheddar Cheese Ball

8 ounces cream cheese
3–4 cups grated cheddar cheese
4 green onions, chopped
2 teaspoons paprika

1 cup chopped pecans or walnuts
1 cup sliced black olives
2 teaspoons chili powder

Set aside half of the nuts, and thoroughly mix (mash) all remaining ingredients. Form into a ball. Roll the ball in the remaining nuts and chill. Serve with crackers. (These are only estimated measurements; adjust as desired.)

Melissa Niegocki
International Ministry, AZ

Do not work for food that spoils, but for food that endures to eternal life, which the Son of Man will give you (John 6:27).

Cheese Ball ◷

10 ounces Cracker Barrel sharp
   cheese, grated
2 8-ounce packages cream cheese
1 tablespoon lemon juice
1 tablespoon Worcestershire sauce

2 tablespoons chopped green pepper
2 tablespoons chopped onion
1 tablespoon chopped pimiento
pecans, chopped (optional)

Thoroughly mix all ingredients except pecans, and form two balls. If desired, roll in pecans. Wrap balls in wax paper and refrigerate until ready to serve.

Mary Canada
President's Office, FL

Cheese Fondue

2 tablespoons margarine
3 tablespoons flour
2½ cups milk
1 teaspoon caraway seeds (optional),
   soaked in hot water for 15 minutes
dash Worcestershire sauce

1 pound Swiss or cheddar cheese,
   cubed
1 teaspoon salt
1 tablespoon lemon juice
⅛ teaspoon nutmeg
French or rye bread

Melt margarine in fondue pot. Stir in flour until blended. Add milk, caraway seeds, and Worchestershire sauce. Add cheese gradually, stirring until cheese melts and mixture begins to bubble. Then add salt, lemon juice, and nutmeg. Serve with cubes of crusty French or rye bread.

Optional: Make fondue in a heavy saucepan, and keep warm over hot water; or pour fondue over bread cubes for individual servings.

Karen Horsey
International Ministry, FL

Cheese Rounds

8 ounces sharp cheddar cheese, grated
1 cup margarine

2 cups sifted flour
2 cups Rice Krispies
dash cayenne pepper

Preheat oven to 350 degrees. Mix ingredients well; shape into 1-inch balls, and flatten with a fork. Bake on non-stick baking sheet for 15 minutes. Cool slightly before removing. Freezes well.

Jane Prall
Crusade Family

Chicken Dip

2–3 chicken breasts
8 ounces cream cheese

1 can cream of mushroom soup
2 ounces sliced almonds, toasted

Boil the chicken, cool, then shred. In a saucepan over low to medium heat, blend cream cheese and cream of mushroom soup. Add chicken and toasted almonds. Serve warm with chips or crackers.

Linda Ferrante
Computer Services, FL

Chicken Waldorf Sandwiches

1 20-ounce can crushed pineapple, drained well
2 whole chicken breasts, cooked, skinned, and cut into chunks
1 cup walnut or pecan pieces
1 cup sliced celery

⅓ cup sliced green onion
1 cup non-fat sour cream
1 tablespoon poppy seeds (optional)
½ teaspoon vanilla extract
sweet hot mustard to taste
cinnamon/sugar mix to taste

In large bowl, combine pineapple, chicken, nuts, celery, and onion. In a small bowl, whisk together sour cream, poppy seeds, vanilla, mustard, and cinnamon/sugar mixture. Pour over chicken and toss well. Serve with pita bread or as a dip with crackers.

Cindy Bogan
JESUS Film Project, FL

Chili Con Queso
(Mexican Fondue)

1 cup stewed tomatoes or tomato sauce	chilies or cayenne pepper to taste
	24 slices American cheese

Heat tomatoes and chilies in a fondue pot. Add cheese one slice at a time. When heated, serve with an assortment of "dunkers" such as carrot strips, celery, cauliflower, corn chips, tortillas, bread sticks, and bread cubes.

Karen Horsey
International Ministry, FL

Cocktail Franks

1 can cranberry sauce	¼ cup water
1 jar Heinz chili sauce	2 pounds cocktail franks
¼ cup brown sugar	

In saucepan over low heat, melt the cranberry sauce. Add chili sauce, brown sugar, and water. Bring to a boil. Place cocktail franks in a crock pot, and pour the sauce mixture on top. Cook on low setting for 6 hours. Serve in a chafing dish.

Turner Middleton
New Life Resources, GA

Crabby Cheese Snacks

½ cup butter	1 tablespoon seasoning salt
1 jar Old English cheddar cheese	dash garlic salt
1 can crab meat	English muffins

Preheat oven to 400 degrees. Combine the first 5 ingredients and mix well. Slice English muffins in half. Spread mixture on muffins and cut into quarters. Place on a cookie sheet and bake for 10–15 minutes.

Donna Knopf
International Ministry, FL

Crab Pizza Appetizer

8 ounces cream cheese
1 tablespoon Worcestershire sauce
1 tablespoon lemon juice
2 tablespoons mayonnaise
1 small onion, finely chopped

dash garlic salt
3 tablespoons horseradish
½ bottle chili sauce
3 ounces crab meat
parsley, chopped

Cream well the first 6 ingredients, and spread on the bottom of a serving dish about 8 inches in diameter. Layer horseradish, chili sauce, and crab meat on top. Sprinkle with parsley and refrigerate for 1 hour. Serve with crackers.

Barbara Ball
ChurchLIFE, FL

Each of us should please his neighbor for his good, to build him up (Rom. 15:2).

Curry Dip

1 cup mayonnaise
1 teaspoon vinegar
1 teaspoon curry powder

1 teaspoon horseradish sauce
1 teaspoon diced onion
¾ teaspoon garlic salt

Mix and serve with vegetables.

Crystal Keller
Computer Services, FL

Denise's Fruit Dip

7 ounces marshmallow creme
3 ounces cream cheese (light
    works well)

1 teaspoon lemon juice
orange juice (optional)

Mix marshmallow creme and cream cheese in mixer until smooth. Blend in lemon juice. Serve with apple slices, strawberries, bananas, or grapes. To keep the sliced apples and bananas fresh, dip them into orange juice.

Bev Coggins
Church Dynamics, MD

Dip-In-A-Loaf

1 large or 2 small round unsliced
    bread loaves
3 8-ounce packages cream cheese,
    softened
1 onion, finely chopped

¼ pound pastrami, sliced thin and
    chopped
½ teaspoon pepper
¼ cup Italian dressing

Preheat oven to 250 degrees. Slice loaf across top and hollow out. Combine remaining ingredients and put inside loaf. Replace top. Tightly wrap in foil, and bake for 1½ hours. Serve with bread pieces and your favorite crackers.

Carol Varner
Student Venture, MO

Donna's Fiesta Dip

8 ounces Monterey jack cheese with
    jalapeño peppers
4 ounces longhorn cheddar cheese,
    shredded
2 cloves garlic, minced

½ cup mayonnaise
2 cans artichoke hearts, drained and
    mashed
grated Parmesan cheese

Preheat oven to 350 degrees. Mix all ingredients except Parmesan cheese. Spread into a greased 9×13-inch baking dish. Sprinkle with Parmesan cheese and bake for 30 minutes. Broil to brown if desired. Serve hot with tortilla chips.

Sue McDaniel
International Ministry, FL

Easy Cheesy Nachos

1 can Hormel chili
3 ounces cream cheese
1 bag tortilla chips (round
    work best)

shredded cheese
Optional toppings: sour cream,
    sliced black olives, diced
    tomatoes, onions

Microwave chili and cream cheese in medium bowl. Place chips on a plate, and top with spoonfuls of chili mixture. Sprinkle with cheese. Microwave

1 minute. Top as desired. *Variation:* For a low-fat version, substitute Hormel turkey chili, light cream cheese, reduced-fat chips, low-fat shredded cheese, and low-fat sour cream.

Lin Newman
Athletes in Action, WI

Easy Homemade Salsa

1 small to medium onion, chopped
½ clove garlic, minced
1 green bell pepper, chopped
1 fresh or 1 jar jalapeño peppers, chopped

2 cans diced tomatoes with green chilies
Louisiana hot sauce

In a small, dry saucepan, sauté onion, garlic, bell pepper, and jalapeño pepper. Cook until onion is clear, and set aside to cool. In a large bowl, pour two cans diced tomatoes and green chilies. Stir in saucepan mixture and mix well. Add Louisiana hot sauce to taste (use approximately 1 tablespoons for mild and 2 tablespoons for hot). Chill in refrigerator for 1 hour. Serve with tortilla chips.

Stephanie Farris
Campus, KY

Share with God's people who are in need. Practice hospitality (Rom. 12:13).

Easy Stuffed Mushrooms

18 medium mushroom caps
butter, melted
3 ounces cream cheese

¼ cup grated Parmesan cheese
2 tablespoons milk
almond slivers

Preheat oven to 350 degrees. Remove mushroom stems. Place mushroom caps upside down on a baking sheet and brush with butter. Mix cheeses and milk, and fill caps. Garnish with almond slivers. Bake for 15 minutes.

Alison Druckemiller
Keynote Communications, IN

Georgia Cheese Ring

2 pounds sharp cheddar cheese,
   grated
1 cup minced onion
½ cup chopped pecans

1¼ cup mayonnaise
½ teaspoon salt
½ teaspoon pepper

Mix all ingredients. Refrigerate mixture in an airtight container for 24 hours. Form into the desired shape (a Jell-O mold works well). Serve with crackers.

Turner Middleton
New Life Resources, GA

Herb Spread

1 cup butter
1 tablespoon dehydrated onion
1 tablespoon dehydrated parsley

1 teaspoon sweet basil
2 tablespoons grated Parmesan
   cheese

Soften butter and combine with remaining ingredients. Spread on party rye or Melba toast. Broil and serve.

Charlotte Day
Crusade Family

Holiday Cheese Ball

2 3-ounce packages cream cheese
10 ounces Cracker Barrel extra
   sharp cheddar cheese
1 onion, diced

2 stalks celery, diced
fresh parsley, finely chopped
chopped pecans

Warm cheeses to room temperature, then mix them together. Use a mixer to add onion and celery to cheese. Refrigerate to harden, then shape into a ball. Roll in fresh parsley and pecans.

Belva Lee
JESUS Video Project, CA

Hot and Good Cheese Dip

1 pound ground beef	2 pounds Velveeta, cubed
1 pound pork sausage	1 can cream of mushroom soup
1 large onion, finely chopped	1 can jalapeño relish

Brown ground beef, sausage, and onion; drain. Over medium heat, add Velveeta and the soup. Stir until cheese is melted, then add relish.

Rachael Garland
Corporate Human Resources, FL

Hot Bacon Bites

canned whole water chestnuts	bottled barbecue sauce
thinly sliced bacon	honey

Drain water chestnuts. Wrap each chestnut with half a slice of bacon and secure with a toothpick. Combine 3 parts barbecue sauce and 1 part honey. Broil bacon/water chestnut for a few minutes until bacon begins to brown and some of the fat has cooked off. Brush with barbecue sauce mixture. Broil until bacon is cooked on one side. Turn and brush with sauce again, then broil until bacon is cooked on that side. Serve hot.

Joette Whims
NewLife Publications, CA

Hot Cheese Canapes

1 stick mild Cracker Barrel cheese, grated	1 teaspoon paprika
½ cup margarine	1 cup flour
½ teaspoon salt	small stuffed olives
	cocktail sausages or wieners

Preheat oven to 400 degrees. Combine all ingredients, and mold into walnut-size balls. Stuff an olive into one side of each ball and half a cocktail sausage or piece of wiener into the other side. Bring dough up to cover olives and meat. Place on ungreased cookie sheet, and bake for 8 minutes. Serve piping hot. Makes 3–4 dozen.

Charlotte Day
Crusade Family

Hot Taco Dip

2 cans refried beans
2 cans chili
1 large yellow onion, diced

2 large tomatoes, diced
½ cup shredded cheddar cheese
½ cup shredded mozzarella cheese

Preheat oven to 350 degrees. Layer ingredients in an 11×13-inch glass baking dish. Heat for 10–12 minutes until cheese is bubbly. Serve hot with tortilla chips or spread on warm tortillas.

Angela Rosa
Sunport Ministry Office, FL

Hummus
(Chickpea Dip)

1 15-ounce can chickpeas (garbanzos), drained
4–5 tablespoons Tahini (sesame seed paste)
5 tablespoons lemon juice

2–3 tablespoons olive oil
10 cloves garlic, finely chopped
1 teaspoon cumin
salt (optional)
2–3 tablespoons water (optional)

Put first six ingredients in blender; blend until mixed. Add salt if desired, and adjust other ingredients to your taste. Add water if needed. Serve with French or Italian bread cubes or fresh vegetables (carrots, cauliflower, zucchini) for dipping.

Sue Imbrock
International Ministry, FL

Layered Dip

2 9-ounce cans bean dip
1 11-ounce jar salsa
1 cup sour cream

3–4 green onions, sliced
1 4½-ounce can sliced black olives
2 cups shredded cheddar cheese

Spread bean dip on the bottom of a serving bowl or dish. Mix salsa with sour cream, and spread over bean dip. Top with onions, olives, and cheese. Serve cold with tortilla chips.

Becky Leppard
International Ministry, FL

Mango Salsa

½ ounce (1 tablespoon) fresh ginger, finely chopped
¼ cup honey
zest of 2 limes, finely chopped
½ cup rice vinegar
2 ortega chilies, seeded and finely chopped
1–3 fresh jalapeños, seeded and finely chopped

1 bunch cilantro, stemmed and finely chopped
½ bunch fresh mint, sliced into thin strips
2 large cloves garlic, minced
1 sweet red pepper, finely chopped
½ cup fresh lime juice
2 medium mangos, medium dice
1 medium purple onion, medium dice

Place ginger, honey, lime zest, and rice vinegar in a non-corrosive saucepan. Cook over medium heat until liquid is reduced by half. Set aside to cool. Place all remaining ingredients in a bowl. Add liquid after it has cooled, and stir gently. Cover and refrigerate at least 30 minutes. Serve with grilled chicken or fish. Makes 8 servings: 75 calories; 0 g fat; 54 mg sodium. *Variation:* Papayas, peaches, or melon can be substituted for mangos.

Lois Mackey
CoMission, CA

To cook is one thing I adore.
I collect recipes galore.
I can put on a stew and be on my way
While it slow-cooks the live long day.

If I dash in, no cause to worry,
I can microwave something in a hurry.

Cooking is easy, no chance of a blunder.
But my husband does say he has cause to wonder
If all this be true without a doubt,
Why are we always eating out?

— Lois Eger

Mozzarella Dip

1 medium red Bermuda onion,
   chopped
1 package pepperoni, chopped

¼ cup grated Parmesan cheese
1 cup mayonnaise
2 cups shredded mozzarella cheese

Combine all ingredients and mix well. Serve with crackers.

Donna Knopf
International Ministry, FL

New York Cheese Ball

1½ pounds Velveeta cheese
2 3-ounce packages cream cheese
2 tablespoons Durkee's salad
   dressing

½ cup chopped pecans
1½ cloves garlic, finely crushed
chili powder
Ritz crackers

Mix the first 5 ingredients in a blender. With dampened hands, shape mixture into balls or logs and roll in chili powder. Place in the center of a platter, and surround with warmed Ritz crackers.

Carol Williams
Crusade Family

Nuts & Bolts

1 pound butter or margarine, *divided*
2 teaspoons beau monde
2 teaspoons seasoning salt
1 teaspoon marjoram
1 teaspoon summer savory
½ teaspoon garlic powder
½ teaspoon onion powder
⅛ teaspoon cayenne pepper
parsley flakes

1 box Cheerios
1 box Rice Chex
1 box Corn Chex
1 box Wheat Chex
2 cups pretzel sticks
3 cups salted peanuts
1 cup pecans
2 cups mixed nuts

Preheat oven to 300 degrees. Melt half the butter and add spices. Pour over dry ingredients and mix well. Put into shallow baking pan; dot remaining butter on top. Bake for 1 hour, stirring occasionally.

Cindy Bogan
JESUS Film Project, FL

Olive-Cheese Snacks

1 5-ounce jar bacon cheese
4 tablespoons butter or margarine
dash hot pepper sauce
dash Worcestershire sauce

¾ cup sifted flour
1 4½-ounce jar medium-size stuffed
    olives (or ripe olives)

Preheat oven to 400 degrees. Blend cheese and margarine until light and fluffy. Add hot pepper sauce and Worcestershire sauce; mix well. Stir in flour; mix to form a dough. Shape around olives, using about one teaspoon of dough for each. Place on an ungreased baking sheet. Bake for 12–15 minutes or until golden brown. Makes about 30.

Jerri Younkman
International School of Theology, CA

Oriental Chicken Wings

3 pounds chicken wings
2 eggs, slightly beaten
1 cup flour
½ cup butter or margarine
½ cup vinegar

3 tablespoons soy sauce
3 tablespoons water
⅔ cup sugar
½ teaspoon salt or seasoning salt

Preheat oven to 350 degrees. Cut wings in half at the joint. Dip in egg, then in flour. Fry in butter until crisp and brown. Place wings in a shallow roasting pan. To make sauce, combine vinegar, soy sauce, water, sugar, and salt. Pour sauce over wings, and bake for 30 minutes. Baste occasionally during cooking. Serve warm or cold.

Sue Imbrock
International Ministry, FL

Roquefort Tomato Vegetable Dip

½ cup salad oil
4 ounces (½ cup) Roquefort cheese
1 clove garlic (or 2 teaspoons
    garlic powder)
½ teaspoon salt

½ teaspoon paprika
1 tablespoon lemon juice
8 ounces tomato sauce
¼ cup Heinz chili sauce

Blend all ingredients in a blender. Use as a dip for radishes, cauliflower, celery sticks, carrot strips, and raw turnips.

Carol Williams
Crusade Family

Salsa

4 pounds fresh tomatoes, chopped
4–5-ounces chopped jalapeño peppers (or 2 fresh)
4–5 ounces chopped green bell pepper (or half a fresh pepper)
1 medium yellow onion, chopped
½ bunch cilantro, stemmed and chopped

1 tablespoon salt
2 teaspoons sugar
1 teaspoon cumin
1 tablespoon crushed red pepper
¼ cup vinegar
2–3 cloves garlic, minced
8 ounces tomato paste (optional)

Mix all ingredients except tomato paste and refrigerate. Adjust amounts to taste. Tomato paste may be added to thicken.

Jane Hursch
World Changers Radio, FL

Sausage Balls

1 pound hot breakfast sausage
2 cups Bisquick

8 ounces sharp cheddar cheese, shredded

Preheat oven to 350 degrees. Mix all ingredients in a large bowl (it's easiest to use your hands). Shape into small balls and bake for 20 minutes.

Cherie Allen/Malinda Collins
CoMission, FL/Church Dynamics, CA

> *Never be lacking in zeal, but keep your spiritual fervor, serving the Lord (Rom. 12:11).*

Sausage Cheese Balls

3 cups flour
1½ teaspoons salt
1½ teaspoons baking powder
¾ teaspoon baking soda

6 tablespoons shortening
8 ounces cheddar cheese, grated
1 pound sausage

Preheat oven to 375 degrees. Cut together flour, salt, baking powder, soda, and shortening until it looks like meal. Mix with cheese and sausage to make a stiff dough. Pinch off to make balls. Place in an ungreased pan, and bake for 15 minutes until brown.

Jill Coble
International Ministry, Africa

Seafood Spread

2 8-ounce packages low-fat cream
   cheese
8 ounces flaked crab or imitation
   crab meat
2 tablespoons finely chopped onion

1 tablespoon horseradish
1 teaspoon Worcestershire sauce
4–5 drops Tabasco
¼ cup finely chopped walnuts
paprika

Preheat oven to 375 degrees. With an electric mixer, beat cream cheese 1–2 minutes until creamy. Blend remaining ingredients except walnuts and paprika. Spread mixture in a 9-inch pie plate. Top with walnuts and sprinkle with paprika. Bake uncovered for 20 minutes or until golden brown. Makes approximately 3 cups.

Michelle Treiber
NewLife Publications, FL

As God's partners, we beg you not to toss aside this
marvelous message of God's great kindness (2 Cor. 6:1).

Seven-Layer Dip

1 can refried beans	¼ cup chopped onion
Guacamole	½ cup sliced black olives
1 tomato, chopped	tortilla chips
6 ounces cheese, shredded	

Layer all ingredients but the chips in order given on a platter, placing each layer ½-inch from edge of previous layer. Arrange tortilla chips around outer layer.

Guacamole:

1 avocado, mashed	½ teaspoon lemon juice
¾ cup sour cream	

Blend all ingredients.

Sus Schmitt
Computer Services, FL

Shrimp Dip

8 ounces cream cheese	3 tablespoons chili sauce
¼ cup Miracle Whip	1 small can shrimp, drained and
3 tablespoons minced onion	flaked well

Blend cheese and Miracle Whip; add onion and chili sauce, then stir in shrimp. Serve with Ritz crackers.

Arlyne Lockard
History's Handful, CA

Shrimp Roll

1 cup (½ pound) soft margarine	2 cloves garlic, pressed
1 6-ounce can shrimp	chopped onions or almonds

Beat together margarine, shrimp, and garlic. Chill. Roll in onions or almonds; refrigerate. Slice roll like butter and spread on crackers.

André Rabe
Crusade Family

Spinach Artichoke Dip

2 packages frozen, chopped spinach
2 4-ounce jars artichokes marinated
  in oil

1 cup mayonnaise
1 cup grated Parmesan cheese

Thaw chopped spinach. Separate artichoke leaves using only the tender leaves, and set aside. (You may omit oil or add a small amount.) In a saucepan, add chopped spinach, artichokes, mayonnaise, and Parmesan cheese. Heat through. Serve with Triscuit crackers, or any other crackers or chips.

Linda Ferrante
Computer Services, FL

Spinach Balls

2 packages frozen chopped spinach
4 eggs
2 cups dry stuffing mix
¾ cup butter

½ cup grated Parmesan cheese
½ teaspoon garlic powder
½ teaspoon thyme

Preheat oven to 375 degrees. Cook spinach; drain thoroughly and allow to cool. Mix all ingredients well. Form into walnut-size balls. (At this point, you can freeze on flat sheets, then store in freezer in Ziploc bags until needed.) Bake on a greased cookie sheet for 10–15 minutes.

Wendy Hill
National Ministry, FL

Stuffed Cheese Roll

1 pound mild jalapeño Velveeta
  cheese at room temperature
8 ounces cream cheese, softened

1 4-ounce can chopped green chilies
1 4¼-ounce jar chopped pimientos
1 4¼-ounce can chopped ripe olives

Place Velveeta between two sheets of wax paper and roll into an 8×4-inch rectangle. Spread with cream cheese. Mix chilies, pimientos, and olives, and spread over the cheese mixture. Fold over the two ends to the middle. Place on a serving plate with seam side down. Serve with assorted crackers.

Barbara Ball
ChurchLIFE, FL

Sweet Party Mix

1 cup brown sugar
½ cup margarine
½ cup light corn syrup
½ teaspoon salt
½ teaspoon baking soda
1 12-ounce box Crispix cereal
1 can fancy nuts
2–3 cups pretzels and/or Cheerios

Put brown sugar, margarine, corn syrup, and salt into a 2-quart baking dish. Microwave for 2½ minutes. Stir, then cook another 2½ minutes. Add baking soda and stir until mixture bubbles. Combine cereal, nuts, and pretzels in a large paper bag. Pour caramel mixture over the top. Shake and mix well. (Cut off the top of the bag if it's too bulky.) Microwave for 1½ minutes; shake and mix well. Microwave 1½ minutes more; shake and mix well. Cool on a cookie sheet or aluminum foil.

Debbie McGoldrick
Student Venture, GA

Terri's Egg Rolls

1 can chicken
1 teaspoon Italian seasoning
⅓ cup grated cheese
½ teaspoon garlic powder
¼ teaspoon pepper
1 teaspoon sesame oil
1 tablespoon soy sauce
1 cup grated cabbage and carrots
about 14 7-inch egg roll wrappers

Mix all ingredients and stuff into egg roll wrappers. Fry until golden brown. Serve with brown sauce.

Liesl Buck
International Ministry, FL

Yummy Easy Apple Dip

8 ounces cream cheese   1 teaspoon vanilla
¾ cup brown sugar   chopped nuts (optional)

Mix and serve with apple slices.

Debbie McGoldrick
Student Venture, GA

Zesty Party Crunch

¾ cup margarine   1 16-ounce package Quaker
½ cup grated Parmesan cheese   Oat Squares cereal
1½ teaspoons Italian seasoning 1½ cups peanuts
1½ cups thin pretzel sticks

Preheat oven to 325 degrees. In a 9×13-inch baking pan, heat margarine in oven until melted. Stir in cheese and seasoning. Add pretzels, cereal, and peanuts, stirring until well coated. Bake for 20 minutes, stirring occasionally during baking. Cool. Store in a tightly covered container. Makes approximately 11 cups.

Barbara Ball
ChurchLIFE, FL

Beverages

Almond Tea

9 regular-size tea bags   1 12-ounce can frozen lemonade
8 cups boiling water   concentrate
¾ cup sugar   1–2 teaspoons almond extract

Steep the tea in boiling water. Add sugar, lemonade concentrate, and almond extract, stirring until sugar dissolves. Pour into a 1-gallon container, adding enough water to fill. Serve over ice. Makes 1 gallon.

Wendy Hill
National Ministry, FL

Banana Shake

2 ripe bananas
⅓ cup lemon juice
1 cup water

1 14-ounce can Eagle Brand
    sweetened condensed milk
2 cups crushed ice

Blend ingredients to the desired consistency, then serve. Makes approximately 5 cups.

Crystal Keller
Computer Services, FL

Best Ever Punch

2 small packages Jell-O (flavor
    determines punch color)
1 cup sugar
juice of 2 lemons
2 ounces almond extract

1 12-ounce can frozen orange juice
    concentrate
1 46-ounce can pineapple juice
ginger ale

Mix the first 6 ingredients and freeze (mixture will still be mushy). Then mash or chip mixture, and place into plastic bags. Freeze. When you're ready to make punch, empty a bag into a punch bowl and pour ginger ale over it, breaking the mixture with a serving spoon. For thinner punch, add more ginger ale.

Rachael Garland
Corporate Human Resources, FL

Bride's Punch

3 12-ounce cans frozen orange
    juice concentrate
3 12-ounce cans frozen lemonade
    concentrate

5 quarts cold water
2 quarts ginger ale, chilled
2 packages frozen strawberries
    or other fruit

Mix juice concentrates and water. Chill. Add ginger ale and berries just before serving. If desired, float a frozen fruit ring in bowl. Serves 100.
Optional: For greater economy, add prepared Kool-Aid to the punch.

Lois Mackey
CoMission, CA

Bubbling Jade Punch

1 small package lime Jell-O
1 cup hot water
2 cups cold water
1 6-ounce can frozen lemonade
   concentrate

1 cup pineapple juice
1 2-liter bottle ginger ale
1 10-ounce package frozen
   strawberries
ice cubes

Dissolve Jell-O in hot water. Add cold water, lemonade, and pineapple juice; blend well. Just before serving, add ginger ale, strawberries, and ice cubes. *Optional:* For a bubbling and smoking effect, place a small piece of dry ice on aluminum foil and float in punch bowl. Serves 25.

Lois Mackey
CoMission, CA

Christmas Cheer

1 quart apple cider or apple juice
2 cups orange juice
½ cup lemon juice

½ package red hot candies
cinnamon sticks (optional)

Mix juices and candies over low heat, stirring occasionally until candies melt. Pour into cups and garnish with cinnamon sticks. Serves 8.

Ann Tormanen
International Ministry, FL

Cranberry-Raspberry Cooler

2 cups Ocean Spray Cran-Raspberry
   drink
2 cups orange sherbet

1 teaspoon lemon juice
lime slices

Place all ingredients in blender, and blend on high until smooth and slushy. Pour into tall glasses; garnish with lime slices. Makes four 8-ounce servings.

Ginni Christopher
Executive Ministry, FL

Cranberry Tea

4 cups or 1 pound fresh cranberries
2½ quarts water, *divided*
2 scant cups sugar

1 cup orange juice
30 whole cloves

Cook cranberries and cloves in 2 quarts water until cranberries all pop; strain. Save juice and discard cranberries and cloves. Dissolve sugar in 2 cups water and add to cranberry juice. Stir in orange juice. Serve hot. (If drink is too thick or strong, add plain tea.) Serves 12.

Marilyn Heavilin
Crusade Family

Frosty Cocorange Juice

crushed ice
orange juice

½ can coconut cream

Fill blender half full with crushed ice. Pour orange juice in blender to ¾ capacity, then add coconut cream. Blend until slushy.

Debbie McGoldrick
Student Venture, GA

Hot Cranberry Punch

1 pound fresh cranberries
2 quarts water
2 tablespoons grated orange peel
6 cinnamon sticks

12 whole cloves
4 cups orange juice
1 cup lemon juice
½ cup sugar

Combine cranberries, water, orange peel, cinnamon sticks, and cloves in large saucepan. Cook until cranberries are soft. Cool and strain. In saucepan, heat cranberry juice mixture, orange and lemon juices, and sugar to boiling. Serve hot. Makes about ¾ gallon.

Wendy Hill
National Ministry, FL

Hot Spiced Tea

1 teaspoon whole cloves
1 cinnamon stick
½ teaspoon allspice
1 gallon water
2½ tablespoons tea leaves or
   3 tea bags

1 6-ounce can (or more) frozen
   orange juice concentrate
1 6-ounce can frozen lemonade
   concentrate
1½ cups sugar

Tie spices loosely in a cheesecloth bag, and bring to a boil in water. Add tea tied loosely in a bag, and steep for 5 minutes. Remove bags; add juice concentrates and sugar. Bring to a boil, then serve. (For a spicier taste, return bag of spices to steep.) May be made ahead and stored in refrigerator; reheat when ready to serve.

Dorothy Brooks
Here's Life America, MA

Lime-Raspberry Punch

1 12-ounce can frozen limeade
   concentrate or 2 packages
   Kool-Aid

2 bottles ginger ale
1 quart raspberry sherbet
ice cubes

Combine all ingredients in a bowl, and blend with a mixer. Pour into ice-filled glasses. Serves 30.

Lois Mackey
CoMission, CA

Jesus said to them, "Can you drink the cup I am going to drink?"
(Matt. 20:22).

Mocha Coffee Mix

1 cup dry milk powder	¼ cup brown sugar
¾ cup sugar	1 teaspoon cinnamon
¾ cup powdered non-dairy creamer	¼ teaspoon salt
½ cup unsweetened cocoa	¼ teaspoon nutmeg
⅓ cup instant coffee, pressed through fine sieve	boiling water

Combine all dry ingredients in a large container. Dissolve ¼ cup of mixture in ¾ cup of boiling water.

Ethel Opie
Church Dynamics International, CA

God has given each of you some special abilities; be sure to use them to help each other, passing on to others God's many kinds of blessings (1 Peter 4:10).

Party Pineapple Punch

1 46-ounce can unsweetened pineapple juice, chilled	1 ounce almond extract
	1 quart ginger ale, chilled

Mix all ingredients in a punch bowl, and add ice or an ice ring.

Nina Locke
Crusade Family

Party Punch   ○

1 tablespoon almond extract	1½ cups sugar
1 46-ounce can pineapple juice	1 liter ginger ale, chilled
1 quart cranberry juice cocktail	

Mix first four ingredients. Pour into a mold and freeze until very icy. When ready to serve, place icy mixture into a punch bowl and pour ginger ale over it.

Brenda Morrow
ChurchLIFE, NC

Pineapple Wassail

4 cups pineapple juice
4 cups apple juice
3 cups orange juice

3 cinnamon sticks, broken
1 teaspoon whole cloves

Heat all ingredients to a boil, and simmer 20 minutes. Makes approximately 10 servings.

Maggie Bruehl
Special Representative, FL

I was hungry and you gave me something to eat, I was thirsty and you gave me something to drink (Matt. 25:35).

Prudence's Party Punch

1 46-ounce can unsweetened
    pineapple juice
4 bananas, mashed
2 12-ounce cans frozen orange juice
    concentrate

3 cups water
juice of 3 lemons
3 23-ounce bottles sparkling apple
    cider

Blend all ingredients except the sparkling apple cider. Freeze overnight.
Thaw at room temperature 2 to 3 hours, then add cider just before serving.

Mary Graham
Women Today International, FL

Punch Base

1 12-ounce can frozen orange juice
    concentrate
3 12-ounce cans frozen limeade
    concentrate
2 12-ounce cans frozen lemonade
    concentrate
2 quarts cranberry juice

2 46-ounce cans pineapple juice
4 quarts water
1 large package raspberry or
    strawberry Jell-O
ginger ale
sugar (optional)

To make base, combine juice concentrates, juices, water, and Jell-O mix. To serve punch, mix 2 quarts punch base and 2 quarts ginger ale. Add more water if needed and sugar to taste. *Optional:* To make a green punch, substitute apple juice for the cranberry juice and lime or apple Jell-O for red Jell-O.

Lois Mackey
CoMission, CA

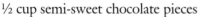

Real French Chocolate

½ cup semi-sweet chocolate pieces
½ cup white corn syrup
¼ cup water

1 teaspoon vanilla
1 pint whipping cream
2 quarts milk

Blend chocolate, syrup, and water over low heat until melted. Pour into a cup and refrigerate until cool. Add vanilla. In a large bowl, whip cream at medium speed, then gradually add chocolate mixture. Continue beating until mixture mounds. Spoon into a serving bowl, such as a punch bowl, and chill. Scald the milk, and pour it into a heated coffee pot. Spoon about 2 tablespoons of the chocolate cream mixture into each cup and pour hot milk over chocolate. Stir. Serves 16.

Lee Etta Lappen Dickerson
Prayer Works, AZ

Russian Tea

16 cups water
10 tea bags
3 cinnamon sticks
2 teaspoons whole cloves
2 cups sugar

1 cup lemon juice
1 46-ounce can pineapple juice
1 6-ounce can frozen orange juice
    concentrate

In a large pan, boil water, tea bags, cinnamon, and cloves. Steep for 15 minutes. Add sugar and juices. Serve hot or cold.

Donna Knopf
International Ministry, FL

Spiced Holiday Tea

2 cups Tang	1 package lemonade mix
2 cups sugar	2 teaspoons cinnamon
½ cup instant tea	2 teaspoons ground cloves

Mix ingredients and store in an air-tight container. Add 2 tablespoons dry mixture with boiling water in a cup for a single serving, or prepare in a crock pot for a party. Float sliced fruit such as oranges or apples on top for a sweet aroma.

Mary Canada
President's Office, FL

Strawberry-Orange Cooler

1 10-ounce box frozen strawberries, thawed	1 liter ginger ale
	crushed ice
1 12-ounce can frozen orange juice concentrate	

Purée strawberries in their juice. Strain out seeds and add orange juice concentrate. Gently stir in ginger ale and crushed ice to taste.

Joette Whims
NewLife Publications, CA

Swedish Egg Coffee

10–12 cups water	1 egg
1 cup regular-grind coffee	1 cup ice cold water

Bring water to a boil and remove from heat. In a small bowl, mix coffee and egg. Add a little hot water to coffee and egg mixture, then pour mixture into hot water. Stir and heat until it comes to a rolling boil. Remove from heat and pour in 1 cup of ice cold water. Let set for 10 minutes before serving. (The egg and grounds settle to the bottom, leaving the coffee a dark honey color.)

Howard Ball
ChurchLIFE, FL

Switzel

½–2 teaspoons apple cider vinegar   cold water
pinch of ginger

Old-fashioned Switzel, a refreshing hot-weather drink, is made by adding a small amount of apple cider vinegar and a pinch of ginger to a glass of cold water. In the "olden days," this was often carried to the harvesters working in the fields. A good rule to follow in the use of Switzel is, if it tastes good to you, drink it.

Dorothy Gregory
Crusade Family

Wassail

4 cups water
1 cup sugar
1–3 cinnamon sticks
5 whole cloves
1 teaspoon whole allspice

1 6-ounce can frozen lemonade
   concentrate
1 12-ounce can frozen orange juice
   concentrate
2 quarts apple juice

Boil water, sugar, and spices for 10 minutes. Add lemonade and orange juice concentrates and apple juice; heat. For a holiday drink, keep a half recipe warm in a crockpot.

Sus Schmitt
Computer Services, FL

 A woman is like a tea bag. It's only when she's in hot water that you realize how strong she is. — Nancy Reagan

Watermelon Punch Korean Style

1 watermelon
1 cup water
1 cup sugar

1 2-liter bottle Sprite or apple cider
pine nuts

Cut off the upper half of a watermelon in a sawtooth design. With a melon baller, scoop out watermelon balls from the lower half. (Estimate how many balls you want compared to how much watermelon juice you will need for the punch; make more or fewer balls accordingly.) Boil water with sugar to make a syrup. Soak the watermelon balls in the syrup.

Scoop out the remaining watermelon, wrap it in a cloth, and squeeze the juice into a bowl. Combine the watermelon juice, syrup, and cider or Sprite. Place punch into the lower half of the watermelon shell along with the watermelon balls. Float ice cubes on top. Serve with a bowl of pine nuts to sprinkle on the punch.

Hyang Sook Kim
Finance, FL

Soups & Breads

Soups

Autumn Soup

2 15-ounce cans diced or stewed
   tomatoes
4 tablespoons beef base or
   4 beef bouillon cubes

2 quarts water
2 bay leaves
salt and pepper to taste
vegetables of your choice (optional)

Combine ingredients in a crockpot. Cook on low all day. *Optional:* Add
1½ pounds ground beef (sautéed and drained) or cut-up roast beef or
stew meat.

Debbie McGoldrick
Student Venture, GA

Avocado Soup

1 medium-size ripe avocado
1 cup light sour cream
1 teaspoon lemon juice

¼ teaspoon Tabasco
1 envelope chicken-flavored bouillon

Combine ingredients in a food processor. Process for one minute. Pour into
bowls and serve cold. Goes well with *Beef Tortillas.*

Barbara Ball
ChurchLIFE, FL

Bachelor's Chili

1½ pounds lean ground beef
3–4 onions, chopped
1 clove garlic, minced
1–3 tablespoons chili powder
⅛ teaspoon cayenne
3 whole cloves
1 bay leaf
2 teaspoons salt (or more)

1 tablespoon Worcestershire sauce
1 can tomato soup
1 can vegetable soup
vegetables of your choice, cut into bite-size pieces
4–6 cups water
1 large potato, thinly sliced
1 can kidney beans

Brown beef, onions, and garlic. Heat seasonings, Worcestershire sauce, soups, vegetables, and water in a large soup kettle. Add meat mixture and potatoes. Cover and simmer about 3 hours. Remove whole cloves and bay leaf. Add beans and heat thoroughly. Serves 10–12.

Joette Whims
NewLife Publications, CA

Beef Barley Stew

1½ pounds lean beef stew meat, cubed
1 medium onion, chopped
1 tablespoon canola oil
3 14½-ounce cans beef broth, chilled and defatted
1 cup medium pearl barley

4 (or more) medium carrots, sliced
1 teaspoon dried thyme
½ teaspoon dried marjoram
¼ teaspoon dried rosemary, crushed
¼ teaspoon pepper
2 tablespoons chopped fresh parsley

In a large Dutch oven, over medium heat, brown the meat and onion in the oil. Add broth, barley, carrots, and spices. Bring to a boil. Reduce heat; cover and simmer for 1 hour and 45 minutes (or until meat and vegetables are tender). Add parsley just before serving.

Ellen Armstrong
Board of Director's Wife

The eyes of all look to You, and You give them their food at the proper time (Psalm 145:15).

Bouillabaisse

¼ cup olive oil
1 onion
2 tablespoons fresh parsley
1 clove garlic, minced
2 leeks (white part only)
1 15-ounce can tomatoes
1 tablespoon salt
1½ cups water
1½ cups clam juice
2 bay leaves
1 carrot, chopped

½ teaspoon thyme
¼ teaspoon basil
⅛ teaspoon saffron
1 teaspoon lemon juice
1 pound large raw shrimp
1 pound fresh or frozen white fish,
    cut into 2-inch pieces
3 medium lobster tails, cut into
    2-inch pieces
1 pound fresh clams
oysters (optional)

Combine all ingredients except seafood in a large crockpot. Cook on low for 6–8 hours. Set cooker to high. When broth boils, add the seafood. Cover and heat 15–20 minutes or until the seafood is cooked.

Barbara Ball
ChurchLIFE, FL

It is better to eat soup with someone you love than steak with someone you hate (Prov. 15:17).

Bright's Traditional Chili

1 pound ground turkey or
    chicken breast
1 can stewed tomatoes

1 package Heinz chili mix without
    preservatives

Brown the meat in a little oil. While meat is browning, purée the tomatoes in a food processor or blender. Add chili mix to browned hamburger, then mix in tomatoes. Simmer for 20 minutes. Turn heat to low and cook for at least 1 more hour or until ready to serve.

Vonette Bright
Co-founder, Campus Crusade for Christ
Executive Director, Women Today International, FL

SOUPS

Broccoli Cheese Noodle Soup

¾ cup chopped onion
2 tablespoons salad oil or margarine
6 cups water
6 chicken bouillon cubes
8 ounces fine egg noodles
1 teaspoon salt
⅛ teaspoon garlic powder

2 10-ounce packages frozen
    chopped broccoli
6 cups milk
1 pound processed American cheese
    (packaged like Velveeta), cubed
pepper to taste

Sauté onion in oil. Add water and bouillon cubes; heat to boiling to dissolve cubes. Add noodles and salt, and cook for 3 minutes. Stir in garlic powder and broccoli, and cook for 4 more minutes. Add milk, cheese, and pepper, stirring until cheese melts. Makes 4 quarts. Can be frozen.

Maggie Bruehl
Special Representative, FL

Broccoli Cheese Soup

1½ pounds fresh broccoli
1 pint half & half
2 cups water
1 pound Velveeta cheese

¾ teaspoon salt
½ teaspoon pepper
½ tablespoon cornstarch
1 cup cold water

Steam broccoli until tender. Place half & half and water in the top of a double boiler. Add cheese, salt, and pepper. Heat until cheese is melted. Add broccoli. Mix cornstarch and cold water in small bowl. Stir into cheese mixture and heat until thickened. Makes 10 1-cup servings.

Andrea Cannon
Student Venture, FL

Cabbage and Rice Soup

1 inner white part of a small celery
    with its tender leaves
¼ pound pancetta, sliced (optional)
¼ cup virgin olive oil
2 tablespoons chopped fresh parsley
2 cloves garlic, finely chopped
½ medium cabbage head (about
    1 pound), chopped

4 cups canned chicken broth
4 cups water
fresh ground pepper to taste
¾ cups rice
olive oil
1 cup fresh grated Parmesan cheese

Chop the celery and leaves very fine. Chop the pancetta. Heat the oil in a large saucepan, and add the celery, pancetta, parsley, and garlic. Cook over medium heat for 3–4 minutes. Add the cabbage; stir and cook a few minutes longer. Add broth and water, and season with several grindings of pepper. Cover; simmer gently for 15–20 minutes.

Add rice and cook 10–15 minutes longer or until the rice is tender but firm. Just before serving, dribble a little olive oil into soup and add ⅓ cup Parmesan. Stir to blend. Taste for seasoning and serve hot with the remaining Parmesan. Serves 6–8.

Barbara Ball
ChurchLIFE, FL

Cheeseburger Chowder

1 pound ground beef
1 medium onion, chopped
2–3 cups water
2–3 potatoes, cubed

2 stalks celery, chopped
salt and pepper to taste
1½ cups milk
1 cup cheddar cheese, shredded

Brown beef and onion; drain grease. Add water, potatoes, celery, salt, and pepper. Simmer until potatoes are tender. Add milk and cheese, and heat through. (Don't let milk boil or it will curdle.) Serve immediately with cornbread or muffins.

Barbara Bennett
Christian Leadership, TN

Chicken Chili Corn Chowder

2 cans cream of chicken soup
1 tablespoon flour
2 soup cans of milk, *divided*
2 cups peeled and cubed potatoes
   (2 large)

1 can sweet corn, drained
¾ cup chopped green chilies
1 cup cubed cooked chicken
2 teaspoons garlic salt
pepper to taste

Place cream of chicken soup in a large pot. Mix flour with 3 tablespoons of milk, and add to pot with the rest of the milk. Add remaining ingredients. Cook on medium heat until thickened and potatoes are tender. Serve with flour tortillas. Serves 4.

Carlyn L. Smith
Keynote Communications

Chunky Split Pea Potato Soup

8 cups water
½ cup split green peas
½ cup split yellow peas
½ cup lima beans
¼ cup uncooked barley
1 large yellow onion, chopped
2 bay leaves
1 teaspoon celery seed
2 carrots, chopped

2 stalks celery, chopped
2 white potatoes, chopped
½ teaspoon paprika
2 tablespoons parsley flakes or
   ½ cup chopped fresh parsley
1 teaspoon dried basil
1 teaspoon ground black pepper
dash ground white pepper

Place the water in a large pot. Add the peas, lima beans, barley, onion, bay leaves, and celery seed and simmer for 1½ hours. Add the remaining ingredients, and cook an additional 45–60 minutes. Remove bay leaves before serving. This healthy, hearty soup is wonderful on a cold day with crusty sourdough or whole wheat bread.

Patti Brown
International School of Theology, CA

Corn Chowder With Shrimp and Roasted Peppers

1 red pepper
1 poblano chili
¼ cup butter
½ cup chopped onion
1½ teaspoons minced garlic
1½ tablespoons cornstarch

¼ cup cold water
2 cups milk
2 10-ounce packages frozen whole
    kernel corn, *divided*
1 cup cream
1 pound raw medium-size shrimp

Broil whole pepper and chili, turning until blackened on all sides. Cool about 10 minutes, then peel and chop. Sauté butter and onion; add garlic. Put in pot with cornstarch, water, milk, and 3 cups of corn. Heat on low for 20 minutes. Puree in blender. Return to pot, and add remaining corn, peppers, cream, and shrimp. Cook 10 minutes. Serve with sourdough baguette.

Barbara Ball
ChurchLIFE, FL

A righteous man may have many troubles, but the Lord delivers him from them all (Psalm 34:19).

Country Pea Soup

1 pound split green peas
8 cups water
1 quart tomato juice (or 1 small can
    tomato sauce and 3 cups water)
1 cup diced ham
1 ham bone or ham hock
1½ cups diced potatoes

1 cup diced celery
1 cup diced onion
1 cup diced carrot
1 bay leaf
1 teaspoon salt
¼ teaspoon pepper

Combine all ingredients in a large kettle. Bring to boiling; lower heat and simmer, stirring occasionally for 1½ hours or until peas are tender. Remove ham bone. Cut off any meat and include in soup. Remove bay leaf. Makes 16 cups.

Darlene Young
Church Dynamics, CA

Darlene's Wild Rice Soup

1 large onion, chopped	1 cup flour
1 cup chopped celery	2 cups cooked wild rice
1 can mushrooms, drained, or	8 cups water
1 cup fresh mushrooms, sliced	9 chicken bouillon cubes
¾ cup margarine or butter	1 cup whipping cream

Sauté onion, celery, and mushrooms in margarine until tender. Sprinkle flour over vegetables until well coated. (Mixture will be pasty.) To the cooked rice, add water and bouillon cubes. Add coated vegetables and whipping cream. Heat and stir until vegetables are blended into the soup. Do not boil.

Optional: Add ½ cup or more cubed Velveeta or Velveeta Light cheese. Also add chopped green and/or red bell pepper and diced or grated carrots, zucchini, and potato.

Lighter variation: Substitute chicken broth for bouillon. Use milk or Coffeemate Light instead of cream. Omit half of the butter.

Darlene Young
Church Dynamics, CA

Taking the five loaves and the two fish and looking up to heaven, he gave thanks and broke the loaves (Matt. 14:19).

Fish Stew

1 cup chopped onion	1 teaspoon grated lemon peel
1 clove garlic, minced	½ teaspoon basil
1 tablespoon olive oil	¼ teaspoon red pepper flakes
1 28-ounce can diced tomatoes	1 pound firm white fish
1 8-ounce bottle clam juice	12 small clams in shells
½ cup parsley	2 cups tortellini

Sauté onion and garlic in olive oil. Add tomatoes, clam juice, parsley, lemon peel, basil, and red pepper flakes. Bring to a boil, then cover and simmer for 25 minutes. Add fish, clams, and tortellini, and return to boiling. Simmer until clams open and tortellini is done al dente.

Barbara Ball
ChurchLIFE, FL

Garden Chowder With Fresh Dill

8 slices bacon, coarsely chopped
1 medium onion, chopped
1 medium green pepper, chopped
2 cans condensed cream of potato soup
1 can chicken broth
1 cup heavy cream
1 cup milk
1 10-ounce package frozen corn

1 10-ounce package frozen chopped broccoli
1 10-ounce package frozen chopped cauliflower
½ teaspoon salt
⅛ teaspoon pepper
1 tablespoon snipped fresh dill

In a 5-quart Dutch oven over medium-high heat, sauté chopped bacon 3 minutes or until crisp. With slotted spoon, remove bacon; set aside. Remove all but 2 tablespoons grease. Add onion and green pepper; sauté 3 minutes longer. Stir in potato soup, broth, cream, and milk; bring to a boil. Add broccoli, cauliflower, and corn. Cover and simmer 10–12 minutes or until vegetables are tender. Add bacon, salt, pepper, and dill. Makes 8–10 servings.

Bobbi Jo Hasz
Campus Ministry, WI

Gazpacho
(a cold Spanish soup)

2 cups tomato juice
1 large clove garlic, pressed
5 tomatoes, chopped
½ cup olive oil
3 tablespoons cider vinegar

1 green pepper, chopped
2 cucumbers, peeled and chopped
1 onion, chopped
dash of Tabasco
salt to taste

In blender, purée tomato juice, garlic, and tomatoes. Add remaining ingredients and chill before serving.

René Drygger
JusticeLINC, WI

Grandma Knopf's German Potato Soup

3 slices cooked bacon, crumbled
1 small onion, chopped
1 can cream of potato soup

1 can condensed milk
2 tablespoons wine vinegar or
   cider vinegar

Sauté onion in bacon grease. Combine remaining ingredients; simmer until heated through.

Donna Knopf
International Ministry, FL

Hamburger Soup

1 pound lean ground beef
1 cup diced onion
½ cup cubed raw potatoes
½ cup chopped celery
1 8-ounce can tomato sauce
1 small bay leaf, crushed
½ teaspoon basil

1 cup sliced carrots
1 cup shredded cabbage
¼ cup uncooked rice
½ teaspoon thyme
1 tablespoon salt
1½ quarts water
dash black pepper

Brown beef and onion; drain the fat. Combine remaining ingredients in a large kettle. Cover and simmer at least 1 hour.

Sarah Willis
International Ministry, FL

Hamburger Vegetable Chowder

½ pound ground beef
1 cup canned tomatoes with juice
1½ cups water
1 cup cubed potatoes
½ cup diced carrots

½ cup diced celery
1 onion, chopped
¼ cup barley
2 teaspoons salt
½ teaspoon pepper

Brown beef in large skillet. Add remaining ingredients. Bring to a boil, then simmer covered for 45–60 minutes, or until vegetables are tender. Serve with green salad and cornbread sticks or muffins.

Lee Etta Lappen Dickerson
Prayer Works, AZ

Healthy Split Pea Soup

1 pound split peas
3 medium yams, peeled and diced
3 leeks, chopped
2 tablespoons ground ginger
4 celery stalks, chopped
3 carrots, chopped

1 teaspoon salt
3 tablespoons Braggs Aminos
(obtain from health food store,
or substitute low-fat soy sauce)
water
cayenne pepper

Place all ingredients except cayenne in a pot, and add enough water to cover.
Cover pot and boil 2 hours. Season with cayenne and serve.

Barbara Ball
ChurchLIFE, FL

Hearty Bean Soup Mix

For bean mixture:

1 pound black beans
1 pound northern beans
1 pound baby lima beans
1 pound split peas

1 pound kidney beans
1 pound pinto beans
1 pound black-eyed peas
1 pound lentils

Mix together and store in a large container. *Tip:* As a gift idea, divide dry
bean mix into jars or small bags with soup recipe attached.

For soup:

2 cups bean mixture
2 quarts water
meaty beef or ham bones
1 large can tomatoes
¼ teaspoon garlic powder or
2 fresh cloves garlic, minced

1 onion, chopped
1 teaspoon chili powder
1 tablespoon lemon juice
dash Tabasco
salt and pepper to taste

Wash bean mixture and drain; soak overnight and drain again. Add water
and beef or ham bones. Bring to a boil; simmer 3–4 hours. Add remaining
ingredients and simmer 30 minutes or more. Remove remaining meat from
bones and discard bones. Serves 8–10.

Variations: Instead of bones, add your choice of meat the last 30 minutes of
cooking: two diced (raw or cooked) chicken breasts, 1 pound diced ham,
smoked sausage, or any leftover meat.

Laurie Killingsworth
New Life Center, FL

Jennie's Bean Soup

1 pound dried beans
2 quarts cold water
meat (optional)
1 bay leaf
6 peppercorns

¼ teaspoon salt
vegetables
2 tablespoons cornstarch or
   arrowroot powder (optional)

Wash dried beans in cold water and soak overnight (or simmer 2 minutes and remove from heat; cover and let stand 1 hour). Don't drain. Add meat if desired, bay leaf, peppercorns, and salt. Cover and simmer 2½ hours. Add water as needed. Add vegetables and seasoning. Cover and simmer 30 minutes more. Remove any bones and the bay leaf. If desired, thicken soup by adding 2 tablespoons cornstarch or arrowroot powder mixed with water.

Variations:

Meat: Turkey carcass; browned ground turkey; browned sausage; leftover beef or chicken and 4 bouillon cubes.

Beans and grains: Lentils; yellow or green split peas; pinto, black, kidney, navy, lima, or red beans; pearl barley; brown rice.

Vegetables: 1 large chopped onion; 1 cup chopped celery; ½ cup sliced carrots; 1 or 2 minced cloves garlic; 1 cup chopped cabbage; 1 14½-ounce can stewed tomatoes; 8 ounces tomato sauce; or 1 medium zucchini, cubed.

Seasoning: 3 tablespoons liquid amino (or soy sauce); 2 tablespoons lemon juice (or vinegar); ½ teaspoon lemon pepper; dash of cayenne pepper; ¼ teaspoon thyme; 2 tablespoons chopped parsley; ¼ teaspoon ginger; ½–1 teaspoon chili powder; ½ teaspoon crushed red pepper pods; or 1 teaspoon green chili.

Jennie Mitchell
Josh McDowell Ministry, CA

Lentil and Brown Rice Soup

5 cups chicken or vegetable broth
3 cups water (or more if needed)
1½ cups lentils, rinsed
3 carrots, chopped
1 large onion, chopped
1 large celery stalk, chopped (½ cup)
3 large cloves garlic, minced
⅓ teaspoon dried basil

1 cup long-grain brown rice
1 28-ounce can diced tomatoes
½ teaspoon dried oregano
½ teaspoon dried thyme
1 bay leaf
½ cup minced fresh parsley
2 tablespoons cider vinegar
salt and fresh pepper to taste

Bring all ingredients to a boil except parsley, vinegar, salt, and pepper. Reduce heat; cover and simmer, stirring occasionally for 45–55 minutes or until lentils and rice are tender. Remove bay leaf and discard. Stir in parsley, vinegar, and salt and pepper if desired. Freezes well. Serves 8–10.

Juanita Wyatt
JESUS Film Project, CA

Meatball Vegetable Soup

For meatballs:

1½ pounds ground chuck
1 egg
½ cup soft bread crumbs
¼ teaspoon salt

1 tablespoon chopped parsley
3 tablespoons water
butter

Combine all ingredients except butter, and shape into 24 balls. Sauté in butter in 4½-quart kettle. Drain off fat; set meatballs aside.

For soup:

2 cups water
2 cups condensed beef broth
1 14½-ounce can tomatoes,
    undrained
1 envelope onion soup mix
2 cups sliced, pared carrots
1 bay leaf

¼ cup chopped celery tops
¼ cup chopped parsley
¼ teaspoon pepper
¼ teaspoon dried oregano
¼ teaspoon dried basil
meatballs

In same kettle, combine all ingredients except meatballs. Bring to a boil; reduce heat and cover. Simmer 30 minutes, stirring occasionally to break up tomatoes. Add meatballs; simmer 20 minutes longer. Serve with warm, buttered garlic bread. Makes 8 servings.

Marilyn Heavilin
Crusade Family

Microwave Corn and Potato Chowder

½ pound ham, diced
2 tablespoons minced onion
5 cups potatoes, peeled and diced
¼ cup water
3 teaspoons chicken bouillon

1 20-ounce package frozen corn
2½ cups skim milk
1 teaspoon salt
¼ teaspoon pepper
½–1 cup shredded cheddar cheese

Cook ham with onion in microwave for 2–3 minutes. Add potatoes and water; cook for 10–12 minutes or until potatoes are tender. Add chicken bouillon, corn, milk, salt, and pepper. Cook for 10–11 minutes on level 8 (80%) power. Add cheddar cheese; stir and heat to melt.

Chris Sather
Student Venture, MN

Potato Leek Soup

½ teaspoon olive oil
1 medium onion, finely chopped
1 ounce Canadian bacon, finely
   chopped
8 ounces leeks, chopped
3–3½ cups chicken broth

2 large potatoes, peeled and
   quartered
2 tablespoons fresh dill, finely
   chopped
salt and pepper to taste

Heat oil in a large pot over medium heat. Add onions, bacon, and leeks, and cover pot. Let simmer for about 10 minutes, stirring once or twice. Add chicken broth, potatoes, and dill; continue simmering until potatoes are soft (about 30 minutes). Remove the potatoes with a slotted spoon, and place in a blender. Add about a cup of the broth and blend.

Stir puréed mixture back into the remaining broth in the pot. Season with salt and pepper if desired, and serve.

Michelle Treiber
NewLife Publications, FL

Scandinavian Fruit Soup

1 cup dried apricots
¾ cup dried apples (or fresh apples, chopped)
½ cup dried peaches
1 cup prunes, pitted and cut in half
½–¾ cup raisins

2 quarts water
¼ cup sugar (optional)
3 tablespoons tapioca
1 cinnamon stick
1 teaspoon grated orange peel
2 cups cranberry or cranapple juice

Rinse the fruits well. (You may vary the amounts of each fruit.) Soak the fruit in water for 2–3 hours in a large, heavy saucepan. Add sugar, tapioca, cinnamon stick, and orange peel. Bring to a boil, then reduce heat. Cover and simmer until fruit is tender (about 1 hour). Remove from heat. Stir in juice and remove cinnamon stick. Serve hot or cold as soup before dinner or as dessert. When serving as a cold dessert, top with whipped cream. Makes 3 quarts.

Judy Douglass
U.S. Staff Women, FL

I am the vine; you are the branches. If a man remains in me and I in him, he will bear much fruit (John 15:5).

Southwest Chicken Hominy Stew

2 teaspoons dried oregano
1 cup chopped red onion, *divided*
3½ cups defatted chicken stock, *divided*
⅛ teaspoon salt
1 clove garlic, minced
1 teaspoon chili powder

1 15-ounce can yellow or white hominy, drained and rinsed
1 15-ounce can black beans, drained
¾ pound skinless, boneless chicken breasts
1 cup shredded green cabbage
1 lime, cut into wedges

In small, dry skillet, heat oregano until fragrant (30–40 seconds). Transfer to a saucer to cool. In a small bowl, combine 1 tablespoon of toasted oregano with ¼ cup of onions, and set aside. In a medium saucepan, combine remaining onions with 3 tablespoons of stock and salt. Cover and cook over medium heat until onions are translucent (3 minutes). Add garlic and cook for 1 minute. Add remaining oregano and chili powder; cook for 1 minute. Add hominy and the remaining chicken stock; simmer for 5 minutes. Add black beans and chicken. Return to simmer and cook until chicken is not pink (about 5 minutes).

Pour into bowls; top with shredded cabbage, reserved onion-oregano mixture, and squeeze of lime juice. Serve with quesadillas. Makes 4 servings.

Barbara Ball
ChurchLIFE, FL

The Lord your God is bringing you into a good land…a land with wheat and barley, vines and fig trees, pomegranates, olive oil and honey; a land where bread will not be scarce and you will lack nothing (Deut. 8:7–9).

Split Pea and Barley Stew

2 quarts chicken stock or water
1 pound dry split peas
½ cup pearl barley
2 cups chopped carrots
1 onion, chopped
3 stalks celery, chopped
2 cups cubed potatoes
10 ounces fresh spinach or other greens
1 bay leaf
2 cloves garlic, minced
¼ cup oil
salt and pepper to taste

Bring stock or water to boil, and slowly add split peas and barley. Reduce to a simmer and cook 1 hour. Add remaining ingredients and cook until tender.

Pat McDaniel
International Ministry, FL

Split Pea Soup

2 pounds split peas
5 quarts cold water
Honey Baked Ham bone
2 cups minced onion
2 cups minced celery
2 bay leaves
Creole seasoning to taste
salt to taste
1 cup minced carrots

The secret of the flavor in this soup is in the Honey Baked Ham bone (purchase at a Honey Baked Ham Store); another bone will not do. Soak peas overnight. Drain and combine peas, water, and ham bone in a kettle or Dutch oven. Cover and bring to a boil. Add onion, celery, and spices. Simmer until the peas have dissolved (about 8 hours). Add carrots about 1 hour before serving. Remove bone and bay leaves. If you cook it less time, you may need to purée the soup. Makes 12–16 servings.

Mary Thompson
JusticeLINC, GA

Taco Soup

1 pound ground beef or turkey	1 can kidney beans
1 medium onion, chopped	1 can hominy
1 package taco seasoning	1 can corn
1 package Original Ranch dressing mix	1 cup chopped fresh green chilies
1 can pinto beans	3 cans stewed tomatoes

Brown beef or turkey with onion. Combine all ingredients and heat. Freezes well. Recipe can be doubled, although I do not double the turkey. Makes 6 hearty servings.

Vonette Bright
Co-founder, Campus Crusade for Christ
Executive Director, Women Today International, FL

Tomato Bisque

1 small onion, chopped	pinch dried basil
2 celery stalks, chopped	pinch thyme
1 carrot, chopped	pinch celery seed
2 cloves garlic, minced	dash of cayenne (optional)
1 tablespoon or less olive oil	½ cup heavy cream
2 15-ounce cans plum tomatoes, drained	green onion, finely chopped (optional)
1¼ cups chicken stock	croutons (optional)
pinch fresh parsley	

Sauté raw vegetables and garlic in oil until soft. Add tomatoes and chicken stock. Stir in parsley, basil, thyme, and celery seed to taste. For a little more spice, add a dash of cayenne. Simmer for 15 minutes. Stir in heavy cream.

Cool a little, then liquefy in a blender. When ready to serve, reheat over low heat, stirring often to avoid scorching. Top with green onions or croutons. Tastes better than a can of Campbells! Serves 4.

Nina Locke
Crusade Family

Zucchini Soup

1 large onion, coarsely chopped
1 clove garlic, minced
1 tablespoon olive oil
1 can consommé
2½ cups water
½ teaspoon salt

¼ cup fresh parsley
1 tablespoon fresh basil or
   1 teaspoon dried basil
freshly ground pepper
6 medium zucchini, sliced
grated Parmesan cheese

Brown onion and garlic slightly in olive oil. Add remaining ingredients except Parmesan, and simmer until zucchini is barely tender. Cool. Put in a blender a little at a time and purée. To serve cold, refrigerate for several hours or overnight. To serve hot, gently reheat and garnish with Parmesan cheese. This is an easy make-ahead soup, and makes a nice first course served cold in demitasse cups.

Nina Locke
Crusade Family

Breads

Angel Biscuits

1 package yeast
2 tablespoons lukewarm water
5 cups sifted flour
1 teaspoon baking soda
3 tablespoons baking powder

¼ cup sugar
1 teaspoon salt
1 cup shortening
2 cups buttermilk

Preheat oven to 400 degrees. Dissolve yeast in water. Sift together dry ingredients. Cut in shortening. Blend in yeast mixture and buttermilk. Knead just enough so that dough holds together. Roll dough to desired thickness. Cut with biscuit cutter and fold each biscuit in half. Place on ungreased cookie sheet. Bake for 20 minutes.

Barbara Ball
ChurchLIFE, FL

Anise Rye Bread

1 package yeast
2 cups warm water
2 cups rye flour
1 teaspoon salt
1½ teaspoons anise

2 rounded tablespoons shortening
½ cup sugar
½ cup molasses
4½ cups white flour

Dissolve yeast in warm water. Sift together rye flour, salt, and anise. Add to yeast mixture along with shortening, sugar, and molasses. Add white flour and knead 5 minutes. Let dough sit overnight in a covered bowl. Divide into 2 loaves and bake at 350 degrees for 1 hour.

Barbara Ball
ChurchLIFE, FL

BREADS

Apple Oatmeal Muffins

1 cup uncooked rolled oats
½ cup raisins or chopped walnuts
1 egg, slightly beaten
⅔ cup water
⅓ cup plain yogurt
1 cup whole grain flour (wheat, spelt, kamut, or other flour)

1 teaspoon fructose or other sweetener (optional)
1½ teaspoons baking powder
1½ teaspoons cinnamon
½ teaspoon salt
1 apple, cored and grated

Preheat oven to 375 degrees. Thoroughly combine oats, raisins or walnuts, egg, water, and yogurt, and set aside. In a separate bowl, mix flour, fructose, baking powder, cinnamon, and salt. Gently blend dry ingredients and liquid ingredients. Fold apple into mixture. Pour into lightly greased muffin tins. (Fill any empty cups halfway with water.) Bake for 30 minutes. Makes 10 large or 12 medium-size muffins.

Jennie Mitchell
Josh McDowell Ministries, CA

> *Do not forget to entertain strangers, for by so doing some people have entertained angels without knowing it (Heb. 13:2).*

Baking Powder Biscuits

1¾ cups flour   ⅓ cup shortening
2½ teaspoon baking powder   ¾ cup milk
¾ teaspoon salt

Preheat oven to 450 degrees. With a whisk, combine the dry ingredients in a bowl. Using a fork, cut the shortening into the flour. (Do not mix, other than to cut in the shortening.) Add milk. Mix all ingredients with a spoon; then knead to work in ingredients. If mixture is too dry and crumbly, add additional milk sparingly. If mixture is too sticky to manage, add flour sparingly. On a floured board, roll dough ½-inch thick, and cut with 2-inch biscuit cutter or a drinking glass. Place rounds on ungreased cookie sheet, and bake for 10–12 minutes.

Lori Burns
Staff & Ministry Opportunities, FL

Banana Apple Muffins

1 cup whole wheat flour   1 egg, beaten
1½ teaspoons baking powder   2 tablespoons melted butter
½ teaspoon cinnamon   1 tablespoon vanilla
½ teaspoon ginger   ¼ cup apple juice concentrate
1 cup rolled oats   1 apple, cored and grated
½ cup papaya bits or raisins (optional)   1 cup mashed ripe bananas

Preheat oven to 400 degrees. Combine dry ingredients. Stir in oats. In a separate bowl, mix remaining ingredients; add to dry ingredients all at once. Stir just to moisten. Fill cups ⅔ full in greased muffin tin. Bake 20 minutes.

Sherry Slaughter
Campus Ministry, CA

Banana Bread

1 cup sugar   1 teaspoon baking soda
½ cup shortening   1 teaspoon baking powder
1 egg, well beaten   pinch of salt
3 over-ripe bananas, mashed   2 cups flour
3 tablespoons milk

Preheat oven to 350 degrees. Cream sugar and shortening. Add egg, bananas, and milk. Add remaining ingredients. Bake in greased loaf pan for 45 minutes.

Lee Etta Lappen Dickerson
Prayer Works, AZ

Banana Nut Muffins

1¼ cups whole wheat flour
1 cup oat bran
¼ cup brown sugar
1 tablespoon baking powder
¼ cup chopped walnuts or pecans

1¼ cups skim milk
2 very ripe bananas, mashed
1 egg or 2 egg whites
2 tablespoons vegetable oil

Preheat oven to 350 degrees. Mix dry ingredients in a large bowl. In a separate bowl, mix milk, bananas, egg, and oil. Combine both mixtures, and pour batter into muffin tins. Bake 17 minutes. Makes 12 muffins.

Iris Cutshall
International Resource Ministry, FL

Bea's Pumpkin Bread

3 cups sugar
1 cup oil
4 eggs, beaten
1 pound canned pumpkin
2 scant teaspoons salt
1 teaspoon allspice

2 teaspoons baking soda
1 teaspoon cinnamon
½ teaspoon ground cloves
1 teaspoon nutmeg
3½ cups flour
⅔ cup water

Preheat oven to 350 degrees. Mix sugar, oil, and eggs; add pumpkin. Add dry ingredients, then water, stirring just until mixed. Pour batter into two greased and floured 9×5-inch loaf pans. Bake for 1 hour.

Bea Chandler
ChurchLIFE, NC

Butterhorns

1 cup milk, scalded	1 package yeast or 1 cake fresh yeast
½ cup shortening or margarine	3 eggs, beaten
½ cup sugar	4½ cups flour
1 teaspoon salt	melted butter

Combine milk, shortening, sugar, and salt. Allow to cool until it's lukewarm. Add crumbled yeast or dry yeast that has been softened in 2 tablespoons warm water. Add eggs, then flour. Mix to a smooth, soft dough; knead slightly. Place dough on greased board. Cover, and let rise until double. Divide dough into thirds. On a lightly floured surface, roll each third into a 9-inch circle. Brush with melted butter. Cut each circle into 12–16 wedges. Roll up each wedge from wide end to point. Arrange in pan; brush again with melted butter. Cover and let rise until very light. Bake at 400 degrees for 15 minutes.

Darlene Young
Church Dynamics, CA

Buttermilk Bran Muffins

2 cups boiling water	1 teaspoon salt
2 cups 100% All-Bran cereal	4 eggs
3 cups sugar	5 cups flour
1 cup plus 2 tablespoons shortening	1 quart buttermilk
5 teaspoons baking soda	4 cups Bran Buds

Preheat oven to 350 degrees. Mix water and All-Bran, and soak. Combine remaining ingredients except for Bran Buds. Then add the bran/water mixture. Add Bran Buds last so they don't get mashed. Pour into muffin pans and bake for 15 minutes.

Marlyse Milburn
Milburn Projects, CA

Keep falsehood and lies far from me, give me neither poverty nor riches, but give me only my daily bread (Prov. 30:8).

Buttermilk Scones

3 cups sifted flour
⅓ cup sugar
2½ teaspoons baking powder
¾ teaspoon salt
½ teaspoon baking soda

¾ cup cold butter
¾ cup currants or raisins
1 teaspoon *bottled* orange peel
1 cup buttermilk
1 egg, beaten with a little water

Preheat oven to 450 degrees. (The oven must be hot when you put in the scones.) Sift dry ingredients; cut in butter until the mixture resembles cornmeal. (A food processor works best.) Add currants or raisins and orange peel. Make a well and add buttermilk all at once. Stir with a fork until dough leaves the side of the bowl. Knead three or four times on a floured surface; roll or pat out into a 1-inch-thick circle. Cut with a 2-inch biscuit cutter. Place on a greased metal sheet, being careful not to let biscuits touch. Brush with egg wash. Bake for about 12 minutes. Makes 11–12. Serve warm with jam and whipped cream. Store extras in a ziplock bag as soon as they cool. Scones freeze well and can be reheated in a microwave.

Pam Davis
National Ministry, FL

Buttermilk Wheat Bread

2 packages dry yeast
½ cup very warm water
¼ cup honey, *divided*
2 cups buttermilk
2 tablespoons oil

1 tablespoon salt
½ teaspoon baking soda
1 cup cracked wheat
6 cups stone ground or wheat
  flour, *divided*

Soften yeast in water. Stir in 1 teaspoon honey. Heat the remaining honey, buttermilk, oil, and salt until lukewarm. Add to yeast mixture. Stir in soda, cracked wheat, and 3 cups flour. Beat in enough of the remaining flour to make a soft dough. Knead until smooth. Let rise until doubled. Punch down, divide, and form into 2 loaves. Place in greased pans; let rise again until doubled. Bake at 375 degrees for 35 minutes or until light brown.

Helen Koopman
JESUS Film Project, FL

BREADS

Carrot Bread

¾ cup shortening
½ cup brown sugar
2 eggs
3 cups grated carrots

1¼ cups flour
1 teaspoon baking powder
½ teaspoon baking soda

Preheat oven to 325 degrees. Mix shortening, sugar, eggs, and carrots. Add dry ingredients. Bake in a small loaf pan for 1 hour. (Tastes like cornbread.)

Sus Schmitt
Computer Services, FL

Cheese Scones

1 cup self-rising flour, sifted
1 cup grated cheese
1 egg

about 1 cup milk
¼ cup oil
pinch of salt

Preheat oven to 425 degrees. Blend flour and cheese. Break egg into a measuring cup; add milk to fill to 1 cup. Add oil and a pinch of salt. Combine with flour mixture. Do not over mix. Pat out dough to ¼-inch thickness. Cut out rounds with a biscuit cutter. Place biscuits on a cookie sheet sprayed with non-stick spray. Bake for 10 minutes.

Jeanette Antrobus
International Ministry, South Africa

Chili Bacon Bread Sticks

1 pound bacon
30 whole Grissini (long, thin)
   bread sticks

⅓ cup light brown sugar
3 tablespoons chili powder

Preheat oven to 350 degrees. Let bacon stand at room temperature for 10 minutes. Gently wrap 1 bacon slice in a spiral around each bread stick. In a shallow dish, stir together sugar and chili powder. Roll each bread stick in sugar mixture, and pat it until well coated. Arrange bread sticks about ½-inch apart on a rack in a broiler pan. Bake 20 minutes until coating is caramelized and bacon is a deep gold. Remove with a spatula and cool 10–15 minutes; sticks become crisp as they cool. Cut sticks in half for a nicer serving portion, and serve at room temperature.

Nina Locke
Crusade Family

Coffee Can Bread

1 package yeast
½ cup warm water
1 tablespoon sugar
½ teaspoon ginger
1 tablespoon honey
1 teaspoon salt

2 tablespoons oil
1 can evaporated milk
2 cups whole wheat flour, *divided*
2–2½ cups white flour, *divided*
butter

Dissolve yeast in warm water and sugar. Stir in ginger and honey. Let stand in a warm place until bubbly (about 20 minutes). Add remaining ingredients except flour. With electric mixer, beat in 2 cups of wheat flour and 1 cup of white flour, a cup at a time. With a heavy spoon, stir in 1 more cup of white flour. Add more flour until dough is very heavy but too sticky to knead.

Divide dough into two parts, and put each into a well-greased coffee can. Cover with plastic lids. Let cans stand in a warm place until the lids pop up. Remove lids and bake the bread in the cans at 350 degrees for 45 minutes. Cool 5 minutes, then loosen edges of bread with a knife and remove from cans. Crust will be very brown. Brush crust with butter. Slice and eat while warm or toast slices when cooled.

Joette Whims
NewLife Publications, CA

Cornbread

1 cup corn meal
1 cup flour
½ cup sugar
½ teaspoon salt
1 tablespoon baking powder

½ teaspoon baking soda
2 eggs, beaten
2 tablespoons butter, melted
1 cup buttermilk

Preheat oven to 350 degrees. Mix all dry ingredients. Add eggs, butter, and buttermilk. Pour into a greased 9×9-inch baking dish and bake 30 minutes.

Judy Douglass
U.S. Staff Women, FL

Cranberry Nut Bread

2 cups flour
1 cup sugar
1½ teaspoons baking powder
½ teaspoon baking soda
1 teaspoon salt
¼ cup shortening

¾ cup orange juice
1 tablespoon orange rind
1 egg, well beaten
½ cup chopped pecans
1 cup chopped cranberries

Preheat oven to 350 degrees. Sift together the dry ingredients. Add shortening, orange juice, orange rind, and egg; mix. Fold in the pecans and cranberries. Pour into 2 greased loaf pans. Bake for 1 hour. (To triple this recipe to make 8 small loaves and 1 medium loaf, use a 1-pound bag of cranberries.)

Debbie McGoldrick
Student Venture, GA

Creamy Cornbread

½ cup oil, *divided*
2 boxes Jiffy cornbread mix
¼ teaspoon salt

1 can cream style corn
1 pint sour cream
4 eggs

Preheat oven to 350 degrees. Grease a large baking pan with part of the oil, then mix the remaining oil with all other ingredients. Bake for 30–45 minutes or until golden brown. Serves 15–20. It tastes like dessert!

Leonora T. Gay
ChurchLIFE, FL

Jesus declared, "I am the bread of life. He who comes to me will never go hungry, and he who believes in me will never be thirsty" (John 6:35).

Crescent Rolls

½ cup milk
2 tablespoons sugar
½ teaspoon salt
¼ cup vegetable oil

1 egg, beaten
1 package dry yeast
2 cups sifted flour
2 tablespoons melted butter

Scald milk and set aside. In mixing bowl, combine sugar, salt, and oil. Stir in cooled (105–115 degrees) milk and beaten egg. Dissolve yeast in milk mixture. Add flour and mix well. Cover and let rise 2 hours. Place dough on a lightly floured board, and roll into a 15-inch circle. Brush with melted butter. Cut into 16 pie-shaped wedges, and roll up each from the wide end to the narrow end. Place rolls on a baking sheet, and let rise 2 hours. Bake at 400 degrees for 6–8 minutes (watch closely because these rolls burn easily).

Anne Lawrence
World Changers Radio, FL

Delicious Arkansas Cornbread

cooking oil
1 cup corn meal
½ teaspoon salt
½ teaspoon baking powder

¼ teaspoon baking soda
1 cup buttermilk
1 egg

Preheat oven to 400 degrees. Cover bottom of a medium-size cast iron skillet with ⅛-inch oil, and heat the oil. In a bowl, mix all ingredients. Carefully pour oil into other ingredients (don't scrape the oil from the pan) and mix. Pour batter back into pan. Place in oven and bake 15 minutes. Turn oven to broil to brown the top. It takes only a minute, so keep an eye on it; cornbread can burn very quickly. *Tip:* Instead of buttermilk, you can substitute plain yogurt, or mix 1 cup milk and 2 tablespoons vinegar and let set for 20 minutes.

Susan Heckmann
President's Office, FL

Dilly Bread

1 package dry yeast
¼ cup warm water
1 cup warm creamed cottage cheese
2 tablespoons sugar
1 tablespoon instant minced onions

1 tablespoon butter
2 teaspoons dill seed
1 teaspoon salt
1 egg
2¼–2½ cups flour

Dissolve yeast in warm water. Mix in cottage cheese. Add remaining ingredients. Beat and form into stiff dough. Cover and let rise in warm place for 1 hour. Stir down. Put into a well-greased, 8-inch-round casserole dish. Let rise 30–40 minutes. Bake at 350 degrees for 40–45 minutes. Brush with melted butter and sprinkle the top with salt. Serve hot (goes well with beef fondue or steak). Serves 12.

Cinny Hicks
Crusade Family

Flavorful Cornbread

1 box Jiffy cornbread
2 tablespoons Ranch or
   Bleu Cheese dressing

3 tablespoons butter
2 tablespoons salsa
¼ cup shredded cheddar cheese

Preheat oven to 375 degrees. Mix cornbread according to package directions, then add remaining ingredients. Pour into muffin pan or shallow baking dish. Cook as directed. This is a family favorite that goes great with Mexican meals.

Kelly Hall
Corporate Human Resources, FL

Gourmet Garlic Bread

1 large onion, minced
8 cloves garlic, minced
¼ cup butter
2 cups grated mozzarella cheese

½ cup grated Parmesan cheese
1 cup mayonnaise
2 long loaves French bread, cut
   into ¾-inch diagonal slices

Sauté onion and garlic in butter until tender. Set aside to cool. Mix cheeses and mayonnaise. Spread butter mixture then cheeses onto sliced bread, and broil until bubbly and slightly browned.

Lana Jones
International Ministry, HI

Grandmother's Banana Nut Bread

1 cup sugar
½ cup margarine, softened
2 eggs
3 ripe bananas, mashed

2 cups sifted flour
1 rounded teaspoon baking soda
½ cup nuts

Preheat oven to 350 degrees. Grease the bottom of a loaf pan. Beat together sugar, margarine, then eggs and bananas. In a separate bowl, sift together the flour and soda. Combine all ingredients. Bake for approximately 1 hour. Let cool for 5 minutes, then remove from pan.

Patsy Morley
Board of Director's Wife

 Give us this day our daily bread (Matt. 6:11).

Hardtack

⅛ teaspoon baking soda
3 tablespoons buttermilk
1 cup flour

4 teaspoons real maple syrup
⅜ teaspoons salt
1½ tablespoons shortening

Preheat oven to 425 degrees. Mix soda and buttermilk; set aside. Combine flour, syrup, and salt, then cut in shortening. Add buttermilk mixture. Roll out very thin and score rectangles in the dough without cutting all the way through. Prick each rectangle several times with a fork. Bake on an ungreased cookie sheet for 5–10 minutes or until golden brown.

Mary Ann and Bob Lepine
FamilyLIFE, AR

Harvest Bread

½ cup sugar
¼ cup melted margarine
1 egg
½–1 ripe banana, mashed
½ zucchini, grated

1¼ cups flour
1 teaspoon baking soda
⅓ cup crushed walnuts
½ cup chocolate chips

Preheat oven to 350 degrees. Mix ingredients in the order given. Bake approximately 45 minutes.

Janet M. Evans
Student Venture, FL

Health Bread

¾ cup soy flour
1 cup whole wheat flour
1 cup unbleached all-purpose flour
½ cup wheat germ
⅓ cup powdered milk
¼ cup bran flakes
1 teaspoon baking soda
½ teaspoon salt

¾ cup chopped dates
¾ cup chopped nuts
1 cup yogurt
1 egg, beaten
¼ cup canola oil
¼ cup molasses
¼ cup honey
½ cup orange juice

Preheat oven to 350 degrees. Mix dry ingredients, dates, and nuts. In a separate bowl, mix yogurt, egg, oil, molasses, honey, and orange juice. Stir both mixtures together just until well blended. Bake 1 hour in loaf pan. Cover loosely with foil the last 20 minutes to prevent over-browning.

Gayle Anne VanFulpen
NewLife Publications, FL

Herb Bread

2 cups milk, scalded
1 package yeast
¼ cup sugar
1 tablespoon salt
2 eggs, beaten
1 teaspoon nutmeg

2 teaspoons sage
4 teaspoons caraway seeds or
   fine herbs
6–6½ cups flour, *divided*
¼ cup melted butter

Cool scalded milk to lukewarm. Add yeast and stir to dissolve. Add sugar and salt. Mix in eggs, spices, and 3 cups flour; stir until smooth. Add butter and remaining flour. Knead until smooth and elastic. Let rise until dough doubles in size. Divide and shape into rolls or loaves. Let rise until double again. Bake at 375 degrees for 25–30 minutes.

Barbara Ball
ChurchLIFE, FL

Honey Wheat Germ Bread

2 packages dry yeast
1 cup warm water
2 tablespoons brown sugar
½ teaspoon salt
4 cups white flour, *divided*

1¼ cups scalded milk
¼ cup honey
2 teaspoons salt
1¾ cups whole wheat flour
¼ cup wheat germ

In a large mixing bowl, combine yeast, water, brown sugar, salt, and ½ cup white flour. Beat until smooth. Cover and let stand in warm place for 15 minutes. To this mixture, add the milk (which has been cooled to warm), honey, salt, whole wheat flour, and wheat germ. Beat 2 minutes with electric mixer, and gradually stir in the remaining white flour. On a floured surface, form into a smooth ball.

Cover with bowl and let rise for 10 minutes. Knead thoroughly and divide into 2 or 3 balls. Cover and let rise again. Shape each ball into a loaf, and place into 2 greased standard loaf pans or 3 8×4-inch pans. Cover and let rise in warm place for 45–60 minutes or until doubled in size. Bake at 375 degrees for 35–40 minutes.

Helen Koopman
JESUS Film Project, FL

You would be fed with the finest of wheat; with honey from the rock I would satisfy you (Psalm 81:16).

BREADS

Irish Soda Bread

3 cups flour   ½ cup raisins (or more)
¼ cup sugar   1⅓ cups buttermilk
1 tablespoon baking powder   1 teaspoon baking soda
pinch of salt

Preheat oven to 350 degrees. With a wooden spoon, mix the first 5 ingredients in a medium bowl. Make a well in the middle. In a small bowl, stir together the buttermilk and baking soda until it is frothy. Pour the buttermilk mixture into the dry ingredients all at once. Stir all together (about 40 strokes) until dough forms one lump. Batter will be lumpy but pliable, similar to biscuit dough, but not too sticky. Place on a floured board, and knead 10–15 times.

Shape into an 8- to 10-inch circle (about 1½-inches thick). Use a sharp knife to cut a cross over the top, about ¼-inch deep. Bake for 35–45 minutes, or until it is a light brown and sounds hollow when thumped. Lean loaf on its side to cool or on a rack so the bottom crust does not get tough. To slice, cut the circle in half, then place the cut side down on a cutting board and slice straight down. Eat within one or two days. (This recipe is from my mother, who immigrated from Ireland in 1955.)

Marjorie Haley
JESUS Film Project, FL

Italian Bread

2 cups warm water   2 tablespoons sugar
2 packages (2 tablespoons) dry yeast 5–6 cups flour
2 teaspoons salt

Mix water, yeast, salt, and sugar in a large bowl; add flour gradually until dough is stiff. Knead about 5 minutes and divide in half. Roll out into a rectangle; roll up dough and pinch ends. Place on greased cookie sheet, and let rise 20 minutes. Bake at 400 degrees for 10 minutes, then lower temperature to 325 degrees for 10 minutes. (You'll never buy store-bought again.)

Variations:

■ Children love to mold it into shapes and eat their creations.

- For cinnamon rolls, roll dough out flat. Spread with butter, chopped nuts, ⅓ cup sugar mixed with 1 teaspoon cinnamon, and raisins (optional) or shredded apple (optional). Roll like a jelly roll and slice. Place slices in greased pan. After dough has doubled, bake at 375 degrees for 25 minutes.

- For pull-aparts, roll walnut-size dough balls in cinnamon sugar. Place a single layer into a greased loaf pan. Sprinkle with chopped nuts. Add another layer of cinnamon balls until pan is ¾ full. Let rise. Bake at 350 degrees for 45 minutes.

- For pizza dough, roll out flat in greased pan. Bake at 425 degrees for 10 minutes. Put pizza ingredients on top. Return to oven for 10 more minutes.

- For calzone, roll flat into 8-inch circles. Fill with cheese. Fold in half and seal edges; brush crust with garlic butter. Sprinkle with grated Parmesan cheese. Bake at 350 degrees for 20 minutes. Serve with hot pizza sauce for dipping.

- For pocket sandwiches, follow calzone directions, using pocket sandwich recipes for fillings.

Sus Schmitt
Computer Services, FL

Lefse

2 cups cold mashed potatoes	¼ cup milk (optional)
1 cup flour	½ cup butter (optional)
1 teaspoon salt	

Mix all ingredients. (Add milk and butter if they were not used when making the mashed potatoes.) Take a 2-inch ball of dough and roll it out quite thin on a floured board. The lefse should be the consistency of pie crust dough. Fry in a dry skillet or griddle until brown spots appear. Serve with any fish dinner. I prefer lefse warm and soft, spread with butter and rolled up. It can also be spread with butter and sprinkled with brown sugar, spread with sour cream, or wrapped around fish with tartar sauce.

This Norwegian "tortilla" was a tradition in our home every Christmas Eve, along with lutefisk. Lefse freezes well and can be warmed in a microwave.

Sus Schmitt
Computer Services, FL

Lemon Bread

1 cup butter
1 cup sugar
3 eggs
½ teaspoon baking soda
½ tablespoon hot water

2½ cups flour
1½ ounces lemon extract
1 cup pecans, chopped
1 cup white raisins

Preheat oven to 250 degrees. Cream butter; gradually add sugars, then add eggs one at a time. Mix soda in water, and add to the butter mixture. Alternately add flour and lemon extract. Stir in nuts and raisins. Bake in loaf pans (1 large and 1 small) for 1 hour and 15 minutes.

Nancy Scott
JESUS Film Project, NC

Mary's Special Carrot Bran Muffins

1 cup oil
1½ cups brown sugar or 1 cup honey
3 eggs
1½ cups buttermilk
1½ teaspoons baking soda
3 cups bran

1½ cups wheat flour
1½ teaspoons cinnamon
dash of salt
2 cups grated carrots
1–2 cups diced prunes
2 cups diced walnuts

Preheat oven to 400 degrees. Combine oil and brown sugar. Mix in eggs one at a time. Combine buttermilk and soda, then add to brown sugar mixture. Add bran and allow to stand 2 minutes. Mix flour, cinnamon, and salt; add to brown sugar mixture. Stir in carrots, prunes, and nuts. Mix well. (For moister muffins, add more buttermilk.) Fill foil muffin cups. Bake for 20 minutes.

Mary L. Walker
JESUS Film Project, CA

Jesus answered, "It is written: 'Man does not live on bread alone, but on every word that comes from the mouth of God'" (Matt. 4:4).

BREADS

Mushroom Bread

1 loaf Vienna or Italian bread
8 ounces fresh or canned mushrooms, sliced
¾–1 pound Swiss or mozzarella cheese
1 cup butter
2 tablespoons poppyseeds (optional)
1 teaspoon salt
½ teaspoon lemon juice
1 tablespoon dry mustard

Preheat oven to 350 degrees. Cut loaf diagonally both ways about 1 inch apart without cutting through at the bottom of the loaf. Place on foil. Stuff cuts with mushrooms and cheese. Melt butter with seasonings. Drizzle on bread. Wrap in foil and bake for 30–40 minutes.

René Drygger
JusticeLINC, WI

Mustard French Bread

1 tablespoon reduced-calorie mayonnaise
1 teaspoon Dijon mustard
2 slices French bread
1 tablespoon snipped fresh parsley
2 teaspoons grated Parmesan cheese

In a small bowl, combine mayonnaise and mustard. Spread onto one side of the bread slices; sprinkle with parsley and Parmesan cheese. Broil about 5 inches from heat for 3–4 minutes or until golden. Serve warm (good with chicken or turkey salads). Makes 2 servings.

Bobbi Jo Hasz
Campus Ministry, WA

Oatmeal Bread

1 cup hot water
1 cup uncooked oatmeal
1 package yeast
¼ cup warm water
1 teaspoon sugar
2–3 tablespoons honey
1 teaspoon salt
¼ cup shortening
¼ cup brown sugar
1 cup water
5–6 cups flour

Pour hot water over oatmeal. Let stand a few minutes. Dissolve yeast in warm water; add sugar and let stand a few minutes. Add honey, salt, shortening, brown sugar, and water to oatmeal mixture, then add yeast mixture. Mix in the flour until the dough is smooth and elastic. Knead. Place into a greased bowl; turn once so all of dough is greased. Cover and let rise until double (about 1 hour).

Punch down. Divide into 2 loaves and put into greased pans. Let rise until no more than 1 inch above pan. Bake at 350 degrees for about 20–25 minutes until loaf sounds hollow when tapped.

Sara Ely
Campus Ministry, SD

Oatmeal Muffins

1 cup rolled oats	1 cup flour
1 cup sour milk	1 teaspoon baking powder
1/3 cup soft butter	1/2 teaspoon baking soda
1/2 cup brown sugar	1 teaspoon salt
1 egg	

Preheat oven to 400 degrees. Soak oats in sour milk. (To make sour milk, add 1 tablespoon vinegar to sweet milk.) Mix in butter, sugar, and egg. Sift dry ingredients and gradually add to oat mixture. Mix well. Fill muffin tins 2/3 full. Bake for 20–25 minutes.

Marilyn Klein
National Ministry, CA

 The Lord said to Moses, "I will rain down bread from heaven for you" (Exodus 16:4).

Onion Herb Bread

1/2 cup butter or margarine	1 teaspoon beau monde
2 tablespoons minced onion or	1 tablespoon poppyseeds
instant onion flakes	slices of jack cheese
1 tablespoon prepared mustard	loaf of French bread or
2 tablespoons lemon juice	petit French rolls

Preheat oven to 350 degrees. Mix the first 6 ingredients. Slice bread lengthwise, cutting from top to bottom but not all the way through. Insert cheese into the slice. Place herb mixture on top of loaf, or spread on the roll. Wrap in foil (if petit roll, wrap each roll individually). Bake for 25–30 minutes. Serve immediately. (Leftover herb mixture may be refrigerated for later use.)

Carol Herron
Church Dynamics, CA

Overnight Refrigerator Rolls

2 packages yeast
2½ cups warm water
¾ cup melted shortening
¾ cup sugar

2 eggs, well beaten
8–8½ cups flour, *divided*
2½ teaspoons salt

Soften yeast in warm water. Stir in shortening, sugar, eggs, 4 cups flour, and salt. Beat until smooth (about 1 minute). Stir in remaining flour. Cover tightly and store in refrigerator overnight or until needed. When ready to use, punch down dough, and pinch off amount needed. Shape into rolls and place in a greased baking pan or cupcake pan. Cover and let rise in warm place 1 hour. Bake at 400 degrees for 15–20 minutes.

Variation: For wheat rolls, use 5 cups white flour and 3 cups wheat flour.

Midge Piedot
Crusade Family

Pumpkin Muffins

3 cups dark brown sugar
1 cup oil
4 eggs, beaten
1 16-ounce can pumpkin
3½ cups flour
2 teaspoons baking soda
2 teaspoons salt

1 teaspoon baking powder
1 teaspoon nutmeg
1 teaspoon allspice
1 teaspoon cinnamon
½ teaspoon ground cloves
⅔ cup water

Preheat oven to 350 degrees. Cream sugar and oil. Add eggs and pumpkin; mix well. Sift together dry ingredients. Add to pumpkin mixture alternately with water. Bake for 10–15 minutes.

Debbie McGoldrick
Student Venture, GA

Quick Banana Bread

3 medium bananas, mashed
(about 1 cup)
2 cups flour
3½ teaspoons baking powder
1 teaspoon salt

3 tablespoons oil
¾ cup milk
1 egg
1 cup sugar
1 cup nuts (optional)

Preheat oven to 350 degrees. Mix all ingredients in a large bowl. Beat 30 seconds at medium speed, scraping bowl constantly. Pour into a greased loaf pan, approximately 9×5×3 inches. Bake for 55–65 minutes. Check for doneness with a wooden toothpick; toothpick will pull out clean when bread is done.

Mike and Lori Burns
Staff & Ministry Opportunities, FL

Quick Bread

3 cups self-rising flour
3 tablespoons sugar

1 can unflavored selzer at
room temperature

Preheat oven to 400 degrees. Mix ingredients and place in a greased bread pan. Let rise about 15 minutes. Bake for 30 minutes or until brown.

Ingrid Bunner
Board of Director's Wife

Quick Onion Rolls

2 packages dry yeast
½ cup warm water
1 teaspoon sugar
1 cup milk, scalded
½ cup margarine

3 eggs
½ cup sugar
1 teaspoon salt
4–4½ cups flour
1 package dry onion soup mix

Dissolve yeast in warm water with 1 teaspoon sugar. Scald milk and add margarine. Mix eggs, ½ cup sugar, and salt in large bowl. Add cooled milk and margarine; mix in yeast. Blend in flour and onion soup; mix thoroughly. (This is a soft dough.) Cover and let rise in warm place until double (about

2 hours). Roll out onto a heavily floured board to about ½-inch thickness. Cut with round cutter, and place rolls on a greased cookie sheet. Cover with a towel and let rise again.

Bake at 350 degrees for 10–12 minutes. Rub margarine across the tops of rolls while hot. Serve warm. These rolls are light as a feather, and are good for sloppy joes, hamburgers, or dinner rolls. They're also good without adding the onion soup mix.

Midge Piedot
Crusade Family

Rainey's Hardtack

⅛ teaspoon baking soda
3 tablespoons buttermilk
1 cup flour

⅜ teaspoon salt
¼ cup maple syrup (not imitation)
1½ tablespoons shortening

Preheat oven to 425 degrees. Mix baking soda and buttermilk, and set aside. Mix flour, salt, and maple syrup, then cut in shortening. Add the buttermilk mixture. Roll out very thin, then score rectangles in the dough without cutting all the way through. Prick each rectangle several times with a fork. Bake on an ungreased cookie sheet for 5–10 minutes or until golden brown.

Dennis and Barbara Rainey
FamilyLIFE, AR

Raisin and Oat Health Bread

1 cup raisins
1 cup bran
water
1 teaspoon baking soda
1½ cup sour milk or yogurt

¾ cup sugar
pinch of salt
1 egg
1 cup oats
1 cup whole wheat flour

Preheat oven to 350 degrees. Boil raisins and bran in water until softened; drain. Add baking soda to the milk. (You can create sour milk by combining half yogurt and half powdered milk made with the water from the raisins.) Combine raisin mixture, sugar, salt, egg, oats, and flour in order. Pour the milk mixture over ingredients and stir. Bake in a greased loaf pan for 50 minutes.

Bob and Ilene Bradberry
JESUS Film Project, CA

Raisin Bran Bread

1½ cups unbleached flour, *divided*
1 tablespoon dry yeast
¼ teaspoon salt
½ cup hot water
½ cup skim milk
2 tablespoons canola oil

¼ cup honey
2 large egg whites
1 cup Raisin Bran cereal
½ cup wheat germ
1 cup whole wheat flour

Mix 1 cup unbleached flour, dry yeast, and salt in a large bowl. Add water, milk, oil, and honey, then fold in egg whites. Beat with a mixer for approximately 3 minutes at high speed. Fold in Raisin Bran, wheat germ, remaining unbleached flour, and whole wheat flour. Divide dough and let rise for 45 minutes in non-stick loaf pans. Bake at 375 degrees for 35–40 minutes. Let cool before serving. *Optional:* Lightly sprinkle top of bread with cinnamon sugar before baking.

Gayle Anne VanFulpen
NewLife Publications, FL

I have treasured the words of his mouth more than my daily bread (Job 23:12).

Scones

2 cups flour
½ teaspoon salt
4 teaspoons baking powder
¼ cup butter or margarine

¾ cup sour milk
1 cup firmly packed grated cheese
   or raisins (optional)

Preheat oven to 475 degrees. Sift together dry ingredients; using your fingers, crumble together with the butter or margarine. Add milk. (To make sour milk, add a little lemon juice or vinegar to sweet milk.) Stir into a very soft dough. Add cheese or raisins if desired. Pat dough out on a floured board, working the dough as little as possible. Cut into rounds. Bake on an ungreased cookie sheet for 10–12 minutes until pale gold.

Lita Barnes and Doris Jones
International Prayer Ministry, FL

Sour Cream Banana Bread

½ cup butter, softened
1 cup sugar
2 eggs
2 bananas, mashed
1 cup sour cream
1 teaspoon vanilla

2 cups flour (or 1½ cups whole
    wheat flour)
1 teaspoon baking soda
pinch salt
1 cup walnuts (optional)

Preheat oven to 350 degrees. Cream together butter, sugar, and eggs; add bananas, sour cream, and vanilla. Combine flour with soda and salt, and add to banana mixture. Stir in nuts. Put into 2 greased and floured loaf pans. Bake 1 hour.

Shirley Heinmets
International Ministry, Europe

South African Overnight Bread

2 cakes compressed yeast or
    2 packages dry yeast
2½ quarts water
3 cups sugar
1 pound margarine or butter

1 can condensed milk
2 teaspoons salt
10 pounds flour
4 eggs, well beaten

Heat together the yeast, water, sugar, butter, and condensed milk. Mix the salt and flour. Add the eggs and the milk mixture to the flour, and knead well. Cover and let rise in a warm place overnight. Form into balls and place on baking pans. Cover and let rise well again. Bake for approximately 45 minutes at 375 degrees.

Babs Oosthuizen
International Ministry, South Africa

Spiced Carrot Muffins

1½ cups flour	½ cup brown sugar
1 teaspoon baking soda	1 egg
1 teaspoon baking powder	½ cup buttermilk or sour milk
½ teaspoon cinnamon	⅓ cup oil
½ teaspoon salt	½ teaspoon vanilla
¼ teaspoon nutmeg	1½ cups grated carrots
pinch ginger	½ cup raisins
pinch allspice	½ cup nuts

Preheat oven to 400 degrees. Measure the dry ingredients into a large bowl. In a separate bowl, beat together the egg, buttermilk, oil, and vanilla. Add to the flour mixture, and stir in the remaining ingredients. Do *not* over mix. Bake in greased muffin tins for 20 minutes.

Bob MacLeod
Finance, FL

Spiced Coconut Carrot Muffins

2 cups flour	1 cup sweetened coconut
1 tablespoon baking powder	1 cup shredded carrots
1 tablespoon cinnamon	1 cup raisins
¼ teaspoon ground cloves	1 small, tart green apple, peeled
¼ teaspoon ginger	and coarsely chopped
¼ teaspoon nutmeg	½ cup chopped walnuts
¼ teaspoon salt	1 cup vegetable oil
1 cup firmly packed dark brown sugar	3 large eggs
¾ cup sugar	1 tablespoon vanilla

Preheat oven to 375 degrees. Sift the first 7 ingredients into a large bowl. Mix in both sugars, coconut, carrots, raisins, apple, and nuts. Whisk oil, eggs, and vanilla in a small bowl to blend. Gradually add oil mixture to dry ingredients. Pour into muffin cups lined with foil liners. Bake for 25 minutes. Makes 18 muffins.

To enjoy what I call the "Coffee Chat With Muffins," call your neighbors and friends one or two days before baking these muffins, and invite them over to chat. Then just put on a pot of coffee or tea, set out the muffins and your favorite tea service, and get to know your neighbors!

Barbara Ball
ChurchLIFE, CA

Spicy Apple Wheat Germ Muffins

1½ cups unsifted unbleached flour
½ cup wheat germ
1 tablespoon baking powder
½ teaspoon salt
½ teaspoon cinnamon
½ teaspoon nutmeg

½ cup raw sugar or honey
¼ cup margarine
2 eggs
1 cup finely chopped apple
⅓ cup raisins (optional)
½ cup milk

Preheat oven to 400 degrees. Measure flour, wheat germ, baking powder, salt, and spices. Stir well to blend. Cream sugar, margarine, and eggs thoroughly. Stir in apple and raisins. Add blended dry ingredients to creamed mixture alternately with milk; stir until moistened. Fill oiled muffin tins. Bake for 20 minutes. Makes 15 muffins.

Arlene Dennison
Crusade Family

Stromboli

1 loaf frozen bread dough
1 egg, beaten
1 tablespoon oregano or
    Italian seasoning

2 teaspoons grated Parmesan cheese
⅓ pound sliced provolone
⅓ pound sliced pepperoni

Preheat oven to 350 degrees. Completely thaw bread dough. Roll it out flat on a greased surface. Brush dough with beaten egg, sprinkle with seasoning and Parmesan cheese. Layer with provolone and pepperoni. Roll up like a jelly roll and tuck edges under. Egg wash the outside of the loaf, and sprinkle with Parmesan and seasoning. Bake for 25 minutes or until brown. Slice and serve.

Chris Sather
Student Venture, MN

Now he who supplies seed to the sower and bread for food will also supply and increase your store of seed and will enlarge the harvest of your righteousness (2 Cor. 9:10).

Swedish Coffee Bread

2½ cups water
⅔ cup sugar
2 teaspoons salt
⅓ cup butter

6–8 cups flour, *divided*
2 packages yeast
2 eggs, well beaten
1 teaspoon cardamom (optional)

Bring water, sugar, and salt to a boil; stir. Add butter to mixture and cool to 130 degrees. Mix 2½ cups flour and yeast, and add to above mixture. Beat 3 minutes with mixer on high. Add eggs and cardamom at medium speed. Lower speed; add enough additional flour to make a firm dough that is not sticky when kneaded. With mixer, beat in flour as much as possible. (Dough hooks are helpful but not necessary.)

On a floured surface, knead in enough of the remaining flour so it is not too sticky (about 10 minutes). Place dough in a greased bowl and cover with a cloth or plate; let rise until doubled in size. Punch down and let rise again. Make into braided rings, rolls, etc. Let rise and bake at 350 degrees for 10–12 minutes. Brush with butter after baked. Cool on a rack.

Joan Tungseth
Computer Services, FL

Sweet Potato Biscuits

¾ cup whole wheat flour
¾ cup unbleached all-purpose flour
2½ teaspoons baking powder
½ teaspoon salt
2 tablespoons brown sugar, packed
1 teaspoon cinnamon

½ teaspoon nutmeg
⅓ cup butter
¼ cup milk
½ cup cooked or canned sweet
    potatoes, mashed

Preheat oven to 425 degrees. Mix dry ingredients; cut in butter until mixture is coarse. Stir in milk and sweet potatoes. Knead gently 12 times. Roll dough ½-inch thick. Cut into 2- to 3-inch rounds, and sprinkle with additional cinnamon or sugar if desired. Bake on ungreased baking sheet for 10–12 minutes.

Gayle Anne VanFulpen
NewLife Publications, FL

Sweet Potato Muffins

½ cup butter
1¼ cups sugar
2 eggs
1¼ cups canned sweet potatoes,
    mashed
1½ cups all-purpose flour
2 teaspoons baking powder

½ teaspoon salt
1 teaspoon cinnamon
¼ teaspoon nutmeg
1 cup milk
¼ cup chopped pecans or walnuts
½ cup chopped raisins

Preheat oven to 400 degrees. Cream butter and sugar. Add eggs and mix well. Blend in the sweet potatoes. Sift flour with baking powder, salt, cinnamon, and nutmeg. Add alternately with milk. (Do not over mix.) Fold in nuts and raisins. Fill cups ⅔ full in greased muffin tin. Bake for 25 minutes. (The key to making these successfully is to use four muffin tins with cups measuring about 1½ inches across the bottom and 2 inches across the top.)

Peggy Hawkins
JESUS Video Project, FL

Wheat Germ Zucchini Bread

3 eggs
1 cup salad oil
1 cup granulated sugar
1 cup brown sugar
1 tablespoon maple flavoring
2 cups shredded zucchini

2½ cups flour
½ cup toasted wheat germ
2 teaspoons baking soda
½ teaspoon baking powder
1 cup chopped nuts
⅓ cup sesame seeds

Preheat oven to 350 degrees. With mixer, beat eggs, oil, sugars, and flavoring until thick and foamy. Use spoon to stir in zucchini. In a separate bowl, mix dry ingredients. Add flour mixture and nuts to zucchini mixture. Pour into two 5×9-inch greased and floured loaf pans. Bake for 1 hour. Insert a toothpick to test for doneness. If it comes out clean, bread is done. Let bread stand for 10 minutes after baking, then remove from pans. Sprinkle with sesame seeds.

Cheryl Henderson
Contributions and Postal Services, FL

Whole Wheat Rusks

½ cup vinegar
1 quart milk
3 cups bran
8 cups unsifted meal (flour),
   Wheaty Treat, or Nutty Wheat

3 cups white flour or cake flour
⅓ cup baking powder
2 teaspoons salt
1 cup sugar
1 pound butter or margarine, melted

Add vinegar to milk before measuring dry ingredients to allow milk to sour
(or use sour milk). Mix dry ingredients in a bowl. Combine soured milk and
margarine, and warm. Stir into dry ingredients. Line pan with waxed paper
or greased brown paper. (Baking pan must be paper lined or the rusks will
stick to the pan.) Put dough in pan. Bake at 360 degrees for 1 hour, then at
150 degrees for 30 minutes. Test for doneness with a toothpick. When
cooked, remove from pan. Cool. Slice thinly and dry in the oven at 200–250
degrees for 4–5 hours.

Variations: Add 2 teaspoons barley sweetener and 1 tablespoon vanilla; or
substitute 8 teaspoons baking powder and 2 teaspoons soda for the ⅓ cup
baking powder; or substitute 1 teaspoon cinnamon, 1 teaspoon nutmeg, and
8 cups ground oven wheat flour for the 8 cups unsifted meal.

Leta Barnes
International Ministry, South Africa

*Keep my commands and you will live; guard my teachings
as the apple of your eye (Prov. 7:2).*

Zucchini Muffins

2 eggs, slightly beaten
2 cups shredded zucchini
1¾ cups flour
¾ cup sugar

1½ teaspoons baking soda
½ teaspoon cinnamon
1 cup chopped pecans or walnuts

Preheat oven to 375 degrees. Combine all ingredients. Do not over mix;
mixture should be lumpy. Bake in greased muffin pan for 20–25 minutes
until a toothpick comes out clean. Makes 1 dozen. *Variation:* Carrots can be
substituted for the zucchini.

Sus Schmitt
Computer Services, FL

Breakfasts & Brunches

Apple Pancake Tier

6 eggs
1 cup flour
1 teaspoon salt
½ teaspoon nutmeg
1 cup milk
½ cup melted butter, *divided*

6 cooking apples, peeled, cored,
and sliced
½ cup sugar
2 teaspoons grated lemon peel
confectioners sugar

Preheat oven to 350 degrees. Beat eggs thoroughly. Mix in flour, salt, and nutmeg on low speed until moistened. Then mix in milk and ¼ cup melted butter. Pour 1 cup batter into each of 3 greased 9-inch pie pans. Bake until pancakes are light brown and puffy (15–20 minutes). While pancakes bake, add apples to remaining butter and cook on low for 5 minutes, stirring occasionally; then stir in sugar. Cook until apples are tender (about 10 minutes). Place one pancake on a serving plate and top with ⅓ of apple mixture and ⅓ of lemon peel. Repeat twice. Garnish with confectioners sugar. Cut into 4 pieces to serve. Top with warm syrup.

Michelle Leichty
Campus Ministry, IL

Baked Chili Relleno

2 large cans Ortega green chilies,
drained and chopped
8 ounces Monterey Jack cheese, grated
8 ounces cheddar cheese, grated

2 eggs, beaten
2 tablespoons flour
1 large can evaporated milk
1 can Ortega green chili salsa

Preheat oven to 350 degrees. In a greased 8-inch square pan, place a layer of chilies, then a layer of each cheese. Alternate layers of chilies and cheeses until all is used (about 3 layers). Mix eggs, flour, and evaporated milk. Pour egg mixture over chilies. Bake for 40 minutes. Remove from oven. Pour salsa over top. Return to oven and bake 10 more minutes.

Susan Heckmann
President's Office, FL

Barbara's Brunch Casserole

1 box seasoned croutons
1 pound any variety Jimmy Dean sausage, browned, drained, and crumbled
6 eggs
3 cups milk
1 can cream of mushroom soup

1 16-ounce package frozen Italian-style vegetables
1 cup grated cheddar cheese
1 cup grated Monterey Jack or mozzarella cheese

Preheat oven to 350 degrees. Spray a 9×13-inch pan with non-stick spray, and line the bottom with croutons. Sprinkle cooked sausage over croutons. Beat eggs and milk in a large bowl until thoroughly mixed. Add remaining ingredients, mixing well with a spoon. Pour egg mixture over the sausage. Bake for 1 hour. This recipe may be prepared ahead and refrigerated overnight before baking. Serves 10–12.

Barbara Nigh
Contributions and Postal Services, FL

Biscuits and Sausage Gravy

2 cups flour
1 teaspoon salt
3 teaspoons baking powder

$\frac{1}{3}$ cup Crisco
$\frac{3}{4}$ cup milk
Sausage Gravy

Preheat oven to 450 degrees. Combine flour, salt, and baking powder. Cut in Crisco until about the size of peas. Stir in milk until just mixed. Knead dough 10 times on a floured surface. Pat out dough until it is about 1-inch thick, and cut biscuits with biscuit cutter or a glass. Spray a baking sheet with cooking spray. Place biscuits close together and bake for 10–15 minutes or until light brown. Serve with *Sausage Gravy*.

Sausage Gravy:

1 pound ground sausage	2½ cups milk, *divided*
3 tablespoons flour	

Fry sausage until well browned; remove from pan. Drain off grease, reserving 3 tablespoons in pan. Sprinkle flour into pan. Cook for 2 minutes, stirring constantly. Add 1 cup milk, whisking rapidly to avoid lumps. Add remaining milk, stirring constantly. Add sausage, and boil for 2 minutes. Serve over biscuits.

Carol and Gary Culbertson
President's Office, FL

Better a dry crust with peace than a house full of feasting with strife (Prov. 17:1).

BREAKFASTS

Breakfast Oven Cakes

2 cups packaged pancake mix	2 tablespoons oil
1½ cups milk	½ teaspoon cinnamon
1 egg	½ cup chopped walnuts

Preheat oven to 350 degrees. Mix all ingredients, and pour into a greased 9×13-inch pan. Bake 13 minutes. Remove from oven, and cut into squares. Serve with or without syrup.

Sus Schmidt
Computer Services, FL

Buttermilk Beauties Waffles or Pancakes

1 cup white flour	2 teaspoons oil
1 cup whole wheat flour	2 eggs
1 teaspoon soda	1 cup plain yogurt
2 teaspoons baking powder	1 cup buttermilk

Combine all ingredients, and cook pancakes on a hot griddle. Batter can also be used to make thick, crisp waffles.

Becky Leppard
International Ministry, FL

Buttermilk Pancakes

1 cup buttermilk
1 egg
3 tablespoons canola oil

¾ cup flour
¼ teaspoon salt
1 teaspoon baking soda

Mix all ingredients. Pour about ½ cup batter on a hot griddle, turning when bubbles start to form and pancake is nicely browned. Brown the second side and remove from griddle. Serve with butter and maple syrup.

Anne Lawrence
World Changers Radio, FL

Cheese Egg Casserole

10 slices bread
3 ounces mushrooms, sliced and
     sautéed
1½ pounds cheese, grated
2 cups diced ham
2½ cups half & half
6 eggs, beaten

1 tablespoon brown sugar
1 small onion, chopped
½ teaspoon paprika
½ teaspoon Worcestershire sauce
½ teaspoon dry mustard
1 teaspoon salt
1 teaspoon celery salt

Remove bread crusts and cut bread into cubes. In a buttered 9×13-inch casserole, layer half the mushrooms, bread, cheese, and ham. Layer again. Mix remaining ingredients. Pour egg mixture over layers. Refrigerate overnight. Bake at 350 degrees for 1 hour. Serves 8.

Ray Van Tuinen
History's Handful, FL

Chili Relleno Casserole

5 eggs
3 tablespoons flour
¼ cup milk
1 tablespoon cumin
1 teaspoon Mexican seasoning
    or chili powder

1½ cups grated Monterey Jack
    or cheddar cheese
1 can diced chilies
salsa
sour cream

Preheat oven to 350 degrees. Mix eggs, flour, milk, and seasonings. In a greased 9-inch pan, layer ½ of cheese, then chilies. Layer remaining cheese on top. Pour the egg mixture over layers and bake for 30 minutes. Cut into squares and serve with salsa and sour cream for a late breakfast.

Sandra Auer
International Ministry, FL

Cold Oatmeal

2 cups dry oatmeal
1 cup applesauce
1 cup apple juice

1 cup milk
¼ cup raisins
1 teaspoon cinnamon

Mix all ingredients; cover and store in refrigerator overnight. Serve with milk. *Optional:* Add finely chopped apples, coconut, nuts, or whatever your family likes.

Krissa Webb
Finance, FL

Corn Cakes With Goat Cheese
and Red Pepper Sauce

Red Pepper Sauce:

1 large red bell pepper
2 shallots, minced (about ¼ cup)
1 clove garlic, minced
2 tablespoons unsalted butter

1 teaspoon tomato paste
pinch cayenne
½ cup half & half
salt and pepper to taste

Broil pepper directly under heat for five minutes until blackened, then turn and broil the other side. Place pepper into a paper bag to steam for 15 minutes. Remove the pepper; peel, seed, and chop it. In a small saucepan, cook shallots and garlic in butter over moderately low heat, stirring until softened. Stir in remaining ingredients; cook until heated through. In a blender, purée mixture with roasted pepper until smooth. Transfer sauce to pan and heat over moderate heat until hot. *Do not boil!* Sauce may be made a day ahead, covered, and chilled; gently reheat before serving. Makes about 1¼ cups.

Corn Cakes:

1 cup fresh corn cut from about 2 ears
1 large egg, beaten
3 tablespoons unsalted butter, melted
¾ cup milk
½ cup flour
½ cup yellow cornmeal
1 teaspoon baking powder
1 teaspoon salt
¼ teaspoon sugar
1 4-ounce log soft mild goat cheese, quartered
red and yellow bell peppers, finely diced
fresh dill blossoms, finely diced
Red Pepper Sauce

Preheat oven to warm. In a bowl, stir together corn, egg, butter, and milk. In another small bowl, whisk together flour, cornmeal, baking powder, salt, and sugar. Stir flour mixture into milk mixture until well combined. Heat a griddle over moderate heat until drops of water scatter over the surface. Brush with butter. Working in batches, drop ⅛ cup batter onto griddle, and cook cakes until golden (1–2 minutes on each side). As they finish cooking, transfer corn cakes to a baking sheet, and keep warm in oven. Reheat *Red Pepper Sauce*, and divide it among 4 plates. Divide corn cakes and goat cheese among plates, and garnish with bell peppers and dill blossoms. Makes 12 corn cakes, serving 4 as a first course or a brunch main course.

Barbara Ball
ChurchLIFE, FL

Taste and see that the Lord is good; blessed is the man who takes refuge in him (Psalm 34:8).

Corny Cakes

½ cup instant masa
½ cup warm water
½ cup cake flour
1 teaspoon baking powder
1 teaspoon baking soda
3 cups fresh corn kernels, cut from
    about 4 medium-large ears

8 ounces low-fat plain yogurt
1 tablespoon sugar
¼ teaspoon salt
1 large egg plus 1 large egg white
3 tablespoons oil, *divided*
warm maple syrup

Combine masa and warm water in a large mixing bowl. Add flour, baking powder, baking soda, corn kernels, yogurt, sugar, salt, egg and egg white, and 2 tablespoons oil. Mix well. To cook, heat 1 tablespoon oil on a non-stick griddle over medium heat. When hot, pour a scant ¼ cup for each cake. Cook until bubbly on top (about 3 minutes). Turn over and brown the other side, about 3 more minutes. Keep cakes warm in a 200 degree oven while cooking the remaining cakes, adding more oil to the griddle as needed. Serve warm with warm maple syrup. Makes 14–16 (4-inch diameter) cakes.

To cook in oven, preheat generously oiled baking sheets at 425 degrees until very hot (about 10 minutes). Use a scant ¼ cup batter for each cake. Bake cakes until bubbly on top and well-browned on bottom (about 5 minutes). Turn over and brown the other side (about 3 minutes). Turn baking sheets around if cakes are baking unevenly.

Variation: Add ½ minced jalapeño pepper (seeded, if desired) and 2 minced large green onions to batter. Cook as instructed above. When cakes have been turned, sprinkle 1 tablespoon shredded Monterey Jack or cheddar cheese on each. Cover griddle for remaining 3 minutes or bake cakes uncovered for 3 minutes more. Garnish each cake with cilantro leaves and a dollop of salsa. You can also add crab.

Lois Mackey
CoMission, CA

Crepes Ensenadas

12 flour tortillas
12 thin slices ham
1 pound Monterey Jack cheese, cut
    lengthwise into ½-inch sticks

1 7-ounce can green chilies, cut
    into ¼-inch strips
Cheese Sauce
paprika

Preheat oven to 350 degrees. Place 1 ham slice on each tortilla. Put 1 cheese stick in center, and top with chili strip. Roll up tortilla, and place seam-side down in a greased 9×13-inch dish. Cover well with *Cheese Sauce*. Bake for 45 minutes. Sprinkle with paprika. Makes a great accompaniment with eggs for brunch.

Cheese Sauce:

½ cup butter
½ cup flour
1 quart milk
¾ pound cheddar cheese, grated

1 teaspoon prepared mustard
½ teaspoon salt
dash of pepper

Melt butter and blend in flour. Add remaining ingredients. Cook until smooth.

Barbara Ball
ChurchLIFE, FL

Crustless Quiche

4 ounces cheese, grated
5–6 slices bacon, fried and crumbled
chopped ham
chopped broccoli
sliced mushrooms
4 unbeaten eggs
½ cup chopped onions

1½ cups milk
½ cup flour
2 tablespoons butter or
    margarine (optional)
½ teaspoon salt
dash pepper

Preheat oven to 350 degrees. Butter a 10-inch pie plate, then sprinkle with cheese. Top with crumbled bacon, ham, broccoli, mushrooms, or whatever you would like (even a little leftover chili is good). Put remaining ingredients into a blender; blend for 1 minute. Pour over ingredients in the pie plate, and bake for 35 minutes. If using a glass pie plate, quiche may need to cook longer. Let stand 3–4 minutes before serving.

Jan Gidel
International Ministry, FL

*"Which of you fathers, if your son asks for a fish,
will give him a snake instead? Or if he asks for an egg,
will give him a scorpion?" (Luke 11:11,12)*

Crustless Spinach Quiche

2 slices day-old bread
1 10-ounce package frozen
   chopped spinach
8 ounces grated Gruyère cheese
6 eggs, slightly beaten

4 teaspoons grated onion
¼ teaspoon nutmeg
salt and pepper to taste
sour cream (optional)

Preheat oven to 350 degrees. Remove crusts from bread and tear bread into small pieces. Place spinach in a colander to thaw, then press out all the moisture. Mix spinach and bread in a bowl; add remaining ingredients except sour cream. Pour into a 9-inch buttered pie plate and bake for 25–30 minutes. Top with sour cream if desired.

Karen Virtue
Campus Ministry, CA

Deviled Egg Casserole

eggs, hard-boiled
mayonnaise
mustard
salt and pepper to taste

vinegar or pickle juice
medium *Basic White Sauce*
grated cheese
garlic

Preheat oven to 350 degrees. Remove shells from eggs, cut eggs in half lengthwise, and separate yolks from whites. Place yolks in a bowl, and mash with a fork. Season with mayonnaise, a small amount of mustard, salt and pepper, and vinegar or pickle juice to taste. Refill egg whites with yolk mixture. Place in a single layer in a baking dish.

To prepare cheese sauce, make a medium *Basic White Sauce* (see Accompaniments), and mix with grated cheese. Adjust amounts for the number of eggs you're using. Season with mustard and garlic to taste. Pour cheese sauce over the deviled eggs and bake until bubbly (about 30 minutes).

Vonette Bright
Co-founder, Campus Crusade for Christ
Executive Director, Women Today International, FL

BREAKFASTS

Easy Sourdough Flapjacks

1 package yeast
¼ cup warm water
1 egg, beaten

2 cups milk
2 cups biscuit mix

Soften yeast in warm water. To egg, add milk and biscuit mix. Beat with rotary beater until blended. Stir in softened yeast. Allow batter to stand at room temperature 1 hour and 30 minutes; do not stir. Bake on a hot, lightly greased griddle or in a skillet. Turn when surface bubbles break. Makes 2 dozen cakes.

Lois Mackey
CoMission, CA

Egg-stra Healthy

2 egg whites
diced tomatoes
diced onion

fresh mushrooms, sliced
½ ounce Jarlsberg cheese, grated

Beat egg whites until stiff. Pour into preheated pan that has been sprayed with non-stick spray. Sprinkle with vegetables. Cook over medium heat until eggs are cooked well on bottom. Lay cheese over vegetables, and fold omelette in half. Allow cheese to melt completely.

Gayle Anne VanFulpen
NewLife Publications, FL

Finnish Pancakes

¼ cup butter
3 eggs
2 cups milk
¾ teaspoon salt
2 teaspoons honey

1 cup flour
fresh strawberries, sliced
whipped cream
honey

Preheat oven to 350 degrees. In oven, melt butter in a 9×13-inch pan. Blend the next 5 ingredients in a blender; pour on top of butter. Bake for 45 minutes. Serve with strawberries and whipped cream sweetened with honey.

René Brygger
JusticeLINC, WI

French Brie Quiche Topped With Berries and Toasted Almonds

1 deep-dish pie shell
½ pound slightly under-ripe French brie cheese
4 eggs
1 cup cream
salt to taste

1 3-ounce package cream cheese with chives, cubed
⅓ cup sliced almonds
1½ cups fresh or frozen berries (strawberries, raspberries, blackberries, blueberries, etc.)

Preheat oven to 400 degrees. Bake pie shell for 8 minutes or until very lightly browned. While the brie is cold, use a sharp knife to remove the outer rind (mold) and dice the remaining brie. Distribute brie evenly in the pie shell. Beat eggs with cream and salt until blended, and pour over brie. Place cream cheese pieces into egg mixture, spacing them evenly. Reduce temperature to 350 degrees. Place quiche on a cookie sheet and bake for 20 minutes. Sprinkle top with sliced almonds, and continue baking for 15–20 minutes or until custard is set and almonds are browned. (Tent lightly with foil if almonds are browning too quickly.) Remove from oven and top with berries; serve immediately. Serves 4 as an entree or 12 as an appetizer. Howard loves it!

Barbara Ball
ChurchLIFE, FL

Fruit and Yogurt Smoothie

1 cup frozen unsweetened berries or other fruit
½ cup plain yogurt

orange extract or orange rind
honey (optional)

Blend the first 3 ingredients to a soft consistency. Add honey to sweeten if desired.

Jeannie Mitchell
Josh McDowell Ministry, CA

BREAKFASTS

Fruit Swirl Coffee Cake

4 cups Bisquick
½ cup sugar
½ cup plus 1–2 tablespoons milk, *divided*
1 teaspoon almond extract
1 teaspoon vanilla

¼ cup butter, melted
3 eggs
1 can raspberry pie filling (or other flavor)
1 cup powdered sugar
fresh berries (optional)

Preheat oven to 350 degrees. Grease a jelly roll pan (15½×10½ inches) or 2 9-inch square pans. Mix Bisquick, sugar, ½ cup milk, almond extract, vanilla, butter, and eggs. Beat vigorously for 30 seconds. Spread ⅔ of batter in jelly roll pan or ⅓ in each square pan. Spread pie filling over batter. Drop remaining batter by tablespoons onto pie filling. Bake for 20–25 minutes. Mix powdered sugar and 1–2 tablespoons milk to glaze consistency. Drizzle over coffee cake while warm. Serve warm or cool. Top with fresh berries.

Ann Tormanen
International Ministry, FL

Gingerbread Hotcakes

2½ cups flour
1½ teaspoons soda
1 teaspoon cinnamon
1 teaspoon ginger
½ teaspoon ground cloves
½ teaspoon salt

½ cup butter
1¾ cups light molasses
1 egg
¾ cup black coffee
coconut syrup
whipped cream

Sift together the dry ingredients. In a separate bowl, combine butter, molasses, egg, and coffee, and beat until well blended. Combine dry ingredients with molasses mixture, and beat until thoroughly blended. Bake on medium griddle. Serve with coconut syrup and whipped cream. If you want a real crazy Sunday morning breakfast, this is it!

Dorothy Gregory
Crusade Family

Good-For-You Hotcakes

1 cup whole wheat flour
¼ cup wheat or oat bran
½ teaspoon salt
1 teaspoon baking powder
¾ cup buttermilk

1 egg plus 1 egg white, beaten
½ teaspoon baking soda
1 tablespoon honey
¼ cup canola oil
milk (optional)

Mix flour, bran, salt, and baking powder. In another bowl, mix buttermilk, eggs, soda, honey, and oil. Add liquid mixture to dry ingredients, stirring only until blended. Add a little milk if you desire thinner pancakes. Heat griddle to medium, and coat with thin layer of oil. Pour ½ cup batter on griddle for each pancake, and cook until bubbles form. Turn and cook the other side.

Mary Jean Jennings
International Prayer Ministry, FL

Your home is the most natural place for life sharing. You and your guests are most comfortable there. —Vonette Bright

Grandma L's Perfect Pancakes

1¼ cups flour
2 teaspoons baking powder
2 tablespoons cooking oil

1 egg
1¼ cups milk (or more)

Using a whisk, mix flour and baking powder well. Add remaining ingredients, and beat well. Mix should pour readily, but not be runny. (If mix is too thick, the top of each pancake may still be too runny to turn, even though the bottom is browned and ready. If necessary, thin the mix with more milk to make pancakes thinner.) Heat greased griddle or large frying pan to medium heat. Control heat carefully; pan is ready for cooking when a water drop sizzles. Add about ½ cup batter per pancake. Turn pancakes after bubbles have surfaced and bottom is browned.

Lori Burns
Staff & Ministry Opportunities, FL

BREAKFASTS

> How sweet are your words to my taste, sweeter
> than honey to my mouth! (Psalm 119:103)

Homemade Granola

4 cups old-fashioned oatmeal
½ cup wheat germ
½ cup wheat bran
½ cup shredded coconut
½ cup sunflower seeds
½ cup chopped almonds
½ cup chopped walnuts

¼ cup honey
¼ cup canola oil
1 tablespoon molasses
1 teaspoon vanilla
¼ teaspoon nutmeg
½–¾ teaspoon cinnamon
raisins

Preheat oven to 275 degrees. Mix the first 7 ingredients. In another bowl, mix honey, oil, molasses, vanilla, nutmeg, and cinnamon. Heat in microwave for 20 seconds. Combine both mixtures, and bake on a large cookie sheet for 1 hour. After baking, add raisins and stir.

Mary Jean Jennings
International Prayer Ministry, FL

Hot Shrimp Sandwich

1 6½-ounce can shrimp pieces
¼ cup finely diced celery
1 tablespoon chopped green onion
2 tablespoons French dressing
¼ cup mayonnaise

dash chili powder
8 slices whole wheat bread
3 eggs, beaten, or egg substitute
1 tablespoon milk
¼ cup melted margarine

In a small bowl, mix shrimp pieces, celery, green onion, French dressing, mayonnaise, and chili powder. Spread on 4 slices of bread, and top with 4 slices. Stir together eggs and milk, and place in shallow bowl. Dip sandwiches into egg mixture, and fry in margarine over medium heat until lightly brown on each side. Makes 4 sandwiches. Great for special luncheons!

Yvonne Bibby
International Ministry, FL

Jan's Hominy Grits

1½ cups quick grits
6 cups boiling water
¾ cup butter
1 pound sharp cheddar cheese, shredded

3 eggs, beaten
1 tablespoon Lawry's seasoned salt
dash Tabasco
paprika

Preheat oven to 350 degrees. Cook grits in boiling water. Melt butter and add cheese, eggs, salt, and Tabasco. Mix with cooked grits. Place into casserole dish, and bake for 50 minutes. Sprinkle paprika on top and bake for 10 more minutes.

Vonette Bright
Co-founder, Campus Crusade for Christ
Executive Director, Women Today International, FL

Land of Nod Cinnamon Rolls

20 frozen dough rolls (Rich's)
½ cup brown sugar
½ box butterscotch pudding

2 teaspoons cinnamon
¾ cup raisins
½ cup butter, melted

Grease a 10-inch Bundt pan. Add frozen rolls; sprinkle with brown sugar, pudding powder, cinnamon, and raisins. Pour melted butter over all. Cover with clean, damp cloth (cheesecloth works best). Leave on the counter overnight. Bake at 325 degrees for 25 minutes. Let cool 5 minutes, then turn out onto a platter. Serves 10. These are great to serve for early morning meetings.

Renee Clifford
Campus Ministry, KY

Mama Sandra's Granola

12 cups rolled oats
2 cups flaked coconut
1 cup sunflower seeds

½ cup honey
½ cup water
1 cup oil

Preheat oven to 325 degrees. Mix dry ingredients in a large bowl, then add honey, water, and oil. Stir well. Spread mixture onto 3 or 4 cookie sheets.

BREAKFASTS

Bake for about 1 hour, stirring each pan from outside edges into center every 15 minutes. This is a hearty cereal that's not too sweet or fat-laden.

Sandra Auer
International Ministry, FL

Morning Energizer

1 cup cooked rice
1 cup drained pineapple,
   blueberries, or strawberries
½ cup skim milk

2 egg whites
2 packets Sweet'n Low
   or 2 tablespoons sugar

Preheat oven to 375 degrees. Spray a small casserole dish with vegetable spray. In a small bowl, mix all ingredients, then pour into casserole. Bake for approximately 25 minutes or until milk is absorbed.

Kelly Hall
Corporate Human Resources, FL

Old-Fashioned Crumb Cake

2 cups brown sugar
3 cups flour
½ cup margarine plus more for topping

1 cup buttermilk
cinnamon

Preheat oven to 375 degrees. With fingers, crumble together brown sugar, flour, and margarine to coarse meal. Set aside 1 cup mixture for topping. Add buttermilk to remaining mixture. Place in 2 greased 8-inch square pans or pie tins. Sprinkle with reserved topping. Dot with chunks of butter, and generously sprinkle with cinnamon. Bake for 30–40 minutes. This easy breakfast cake is so good!

Charlotte Day
Crusade Family

Orange French Toast

¼ cup butter
⅓ cup sugar
½ teaspoon cinnamon
1 teaspoon grated orange rind
4 eggs, slightly beaten

⅔ cup orange juice
15 1-inch slices French toast
flaked coconut (optional)
Orange Syrup

Preheat oven to 400 degrees. Place butter in a jelly roll pan, and melt in oven. Combine sugar, cinnamon, and orange rind. Sprinkle evenly over butter. Mix eggs and juice. Dip bread into egg mixture, soaking well. Arrange bread slices in pan on top of sugar mixture. Bake for 25 minutes. Let stand 1 minute, then lift out and serve sugar side up. Sprinkle with flaked coconut, and serve with a pitcher of *Orange Syrup*.

Orange Syrup:

1 6-ounce can frozen orange
   juice concentrate

⅓ cup butter
1⅓ cups sugar

Heat ingredients to boiling, stirring constantly. Cook until slightly thickened. Serve hot.

Joette Whims
NewLife Publications, CA

Overnight Coffee Cake

⅔ cup shortening
¾ cup sugar
½ cup brown sugar
2 eggs
1 teaspoon baking powder
1 teaspoon baking soda

1 teaspoon cinnamon
½ teaspoon salt
2 tablespoons powdered milk
2 cups flour
1 cup buttermilk
Brown Sugar Topping

Cream shortening and sugars. Beat in eggs. Add dry ingredients and buttermilk. Place into an oblong pan. Top with *Brown Sugar Topping*. Cover and refrigerate overnight. Bake at 350 degrees for 30–40 minutes. This is great for making ahead and serving to breakfast guests or for a brunch.

Brown Sugar Topping:

⅔ cup brown sugar   ½ cup chopped nuts
¾ teaspoon cinnamon   2 tablespoons flour
1 teaspoon nutmeg   ¼ cup butter

Mix all ingredients thoroughly.

Jeannette Entz
Campus Ministry, TX

Quesadilla Quiche

2 4-ounce cans chopped green   1 cup Bisquick
    chilies, drained   4 eggs
1 pound cheddar cheese, shredded   guacamole
2 cups milk   sour cream

Preheat oven to 425 degrees. Grease a 9×13-inch pan. Sprinkle chilies and
cheese onto the bottom of the pan. Beat milk, Bisquick, and eggs until
smooth; pour over chilies and cheese. Bake for 25–30 minutes. Let stand
10 minutes before cutting. Serve with dollops of guacamole and sour cream.
This is an easy favorite that is great for brunches!

Barbara Ball
ChurchLIFE, FL

Quiche Lorraine

1 9-inch pie crust   ½ teaspoon salt
8 slices bacon   dash nutmeg
8 ounces Swiss cheese, shredded   3 eggs, beaten
1 tablespoon flour   1¾ cups milk

Preheat oven to 450 degrees. Bake pie crust for 7 minutes or until lightly
browned. Remove from oven and reduce heat to 325 degrees. Fry bacon
until crisp; drain and crumble. Reserve 2 tablespoons bacon for garnish. Place
remaining bacon in pie crust, then sprinkle cheese over bacon. In a bowl,
mix the remaining ingredients and pour into crust. Sprinkle reserved bacon
on top. Bake for 35–40 minutes. Let stand for 10–15 minutes before serving. Serves 6–8. This "cheese pie" is good for a ladies' luncheon.

Joan Kendall
Crusade Family

Quiche Montezuma

1 9-inch pie crust	3 eggs, slightly beaten
1½ cups shredded Monterey Jack cheese	1 cup half & half
1 cup shredded mild cheddar cheese	¼ teaspoon salt
1 4-ounce can chopped green chilies	

Preheat oven to 450 degrees. Bake pie crust for 5–7 minutes or until lightly brown. Reduce heat to 325 degrees. Sprinkle all of the Jack and half of the cheddar cheese over the bottom of the pie crust. Distribute chilies over cheeses. Beat eggs with half & half and salt, and pour over contents in crust. Sprinkle remaining cheddar on top. Bake 40 minutes. Shake gently to see if center is set or insert knife blade to see if it comes out clean. Let quiche stand 15 minutes before cutting. Serve hot or cold. *Variation:* I use a 10-inch deep-dish crust and double the filling recipe, but triple the chilies (3 cans), then bake for about 60 minutes. This makes a thick, rich quiche that can be cut into smaller pieces.

Laurie Killingsworth
New Life Center, FL

BREAKFASTS

Do not be anxious about anything, but in everything, by prayer and petition, with thanksgiving, present your requests to God (Phil. 4:6).

Rainey's Thanksgiving French Toast

½ cup margarine	8–9 eggs
1½ cups brown sugar	pinch salt
1 teaspoon cinnamon	1¾–2 cups milk
8–12 slices bread	

Melt margarine in a 9×13-inch pan. Add brown sugar and cinnamon; stir. Lay bread slices on mixture. Beat eggs and salt together, then add milk. Pour over bread. Cover and refrigerate overnight. The next morning, uncover and bake at 350 degrees for 45 minutes. Cut into squares and place upside down on a plate so margarine and cinnamon are on top.

Dennis and Barbara Rainey
FamilyLIFE, AR

Robbyn's Baked French Toast

6 large eggs
1½ cups milk
1 cup half & half
1 tablespoon vanilla
1 teaspoon cinnamon
1 teaspoon nutmeg

1 loaf French bread
¼ cup melted butter
½ cup brown sugar
½ cup chopped walnuts
1 tablespoon corn syrup

Cut bread into slices, and place on the bottom of a greased 9×13-inch pan. Mix eggs, milk, half & half, vanilla, cinnamon, and nutmeg. Pour over bread. Refrigerate overnight. In the morning, mix melted butter, brown sugar, walnuts, and corn syrup. Sprinkle over French toast. Bake at 350 degrees for 40 minutes. This recipe is a must for our family's get-togethers.

Barbara Ball
ChurchLIFE, FL

Rosemont Quiche

6 ounces ham, diced
½ cup chopped onion
6 ounces Swiss cheese, grated
1 cup milk
½ cup half & half
½ cup Bisquick

pinch salt
pinch pepper
pinch nutmeg
pinch Italian spices
4 eggs
1 deep-dish pie crust

Preheat oven to 350 degrees. Mix ham, onion, and cheese; set aside. Combine remaining ingredients except eggs and pie crust. Whip in eggs. Add egg mixture to the ham mixture, and put in uncooked pie crust. Bake for 1 hour and 15 minutes. Rotate and bake 5 minutes more.

Sherry Cumpstone
Worldwide Challenge, FL

Saturday Morning Waffles à la Auers

3 eggs
1½ cups buttermilk
1 teaspoon soda
¾ cup whole wheat flour

1 cup flour
2 teaspoons baking powder
½ teaspoon salt
½ cup oil

Mix eggs and buttermilk. Add remaining ingredients and stir well. Pour by cupfuls onto piping-hot waffle iron.

Sandra Auer
International Ministry, FL

Sausage and Egg Souffle

1 pound mild ground sausage
6 eggs
2 cups milk
1 teaspoon salt

1 teaspoon dry mustard
6 slices white bread, cubed
1 cup grated cheddar cheese,
    firmly packed

Crumble and brown sausage; drain grease and cool meat. In a mixing bowl, beat eggs; add milk, salt, and mustard. Stir in bread cubes, then cheese and sausage. Place in an 8×12-inch baking dish. Cover and refrigerate overnight. Bake at 350 degrees for 45 minutes. Let stand for a few minutes, then cut and serve. *Variation:* Use 7 eggs and 3 slices cubed bread, and substitute mozzarella for part of the cheddar cheese.

John Cannon/Lorraine Pettijohn
President's Office, FL/Military Ministry, VA

Sausage Casserole

1 pound sausage, cooked and drained
1 can cream of celery soup
½ bag wide egg noodles, cooked
    and drained

1 can evaporated milk
8 ounces Velveeta cheese, cubed
salt and pepper to taste

Preheat oven to 350 degrees. Mix all ingredients and place in a lightly greased casserole dish. Bake for 25–35 minutes or until hot.

Shelly Martin
Campus Ministry, MN

Savory Eggs

1 cup grated cheese
2 tablespoons butter
½ cup cream
¼ teaspoon salt

pepper to taste
1 teaspoon mustard
6 eggs, slightly beaten

Preheat oven to 325 degrees. Spread cheese in a greased 8-inch square baking dish. Dot with butter. Combine cream, salt, pepper, and mustard. Pour half this mixture over cheese. Pour eggs into baking dish, then add remaining cream mixture. Bake for about 25 minutes. This recipe makes a delicious breakfast for company.

Midge Piedot
Crusade Family

Short Cut Coffee Cake

2 tablespoons soft butter
½ cup packed brown sugar
2 teaspoons cinnamon

½ cup white sugar
2 cans refrigerated biscuits
¼ cup melted butter

Preheat oven to 400 degrees. Crumble soft butter with brown sugar in the bottom of a ring mold. Mix cinnamon and white sugar. Dip each biscuit in melted butter, then in cinnamon-sugar mixture. Stand the biscuits on edge around the mold. Sprinkle remaining butter and cinnamon-sugar over biscuits. Bake for about 25 minutes. Immediately turn upside down on a plate and serve.

Elaine Hannah
History's Handful, CA

Southern Breakfast Casserole

8 slices bread (white or whole wheat), cubed
1 pound sausage, cooked, crumbled, drained, or ¾ pound ham, diced
8 ounces Swiss cheese, grated
8 ounces cheddar cheese, grated

1 cup sliced fresh mushrooms
5 eggs, beaten
1½ cups milk
salt and pepper to taste
1 teaspoon Worcestershire sauce
1 teaspoon dry mustard

Grease a 9×13-inch pan. Cover the bottom with bread cubes. Layer sausage or ham over bread. Add cheeses and mushrooms. In a medium mixing bowl, combine eggs, milk, salt, pepper, Worcestershire sauce, and mustard. Whisk thoroughly. Pour over bread mixture. Refrigerate overnight. The next morning, bake at 350 degrees for 40 minutes. *Optional:* You can lower the cholesterol and fat by using turkey sausage, low-fat cheeses, and 1% or non-fat milk.

Laura Staudt/Sharon Scroggins
Women Today International, FL/ChurchLIFE, FL

> *Only God can fully satisfy the hungry heart of man.*
> — Hugh Black

BREAKFASTS

Spinach Quiche

1 package frozen chopped spinach,
    cooked and drained
4 ounces cream cheese
½ teaspoon pepper
½ teaspoon parsley

2 eggs
¼ cup milk
1 cup grated cheddar cheese
1 9-inch pie crust

Preheat oven to 375 degrees. Combine all ingredients and pour into pie crust. Bake for 35 minutes.

Terry Morgan
Campus Ministry, Mexico

Strawberry Coffee Cake

½ cup butter
½ cup sugar
1½ cups flour
1½ teaspoons baking powder
1 egg, slightly beaten

1 teaspoon vanilla
2 cups sliced strawberries, *divided*
Topping
½ cup sliced almonds
powdered sugar

Preheat oven to 350 degrees. Cream butter and sugar. Combine flour and baking powder; add to creamed mixture. Mix in egg and vanilla. Pat into a greased 9-inch springform pan, and sprinkle with 1½ cups sliced strawberries. Prepare *Topping* and pour it over strawberries. Bake for approximately

1 hour. Before serving, sprinkle remaining strawberries, almonds, and powdered sugar over the cake, ending with the powdered sugar. This is an elegant cake that is great for brunches.

Topping:

2 cups sour cream   ½ cup sugar
2 egg yolks   1 teaspoon vanilla

Combine ingredients and blend well.

Barbara Ball
ChurchLIFE, FL

Swedish Fruit Rolls

1 cup cottage cheese   jam or fresh fruit
3 eggs   cornstarch (optional)
1 tablespoon cooking oil   whipped cream
salt   powdered sugar or coconut
¼ cup flour

Blend cottage cheese, eggs, oil, salt, and flour in a blender for a few seconds. Pour batter on a griddle and cook like pancakes. When done, spread with jam or fill with fresh fruit thickened with cornstarch. Fold in half and roll up. Top with whipped cream, powdered sugar, or coconut. These are great for breakfast or a snack.

Gladys Dickleman
Crusade Family

Swedish Pancakes

4 eggs   2 cups flour
3 cups milk   ¼ cup oil
1 cup sugar (or less)   fruit (optional)
2 teaspoons salt

Mix all ingredients except fruit. Fry on a lightly oiled griddle. Stack on a plate, or top with fruit and roll up like a jelly roll.

Joan Tungseth
Computer Services, FL

Turkish Pancakes

4 eggs, slightly beaten
1½ cups flour
½ teaspoon salt

1½ cups milk
¼ cup butter

Preheat oven to 400 degrees. To eggs, gradually add flour, salt, and milk. Melt butter in a 9×13-inch pan. Pour batter over butter. Bake for 30 minutes.

Doris Maugle
Contributions and Postal Services, FL

Whole Grain Yogurt Pancakes

1 cup plain yogurt
1 cup water
3 eggs
¼ cup canola oil

1 teaspoon baking powder
2 cups flour (rye, oat millet,
buckwheat, or other flour)

In a large bowl, mix yogurt, water, eggs, oil, and baking powder. Add flour and beat until lumps disappear. Cook over medium-high heat on a lightly oiled skillet.

Jennie Mitchell
Josh McDowell Ministry, CA

BREAKFASTS

World Famous Waffles

¼ teaspoon baking soda
¼ teaspoon salt
1 cup white flour, or ½ cup wheat
and ½ cup white flour

1 egg, separated
1 cup buttermilk
¼ cup oil

Preheat waffle iron. Mix dry ingredients. Add egg yolk, buttermilk, and oil. Beat egg white until semi-stiff, and fold into batter. Pour onto waffle iron. Cook until golden brown.

Dick Edie
Church Dynamics International, CA

Yogurt and Grain Smoothie

3 frozen strawberries
5 frozen peach slices
½–1 fresh banana
¼ cup plain yogurt
1 teaspoon honey

cinnamon to taste
2 tablespoons wheat germ
2 tablespoons oat bran
½–¾ cup cranberry juice

Blend all ingredients until smooth. Serve immediately. Makes 1 serving.

Theresa Anstett
Corporate Human Resources, FL

Yogurt Coffee Cake

1½ cups plus 2 tablespoons flour,
   divided
1 cup sugar
2 teaspoons baking powder
½ teaspoon salt
1 cup yogurt (peach is great)

½ cup oil
2 eggs
½ cup brown sugar
2 teaspoons cinnamon
2 tablespoons butter, melted
½ cup chopped nuts

Preheat oven to 350 degrees. Combine 1½ cups flour with the next 6 ingredients and stir until well blended. Pour ½ of the batter into a well-greased 8- or 9-inch pan. Then combine 2 tablespoons flour, brown sugar, cinnamon, butter, and nuts; sprinkle ½ of streusel over batter in pan. Add remaining batter and sprinkle with remaining streusel. Bake for 35–45 minutes.

Terry Morgan
Campus Ministry, Mexico

God is at work within you, helping you want to obey him, and then helping you do what he wants (Phil. 2:13).

Salads
&
Salad Dressings

Salads

Apricot Nectar Jell-O Salad

1 small package orange or
　lemon Jell-O
2 cups liquid (apricot nectar plus
　juice of one lemon), *divided*

1 banana, sliced
1 orange, sliced
¼ cup nuts, chopped
3–4 marshmallows, cut up

Heat 1 cup liquid; add Jell-O, and stir well to dissolve. Add remaining liquid. Mix with all other ingredients and chill.

Vonette Bright
Co-founder, Campus Crusade for Christ
Executive Director, Women Today International, FL

Apricot Salad

3 cups apricot nectar
2 small packages lemon Jell-O
¼ cup lemon juice
½ cup water
½ cup crushed pineapple, undrained

pinch of salt
2 bananas, diced
1 cup mandarin oranges
mayonnaise

Heat nectar to boiling point; add Jell-O and stir until dissolved. Add lemon juice, water, pineapple, and salt. Chill until thickened. Stir in bananas and oranges. Grease mold with mayonnaise; fill with Jell-O mixture. Chill until firm. Serves 10. This salad is nice and tart.

André Rabe Alton
Crusade Family

Aunt Veronica's Pickled Macaroni

2 pounds spiral macaroni
2¾ cups vinegar
½ cup oil
1½ cups sugar
2 tablespoons prepared mustard
1 tablespoon salt
1 teaspoon pepper

1 tablespoon parsley
1 teaspoon celery seed
1 teaspoon garlic powder
1 medium red onion, chopped
1 medium green pepper, chopped
2 medium carrots, grated

Cook macaroni in salted water; drain, rinse, and dry on towels. Coat with oil and stir in remaining ingredients. Let stand at room temperature for 1 hour, stirring occasionally. Cover and refrigerate for 2–3 days for best flavor.

Liesl Buck
International Ministry, FL

Avocado-Orange Salad

1 tablespoon white vinegar
1½ teaspoons olive oil
¼ teaspoon salt

⅛ teaspoon pepper
1 medium avocado, cubed
2 oranges, peeled and cut

About 15 minutes before serving, mix vinegar with oil, salt, and pepper in a small bowl. Mix with freshly cut avocado and orange pieces; toss lightly. Serve in avocado half shells or in small individual bowls. For a family, double the recipe and serve family style, if desired.

René Brygger
JusticeLINC, WI

Bean Waldorf Salad

2 cups cooked chickpeas or 1 can
    chickpeas or beans (white, kidney,
    navy, or pea), rinsed and drained
2 Red Delicious apples, cored,
    unpeeled, and cubed

1 cup diced celery
¼ cup chopped walnuts
¼ cup reduced-calorie mayonnaise
2 tablespoons lemon juice
greens (Boston or romaine lettuce)

Place all ingredients except greens into a mixing bowl; toss well. Cover and chill 2 hours before serving on greens. Makes 6 servings: 159 calories; 4.9 g fat; 1.33 mg cholesterol; 55.8 mg sodium.

Debra Brady
Staff & Ministry Opportunities, FL

Beautiful Green Jell-O

1 large can pears with juice
1 small package lime Jell-O

1 3-ounce package cream cheese
1 package whipped topping, prepared

Drain pears and reserve the juice. Boil pear juice and add lime Jell-O. Stir until dissolved. Mix cream cheese and pears in blender. Add to Jell-O. Let stand until slightly set, then fold in prepared whipped topping. Chill.

Sus Schmitt
Computer Services, FL

 "How beautiful are the feet of those who bring good news!" (Rom. 10:15)

SALADS

Black Bean and Salsa Salad

¼ cup red wine vinegar dressing
1 16- or 20-ounce jar mild salsa
1 15-ounce can black beans,
    rinsed and drained

1 15-ounce can corn, drained
1½ cups chopped celery
½ cup chopped green onions
¼ cup chopped cilantro

Mix the dressing and salsa. In a separate bowl, mix remaining ingredients. Pour dressing mixture over vegetables and toss. Chill and serve. Serves 6–8 as a side dish. I like to double this recipe because many people like seconds, and leftovers are always consumed quickly.

Miriam Phinney
Campus Ministry, MT

Blackened Chicken Salad

½ teaspoon salt
¼ teaspoon paprika
¼ teaspoon ground red pepper
¼ teaspoon black pepper
⅛ teaspoon garlic powder
⅛ teaspoon onion powder
⅛ teaspoon ground cumin

2 tablespoons margarine, *divided*
4 4-ounce skinned, boned chicken
    breast halves
1 cup vertically sliced onion
1½ cups chopped tomatoes
lettuce leaves (optional)

Combine the seasonings in a bowl; rub over chicken. Place a skillet over high heat until hot; add 1 tablespoon margarine, and quickly tilt in all directions so margarine covers bottom. Add chicken; cook 2 minutes on each side or until blackened. Remove chicken. Melt remaining margarine in skillet over medium-high heat; add onion and sauté 1 minute. Reduce heat to medium and cook 5 minutes or until tender, stirring occasionally. Thinly slice chicken; toss with onion and chill. Just before serving, drain the chopped tomatoes, and add to chicken mixture. Serve over lettuce or as a filling for pita bread or croissants. Serves 4.

Laura Staudt
Women Today International, FL

Broccoli Raisin Salad

1 bunch fresh broccoli
½ cup or less yellow raisins

½ cup or less walnuts
Marzetti's or other slaw dressing

Cut broccoli florets into bite-size pieces. Mix in a bowl with raisins and walnuts. Add dressing to taste.

Mary Jane Morgan
Crusade Family

Broccoli Salad

2 bunches raw broccoli florets,
  cut into bite-size pieces
1 pound bacon, fried and crumbled
  (optional)
¼ cup medium red onion, finely
  chopped

1 pound cheddar cheese, grated
½ cup mayonnaise or light Miracle
  Whip salad dressing
2 tablespoons wine vinegar
2 tablespoons sugar

Toss together the broccoli, bacon, cheese, and onion. Mix remaining ingredients and pour over salad just before serving. *Optional:* Add other vegetables such as small fresh mushrooms or cherry tomatoes. I usually double the recipe. *Variations:* Bobbi Jo Hasz (Campus Ministry, WA) uses half the broccoli and adds an equal amount of cauliflower. Cherie Allen (CoMission, FL) omits the cheddar cheese; substitutes 1 bunch chopped green onions for the red onion; and adds ½ cup diced red bell pepper and ½ cup sunflower seeds.

Mitzi Norton
Campus Ministry, NY

Cabbage Nut Slaw

1 cup slivered almonds
½ cup sesame seeds
2 tablespoons margarine
1 large head cabbage, shredded

10 green onions with tops, chopped
2 packages dry Ramen noodles,
  crushed
Slaw Dressing

Sauté almonds and sesame seeds in margarine until brown. When cooled, toss with cabbage and onions. Add noodles and dressing just before serving. *Tip:* Can be made a day ahead and stored in the refrigerator; mix with noodles and dressing when ready to serve.

Slaw Dressing:
¾ cup oil
2 teaspoons salt

1 teaspoon black pepper
⅓ cup Maukan rice vinegar

Shake ingredients in a pint jar until salt is dissolved. Refrigerate until ready to use.

Hilda Swartzwelter
Katherine Bright's grandmother

SALADS

Cafe Figaro Egg-Free Caesar Salad

inner leaves of 2 heads romaine
    lettuce, cut up
Caesar Dressing

Garlic Croutons
2 tablespoons grated Parmesan
    cheese

Place romaine leaves in a bowl. Add *Caesar Dressing* and *Garlic Croutons*. Toss slightly but thoroughly. Sprinkle with Parmesan cheese. Makes 6 servings. *Optional:* Add shrimp, chunks of chicken, or sliced steak.

Caesar Dressing:

¼ cup lemon juice
½ cup freshly grated Parmesan cheese
2–3 canned whole anchovy fillets
2 teaspoons Worcestershire sauce
1 teaspoon red wine vinegar

2 tablespoons Dijon mustard, *divided*
2 tablespoons puréed garlic
salt and pepper to taste
¾ cup olive oil

In a blender, combine all ingredients except olive oil; whir on medium speed. Gradually add olive oil in a continuous stream until dressing is completely blended and smooth. If too thick, thin with up to ¼ cup cold water.

Garlic Croutons:

6 slices whole-wheat bread, crusts
    trimmed and bread cubed

3–4 tablespoons butter, melted
2 teaspoons garlic powder

Toss well. Bake at 400 degrees until browned.

Lois Mackey
CoMission, CA

Cajun Tomato Aspic With Shrimp

1½ envelopes gelatin
¼ cup cold water
2 cups tomato juice
1 bay leaf
1 stalk celery, chopped
¼ onion or 1 green onion, chopped
salt and pepper to taste
lemon juice to taste
Worcestershire sauce to taste

dash hot sauce
1 tablespoon minced parsley
¼ cup finely chopped celery
2 carrots, grated
1½ cups small cocktail shrimp
1 3-ounce package cream cheese,
    softened
3 tablespoons mayonnaise
lettuce leaves

Dissolve gelatin in cold water. Combine the tomato juice, bay leaf, celery, and onion. Bring to a boil and simmer slowly for 5 minutes. Strain out bay leaf, celery, and onion. Add dissolved gelatin to tomato juice; mix well. Add salt, pepper, lemon juice, Worcestershire sauce, hot sauce, parsley, celery, carrots, and shrimp. Pour about half the mixture into a greased mold, and chill until jelled. Mix cream cheese with mayonnaise. Spread a thin layer over the congealed mixture in the mold; top with the remaining tomato juice mixture. Chill until firm. Turn out onto lettuce leaves.

Cathy Oliver
Student Venture, TX

Caribbean Shrimp and Black Bean Salad

1 15-ounce can black beans, rinsed and drained
1 small green pepper, finely chopped
½ cup chopped celery
½ cup sliced purple onion, separated into rings
2 tablespoons chopped fresh cilantro leaves
¼ cup lime juice
2 tablespoons vegetable oil
2 tablespoons honey
¼ teaspoon salt
3 cups water
2 pounds shrimp
lettuce leaves
cherry tomato halves

Combine the first 9 ingredients; toss gently. Cover and refrigerate 8 hours. Bring water to a boil. Add shrimp and cook for 3–5 minutes or until shrimp turn pink. Drain well; rinse with cold water and chill. Arrange shrimp around the edge of lettuce-lined plates. Spoon black bean mixture in the center. Garnish with tomato halves. Serves 4. This recipe is easy to double, and is refreshing on a summer evening.

Barbara Ball
ChurchLIFE, FL

SALADS

Carrot and Walnut Crunch

1 11-ounce can mandarin oranges, drained
1½ cups fresh pineapple chunks
2½ cups shredded carrots
½ cup flaked coconut
½ cup golden raisins
1 cup chopped walnuts
1 8-ounce Dannon Light lemon or vanilla yogurt
red cabbage leaves

Mix all ingredients except yogurt and cabbage leaves; chill 2 hours. Stir in yogurt. Serve on red cabbage leaves.

Gayle Anne VanFulpen
NewLife Publications, FL

Cauliflower Salad

4 cups raw cauliflower florets
1 cup stuffed green olives, chopped
⅔ cup chopped green pepper
½ cup chopped onion
½ cup pimiento (may include ones in stuffed olives)
½ cup salad oil
3 tablespoons lemon juice
3 tablespoons wine vinegar
1 tablespoon salt or less
½ teaspoon sugar
¼ teaspoon pepper

Combine cauliflower, olives, green pepper, onion, and pimiento. Shake remaining ingredients together to make a dressing, and pour over vegetables. Refrigerate 4 hours.

Clara Nell Shirey
President's Office, FL

Cheesy Potato Salad

3 pounds red potatoes, cubed
water
2 cups grated Swiss cheese
1¼ cups grated cheddar cheese
⅓ cup sliced green onion
6 hard-boiled eggs
2½ cups mayonnaise
3 tablespoons milk
1½ teaspoons salt
½ teaspoon pepper

Place potatoes in a large saucepan; cover with water. Cook over medium heat until tender (this can be done the night before). Place potatoes in a large bowl with cheeses and onion. Coarsely chop 5 eggs, and add to the potato mixture. Reserve 1 egg for garnish. Combine mayonnaise, milk, salt, and pepper in a small bowl. Pour over potato mixture, and toss gently. Slice remaining egg and garnish the top. Refrigerate 2 hours. Serves 8–10.

Alison Druckemiller
Keynote Communications, IN

My soul will rejoice in the Lord and
delight in his salvation (Psalm 35:9).

Cherry Delight

1 small package raspberry Jell-O
2 cups hot water, *divided*
1 can cherry pie filling
1 small package lemon Jell-O
1 small can crushed pineapple
1 tablespoon mayonnaise

1 3-ounce package cream cheese, softened
1 cup miniature marshmallows
1 cup whipping cream, whipped
chopped walnuts

Dissolve raspberry Jell-O in 1 cup hot water. Add pie filling and pour mixture into a 9-inch square pan. Refrigerate until set. Dissolve lemon Jell-O in 1 cup hot water; add pineapple. Blend mayonnaise and cream cheese until smooth. Fold in marshmallows and whipped cream, then pour over cherry mixture. Sprinkle with walnuts and chill. Serves 9. This salad can also be served as a dessert.

Connie Van Maanen
Crusade Family

Chicken Salad

1 small package cherry Jell-O
1 cup hot water
1 can jellied cranberry sauce
4 cups diced chicken or turkey
1 cup drained pineapple tidbits
1 cup chopped walnuts

1 cup diced apple
1 cup halved seedless grapes
1 cup chopped celery
1½ cups mayonnaise (not Miracle Whip)
lettuce leaves

SALADS

Dissolve Jell-O in hot water. Mix in cranberry sauce. Pour into a 9×13-inch pan and refrigerate until completely jelled. Mix remaining ingredients except lettuce. Spoon over firm Jell-O base, and refrigerate until ready to serve. Cut into squares and serve on lettuce leaves; goes well with muffins or rolls.

Joanne Austin
International Ministry, FL

Chicken Salad With Almonds and Grapes

¾ cup mayonnaise
¼ cup sour cream
4 cups diced chicken
1 cup finely diced celery
½ cup slivered almonds
salt and pepper to taste

lemon pepper to taste
garlic to taste
⅔ cup halved seedless green grapes
lettuce leaves
tomatoes, quartered
hard-boiled eggs, quartered

Mix mayonnaise and sour cream; whip with a fork. Combine chicken, celery, and almonds in a bowl and pour mayonnaise mixture over. Mix well. Season and refrigerate 2–3 hours. When ready to serve, fold in grapes. Serve on lettuce with tomatoes and hard-boiled eggs for garnish.

Lisa Master
Worldwide Challenge, FL

Chicken Salad With Grapes and Pineapple

4 cups diced chicken
2 cups halved seedless red grapes
1 20-ounce can pineapple chunks,
    drained
⅔ cup coarsely chopped dry
    roasted peanuts

1 cup chopped celery
2 tablespoons lemon juice
2 tablespoons pineapple juice
about 1 cup mayonnaise
lettuce cups

Combine all ingredients except mayonnaise and lettuce cups. Gently fold in mayonnaise. Serve in lettuce cups. Garnish as desired. Best if served immediately after mixing.

Janice Gregory
ChurchLIFE, FL

Chicken Salad With Mandarin Oranges

1½ cups cubed chicken
1 cup mandarin oranges
1 cup chopped celery
salt to taste

½ cup chopped walnuts
salad dressing or French dressing
1 cup cooked rice (optional)
lettuce leaves or sectioned tomato

Combine chicken, oranges, celery, salt, and walnuts. Add rice if desired. Moisten with salad dressing. Serve on lettuce leaves or sectioned tomato.

Laurie Killingsworth
New Life Center, FL

Chinese Chicken Salad

1 head iceberg lettuce, chopped
3 green onions, chopped
1 cucumber, thinly sliced
1 small can mandarin oranges, drained
3 chicken breasts, cooked and cubed
1 package Ramen noodles, crushed

⅓ cup Honey Dijon salad dressing
dash curry powder
dash oregano
dash garlic
¼ cup rice wine vinegar
sesame seeds

Mix vegetables, oranges, chicken, and Ramen noodles in a large bowl. To make dressing, combine salad dressing, seasonings, and vinegar; mix well with salad. Add sesame seeds as garnish; serve immediately. Makes 4 servings.

Angela Rosa
Sunport Ministry Office, FL

SALADS

Are you called to help others? Do it with all the strength and energy that God supplies so that God will be glorified through Jesus Christ (1 Peter 4:11).

Chinese Chicken Salad With Bamboo Shoots

4 cups cooked chicken
1 5-ounce can bamboo shoots, drained
1 5-ounce can water chestnuts, drained
2 11-ounce cans mandarin oranges, drained

1 cup slivered almonds
2 tablespoons dehydrated onion
2 cups mayonnaise
2 cans Chinese noodles

Combine the first 7 ingredients and chill. Serve on Chinese noodles. Serves 6–8.

Doris Maugle
Contributions and Postal Services, FL

Everywhere we go we talk about Christ to all who will listen (Col. 1:28).

Chopped Salad With Chili Vinaigrette

1 head romaine lettuce, torn
2 Belgian endive heads, thinly sliced crosswise
3 stalks celery, chopped
1 small onion, chopped

1 large tomato, chopped
1 cucumber, peeled, seeded, and chopped
Chili Vinaigrette Dressing

Combine lettuce, endive, celery, onion, tomato, and cucumber in a large bowl. Toss with dressing.

Chili Vinaigrette Dressing:

½ cup olive oil
⅓ cup balsamic vinegar or red wine vinegar

4 cloves garlic, minced
1 teaspoon chili powder

Whisk oil and vinegar to blend. Whisk in garlic and chili powder. Season to taste with salt and pepper. Can be prepared 3 hours ahead. Cover and refrigerate.

Barbara Ball
ChurchLIFE, FL

Country-Style Coleslaw

1 cup mayonnaise
3 tablespoons sugar
3 tablespoons cider vinegar
¾ teaspoon dry mustard
¼ teaspoon celery seed

8 cups shredded cabbage
1½ teaspoons salt
grated carrot (optional)
finely diced green pepper (optional)

In a large bowl, mix all ingredients. Toss to coat well. Cover and chill several hours. Makes about 8 cups. For color, add carrot and/or green pepper.

Cheryl Hile
Computer Services, FL

Crab and Shrimp Molded Salad

1 large package lemon Jell-O
2 cups hot water
1 tablespoon lemon juice
½ cup whipping cream, whipped
1 tablespoon grated onion

½ cup mayonnaise
¾ cup diced celery
½ cup stuffed green olives, sliced
Dressing

Dissolve Jell-O in water with lemon juice. When slightly thickened, beat until foamy. Add whipped cream, onion, mayonnaise, celery, and olives. Pour into mold and chill. Serve with dressing. This makes an elegant, lovely salad for a ladies' luncheon.

Dressing:

1 cup Miracle Whip
1 cup mayonnaise
¼–½ cup chili sauce
several sweet pickles, chopped

6 hard-boiled eggs, chopped
1 cup shrimp
1 cup crab

Blend Miracle Whip, mayonnaise, chili sauce, pickles, eggs, shrimp, and crab.

Judy Anderson
Christian Embassy, VA

 Be completely humble and gentle; be patient, bearing with one another in love (Eph. 4:2).

Cranberry Pineapple Salad

1 large package cherry Jell-O
1½ cups boiling water
1 can whole berry cranberry sauce

1 can crushed pineapple with juice
2 cups chopped pecans

Dissolve Jell-O in water. Add cranberry sauce and stir to dissolve. Mix in pineapple. Place in a shallow dish about 1-inch deep and sprinkle nuts on top. Chill overnight or several hours before serving. Serves 10–12.

Ginny Purdy
Military Ministry, VA

Cranberry Salad

2 large packages raspberry Jell-O
3 cups hot water
2 cups cold water
3–4 cups raw cranberries
1 orange

1 cup sugar
1 cup diced celery
1 apple, chopped
½ cup walnuts

Dissolve Jell-O in hot water; add cold water, and set aside until syrupy. Put raw cranberries and orange through food chopper, using the course blade. Stir in sugar and let stand until well mixed. Add to prepared Jell-O along with celery, apple, and nuts. Turn into a mold.

Linda Crone
Josh McDowell Ministry, CA

Date and Apple Salad

1 cup pitted dates
2 apples, diced
1 teaspoon grated orange peel
½ cup diced cheddar cheese

1 cup diced celery
⅔ cup mayonnaise
1 tablespoon orange juice
1 teaspoon seasoned salt

Mix dates, apples, orange peel, cheese, and celery. In a separate bowl, blend mayonnaise, orange juice, and salt. Combine dressing with fruit mixture.

Billie Thurman
Crusade Family

Dilly Artichoke Rice Salad

2 cups chicken broth
1 cup uncooked regular rice
⅓ cup chopped green onion
⅓ cup chopped green pepper
⅓ cup stuffed olives, sliced
⅓ cup chopped celery

1 7-ounce jar marinated artichoke
    hearts, drained and chopped
½ cup mayonnaise
¾ teaspoon dill weed
salt and pepper to taste
lettuce leaves

Bring chicken broth to a boil. Add rice and cook over low heat for 20 minutes or until rice is tender and broth is absorbed; remove from heat. Cool. Combine rice with the next 8 ingredients, reserving a few olives for garnish; chill well. Serve on lettuce, and garnish with sliced olives. Serves 8–10.

Sherry Cumpstone
Worldwide Challenge, FL

Dream Salad

1 small package orange Jell-O
4 cups boiling water, *divided*
1 package miniature marshmallows
1 8-ounce package cream cheese,
    softened

1 15¼-ounce can crushed pineapple
1 cup whipping cream, whipped
1 large package lime Jell-O
2 cups cold water

Dissolve orange Jell-O in 2 cups boiling water; stir marshmallows into Jell-O until dissolved. Chill until slightly thickened; beat in cream cheese and pineapple. Fold in whipped cream. Pour into a large pan and chill until firm. Dissolve lime Jell-O in 2 cups boiling water, and add 2 cups cold water. When cooled to room temperature, pour over orange Jell-O mixture; chill until set.

Laurie Killingsworth
New Life Center, FL

SALADS

Tell the righteous it will be well with them, for they will enjoy the fruit of their deeds (Psalm 3:10).

Dry Jell-O Salad

1 12-ounce carton cottage cheese
1 small package dry raspberry Jell-O

1 large container Cool Whip
1 15¼-ounce can crushed pineapple

Mix all ingredients and refrigerate.

Laurie Killingsworth
New Life Center, FL

Easy Salad

1 can dark cherry pie filling, chilled
½ cup flaked coconut
½ cup pecans, chopped

½ cup miniature marshmallows
2 bananas, sliced

Mix all ingredients. Sprinkle additional coconut on top.

Juli Emory
Military Ministry, VA

Easy Tomato Aspic Salad

1 small box lemon or orange Jell-O
1 cup boiling water
1 8-ounce can tomato sauce
1½ tablespoons cider vinegar
salt and pepper to taste

dash Tabasco
½ teaspoon dill
½–1 teaspoon horseradish sauce
lettuce leaves
mayonnaise

Dissolve Jell-O in boiling water. Add the next 6 ingredients, and chill until jelled. Cut into 4–6 squares, and serve on lettuce leaves. Top with a dollop of mayonnaise. This recipe can be doubled or tripled. *Optional:* Add other ingredients that you have on hand or that you like, such as ½ cup chopped celery, ½ cup chopped fresh tomatoes, ¼ cup chopped olives, ¼ cup chopped green pepper, ½ cup shredded carrots, ¼ cup chopped cucumbers, ½ cup cottage cheese. The combinations are limitless.

Nina Locke
Crusade Family

Exotic Chicken Salad

2 cups mayonnaise
1 tablespoon Dijon mustard
¼ cup oriental sesame oil
¾ cup tamari, *divided*
1 pound Capellini (angel hair pasta)
¼ cup peanut oil
1½ cups cooked chicken, chopped

1 large carrot, chopped
1 red pepper, chopped
1 can bamboo shoots, drained
1 can mini corn, drained
½ cup fresh cilantro
½ pound snow peas, blanched
    and chilled

Combine mayonnaise, mustard, sesame oil, and ½ cup tamari; refrigerate. Cook Capellini al dente, approximately 8–10 minutes. Drain and toss with ¼ cup tamari and peanut oil. Cool to room temperature. Combine with chicken, carrot, pepper, bamboo shoots, corn, and cilantro; mix gently but thoroughly. Add mayonnaise mixture and toss in snow peas.

Ann Wright
Women Today International, FL

Exotic Luncheon Salad

2–3 cups mayonnaise
1 tablespoon curry powder
2 tablespoons lemon juice
1 tablespoon soy sauce
8 cups cut-up chicken or turkey
1 teaspoon salt
¼ teaspoon pepper

2 small cans sliced water chestnuts
2 pounds seedless grapes
2 cups diced celery
lettuce leaves
pineapple spears, chilled
litchi nuts

Mix mayonnaise, curry powder, lemon juice, and soy sauce with chicken. Add seasonings, water chestnuts, grapes, and celery. Serve on lettuce leaves. Garnish with chilled pineapple spears or chunks and litchi nuts. Serves about 8.

Charlotte Day
Crusade Family

SALADS

Everything else is worthless when compared with the priceless gain of knowing Christ Jesus my Lord (Phil. 3:8).

Fonduloha
(Paradise Chicken Salad)

2 fresh pineapples with fresh green leaves
2½ cups cut-up chicken or turkey
¾ cup diced celery
¾ cup mayonnaise or yogurt
2 tablespoons chopped chutney
1 teaspoon curry powder
1 medium banana, sliced
⅓ cup salted peanuts
½ cup flaked coconut
1 11-ounce can mandarin oranges, drained

To prepare pineapple boats, remove any brown leaves from the green top with a sharp knife. Cut each pineapple in half lengthwise through the green top, then cut in half again, making 4 pieces, each with part of the green top. Remove fruit; cut away eyes and fibrous shells. Cut fruit into chunks. Drain pineapple shells and fruit on paper towels. Combine pineapple, chicken, and celery in a large bowl; cover and chill. In a separate bowl, blend mayonnaise, chutney, and curry. Cover and refrigerate. Just before serving, drain pineapple mixture. Toss lightly with mayonnaise mixture, banana, and peanuts. Fill pineapple boats. Sprinkle with coconut and garnish with oranges. Serves 8. This dish is fun to make and delightful to serve.

Nancy Wilson/Barbara Ball
Student Venture/ChurchLIFE, FL

Whatever a person is like, I try to find common ground with him so that he will let me tell him about Christ and let Christ save him (1 Cor. 9:22).

Fresh Spinach Salad

fresh spinach leaves
1 hard-boiled egg, chopped
2 slices bacon, fried and crumbled
sliced mushrooms
2 scallions, chopped

Clean fresh spinach; blot with a paper towel. Place in a plastic bag and refrigerate until crisp. Break spinach leaves if needed. Fill a large individual salad bowl with the desired amount of spinach. Sprinkle each of the other items over spinach. Makes 1 serving. Good with *Bacon Buttermilk Dressing*.

Mary Canada
President's Office, FL

Frozen Cherry Salad

1 cup whipping cream, whipped
1 can Eagle Brand condensed milk
1 can cherry pie filling

1 large can crushed pineapple, drained
lettuce leaves

Mix all ingredients well except lettuce; freeze in a 9×13-inch covered pan. Slice and serve on lettuce leaves.

Ginny Purdy
Military Ministry, VA

Frozen Cranberry Salad

1 can whole berry cranberry sauce
1 8-ounce can crushed pineapple
1 8-ounce carton Lite Cool Whip

1 8-ounce package low-fat cream cheese
2 ounces (⅓ cup) walnut pieces

In a large bowl, mix all ingredients and pour into a glass loaf pan. Freeze until ready to serve, then slice like bread.

Sally Tanner
NewLife Publications, FL

Frozen Delight

2 packages frozen strawberries
1 package frozen pineapple chunks
1 3-ounce package cream cheese, softened

½ cup mayonnaise
1 cup miniature marshmallows
½ cup chopped pecans
½ cup whipping cream, whipped

Defrost and drain strawberries and pineapple. Cut pineapple chunks smaller. Blend cream cheese and mayonnaise. Add fruit, marshmallows, and pecans. Fold in whipped cream. Place in a salad mold or large refrigerator tray and freeze.

Cindy Bogan
JESUS Film Project, FL

SALADS

Fruit Salad

1 11-ounce can mandarin oranges
1 cup miniature marshmallows
1 13-ounce can pineapple tidbits
⅓ cup maraschino cherries, halved

½ cup flaked coconut
1 banana, sliced
1 cup sour cream

Mix the first 5 ingredients. Chill at least 2 hours or overnight. Before serving add banana. Mix sour cream with a little of the cherry juice and toss with fruit. Serve.

Cathy Emmans
Contributions and Postal Services, FL

Garden Pasta Salad

16 ounces uncooked rotini
1 16-ounce bag frozen broccoli,
    cauliflower, and carrot mix,
    thawed (or fresh vegetables,
    slightly cooked)
1 bunch green onions, thinly sliced

1 cup pitted ripe olives, halved
10 or more cherry tomatoes, halved
½ cup Parmesan cheese
½ teaspoon Italian seasoning
½ teaspoon garlic powder
1 cup oil and vinegar salad dressing

Cook pasta; drain and rinse with cold water. In a very large bowl, combine pasta, vegetables, cheese, Italian seasoning, and garlic powder. Add dressing and mix. Serve at room temperature.

Jeanie Stedman
Military Ministry, VA

Great-For-You Salad

cauliflower
broccoli
zucchini and/or other squash
carrots
red or yellow onion
2–3 kinds of sprouts
2–3 kinds of lettuce (not iceberg), torn
sunflower seeds
sesame seeds

pumpkin seeds
raisins (optional)
avocado (optional)
1–2 tablespoons flax seed or
    virgin olive oil
1–2 tablespoons apple cider vinegar
Braggs amino acid (purchase at
    health food store)

Chop cauliflower and broccoli into small pieces. Finely grate zucchini, carrots, and onion. Mix vegetables with lettuce, seeds, raisins, and avocado. Toss mixture with flax seed or olive oil and apple cider vinegar. Sprinkle on Braggs amino acid. Serve with whole wheat bread. This salad is best if organically grown items are used.

Juanita Wyatt
CoMission, CA

> If your enemy is hungry, give him food to eat, if he is thirsty, give him water to drink (Prov. 25:21).

Greek Salad

2 heads Boston lettuce, torn	6 green onions, chopped
4 ounces feta cheese, crumbled	3 stalks celery, chopped
18–20 Greek Calamata olives	1 green pepper, chopped
6 Roma tomatoes, quartered	1 box croutons (optional)

Toss lettuce with remaining salad ingredients. Garnish with *Vinaigrette Dressing* as desired. Serves 6.

Vinaigrette Dressing:

¾ cup olive oil	¼ teaspoon paprika
1 clove garlic, minced	¼ teaspoon oregano
¼ cup red wine vinegar	½ teaspoon sugar
1 teaspoon salt	1 tablespoon Dijon mustard or
¼ teaspoon pepper	1 teaspoon dry mustard

Marinate garlic in oil for 1 hour. Add remaining ingredients, and shake well. Chill.

Cathy Oliver
Student Venture, TX

SALADS

Green Salad Vinaigrette

2 tablespoons red wine vinegar or
   fresh lemon juice
2 tablespoons oil
2 tablespoons defatted chicken stock
½ teaspoon garlic powder
½ teaspoon Dijon mustard

1 tablespoon parsley
1 tablespoon tarragon
1 tablespoon chopped chives or
   basil
salt and pepper to taste
8 cups mixed greens, torn

In a large salad bowl, whisk all ingredients except greens until blended. Add greens and toss. Serves 4.

Barbara Ball
ChurchLIFE, FL

Grilled Chicken Salad

3 chicken breasts, boned and skinned
2 tablespoons olive oil
1 tablespoon oregano
1 teaspoon cumin
½ teaspoon garlic
salt and pepper
1 head romaine lettuce, torn

4 tomatoes, diced
2 cups corn
1 can black beans, rinsed and drained
1 red onion, thinly sliced into rings
1 cup shredded cheddar cheese
salsa

Combine chicken, oil, and seasonings in a bowl and marinate 1 hour. Prepare a large platter with the lettuce, vegetables, and cheese decoratively layered. Grill chicken breasts over high heat; remove from grill and slice. Lay slices over salad. Serve with mild or medium salsa as a dressing on the side.

Judy Anderson
Christian Embassy, CO

Holiday Cranberry Salad

1 large package raspberry Jell-O
2 cups hot water
2 cups liquid (water and pineapple
   juice)
1 cup crushed pineapple, drained

1 can whole berry cranberry sauce
1 3-ounce package cream cheese,
   softened
1 cup sour cream
nuts

Dissolve Jell-O in hot water. Add liquid. Mix in pineapple and cranberry sauce. Chill to thicken. Make a topping by blending cream cheese and sour cream; spread on set Jell-O. Sprinkle nuts over salad.

Donna Brandt
Here's Life World, FL

"Blessed is the man who will eat at the feast in the kingdom of God" (Luke 14:15).

Hot Almond Chicken Salad

2 cups cubed chicken
2 cups sliced celery
½ cup slivered almonds
1 cup mayonnaise
2 tablespoons grated onion
2 teaspoons lemon juice

½ teaspoon salt
½ cup grated cheese
1 cup crushed potato chips
3 hard-boiled eggs, sliced
fresh parsley

Preheat oven to 400 degrees. Combine chicken, celery, and almonds in a mixing bowl. Add mayonnaise, onion, lemon juice, and salt; mix well. Place in a baking dish. Top with cheese and potato chips. Bake for 20–25 minutes. Garnish with egg slices and parsley.

Doris Maugle
Contributions and Postal Services, FL

Individual Mexican Salads

2 cups lettuce per salad
1 cup chopped tomatoes
½ green pepper, chopped
1 small onion, chopped

1 8-ounce can refried beans
1 cup shredded cheddar cheese
2 taco shells per salad, cooked
2 teaspoons fat-free sour cream

In medium salad bowls, distribute lettuce, tomatoes, and half the green peppers and half the onions. Spray a medium saucepan with non-stick spray, and sauté the remaining onions and peppers. Add refried beans and cook until hot. Sprinkle salad bowls with cheese. Crush 2 taco shells per salad, and mix with cheese and greens. Top each salad with a scoopful of refried beans and sour cream. This salad is very filling and delicious.

Kelly Hall
Corporate Human Resources, FL

Kiwi and Tomato Salad

1 ½ tablespoons olive oil
1 tablespoon white wine vinegar
1 ½ teaspoons lime juice
¼ teaspoon dry mustard
¼ teaspoon salt

1 head red leaf lettuce, separated
1 endive, separated
1 large tomato, sliced
1 kiwi fruit, pared and sliced
2 tablespoons chopped pecans

To make dressing, whisk together oil, vinegar, lime juice, mustard, and salt. Arrange lettuce leaves and endive on individual plates. Top with tomato and kiwi. Drizzle dressing over salad. Sprinkle with pecans. Serves 6.

Barbara Ball
ChurchLIFE, FL

Layered Salad

½ head lettuce, torn
1 can sliced water chestnuts
1 cup chopped celery
½ cup diced green pepper
½ cup diced radishes

¼ cup chopped onion
2 cups cooked navy beans
3 cups Hellman's mayonnaise
1 cup grated Parmesan or Romano
    cheese

Layer vegetables in a glass dish. Spread mayonnaise over the top layer and sprinkle with cheese. Refrigerate. Serves 8.

Sherry Cumpstone
Worldwide Challenge, FL

Layered Spinach Salad

1 package fresh spinach
1 pound bacon, fried and crumbled
6 hard-boiled eggs, sliced
1 10-ounce package frozen peas,
    thawed

1 head lettuce, torn
1 small onion, sliced
3 cups salad dressing
1 tablespoon sugar
1 pound Swiss cheese, shredded

Layer the first 6 ingredients in 2 9×13-inch pans. Spread with salad dressing, and sprinkle with sugar and cheese. Cover with plastic wrap, and refrigerate overnight. Makes 2 salads that could easily serve 6–8 people each.

Donna Knopf
International Ministry, FL

Mandarin Orange Salad

1 cup almonds
5 tablespoons sugar
1 bunch romaine or green leaf
   lettuce

1 head red leaf lettuce
3 whole green onions, chopped
2 11-ounce cans mandarin oranges
Dressing

In a small pan, cook almonds and sugar over medium heat, stirring constantly until almonds are coated. (Be careful—almonds burn easily). Mix *Dressing* and chill. Toss all ingredients and serve.

Dressing:

dash salt and pepper
⅓ cup oil
2 tablespoons sugar
3 tablespoons vinegar

2 tablespoons chopped parsley
dash Tabasco
dash juice from mandarin oranges

Mix all ingredients and chill.

Ingrid Bunner
Board of Director's Wife

Mango Salad

3 small packages lemon Jell-O
3 cups boiling water
8 ounces cream cheese, softened

1 large can (approximately
   16 ounces) mangos
Cool Whip or mayonnaise (optional)

Dissolve Jell-O in boiling water. Cool. In a blender, mix cream cheese and mangos with juice. Add blended mixture to cool Jell-O and refrigerate until firm. Top with Cool Whip or mayonnaise, if desired. Serves 12–15, depending on serving size.

Juli Emory
Military Ministry, Virginia

SALADS

Marinated Vegetable Salad

2 cans French-style green beans
1 can kidney beans, drained
2 medium onions, sliced
1 red or green pepper, sliced
4 stalks celery, chopped
1 can pimiento (optional)

1 cup sugar
½ cup salad oil
1 cup vinegar
1 teaspoon paprika
1 teaspoon salt

Mix vegetables and pimiento. To make marinade, blend remaining ingredients. Pour over vegetables and marinate for 24 hours, stirring ingredients several times. Drain the marinade (keep for use on other salads) and serve as individual salads.

Yvonne Bibby
International Ministry, FL

> *Let your conversation be always full of grace, seasoned with salt, so that you may know how to answer everyone (Col. 4:6).*

Mediterranean Rice Salad

2 tablespoons vegetable oil
1 pint large shrimp, peeled and
    deveined
1 large clove garlic, minced
2 green onions, sliced
2 cups water

1 cup long-grain rice
1 teaspoon salt
1 medium cucumber, diced
½ cup crumbled feta cheese
Spicy Vinaigrette

In a 3-quart saucepan, heat 1 tablespoon oil over medium-high heat. Cook half the shrimp, until well browned and tender. With a slotted spoon, remove shrimp and place in a large bowl. Repeat with the remaining shrimp and oil. Reduce heat to medium. In drippings remaining in saucepan, sauté garlic and green onion about 2 minutes, stirring frequently. Add water, rice, and salt to saucepan. Cook to boiling over high heat. Reduce heat to low; cover and simmer 20 minutes or until rice is tender. Meanwhile, add cucumber and feta cheese to the shrimp. Add rice and *Spicy Vinaigrette* to shrimp mixture, and toss well. Serves 6.

Spicy Vinaigrette:

¼ cup olive oil
3 tablespoons cider vinegar
1 tablespoon Dijon mustard

1 teaspoon Tabasco
1 teaspoon salt

In a small bowl, combine all ingredients.

Crystal Keller
Computer Services, FL

Mexican Chef Salad

1 onion, chopped
4 tomatoes, chopped
1 head lettuce, chopped
1 cup shredded cheddar cheese
1 cup Thousand Island or
   French dressing
hot sauce to taste

1 cup crushed Fritos
1 pound ground beef
1 can kidney beans, drained
¼ teaspoon salt
tortilla chips
avocado slices
tomato slices

Toss together onion, tomatoes, and lettuce. Add cheese, dressing, hot sauce, and Frito chips. Brown the ground beef; mix in kidney beans and salt. Simmer 10 minutes; drain. Stir hamburger mixture into cold salad. Garnish with tortilla chips, avocado, and tomato. Serve immediately. This tossed salad with a Mexican flare is good with hard rolls for lunch.

Variation: Substitute 1 6-ounce can tuna and ½ cup sliced ripe olives for the ground beef and kidney beans. In place of the Thousand Island or French dressing, use the following dressing:

Dressing:

½ large ripe avocado, mashed
1 tablespoon lemon juice
½ cup sour cream
⅓ cup salad oil

1 clove garlic, pressed
1 teaspoon sugar
¼ teaspoon salt
⅛ teaspoon Tabasco

Blend together and toss with salad just before serving. Add crushed Fritos.

Charlotte Day
Crusade Family

SALADS

Mexican Salad

1 head lettuce, torn
2 tomatoes, chopped
2–3 green onions or ¼ medium
   onion, chopped
6 ounces sliced ripe olives
1 avocado, sliced
1½ cups grated cheddar cheese

1 can kidney beans, drained
½ green pepper, sliced into rings
2 ounces Ortega chilies, chopped
1 tablespoon chili powder
1 pint sour cream
1½ cups taco-flavored Doritos,
   lightly crushed

Mix all ingredients except chips well; allow flavors to mix for about 30 minutes to 1 hour. Add chips before serving.

Barbara Shearhart
Finance, FL

Mom's Festive Cherry Delight

2 1-pound cans dark sweet
   pitted cherries
2 small cans crushed pineapple

2 small packages cherry Jell-O
1 cup chopped nuts
Cool Whip

Drain the cherries and pineapple, reserving the juices. Add enough water to the juices to make 3 cups liquid. Bring liquid to a boil; add gelatin and dissolve. Stir in nuts and pour into a mold; chill. When set, top with Cool Whip and serve. Serves 12–15. This is perfect for the holidays.

Patsy Morley
Board of Director's Wife

Orange Almond Salad

2 tablespoons sugar
½ cup almonds, walnuts, and/or pecans
½ head iceberg lettuce
½ head romaine lettuce

1 cup chopped celery
2 whole green onions, chopped
1 can mandarin oranges, drained
Poppy Seed Dressing

Place nuts in a non-stick pan with the sugar, and cook until sugar is dissolved and nuts are coated and brown. Cool, then break apart. Mix greens, celery, onion, and oranges; chill. When ready to serve, toss with *Poppy Seed Dressing* and top with candied nuts.

Poppy Seed Dressing:

2 tablespoons sugar
1½ teaspoons Dijon mustard
⅓ cup red wine vinegar
¼ teaspoon salt

1½ tablespoons grated yellow onion
1 cup canola oil
1½ tablespoons poppy seeds

Blend the first 5 ingredients in a food processor or blender for 1 minute. Slowly add oil with processor running. Stir in poppy seeds.

Anne Lawrence
World Changers Radio, FL

Orange Almond Salad With Romaine Lettuce

1 head romaine lettuce, torn
1–2 cans mandarin oranges, drained
2 tablespoons sesame seeds, toasted

2 kiwi fruit, sliced (optional)
slivered almonds
Dressing

Toss together all ingredients. Delicious!

Dressing:

2 tablespoons white wine vinegar
¼ cup salad oil
2 tablespoons sugar or
    3 packets Sweet'n Low

½ teaspoon salt
⅛ teaspoon almond extract
dash pepper

Mix dressing ingredients.

Leonora Gay
ChurchLIFE, FL

SALADS

Orange Cream Fruit Salad

1 20-ounce can pineapple chunks
1 11-ounce can peach slices, cut up
1 11-ounce can mandarin oranges
3 medium bananas, sliced
2 medium apples, chopped

1 small package instant vanilla pudding
3 ounces frozen orange juice
   concentrate (⅓ cup), thawed
1½ cups milk
¾ cup sour cream

Mix all fruits and set aside. Combine dry pudding mix, orange juice, and milk. Beat with mixer for 1–2 minutes until well blended. Beat in sour cream. Fold into fruit. Cover and refrigerate several hours. Makes 10 or more servings.

Marge Vander Berg
Contributions and Postal Services, FL

Oriental Chicken Salad

2 tablespoons sesame seeds
½ cup slivered almonds
1 package dry chicken Ramen
   noodles, crumbled

2 cups cut-up chicken breast
½ head cabbage, shredded
4 green onions, chopped
Dressing

Preheat oven to 350 degrees. Combine sesame seeds and almonds in a shallow pan, and brown in oven for 10–15 minutes. When cooled, stir in Ramen noodles. In a separate bowl, mix chicken, cabbage, and onion. Combine with noodle mixture. Pour dressing over salad just before serving.

Dressing:

2 tablespoons sugar
3 tablespoons vinegar
½ cup oil, or ¼ cup oil
   and ¼ cup water

1 teaspoon salt
½ teaspoon pepper
flavor packet from chicken
   Ramen noodles

Mix ingredients and shake well; refrigerate until ready to serve.

Linda Painton/Jackie Jackson
Travel Department, FL/Finance, FL

Oriental Coleslaw

1 16-ounce package shredded coleslaw
(about 5 cups cabbage and carrots)
4 green onions, thinly sliced
1 3-ounce package chicken Ramen
noodles, crumbled
½–¾ cup slivered toasted almonds

½–¾ cup sunflower seeds
½ cup salad oil
⅓ cup vinegar
1 tablespoon sugar
⅛ teaspoon pepper

Up to 1 hour before serving, combine coleslaw mix, green onions, dry
Ramen noodles, almonds, and sunflower seeds in a salad bowl. Cover and
chill. In a jar, combine oil, vinegar, sugar, pepper, and flavor packet from the
Ramen noodles; cover and shake. Chill. Just before serving, shake dressing
again, pour over salad, and toss to coat. Serves 12. This unique coleslaw is
very good with cookouts and always gets compliments.

Bobbi Jo Hasz
Campus Ministry, WA

Pea Salad

2 packages frozen tiny peas,
thawed and drained
6 slices bacon, fried and crumbled,
or ¼ cup Bacon Bits

1 cup sour cream
3 green onions, sliced
½ cup salted peanuts

Mix all ingredients together except peanuts. Add peanuts just before serving
so they won't get soggy.

Sus Schmitt
Computer Services, FL

SALADS

*God wants to work uniquely in our lives to serve Him and
others. Our creativity will grow as we learn from each other
and as we are led by the Holy Spirit. So go ahead—don't be
afraid to try something new and different. Be creative.*

— Barbara Ball

Pepperoni Salad

1 onion, sliced and separated into rings
1 stick pepperoni, sliced
¼ pound blue cheese
⅔ cup olive oil
⅓ cup vinegar
salt and pepper to taste
1 pound spinach and other greens

Mix the oil and vinegar; add pepperoni and crumbled blue cheese. Season with salt and fresh ground pepper. Marinade at least 12 hours. To serve, toss with freshly washed spinach and other greens.

Ann Wright
Women Today International, FL

Polynesian Chicken Salad

3 cups cubed chicken or turkey
1 15¼-ounce can pineapple chunks, drained
2 stalks celery, thinly sliced
¾ cup low-fat mayonnaise or salad dressing
1 teaspoon curry powder
¼ teaspoon salt
1 banana
½ cup salted peanuts or cashews
lettuce leaves
1 11-ounce can mandarin oranges, drained
½ cup flaked coconut (optional)

In a large bowl, combine chicken, pineapple, celery, mayonnaise, curry powder, and salt; toss lightly. Cover and chill at least 2 hours. Just before serving, slice banana, and add to chicken mixture along with peanuts. Serve on lettuce; garnish with oranges and coconut. Makes 10 ½-cup servings. Good served on croissants as a sandwich or in ¼ or ½ pineapple shell.

Laura Staudt
Women Today International, FL

If we are living now by the Holy Spirit's power, let us follow the Holy Spirit's leading in every part of our lives (Gal. 5:25).

*O God, my heart is quiet and confident. No wonder
I can sing your praises! (Psalm 57:7)*

Potato or Macaroni Salad

4 cups cooked potatoes or macaroni
½ cup chopped celery
chopped sweet pickle

4 hard-boiled eggs, chopped
¼ cup chopped onion
Dressing

Mix ingredients and add dressing.

Dressing:

1 cup mayonnaise
⅓ cup sour cream
1 tablespoon mustard
1 tablespoon parsley

1 teaspoon seasoning salt
1 teaspoon pepper
2 tablespoons wine vinegar
pinch celery seed

Blend all ingredients.

Cathy Emmans
Contributions and Postal Services, FL

Pretzel Salad

2 cups coarsely crushed pretzels
3 tablespoons plus 1 cup sugar, *divided*
¾ cup melted margarine
1 8-ounce package cream cheese,
    softened

1 9-ounce carton Cool Whip
1 16-ounce package frozen
    strawberries, thawed and sliced
1 large package strawberry Jell-O

Preheat oven to 400 degrees. Mix pretzels, 3 tablespoons sugar, and margarine. Press into a 9×13-inch pan. Bake for 8 minutes; don't over bake! Cool. Beat 1 cup sugar into cream cheese; stir in Cool Whip. Spread onto the cooled pretzel crust and refrigerate. Drain strawberries, reserving the liquid. Mix the Jell-O according to directions on the box, using ½ cup liquid from the strawberries as part of the water. Add the strawberries and let stand for 10 minutes. Spread over the cooled cream cheese layer. Refrigerate.

Cindy Bibb/Rachel Garland
Church Dynamics International, FL/Corporate Human Resources, FL

SALADS

Raspberry and Cherry Salad

1 small package raspberry Jell-O
1 cup boiling water
1 cup chopped nuts

1 3-ounce package cream cheese,
　softened
1 can cherry pie filling

Dissolve Jell-O in boiling water. Cream together the nuts and cream cheese. Add cream cheese mixture and pie filling to Jell-O. Pour into a mold and chill until firm. Serves 8.

Juli Emory
Military Ministry, VA

Raspberry Applesauce Jell-O

1 small box raspberry Jell-O
1 cup hot water
1 cup applesauce

1 cup raspberries
1 cup sour cream
1½ cups miniature marshmallows

Dissolve Jell-O in hot water. Add applesauce and raspberries. To make topping, combine sour cream and marshmallows. Chill both mixtures overnight. Spread topping over Jell-O.

Janet Beal
Latin America Office, FL

Raspberry Ring

2 cups boiling water or fruit syrup
1 large package raspberry Jell-O
1 pint raspberry sherbet
1 11-ounce can mandarin oranges,
　drained
1 cup flaked coconut

1 13½-ounce can pineapple chunks,
　drained
1 cup miniature marshmallows
½ cup chopped pecans
1 cup sour cream

Dissolve Jell-O in boiling water; stir in sherbet until melted. Pour mixture into a ring mold, and chill until firm. In a bowl, combine orange segments, pineapple, coconut, marshmallows, and nuts. Fold in sour cream. Chill at least 3 hours. Just before serving, remove Jell-O from the mold and place on a plate; fill the center of the Jell-O ring with fruit mixture. This makes a very pretty salad.

Joette Whims
NewLife Publications, CA

Romaine Salad

1 cup white grapes
few red onion rings
½ cup slivered almonds, toasted

½ cup sesame seeds
2–3 small heads romaine lettuce, torn

Combine grapes, onion, almonds, and sesame seeds. Toss with lettuce. Serve with red wine vinegar dressing, French, Ranch, or Roquefort dressing as desired.

Fay Hendley
Contributions and Postal Services, FL

SALADS

Your beauty should not come from outward adornment…Instead, it should be that of your inner self, the unfading beauty of a gentle and quiet spirit, which is of great worth in God's sight (1 Peter 3:3,4).

Rose Beauty Salad

1 small package black cherry Jell-O
1 small package red raspberry Jell-O
3 cups hot water

1 can cherry pie filling
1 cup sour cream
2 cups miniature marshmallows

Dissolve Jell-Os in hot water. Add cherry pie filling. Pour into an oiled mold and chill. Mix sour cream and marshmallows; leave overnight or until marshmallows are dissolved. Top Jell-O with sour cream mixture. Serves 12–15.

Conda DeVries
International Ministry, FL

Seven-Layer Salad

1 head lettuce, shredded
chopped onions to taste
2 stalks celery, chopped
1 10-ounce package frozen peas,
  thawed

1 pint Hellman's mayonnaise
1½ tablespoons sugar
grated cheese
crumbled bacon
croutons

Layer lettuce, onions, celery, and peas. Put into a 9×13-inch glass dish. Mix mayonnaise and sugar, and spread over salad. Top with cheese and bacon. Refrigerate overnight; sprinkle with croutons before serving.

Debbie McGoldrick
Student Venture, GA

Seven-Up Salad

1 small package lime Jell-O
¾ cup boiling water
1 cup 7-Up
1 8-ounce package cream cheese

1 small can crushed pineapple,
  drained
1 large carton Cool Whip
1 cup sliced almonds

With a beater, mix Jell-O, water, and 7-Up. Add cheese in small pieces; beat until mixed. Reserving some almonds for the top, fold in pineapple, Cool Whip, and almonds. Sprinkle with remaining almonds and refrigerate.

Lynn Copeland
NewLife Publications, OK

Shrimp Salad

8 ounces macaroni shells, cooked
1 cup chopped celery
1 medium onion, chopped
¼ cup chopped green pepper
¼ cup chopped pimiento or red bell
  pepper (optional)

3 hard-boiled eggs, chopped
1⅓ cups small shrimp
½ teaspoon salt
¼ teaspoon paprika
⅓ cup mayonnaise or Miracle Whip
¼ cup French dressing

Place celery, onion, and green and red peppers in a bowl. Add eggs, shrimp, salt, and paprika. Make dressing by blending mayonnaise and French dressing. Combine egg mixture and macaroni; toss with dressing. Chill for several hours or overnight to blend flavors. Great served with cornbread.

Anne Lawrence
World Changers Radio, FL

Southern Corn Bread Salad

1 package Jiffy Corn Bread Mix	1 large tomato, chopped
1 cup chopped celery	½ pound bacon, fried and crumbled
1 green pepper, chopped	garlic powder to taste
1 bunch green onions, chopped	mayonnaise

Bake the bread; cool and crumble. Mix cornbread with remaining ingredients and enough mayonnaise to moisten. Serve.

Bea Chandler
ChurchLIFE, NC

*It doesn't matter to God whether your home is elaborate or simple.
All He needs is your willingness to love others as He does.*
— Vonette Bright

Southern Homestyle Potato Salad

8 medium white potatoes, peeled	½ cup sandwich spread
3 eggs	1 cup mayonnaise
1 medium onion	salt
1 jar pimiento or red bell pepper	paprika

Cut potatoes into small chunks and boil until soft but not mushy; cool. Boil eggs in a separate pot; cool. Finely chop onions, eggs, and pimiento or red bell pepper. In a large bowl, toss all ingredients together except salt and paprika. Salt to taste. Garnish with paprika. Chill in refrigerator for at least 3 hours. Serves 4.

Melvita Chisholm
Intercultural Resources, NY

SALADS

Southwestern Chicken Pasta Salad

2 cups rotini pasta, cooked
4 ounces chicken breast, cooked
    and diced
½ cup chopped celery
½ cup chopped tomatoes
½ cup chopped green onion

⅓ cup fat-free mayonnaise
⅓ cup seasoned rice wine vinegar
2 teaspoons chili seasoning
1 teaspoon lemon juice
1 teaspoon garlic powder

In a large bowl, combine pasta, chicken, celery, tomatoes, and green onion. In a small bowl, mix together mayonnaise, vinegar, chili seasoning, lemon juice, and garlic powder. Stir into rotini mixture. Cover and chill. Makes 4 1-cup servings.

Angela Rosa
Sunport Ministry Office, FL

Spinach Salad With Basil and Dill Dressing

¼ pound fresh spinach, chopped
grated onion to taste
2 strips bacon, fried and chopped

Basil and Dill Dressing
1 hard-boiled egg, quartered

Place spinach in a large bowl. Sprinkle grated onion and bacon over spinach. Shake *Basil and Dill Dressing*; pour over salad and toss lightly. Garnish with egg quarters. Serves 2.

Basil and Dill Dressing:

¾ cup oil
¼ cup vinegar
1 teaspoon salt
½ teaspoon sugar

¼ teaspoon pepper
dash basil
dash dill
½ teaspoon paprika

Mix all ingredients and shake.

Elizabeth Marks
International Ministry, FL

Don't try to get into the good graces of important people, but enjoy the company of ordinary folks (Rom. 12:16).

Spinach Salad With Poppy Seed Dressing

1 pound fresh spinach, torn
1 cup strawberries, halved

1 cup toasted pecan halves
Poppy Seed Dressing

Combine spinach, strawberries, and pecans. Drizzle with *Poppy Seed Dressing* and serve immediately. Makes 6 servings.

Poppy Seed Dressing:

⅓ cup cider vinegar
⅓ cup vegetable oil
¼ cup sugar
1 tablespoon Dijon mustard

1 teaspoon salt
½ teaspoon pepper
1 small onion, chopped
2 teaspoons poppy seeds

Combine the first 7 ingredients in a blender; process until smooth, stopping once to scrape the sides. Stir in poppy seeds. Makes 1 cup.

Carrie Machiela
Executive Ministry, FL

There is no better place to be about the redemption of society than in the Christian servant's home; and the more we deal with the captive, the blind, the downtrodden, the more we realize that in this inhospitable world, a Christian home is a miracle to be shared.
— Karen Burton Mains

SALADS

Spring Pea Salad

1 can French-style green beans
1 can shoepeg white corn
1 can spring peas
1 cup chopped celery
½–1 cup chopped green onion

1 jar pimiento, chopped
¼ cup vinegar
½ cup oil
¾ cup sugar
salt and pepper to taste

Drain and combine all vegetables. Mix in remaining ingredients, and refrigerate for 24 hours.

Grace Swartz
NewLife Resources, GA

Strawberry-Mandarin Dessert Salad

1–2 tablespoons sour cream
1 11-ounce can mandarin oranges, drained

1 16-ounce package frozen sweetened sliced strawberries, thawed

Bring sour cream to room temperature in a mixing bowl. Pour the juice from the thawed strawberries into the sour cream and blend together. Stir in oranges and strawberries; serve immediately or chill until serving time. Serves approximately 4. Very light and refreshing.

Debra Brady
Staff & Ministry Opportunities, FL

Strawberry Nut Delight

2 small packages strawberry Jell-O
1 cup boiling water
2 10-ounce packages frozen strawberries, thawed

1 15¼-ounce can crushed pineapple
4 bananas, diced
1 cup chopped pecans (optional)
1 cup sour cream

Combine Jell-O with boiling water; stir until dissolved. Fold in strawberries with juice, pineapple with juice, bananas, and nuts. Place half of mixture in a 9×13-inch glass dish. Refrigerate until firm. Spread sour cream on top. Place remaining mixture over sour cream. Refrigerate until firm.

Justine Nielsen/Janice Gregory
Student Venture, FL/ChurchLIFE, FL

Strawberry Spinach Salad   🕐

1 pound fresh spinach, torn
1 pint strawberries, sliced
1 cup sugar
¼ cup sesame seeds
2 teaspoons poppy seeds

½ teaspoon Worcestershire sauce
1 cup Puritan canola oil
½ cup vinegar
1 tablespoon minced onion

Toss spinach and strawberries. Combine all remaining ingredients. Pour ½–⅓ of the dressing over salad, according to taste. This will make enough dressing for 2–3 salads.

Karen Virtue/Linda Painton
Campus Ministry/Travel Department, FL

Super Slaw

1 head white cabbage, shredded
1 cup chopped tomatoes

⅓ cup chopped cilantro
Kathy's Dressing

Combine cabbage, tomatoes, and cilantro; chill. Pour half of Kathy's Dressing over the salad. Taste and add more dressing if desired. Serves 6.

Kathy's Dressing:

1–2 cloves garlic, minced
¼ teaspoon salt
1 tablespoon Dijon mustard

freshly ground pepper
3–4 tablespoons red wine vinegar
½ cup olive oil

Mix garlic, salt, mustard, pepper, and vinegar in a bowl. Whisk in olive oil. Add additional seasoning if desired.

Lois Mackey
CoMission, CA

 You constantly satisfy the hunger and thirst of every living thing (Psalm 145:16).

Taco Salad

1 small head lettuce
3 tomatoes, quartered
2 green onions, chopped
1 cup crushed Fritos

2 cups Mexican-style chili beans, drained
1 cup grated cheese
Italian salad dressing

Layer all ingredients except dressing in a salad bowl. Just before serving, top with salad dressing.

Sue Myers
FamilyLIFE, AR

Tomato-Shrimp Mold

1 small package lemon Jell-O
1 cup boiling water
¾ can undiluted tomato soup
1 8-ounce package cream cheese, softened

2 4½-ounce cans shrimp
1 cup chopped celery
¼ cup chopped onion
¼ cup chopped green pepper
1 cup mayonnaise

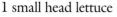

Dissolve Jell-O in boiling water; set aside to cool. Heat soup. Add cream cheese; stir until smooth. Allow to cool, then add shrimp, vegetables, and mayonnaise. Combine with Jell-O. Mold and chill.

Barbara Ball
ChurchLIFE, FL

Tortellini Pasta Salad

1 pound tricolor rotini
½ cup plus 1 tablespoon olive oil
6 cloves garlic, minced
1 bunch broccoli, cut into small florets
2 large zucchini, diced
2 packages frozen snow peas
2 sweet red peppers, diced

1 green pepper, diced
1 6-ounce can sliced black olives
4 tomatoes, diced
1 cup freshly grated Parmesan cheese
½ cup freshly grated Romano cheese
freshly ground pepper
½ pound cheese tortellini, cooked

Cook the pasta; drain and set aside in a large bowl. Place garlic and oil into a saucepan; cook slowly until the garlic is light brown. Set aside to cool. Blanch broccoli, zucchini, and snow peas. Rinse in cold water and set aside. Toss the pasta with garlic oil. Add remaining ingredients and toss gently. Serve at room temperature. Serves 15 or more.

Mary Graham
Women Today International, FL

Tuna Noodle Salad

½ cup mayonnaise
1 tablespoon vinegar
1 tablespoon milk
1 small can tuna
1 3-ounce can Chinese noodles

2 tablespoons chopped onion
3 tablespoons chopped celery
3 tablespoons chopped green pepper
2 tablespoons pimiento
2 hard-boiled eggs, chopped

Blend mayonnaise, vinegar, and milk together for dressing. Mix with remaining ingredients just before serving.

Thelma Stoll
Military Ministry, Retired

24-Hour Slaw

1 medium head cabbage, chopped
2 medium onions, chopped
1 small carrot, grated
¾ cup plus 1 teaspoon sugar, *divided*
½ teaspoon mustard seed

1 teaspoon celery seed
1 teaspoon salt
¾ cup vinegar
½ cup oil

Toss cabbage, onions, and carrot with ¾ cup sugar. In a saucepan, combine seeds, 1 teaspoon sugar, salt, and vinegar. Bring to a rolling boil; stir in oil. Bring to a rolling boil again, and pour slowly over cabbage mixture. Do not stir! Cover and refrigerate 24 hours.

Susan Heckman
President's Office, FL

Vegetable Salad

1 bunch broccoli, cut into bite-size
　　florets
1 head cauliflower, cut into bite-size
　　pieces
½ cup sliced red onion
1 pound bacon, fried and crumbled
　　or 1 jar real bacon bits

1 cup raisins
sunflower seeds
1 cup Hellman's mayonnaise
¼ cup sugar
½ cup sour cream
2 teaspoons white vinegar

Mix vegetables, bacon, raisins, and sunflower seeds. Combine remaining ingredients to make dressing. Mix with vegetables. Cover with plastic wrap and refrigerate overnight.

Betty Van Tuinen
History's Handful, CA

SALADS

Watergate Salad

1 small package pistachio pudding
　　mix
1 large can crushed pineapple
　　with juice

1 cup miniature marshmallows
1 9-ounce container Cool Whip
1 cup sour cream
½ cup chopped nuts (optional)

Mix all ingredients, and chill at least one day or overnight.

Ingrid Bunner
Board of Director's Wife

Salad Dressings

Bacon Buttermilk Dressing

6 slices bacon, diced
1 cup mayonnaise
1 cup buttermilk
2 tablespoons minced scallions
1 tablespoon minced fresh chervil
1 teaspoon minced garlic

½ teaspoon freshly ground black
　　pepper
¼ teaspoon salt
¼ teaspoon paprika
dash Tabasco

Sauté bacon in a skillet until crisp. Drain on paper towels. In a mixing bowl, whisk together remaining ingredients. Add bacon. Cover and refrigerate at least 1 hour. Makes 2 cups.

Barbara Ball
ChurchLIFE, FL

Celery Seed Dressing

1 cup oil
⅓ cup red wine vinegar
⅓ cup sugar
1 teaspoon celery seed

3 tablespoons finely grated onion
1 teaspoon dry mustard
salt and pepper to taste

Mix thoroughly in a blender. It's great on greens.

Cheryl Hile
Computer Services, FL

Dad's Favorite Onion Dressing

1 cup oil
1 cup sugar
1 teaspoon salt
1½ teaspoons poppy seeds (optional)

1 teaspoon dry mustard
1 medium onion, minced
½ cup vinegar

Mix the first 6 ingredients in a blender or food processor on high. Slowly add vinegar and continue to mix for 2–3 more minutes. Serve over salad.

Alison Druckemiller
Keynote Communications, IN

French Dressing

⅔ cup salad oil
¼ cup vinegar
⅓ cup ketchup
½ cup sugar

1 teaspoon salt
1 teaspoon paprika
1 teaspoon grated onion
juice of 1 lemon

Blend oil and vinegar, then add remaining ingredients. Blend until well mixed.

Sue Imbrock
International Ministry, FL

French Salad Dressing

1 cup salad oil
¼ cup vinegar
1 small onion, finely chopped
¾ cup sugar

1 tablespoon Worcestershire sauce
¾ teaspoon salt
⅓ cup ketchup

Mix ingredients in a blender, or place in a jar and shake well.

Cheryl Hile
Computer Service, FL

Frozen Fruit Salad Dressing

1 cup sugar
²/₃ cup light corn syrup
½ cup water
2 egg whites

½ cup mayonnaise
1 tablespoon grated orange rind
1 teaspoon grated lemon rind
⅛ teaspoon salt

Combine sugar, corn syrup, and water; cook to thread stage (234 degrees). Beat egg whites until stiff; slowly add syrup while beating constantly. Cool. Fold in remaining ingredients; freeze. (This does not harden when frozen.) Makes 2 cups dressing. Good served on fruit or Jell-O salads.

Eloise Knippers
Crusade Family

Poppy Seed Dressing

¼–½ cup chopped onion
¾ cup tarragon vinegar
2 tablespoons vegetable oil
1½ tablespoons poppy seeds

1 tablespoon sugar
1 teaspoon salt
1 teaspoon dry mustard
¾ cup vegetable oil

Combine the first 7 ingredients in a blender; mix well. Slowly add vegetable oil, continuing to blend until thick. Pour into a jar with a tight-fitting lid. Chill. Shake before serving.

Cheryl Hile
Computer Services, FL

Ranch Dressing

1 pint mayonnaise
1 pint buttermilk
1 teaspoon salt
½ teaspoon garlic powder

1 tablespoon minced onion or
    1 teaspoon onion powder
½ teaspoon pepper
1½ teaspoons parsley flakes

Mix all ingredients by hand or shake in a jar. Refrigerate for 30 minutes before serving.

Marlene Koslowsky/Jan Gidel
International Ministry, Africa/International Ministry, FL

Russian Dressing

1 cup canola oil
½ cup tomato sauce
2 tablespoons lemon juice
¼ teaspoon dry mustard

1½ teaspoons Bragg's liquid amino
    or soy sauce
2 tablespoons fructose (optional)

Combine all ingredients in a shaker bottle.

Jennie Mitchell
Josh McDowell Ministry, CA

Spinach Salad Dressings

The Good:

⅓ cup fresh orange juice
2 tablespoons olive oil
2 teaspoons Dijon mustard

1 small clove garlic, minced
pinch sugar
salt and pepper to taste

Whisk or shake ingredients together.

The Bad:

¼ cup bacon fat
¼ cup wine vinegar
½ teaspoon seasoned salt

½ teaspoon sugar
¼ teaspoon dry mustard

Heat ingredients to simmering, stirring frequently.

The Beautiful:

6 tablespoons virgin olive oil,
    divided
1 teaspoon grated lemon peel
1 clove garlic, sliced

1 tablespoon drained chopped
    capers
1 tablespoon balsamic vinegar

Heat 2 tablespoons oil in a small pan, and gently fry the lemon peel, garlic, and capers for 3 minutes or until softened. Stir in the vinegar; remove pan from heat and gradually beat in remaining oil. Pour over spinach salad and serve immediately.

Barbara Ball
ChurchLIFE, FL

Sweet and Sour Dressing

1 egg, well beaten   ½ cup vinegar
¾ cup sugar   dash salt

Stir ingredients until mixed well. Cook over medium heat, stirring continually until it starts to boil. Spoon warm dressing generously over salad. Makes 2 servings. May be refrigerated for about 2 weeks. Reheat before serving. If it seems thick when reheating, add a little water.

Mary Canada
President's Office, FL

Thai Peanut Salad Dressing

½ cup chunky peanut butter   ½ teaspoon chopped fresh chili
½ cup cider vinegar   pepper or crushed red peppers
1 cup canola oil   2 tablespoons chopped green onion
12 packets Equal or ½ cup sugar   (optional)

Whisk together all ingredients. Serve as a dressing for spinach or as a sauce with grilled poultry or meat on noodles.

Lana Jones
International Ministry, HI

Entrees

Beef

African Peanut Stew
(Bob's Famous Elephant Stew)

5 tablespoons oil, *divided*
2 pounds well-trimmed beef, cut
    into 1-inch or smaller cubes
flour
½ teaspoon nutmeg
1 tablespoon chili powder
4 medium onions, sliced
1 teaspoon minced garlic

5–6 cups water
up to 1 teaspoon red pepper
¾ cup tomato sauce
carrots and peas (optional)
½ cup chunky peanut butter
steamed rice
hot sauce

In a large heavy kettle, heat 3 tablespoons oil. Roll beef cubes in flour, and brown in hot oil. While this is cooking, add nutmeg and chili powder. When meat is browned, add onion, garlic, water, red pepper to taste, and tomato sauce. Simmer until meat is tender. If desired, add carrots and peas while the stew is simmering. A few minutes before serving, heat peanut butter and the remaining oil (this may be done in the microwave). Stir peanut butter mixture well, and pour it into the beef stew over low heat. Once the peanut butter is well absorbed into the stew (about 15 minutes), serve over steamed rice. Offer hot sauce at the table.

Bob Auer
International Ministry, FL

Armenian Shish-Kebab

½ pound fillet of beef, mutton,
    or lamb
1 medium onion, finely chopped

pinch of thyme
salt and pepper
2 cups hot broth

Cut meat into walnut-size pieces. Mix onion with thyme; spread over meat. Salt and pepper to taste. Allow meat to stand 3 hours. Arrange meat on metal skewers, and broil or grill over hot fire. Place the cooked kebabs into hot broth and simmer for 15–20 minutes. Serve hot.

Rita Harvey
Crusade Family

Barbecue

1 pound ground beef
1 onion, chopped
¾ cup ketchup
1 tablespoon sugar

2 tablespoons vinegar
2 tablespoons Worcestershire sauce
1½ teaspoons mustard

Brown and drain the beef and onion. Add remaining ingredients. Simmer and serve in buns. *Tip:* I make a double recipe and freeze the extra.

Jody Maurer
Campus Ministry, PA

Barbecue Brisket Sandwiches

¾ cup water
¼ cup Worcestershire sauce
1 tablespoon vinegar
1 teaspoon instant beef bouillon
    granules
1 teaspoon chili powder
½ teaspoon dry mustard
¼ teaspoon ground red pepper

2 cloves garlic, minced
2½ pounds fresh beef brisket
½ cup ketchup
2 tablespoons brown sugar
1 teaspoon cornstarch
8 French-style rolls (6–8 inch),
    split and toasted

Combine the first 8 ingredients in a small bowl. Trim any excess fat from the brisket and place in a crockpot (if necessary, cut the brisket to fit). Pour the liquid mixture over meat, reserving ½ cup for the barbecue sauce. Cover and cook brisket on low for 10–12 hours or on high for 4–5 hours. To make sauce, add ketchup, brown sugar, and cornstarch to the reserved liquid mixture, and cook over medium-high heat until thickened and bubbly. Cook and stir 2 minutes more. To serve brisket, remove meat from crockpot and discard cooking liquid. Thinly slice the meat diagonally across the grain. Serve on toasted rolls with sauce. Makes 8 servings. Good served with *Garden Chowder*.

Bobbi Jo Hasz
Campus Ministry, WI

Barbecue Cups

1 pound ground beef
1 small onion, chopped
¾–1 cup barbecue sauce

2 cans refrigerated biscuits
sliced American cheese

Brown ground beef and onion; drain fat. Add barbecue sauce. Simmer for approximately 15 minutes. While ground beef mixture is simmering, flatten each biscuit and spread in a muffin tin to form a cup. Spoon ground beef mixture into biscuit dough. Top with cheese and bake according to biscuit directions.

Cindy Bogan
JESUS Film Project, FL

Barbecued Beef

1 pound ground beef
¾ teaspoon salt
2 tablespoons Grandma's Molasses
2 tablespoons prepared mustard

1 tablespoon Worcestershire sauce
⅛ teaspoon Tabasco
½ cup ketchup
1 package hamburger buns

Sprinkle beef with salt, and brown in skillet. Blend molasses and mustard; stir in Worcestershire sauce, Tabasco, and ketchup, and add to beef. Cook until heated through. Serve on toasted hamburger buns.

Carolyn Justice
Single Life Resources, NC

BEEF

Bean Casserole

1 pound ground beef
½ pound bacon, chopped
1 cup chopped onion
1 16-ounce can pork and beans,
    drained
1 16-ounce can butter beans, drained

1 16-ounce can kidney beans,
    drained
2 teaspoons vinegar
½ cup ketchup
½ cup brown sugar
1 teaspoon mustard

Preheat oven to 350 degrees. Cook ground beef, bacon, and onion together. Add beans and stir. Combine remaining ingredients to make a sauce and add to mixture. Pour into baking dish and bake for 30–45 minutes. Serve with salad and cornbread. *Variation:* Substitute turkey for the beef, use more beans, or add ground sausage.

Cheryl Henderson
Contributions and Postal Services, FL

Beef and Bean Burritos

8 8-inch flour tortillas
1 pound lean ground beef
1 cup onion, chopped
2 cloves garlic, minced
1 16-ounce can black beans or pinto
    beans, rinsed and drained
½ cup salsa
2 teaspoons chili powder

3–4 dashes Tabasco
1 cup (4 ounces) shredded
    reduced-fat cheddar cheese
1½ cups shredded fresh spinach
1½ cups shredded lettuce
salsa (optional)
guacamole (optional)
low-fat sour cream (optional)

Preheat oven to 350 degrees. Stack tortillas and wrap tightly in foil; place in oven for 10 minutes. To make the filling, cook the beef, onion, and garlic until beef is brown. Drain off fat. Stir in beans, salsa, chili powder, and Tabasco; heat through. Spoon about ⅓ cup filling onto each tortilla. Top with 1 tablespoon cheese. Fold bottom edge up and over filling, then fold in the sides. (Secure with toothpicks if desired.) Arrange tortillas, seam-side down, on a foil-lined baking sheet. Cover tortillas with foil and bake until heated through (about 20 minutes). Serve on a bed of shredded spinach and lettuce. If desired, garnish with salsa, guacamole, and sour cream.

Ellen Armstrong
Board of Director's Wife

Beef Barbecue

3–4 pounds chuck roast
1 40-ounce bottle Heinz ketchup
1¼ quarts water
1 stalk celery, chopped
1 tablespoon Worcestershire sauce

1 large onion, chopped
2 tablespoons vinegar
1 tablespoon chili powder
salt and pepper to taste
hot sauce to taste

Preheat oven to 350 degrees. Combine all ingredients in a covered pan. Bake for approximately 3 hours. During cooking, add water if needed. After roast is tender, cool and remove any bone, fat, or gristle. Pull meat apart; place back into the pan and simmer until ready to eat. Makes 20–24 sandwiches. Freezes well.

Janice Gregory
ChurchLIFE, FL

Beef "Porcupine" Balls

1½ pounds ground beef or turkey
2 cups applesauce
1 cup instant rice
½ cup finely chopped onion
salt and pepper to taste

dash of poultry seasoning
1 14-ounce can tomato sauce
½ cup water
¼ cup brown sugar

Preheat oven to 350 degrees. Mix well the ground beef, applesauce, rice, onion, salt and pepper, and poultry seasoning. Shape into balls. Place a single layer in a 9×13-inch baking pan. Mix tomato sauce, water, and brown sugar; pour over meatballs. Bake for 45 minutes covered, then 15 minutes uncovered.

Cathy Hertzler
Computer Services, FL

BEEF

Beef Pot Roast

3–5 pounds chuck roast
1 teaspoon salt
1 teaspoon pepper
⅛ teaspoon ginger

2 onions, sliced
1 cup beef stock or water
potatoes, peeled and quartered
carrots, peeled and cut lengthwise

Rub chuck roast with salt, pepper, and ginger. Brown meat; add onions and beef stock or water. Cover and simmer for 1 hour. Then add potatoes and carrots. Bake covered for 1–2 hours at 325 degrees. Add more stock or water if needed. *Variation:* Brown meat in a Dutch oven and simmer on top of the stove the entire time.

Lori Burns
Staff & Ministry Opportunities, FL

Beef Stroganoff

1 pound ground beef
1 medium onion, chopped
1 clove garlic, minced
¼ cup water

1 can cream of chicken soup
1 can sliced mushrooms
½ cup sour cream

Brown and drain meat. Add onion and garlic, and sauté until golden brown. Add water and stir; add soup and mushrooms. Cook uncovered over low heat, stirring occasionally until thick and meat is tender (about 20 minutes). Just before serving, stir in sour cream and heat through. Serve with noodles, rice, or potatoes. Serves 4.

Lisa Master
Worldwide Challenge, FL

Beef Stroganoff With Mushrooms

2 pounds round steak
Lawry's Meat Tenderizer
4 tablespoons butter, *divided*
1 cup chopped onion
1 clove garlic, minced
½ pound fresh mushrooms or
    1 8-ounce can sliced mushrooms
3 tablespoons flour
1 tablespoon ketchup

2 teaspoons meat extract paste or
    4 teaspoons bottled extract
½ teaspoon salt
⅛ teaspoon pepper
1 can beef consommé
½ teaspoon dried dill
1 pint sour cream
12 ounces wide noodles, cooked,
    or 4–6 cups cooked rice

Tenderize steak with Lawry's tenderizer. Cut meat across the grain in strips and brown in 1 tablespoon butter on high heat. Set meat aside. In 3 tablespoons butter, sauté onion, garlic, and mushrooms; slowly add flour. Then add ketchup, meat extract, salt, and pepper. Gradually add bouillon, stirring constantly. Reduce heat and simmer 5 minutes; add dill and sour cream. Return meat to sauce and heat through. Serve over wide noodles or rice.

Pat Billings
Crusade Family

Beef Tortillas

1 large carrot, peeled
½ small cucumber, peeled
¼ teaspoon salt
1 3-ounce package cream cheese
　with chives, softened
2 tablespoons prepared white
　horseradish

1 tablespoon milk
4 8-inch flour tortillas
Romaine or green leaf lettuce
½ pound cooked roast beef,
　thinly sliced
sliced jalapeño peppers

Into a small bowl, coarsely shred carrot and cucumber. Stir in salt. In another small bowl, mix cream cheese, milk, and horseradish until blended. Spread horseradish mixture along the center of each tortilla. Top with lettuce leaves, then roast beef slices. Sprinkle with shredded vegetables. Fold the two opposite sides of each tortilla over the filling, overlapping slightly. To serve, arrange tortillas seam-side down on a platter and garnish each with a few jalapeño slices. Makes 4 servings. Serve with cold *Avocado Soup*.

Barbara Ball
ChurchLIFE, FL

 My command is this: Love each other as I have loved you (John 15:12).

Beefed-Up Biscuit Casserole

1–1¼ pounds ground round
½ cup chopped onion or 2 tablespoons
　instant minced onion
¼ cup diced green chilies or
　green pepper
1 8-ounce can tomato sauce
2 tablespoons chili powder

½–¾ teaspoon garlic salt
1 8-ounce can refrigerated butter-
　milk or country style biscuits
1½ cups shredded Monterey Jack
　or cheddar cheese, *divided*
½ cup sour cream
1 egg, slightly beaten

BEEF

Preheat oven to 375 degrees. Brown beef, onion, and chilies in a large frying pan. Drain. Stir in tomato sauce, chili powder, and garlic salt. Simmer while preparing dough. Separate biscuit dough into 10 biscuits; pull each apart into 2 layers. Press 10 biscuits to make a layer on the bottom of an ungreased 8- or 9-inch square baking pan. Combine ½ cup of cheese, sour cream, and egg; mix well. Remove meat mixture from heat; stir in sour cream mixture; spoon over dough. Arrange remaining biscuit layer on top; sprinkle with remaining cheese. Bake for 25–30 minutes until biscuits are deep golden brown. Serves 4–5. *Tip:* To reheat, loosely cover with foil, and bake for 20–25 minutes until heated through. This is a bake-off winning entry for most nutritious and most economical dish.

Merry McKean
Crusade Family

The Lord does not let the righteous go hungry but he thwarts the craving of the wicked (Prov. 10:3).

Bierrocks

2 packages dry yeast
2 cups warm water
¼ cup sugar
3 teaspoons salt, *divided*
1 egg
¼ cup margarine, softened

6–6½ cups flour
1½ pounds ground beef
½ cup chopped onion
3 cups finely chopped cabbage
½ teaspoon pepper
cheese slices (optional)

To make dough, dissolve yeast in water. Add sugar, 1½ teaspoons salt, egg, and margarine. Slowly add flour (may use part whole wheat). Knead dough 10 minutes, then chill for several hours. To make meat mixture, brown beef and onion in a skillet. Drain fat and add cabbage, 1½ teaspoons salt, and pepper. Cover skillet and cook on low heat until cabbage is tender. Roll dough into thin sheets. Cut into 5-inch squares. Place 2 tablespoons meat mixture on each square. Pull edges up and pinch together at the top to form a ball around the meat. Place pinched side down on a greased cookie sheet. Let rise 20 minutes, then bake at 350 degrees for 20–30 minutes. Serves 10. Great for freezing and taking in lunch boxes. *Optional:* Place a small piece of cheese on each square before adding meat mixture.

Sarah Willis
International Ministry, FL

Bobotie

1 pound ground beef
1 onion, chopped
1 thick slice of bread
1 cup milk
1 teaspoon curry powder
1 teaspoon turmeric
salt and pepper to taste

¼ cup vinegar (optional)
1 large tablespoon apricot jam,
   chutney, or chopped dried apricot
1 handful raisins
1 cup rice, cooked
1 cup half & half
1 egg

Preheat oven to 350 degrees. Brown beef and onion; drain. Soak bread in milk. Combine meat mixture, bread/milk mixture, seasonings, vinegar, jam, and raisins. Place mixture over rice in a baking dish. Beat together half & half and egg, and pour over entire dish. Bake 30 minutes. This is an Indian/South African recipe that's good!

Sue Patterson
International Ministry, Africa

Burrito Casserole

6 frozen bean and beef burritos
2 large cans chili
½ cup salsa

1½ cups shredded mild cheddar
   cheese
½ cup chopped onion

Preheat oven to 350 degrees. Line the bottom of a retangular casserole dish with the burritos. Evenly pour the chili over burritos, then top with salsa. Add a layer of onion, then top with cheese and bake for 40 minutes. This makes a quick and easy dinner.

Turner Middleton
New Life Resources, GA

Cheese Runzas

1 pound ground beef
1 medium onion, chopped
1 teaspoon margarine
1 medium head cabbage,
   coarsely shredded

water
salt and pepper to taste
2 1-pound loaves frozen bread
   dough, thawed
sliced cheddar or American cheese

BEEF

Preheat oven to 350 degrees. In a skillet, brown ground beef with onion; drain and set aside. In the same skillet, melt margarine then add cabbage and water to cover. Cook slowly until cabbage is soft; drain. Add salt and pepper. Combine beef mixture with cabbage. Roll out dough to ¼-inch thickness. Cut into 6-inch squares. Place a scant ½ cup beef mixture and a slice of cheese in the middle of each square. Pull the four corners together, and pinch edges firmly. Place seam-side down, with edges touching, in a greased cake or jelly roll pan. Bake for 30 minutes or until browned. Serve hot, or freeze after baking and reheat later. Makes about 1 dozen. *Tip:* Double the recipe and freeze them. They reheat well for lunch or dinner.

Kristen Warren
Campus Ministry, FL

Chili

1 pound ground beef
1 onion, chopped
2 cans red kidney beans or
    pinto beans, drained
1 large can tomatoes

1 8-ounce can tomato sauce
1 4-ounce can diced green chilies
2 tablespoons brown sugar
4 tablespoons chili powder

Brown the ground beef with the onion; drain the fat. Add remaining ingredients. Cover and simmer for 30 minutes or more, stirring occasionally.

Grace Swartz
NewLife Resources, GA

Country Garden Casserole

1 pound lean ground beef
1 small onion, finely chopped
1 stalk celery, finely chopped
2 large potatoes, peeled and thinly sliced

1½ cups vegetables of your choice
    (combine 2 if you wish)
1 can tomato soup

Preheat oven to 350 degrees. Brown the ground beef in a frying pan. Add onion and celery, and sauté until done. Spray a casserole dish with vegetable spray. Layer the sliced potatoes, then the vegetables, and add ground beef mixture on top. Pour the tomato soup over the casserole. Cover and bake for 45–60 minutes or until the potatoes are done.

Michelle Treiber
NewLife Publications, FL

Crockpot Beef Ribs

4½ pounds beef ribs
1 tablespoon oil
1 medium onion, sliced
½ cup celery, sliced

½ cup water
1 tablespoon brown sugar
1 can tomato soup
1 tablespoon flour

Brown ribs in oil. Mix onion, celery, and water in a crockpot. Add ribs and remaining ingredients. Cook all afternoon. Serve with rice. *Optional:* Lamb or pork ribs can also be used.

Sus Schmitt
Computer Services, FL

If anyone has material possessions and sees his brother in need but has no pity on him, how can the love of God be in him?
(1 John 3:17)

Crusty Mexican Bean Bake

½ cup flour
1½ teaspoons salt, *divided*
½ teaspoon baking powder
2 tablespoons shortening or
    margarine
½ cup sour cream or yogurt
    (increase flour by 2 tablespoons
    if using yogurt)
1 egg, beaten

¾ pound ground beef
½ cup chopped onion
2 teaspoons chili powder
½ teaspoon Tabasco
2 cups undrained cooked kidney beans
¾ cup (6 ounces) tomato paste
½ cup grated cheese
1–2 cups shredded lettuce
1 cup chopped tomatoes

Preheat oven to 350 degrees. To make crust, combine flour, ½ teaspoon salt, baking powder, shortening, sour cream, and egg. Stir together (mixture may be slightly lumpy). With the back of a spoon, spread thinly on the bottom and sides of a greased shallow, 2-quart casserole. (Crust may be prepared in advance and refrigerated until ready to use.) Brown beef and onion in a skillet. Add 1 teaspoon salt, chili powder, Tabasco, kidney beans, and tomato paste. Fill crust with bean mixture. Bake for 30 minutes. Sprinkle remaining ingredients over pie or serve alongside. Serves 6.

Karen Horsey
International Ministry, FL

BEEF

Deep-Dish Taco Squares

1 pound ground beef
½ cup sour cream
⅓ cup mayonnaise or salad dressing
½ cup (approximately 2 ounces)
    shredded sharp cheddar cheese
1 tablespoon chopped onion

1 cup Bisquick
¼ cup cold water
1–2 medium tomatoes, thinly sliced
½ cup chopped green peppers
paprika (optional)

Preheat oven to 375 degrees. Brown ground beef; drain. Combine sour cream, mayonnaise, cheese, and onion; set aside. Mix Bisquick and water to make a soft dough. Place dough in a greased 8-inch square pan, pressing dough ½ inch up the sides. Layer beef, tomatoes, and green peppers in pan. Spoon sour cream mixture on top. Sprinkle with paprika, if desired. Bake for 25–30 minutes or until edges of dough are light brown. Serves 5–6.

Conda DeVries
International Ministry, FL

Domatelli

2 medium onions, chopped
2 cloves garlic, minced
1 green pepper, chopped
1½ pounds ground beef
1 medium can tomatoes

2 tablespoons grated Parmesan cheese
¼ teaspoon thyme (optional)
⅓ package shell macaroni, cooked
½ pound cheddar cheese, cut into
    8 sticks

Preheat oven to 350 degrees. Sauté onion, garlic, and green pepper until soft; add beef and cook until brown. Drain off grease. Add tomatoes, Parmesan cheese, thyme, and macaroni. Place in a 2½-quart casserole. Stick pieces of cheddar cheese down through the mixture, and sprinkle with additional Parmesan. Bake for 25–30 minutes. This makes a whole meal in one dish. *Variation:* Turkey or chicken can also be used.

Dorothy Brooks
Here's Life America, MA

Double Teriyaki Kabobs

1½ pounds sirloin steak	1 tablespoon ginger
½ cup soy sauce	¼ teaspoon cracked pepper
¼ cup brown sugar	2 cloves garlic, minced
2 tablespoons olive oil	1 can whole water chestnuts

Cut steak into strips ¼-inch thick and 1-inch wide (it works best if meat is partially frozen). Mix the next 6 ingredients, then add strips and stir to coat. Refrigerate for 3 hours. On each skewer, lace 1 strip of meat accordian-style, add 1 chestnut, another strip of meat, and a second chestnut. Cook over hot coals for 10–12 minutes. Turn often and baste with marinade. Serves 4–5.

Joette Whims
NewLife Publications, CA

Earle's Specialty Roast

2–3 pounds chuck roast	½ cup water
1 package dry onion soup mix	

Preheat oven to 350 degrees. Place meat on a large sheet of aluminum foil. Sprinkle with onion soup mix and water. Wrap securely and place in a casserole; bake for 1½–2 hours. *Tip:* Pork chops, chicken, or any other meat can also be used.

Judy Carpenter
Crusade Family

Easy Crockpot Stew

1–2 pounds lean stew beef, cubed	2 medium carrots, thinly sliced
1 envelope onion soup mix	2 stalks celery, chopped
½ cup beef bouillon	3 medium potatoes, cut bite-size
1 can cream of mushroom soup	1 tablespoon dried parsley
1 4-ounce can mushrooms, drained	

Combine all ingredients in a crockpot. Cover and cook on high for 1 hour. Reduce heat to low and cook for 6 more hours. Serves 5–6.

Terry Morgan
Campus Ministry, Mexico

BEEF

Egg Foo Yung

½ pound ground beef
¾ cup finely chopped onion
  or scallions
¼ cup finely diced celery
1 cup canned bean spouts, drained,
  or 2 cups fresh bean spouts
6 eggs, well beaten

1 teaspoon salt
¼ cup soy sauce
1 tablespoon cornstarch
2 teaspoons sugar
2 teaspoons vinegar
¾ cup water or chicken broth

Brown beef in a skillet; drain and reserve 2 tablespoons fat. Combine onion, celery, bean sprouts, eggs, and salt. Add beef. Heat fat in the skillet. Form patties using ¼ cup of mixture and fry in the skillet. Keep patties shaped by pushing egg back into the mixture with a spatula. When brown on one side, turn and brown the other side. To make sauce, combine remaining ingredients in a saucepan. Cook, stirring constantly, until sauce clears. Keep sauce hot. Serve patties hot with rice and sauce. Serves 6–8.

Karen Horsey
International Ministry, FL

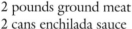

Enchiladas

2 pounds ground meat
2 cans enchilada sauce
2–3 cans tomato sauce
24 hand-made corn tortillas
1 can black olives, chopped

1 large onion, chopped
1 pound yellow cheese, grated
1 pound Monterey Jack cheese,
  grated

Preheat oven to 325 degrees. Brown and drain meat. Combine sauces in a frying pan or pan large enough to hold a tortilla. Heat sauces until simmering. Place a tortilla in sauce for a few seconds; drain slightly on paper towels. Layer 2 tablespoons meat, 1 tablespoon olives, onion to taste, and 1 tablespoon of each cheese on a tortilla. (Vary the ingredients and amounts to suit your taste.) Roll up, and place seam-side down in 2 9×13-inch baking dishes. Repeat with all tortillas. Pour remaining sauce over rolled enchiladas in dish. If desired, add remaining onion and olives and top with remaining cheese. Bake until cheese bubbles (about 30 minutes).

Barbara Ball
ChurchLIFE, FL

Fajitas

1½ pounds sirloin steak
   (1½ inches thick) or chicken
¼ cup plus 2 tablespoons oil
¼ cup red wine vinegar
1 teaspoon sugar
1 teaspoon oregano
1 teaspoon chili powder
½ teaspoon garlic powder
½ teaspoon salt

¼ teaspoon pepper
chopped onions
sliced green pepper
1 package fajita-size flour tortillas
salsa
sour cream
guacamole
shredded cheese

Marinate meat overnight in a mixture of ¼ cup oil, vinegar, sugar, and seasonings. When ready to cook, brush meat with marinade and grill or broil 8 minutes on each side. Sauté onions and green pepper in 2 tablespoons oil. Slice meat into strips. Place meat, onion mixture, salsa, sour cream, guacamole, and cheese into separate bowls. Serve with flour tortillas.

Liz Lazarian
Women Today International, FL

 Your laws are wonderful; no wonder I obey them (Psalm 119:129).

Flank Steak Marinade

½ cup soy sauce
¼ cup brown sugar
1 clove garlic, minced, or
   ½ teaspoon garlic powder
   (optional)

2 tablespoons vegetable oil
1 teaspoon ground ginger
½ teaspoon monosodium
   glutamate (Accent)
flank steak

For marinade, combine all ingredients except steak. Mix well. Score both sides of steak and place in a glass baking dish. Spoon the marinade over the steak, and let stand for at least 2 hours at room temperature, turning the steak over about every 30 minutes. (Steak can be marinated in the refrigerator but will require approximately 4 hours to achieve the same degree of flavor as at room temperature.) Broil steak under broiler or grill over coals. Slice steak across the grain and serve. Marinade is also good with chicken, pork chops, or ribs.

Ronnie Lesher
Military Ministry, VA

BEEF

Glop

1 pound ground beef
diced onion
salt and pepper to taste
2 cans tomato soup

1 can cream of mushroom soup
water
1 package noodles, cooked
cheese slices

Preheat oven to 350 degrees. Brown beef and onion; drain. Add salt and pepper, tomato and mushroom soups, and a little water (for the right consistency) and simmer. Combine noodles and meat mixture, and place in a casserole. Bake for about 25 minutes. Just before it's done, add cheese slices on top and melt.

Liesl Buck
International Ministry, FL

Good and Hearty Barbecue

1½ pounds onions, chopped
1½ bunches celery, chopped
5 pounds ground beef
½ cup butter (optional)
juice of 1½ lemons
1 tablespoon dry mustard

2 tablespoons brown sugar
2 tablespoons vinegar
1½ bottles ketchup
1 bottle chili sauce
1 can tomato soup
salt and pepper

Cook onions and celery together until tender. Brown ground beef in butter. Stir in remaining ingredients, and simmer 10 minutes or longer. Serve on warm hamburger buns. Serves 25. *Tip:* Divide barbecue into family portions and freeze. Handy for emergency meals!

Midge Piedot
Crusade Family

Good Goulash

1 pound ground chuck
salt and pepper to taste
1 small can tomato sauce
1 cup sour cream
1 8-ounce package cream cheese

5 green onions, chopped
1 pint cottage cheese (optional)
5 ounces noodles, cooked
grated cheddar cheese

Preheat oven to 350 degrees. Brown ground beef; salt and pepper to taste. Drain grease and add tomato sauce. Simmer 5–10 minutes. Mix together sour cream, cream cheese, and onions; add cottage cheese if desired. Place cooked noodles in a casserole dish. Add a layer of sour cream mixture, then cover with meat mixture. (Or all ingredients can be combined and placed in a deep casserole dish.) Top with cheese and bake uncovered for 35 minutes.

Linda Dillow
Crusade Family

Hamburger-Onion Pie

1 cup biscuit mix
⅓ cup light cream or evaporated milk
1 pound ground beef
2 medium onions, sliced
1 teaspoon salt
¼ teaspoon pepper

1 teaspoon curry powder
2 tablespoons flour
2 eggs, slightly beaten
1 cup small-curd cottage cheese
paprika

Preheat oven to 400 degrees. With a fork, combine biscuit mix and cream. Knead and roll dough to line a 9-inch pie pan. Sauté beef and onions. Add salt, pepper, curry powder, and flour. Spread meat mixture into the dough-lined pan. Combine eggs and cottage cheese. Pour over meat but *do not* mix. Sprinkle with paprika. Bake 30 minutes. Serves 6–8.

Karen Horsey
International Ministry, FL

Hot Chili

1 pound ground beef
1 medium onion, chopped
1 package McCormick Chili mix
1 30-ounce can Bush's Chili Hot beans

1 28-ounce can peeled whole tomatoes
1 15-ounce can tomato sauce
1 small can tomato paste

Brown beef and onions, then drain. Place in a large pan or crock pot with remaining ingredients. Let simmer for 30–60 minutes or all day. The longer it cooks, the more flavor it will have. Serve over rice or nacho chips with sour cream, cheese, black olives, and fresh tomatoes. *Tip:* Double the recipe to freeze some for another day.

Barbara Bennett
Christian Leadership, TN

Hot Curried Beef

1½ pounds beef, cut across
  grain into thin slices
1 onion, chopped
1 teaspoon cumin
½ teaspoon ginger

1 teaspoon curry powder
¼ cup soy sauce
½–1 teaspoon crushed red pepper
water
medium grain white rice

Heat skillet or wok to high. Cook beef slices until browned. Add onion, cumin, ginger, and curry; stir to coat. Add soy sauce and reduce heat to low. Stir in pepper, then add enough water to cover beef. Simmer at least 2 hours for full flavor (water will cook down into a thick broth). Serve with rice.

Penny Dixon
Campus Ministry, ID

Hungarian Goulash

4 cups cubed beef
1 onion, sliced
1–2 cloves garlic, minced
2–4 tablespoons shortening
¾ cup ketchup
2 tablespoons Worcestershire sauce
1 tablespoon brown sugar

1–2 tablespoons paprika
1–2 tablespoons salt
½ teaspoon dry mustard
dash cayenne pepper
2 cups water, *divided*
cooked noodles or rice

In a large skillet, brown beef, onion, and garlic in shortening. Add ketchup, Worcestershire sauce, brown sugar, seasonings, and 1½ cups water. Simmer 1–2 hours, adding more water if needed. Mix flour and ½ cup water, and stir gradually into meat mixture. Boil for 1 minute to thicken. Serve over hot cooked noodles or rice.

Joanne Austin
International Ministry, FL

Make the most of your chances to tell others the Good News.
Be wise in all your contacts with them (Col. 4:5).

Hungarian Goulash
With Macaroni

1½–2 pounds ground beef
1 medium green pepper,
   finely chopped
1 onion, finely chopped
1 small box elbow macaroni

1 large can tomato sauce
2 sauce cans water
soy sauce
salt and pepper

Brown beef in a skillet; drain. Add green pepper and onion. Cook macaroni according to package directions. Drain water and pour macaroni into a large soup pot. Add tomato sauce and water, then add ground beef mixture. Stir in soy sauce, salt, and pepper to taste.

Crystal Keller
Computer Services, FL

Irish Boiled Dinner

4 pounds corned beef brisket
1 can condensed onion soup
4 whole peppercorns
1 medium clove garlic, minced
1 bay leaf
¼ teaspoon crushed rosemary
6 medium carrots, cut into
   bite-size pieces

7 medium potatoes, quartered
½ cup celery, cut into
   bite-size pieces
1 medium head green cabbage,
   cut into wedges
3 tablespoons water
3 tablespoons flour

Rinse corned beef well. Place in a large heavy pan, and add soup and seasonings. Cover and cook over low heat for 3½ hours. Add carrots, potatoes, and celery. Place cabbage on top. Cover and cook about 1 hour or until all ingredients are tender. Remove meat, vegetables, and bay leaf. Gradually blend water into flour until smooth; slowly stir into the sauce in the bottom of the pan. Cook, stirring until thickened. Makes approximately 8 servings.

Laurie Killingsworth
New Life Center, FL

BEEF

Italian Meatloaf

1½ pounds ground meat
1 egg, beaten
¾ cup cracker crumbs
½ cup chopped onion
1 teaspoon salt

1 cup tomato sauce, *divided*
½ teaspoon oregano
¼ teaspoon pepper
2 cups grated mozzarella cheese
⅔ cup tomato sauce

Preheat oven to 350 degrees. Combine meat, egg, cracker crumbs, onion, salt, ⅓ cup tomato sauce, oregano, and pepper. Shape into a 10×12-inch rectangle on waxed paper. Sprinkle with the cheese. Roll up and press ends to seal. Place in a shallow pan and bake for 1 hour. Pour tomato sauce over the top and bake another 15 minutes.

Lori Burns
Staff & Ministry Opportunities, FL

Jordy's Chili

1–2 pounds ground beef
1 onion, chopped
½ green pepper, diced
2–4 cups diced celery
1½–2 cups tomato juice or V-8
salt to taste

2 teaspoons paprika
1 teaspoon oregano
1 tablespoon chili powder or more
garlic (optional)
1–2 cans French style green beans

Brown and drain ground beef. Add remaining ingredients except green beans, and simmer about 1 hour. Add green beans before serving and heat through. Makes 4–5 servings. This is a low-calorie dish and very tasty. Prepare the night before to allow seasonings to blend.

Helen Koopman
JESUS Film Project, FL

Machaca

2 pounds roast beef
2–3 eggs
3 tablespoons oil
1 onion, chopped

1 4-ounce can chopped green chilies
1–2 tomatoes, chopped
2 cloves garlic, minced
flour tortillas

Cook beef in crock pot or oven until tender. When cooled, shred into bite-size pieces. In a large pan, stir-fry beef with remaining ingredients until eggs are cooked and tomatoes are soft. Serve with soft flour tortillas, burrito style.

Dianne Webb
Finance, FL

Mexican Casserole With Doritos

1½ pounds lean ground beef
1 small onion, chopped
½ teaspoon garlic salt
2 8-ounce cans tomato sauce
1 cup sliced ripe olives
1 cup sour cream

1 cup small curd cottage cheese
3–4 cans green chilies, seeded
  and chopped
1 package crisp tortilla chips (Doritos)
2 cups (¾ pound) grated Monterey
  Jack cheese

Preheat oven to 350 degrees. Brown the beef and onions. Add garlic salt, tomato sauce, and olives; simmer 10 minutes. In a small bowl, combine sour cream, cottage cheese, and chilies. Crush tortilla chips slightly and place ½ on the bottom of a buttered 2½-quart casserole. Add ½ of the meat mixture, cover with ½ of the sour cream mixture, and sprinkle with ½ of the cheese. Repeat layers. Bake uncovered 30–35 minutes until bubbly. *Variation:* Roast beef, leftover chicken, or turkey may be substituted for ground beef.

Lorraine Pettijohn
Military Ministry, VA

Mexican Lasagna

1 large onion, chopped
1½ pounds ground chuck
1 can Rotel diced tomatoes and
  green chilies

1 can cream of chicken soup
1 can ranch-style beans
1 pound Velveeta cheese, cubed
1 package tortillas

Preheat oven to 350 degrees. Brown onion and meat; drain. Mix together all ingredients except tortillas. Layer mixture with tortillas, and bake until hot and bubbly (about 30 minutes).

Juli Emory
Military Ministry, VA

BEEF

Mom's Swedish Meatballs

2 cups dry bread crumbs
2 cups milk plus additional for gravy
1¾ pounds ground beef
¼ pound ground pork
2 eggs
1 onion, diced

1 teaspoon salt
¼ teaspoon pepper
¼ teaspoon nutmeg
flour
2 tablespoons oil

Preheat oven to 350 degrees. Soak bread crumbs in milk for 20 minutes.
Combine all ingredients except flour and oil. Roll mixture into 1-inch balls,
then roll in flour to coat. Place in skillet with oil and brown on all sides;
don't crowd the meatballs while they're browning. Add more oil as needed.
Remove meatballs from oil and drain. Bake for 50–60 minutes in a pan.
Remove meatballs from pan; add milk to drippings to make a gravy. Salt and
pepper to taste. Serve over noodles.

Sue McDaniel
International Ministry, FL

Moussaka

1 large eggplant, unpeeled
melted margarine
salt and pepper
1 pound ground beef
1 onion, chopped
2 cups tomato sauce
⅓ cup tomato paste

1 garlic clove, minced
dash nutmeg
½ teaspoon oregano
1 tablespoon chopped parsley
1 tablespoon chopped mint
   (optional)
½–1 cup grated Parmesan cheese

Preheat oven to broil. Cut unpeeled eggplant into ½-inch slices. Place slices
on a cookie sheet, brush with melted margarine, and sprinkle with salt and
pepper. Broil 5 minutes or until golden. Turn slices, brush and season again,
and brown second side. Remove from broiler and set oven at 350 degrees.
Brown beef and onion together. Add tomato sauce and paste, and seasonings. In a 9-inch square baking dish, layer ½ the eggplant slices and ½ the
meat mixture; repeat with remaining ingredients. Sprinkle with cheese. Bake
for 40 minutes. Serves 6.

Vegetarian option: Sauté onion and garlic in 2 tablespoons oil, and proceed
with tomato sauce mixture. In a separate bowl, combine 1 beaten egg,
2 tablespoons Parmesan cheese, and 1 cup cottage cheese. Place ½ of tomato

sauce mixture in casserole, add ½ of eggplant, all of cottage cheese mixture, remaining eggplant, and remaining tomato sauce, sprinkling layers with Parmesan. Top with additional Parmesan. Omit last ½–1 cup grated cheese. Bake as directed.

Karen Horsey
International Ministry, FL

Norwegian Meatballs

beef soup bone
2 pounds round steak,
ground 3–4 times
4 teaspoons onion, finely ground

salt and pepper to taste
2 tablespoons cornstarch
milk
flour

Boil soup bone and strain the broth; discard bone and bring broth to a boil. Mix meat, onion, salt, and pepper. With a spoon, cream together meat and cornstarch. Add milk gradually until mixture becomes like a thick paste. With wet hands (to keep meat smooth), shape the meat mixture into balls. Drop meatballs into rapidly boiling broth; cook about 20 minutes. (When meatballs are done, they will come to the top of the broth.) Spoon off any fat. Keep meatballs in broth until ready to use. To make gravy, thicken the broth with flour. Serve over mashed potatoes.

Joette Whims
NewLife Publications, CA

 Open my eyes to see wonderful things in your Word (Psalm 119:18).

Oriental Charcoal Broiled Roast

5 ounces soy sauce
2 cups tomato juice
juice of 2 lemons

1 tablespoon dehydrated onion
2–3 pounds chuck roast, cut about
2-inches thick

Combine soy sauce, tomato juice, lemon juice, and onion to make marinade. Marinate roast for several hours or overnight. Grill over hot charcoal; cut into thin slices to serve. Serves 6.

Marilyn Heavilin
Crusade Family

BEEF

Pakistani Kima

1 cup chopped onion
1 clove garlic, minced
3 tablespoons butter or margarine
1 pound ground beef
1 tablespoon curry powder
1½ teaspoons salt
dash pepper

dash cinnamon
dash ginger
dash tumeric
2 cups cooked tomatoes
2 potatoes, diced
2 cups frozen peas or green beans

Sauté onion and garlic in butter. Add beef. Brown well, then stir in remaining ingredients. Cover and simmer 25 minutes. Serve with rice. Makes 5–6 servings.

Karen Horsey
International Ministry, FL

Pizza Meatloaf

2 pounds ground beef
1 cup soda cracker crumbs
2 eggs
1 cup milk
½ cup chopped onions
½ cup grated Parmesan cheese

2 teaspoons seasoning salt
1 teaspoon ground oregano
¼ teaspoon pepper
1 8-ounce can pizza sauce
1 cup grated mozzarella cheese

Preheat oven to 350 degrees. Lightly combine all ingredients except pizza sauce and mozzarella. Press into an 8-inch square pan. Bake for 45 minutes then drain grease. Pour pizza sauce evenly over meatloaf and bake 10 more minutes. Sprinkle mozzarella cheese on top and bake until cheese is melted.

Lisa Master
Worldwide Challenge, FL

If you stay away from sin you will be like one of these dishes made of purest gold—the very best in the house—so that Christ himself can use you for his highest purposes (2 Tim. 2:21).

Polenta Meat Pie

¼ cup finely chopped onion
1 clove garlic, finely minced
1 tablespoon salad oil
1 pound ground round
1 cup fresh bread crumbs
3 eggs, *divided*
2¼ cups buttermilk, *divided*

¼ cup ketchup
2½ teaspoons salt, *divided*
⅛ teaspoon pepper
½ cup yellow cornmeal
1 teaspoon sugar
½ teaspoon baking soda
¼ cup grated sharp cheddar cheese

Preheat oven to 350 degrees. In a medium skillet, sauté onion and garlic in oil until golden; remove from heat. Stir in meat, bread crumbs, 1 egg, ¼ cup buttermilk, ketchup, 1½ teaspoons salt, and pepper. Mix thoroughly. Press onto the bottom and side of a 10-inch pie plate. Bake 15 minutes; pour off excess liquid. Meanwhile, separate the 2 remaining eggs. In a medium saucepan, mix together 2 cups buttermilk, cornmeal, sugar, 1 teaspoon salt, and baking soda. Cook, stirring constantly, until thickened and smooth. Remove from heat; stir in egg yolks. Beat egg whites until stiff; fold into cornmeal mixture. Pour into meat-pie shell; top with grated cheese. Bake 30 minutes or until cheese is lightly browned. Cool 5 minutes before cutting. Serves 6–8.

Midge Piedot
Crusade Family

Quick Chop Suey

1½ pounds ground beef
½ cup chopped onion
1½–2 cups chopped celery
 (½-inch pieces)
1 cup water, *divided*

1 can bean sprouts, drained
1 can sliced water chestnuts, drained
1 teaspoon sugar
2 teaspoons cornstarch
2 tablespoons soy sauce

Brown beef; add onion, celery, and ⅔ cup water. Cover and steam for 5 minutes. Add bean sprouts and water chestnuts. Mix sugar, cornstarch, and soy sauce with ⅓ cup water, and add to beef mixture. Bring to a good boil. Serve on hot rice with soy sauce or chow mein noodles. Good with cooked chicken, also.

Marlyse Milburn
Milburn Projects, CA

BEEF

Rice Meatballs

1 cup uncooked Minute Rice
1 pound ground beef
1 egg, slightly beaten
2 teaspoons marjoram

dash of pepper
2½ cups tomato juice, *divided*
½ teaspoon sugar

Lightly mix the first 5 ingredients with ½ cup tomato juice. Shape into approximately 18 balls. Place in skillet; add sugar and remaining tomato juice. Bring to a boil, then cover and simmer for 15 minutes, basting occasionally. Use additional tomato juice for basting if necessary.

Cindy Bogan
JESUS Film Project, FL

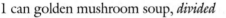

Salisbury Steak for Six

1 can golden mushroom soup, *divided*
1½ pounds ground beef
½ cup fine bread crumbs
1 egg, beaten

¼ cup finely chopped onion
1 teaspoon Tabasco
⅓ cup water

Preheat oven to 350 degrees. Combine ¼ cup soup with remaining ingredients except water. Shape into 6 oblong loaves. Place in a large baking dish and bake for 45 minutes. Spoon off grease. Add water to the remaining soup and pour over loaves; bake 10 minutes longer. *Tip:* Broil loaves for a few minutes to brown them before covering with soup.

Nancy Scott
JESUS Film Project, NC

San Francisco Stew ⏱ 📖

1 pound ground chuck
1 onion, chopped
1 can tomato soup

2 cans pork and beans
1 can Hormel chili without beans
½ cup brown sugar

Preheat oven to 300 degrees. Brown ground chuck with onion. Add tomato soup and pork and beans. Then add chili and brown sugar. Place in a casserole and bake for 1 hour. This tried and tested recipe from early Campus Crusade days is inexpensive and a family favorite.

Joan Kendall
Crusade Family

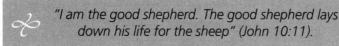

"I am the good shepherd. The good shepherd lays down his life for the sheep" (John 10:11).

Shepherd's Pie

mashed potatoes, *divided*
vegetables
cubes of meat

bread crumbs
gravy
seasoning

Preheat oven to 350 degrees. Line a greased casserole with mashed potatoes. Fill with vegetables and meat, such as broccoli and chicken. Add bread crumbs, gravy, and any desired seasonings. Cover with mashed potatoes and bake for 40 minutes. *Tip:* This is a good way to use leftovers from a holiday meal. If you don't have leftover gravy, beat an egg and stir into 1 cup milk. Pour over meat and vegetables before topping with mashed potatoes.

Karen Horsey
International Ministry, FL

Simply Great Meatloaf

3 tablespoons unsalted butter
¾ cup finely chopped onion
¾ cup finely chopped scallions
½ cup finely chopped carrots
¼ cup finely chopped celery
¼ cup minced red pepper
¼ cup minced green pepper
2 teaspoons minced garlic
1 teaspoon finely ground
   black pepper
½ teaspoon finely ground
   white pepper

¼ teaspoon cayenne pepper
salt to taste
1 teaspoon ground cumin
½ teaspoon nutmeg
3 eggs
½ cup ketchup
½ cup half & half
2 pounds lean ground chuck
12 ounces ground sausage
¾ cup fine fresh bread crumbs,
   toasted

BEEF

Melt butter and add onion, scallions, carrots, celery, peppers, and garlic. Cook, stirring often, until moisture has evaporated (about 10 minutes). Set aside to cool, then refrigerate, covered, at least 1 hour or overnight. Add seasonings and eggs, and beat well. Add ketchup and half & half; blend well. Add ground chuck, sausage, and bread crumbs to the egg mixture, then add vegetables. Mix thoroughly by kneading for 5 minutes, then form into a loaf. Bake for 35–40 minutes at 375 degrees. Serve with mashed potatoes and your favorite green salad. Makes 8–10 servings. *Tip:* Use leftovers in cold meatloaf sandwiches.

Barbara Ball
ChurchLIFE, FL

Six-Hour Stew

1 14½-ounce can tomatoes
3 tablespoons tapioca
½ teaspoon basil
½ teaspoon oregano
¼ teaspoon marjoram
2 tablespoons plus 2 teaspoons
   Worcestershire sauce

2 teaspoons salt
4 stalks celery, cut into large pieces
1 large onion, cut into large pieces
4–5 carrots, cut into large pieces
4–5 new potatoes, cut into large pieces
2 pounds boneless beef stew meat
1 almond-size bay leaf

Preheat oven to 250 degrees. Place all ingredients in a large roaster. Cover and bake for 6 hours. Remove bay leaf before serving.

Evelyn Bromberg
Crusade Family

Spicy Beef and Vegetable Sloppy Joes

1 pound lean ground beef
1 medium onion, chopped
2 cloves garlic, minced
1 cup chopped zucchini
1 cup chopped yellow summer squash
1 cup sliced fresh mushrooms

¾ cup chopped green pepper
1 16-ounce jar salsa
1 teaspoon dried basil, crushed
½ teaspoon dried parsley flakes
½ teaspoon crushed dried rosemary
6–8 Kaiser rolls, split and toasted

In a 10-inch skillet, cook beef, onion, and garlic over medium heat until meat is brown and onion is tender. Drain the fat. Add zucchini, squash, mushrooms, and green pepper. Cover and cook over low heat for 5–7 minutes or until vegetables are tender. Stir in salsa and seasonings. Simmer uncovered for about 10 minutes or until most of the liquid has evaporated. Serve on toasted rolls. Serves 6–8.

Ellen Armstrong
Board of Director's Wife

Spinach Fandango

1 pound ground meat
1 onion, chopped
2 cloves garlic, minced
1 cup cream of celery soup
1 cup sour cream
2 packages frozen spinach, cooked
1 teaspoon oregano
6 ounces grated mozzarella cheese

Preheat oven to 350 degrees. Brown meat, onion, and garlic; drain. Add soup, sour cream, spinach, and oregano. Heat, then put into a casserole dish. Top with cheese. Bake about 20 minutes or until bubbly.

Clara Nell Shirey
President's Office, FL

Streamlined Chimichangas

2 pounds very lean ground beef
1 medium onion, chopped
2 cloves garlic, minced
1 cup medium picante sauce
2 teaspoons ground cumin
1 teaspoon oregano
1 teaspoon salt
1 cup cooked rice
20 8-inch flour tortillas
½ cup butter, melted
sour cream
chopped tomatoes
Quick Guacamole
extra picante sauce

Preheat oven to 475 degrees. Brown meat with onion and garlic; drain. Stir in picante sauce and seasonings; simmer 5 minutes or until most of liquid has evaporated. Add cooked rice. Brush one side of tortillas with butter; spoon heaping ⅓ cup of meat mixture onto center of unbuttered sides. Roll and place seam down in a buttered 9×13-inch baking dish. Bake about 15 minutes or until golden brown. Top with sour cream, tomatoes, *Quick Guacamole*, and picante sauce. Serves 10 (2 per serving). May be frozen and reheated; do not cover to reheat.

Quick Guacamole:

2 ripe avocados
¼ cup picante sauce

2 teaspoons lemon juice
½ teaspoon salt

Peel, seed, and mash avocados; add picante sauce, lemon juice, and salt; mix well.

Karen Horsey
International Ministry, FL

Fix your thoughts on what is true and good and right. Think about things that are pure and lovely, and dwell on the fine, good things in others (Phil. 4:8).

Stuffed Flank or Round Steak

1 cup milk
1 egg
1 teaspoon sage
½ teaspoon salt
2 slices onion, chopped

½ cup diced celery
½ cup walnuts
3 cups bread crumbs
1½–2 pounds flank or round steak

Preheat oven to 350 degrees. Beat the first 6 ingredients for 1 minute. Add walnuts. Stir mixture into bread crumbs. Mix well and arrange stuffing in a strip down the middle of the steak. Roll and fasten with toothpicks. Bake in a well-greased covered baking dish for 1½ hours. Serves 6–8.

Marilyn Klein
National Ministry, CA

Sukiyaki

½ cup water
½ cup soy sauce
1 tablespoon honey
1½ pounds sirloin steak, cut into
¼-inch strips

½ pound fresh mushrooms, sliced
2 green onions, chopped
1 pound bean sprouts
1 8-ounce can sliced water chestnuts
1 8-ounce can bamboo shoots, drained

To make marinade, mix water, soy sauce, and honey. Place steak in a 7×12-inch microwave-safe baking dish. Pour marinade over steak and marinate at room temperature 4–6 hours or overnight in the refrigerator. Place a row of sliced mushrooms down the center of the dish; sprinkle green onions across mushrooms. Divide bean sprouts in ½ and place in opposite corners of the dish. Place water chestnuts in another corner and bamboo shoots in the fourth corner. Cook on high in microwave for 8½ minutes. Cover with plastic wrap to steam the vegetables and let stand for 5 minutes. *Variation:* Use 2 cups chopped chicken instead of steak.

Doris Maugle
Contributions and Postal Services, FL

Summary Casserole

Summer Casserole

1 cup cooked macaroni
1 cup milk
1 cup cream of mushroom soup
3 hard-boiled eggs, chopped

1 small jar pimiento
1 package dried beef, shredded
1 small onion, chopped
1 cup cheddar cheese

Preheat oven to 350 degrees. Mix all ingredients and put in a greased casserole. Bake 1 hour. May be prepared the night before and refrigerated.

Cheryl Hile
Computer Services, FL

Susie's Meatloaf

2 pounds ground round
1 egg
¼ cup grated Parmesan cheese
1 onion, chopped

1 teaspoon garlic powder
1 can cream of mushroom soup
1 cup ketchup

Preheat oven to 350 degrees. In a large bowl, combine ground round, egg, Parmesan, onion, and garlic powder. In a separate bowl, mix mushroom soup and ketchup. Add ½ of this mixture to the beef mixture and combine. Form into a loaf in the center of a 9×13-inch pan; pour the remaining ½ of soup mixture over loaf. Bake for 1 hour. Serves 6. This is my mother-in-law's recipe and is excellent! I never thought I could actually like meatloaf until I tried this one.

Kristen Warren
Campus Ministry, FL

BEEF

Swedish Meatballs

1½ pounds ground beef
1 egg (or egg substitute)
½ cup dry quick oatmeal
½ cup dried bread crumbs

¼ teaspoon celery salt
salt and pepper
1 medium onion, chopped
¼ teaspoon Lawry's seasoned salt

Mix all ingredients and form into 1½-inch balls. Cook in a frying pan coated with non-stick spray, on a heated grill, or under a broiler. *Tip:* Meatballs can be frozen and cooked when needed. If you are going to freeze the meatballs, sauté the onion in butter. Lay raw meatballs side by side on a pan and freeze, then place in a ziplock bag.

Joan Tungseth
Computer Services, FL

Sweet and Sour Stew

3 tablespoons vegetable oil
2 pounds round steak, cut into
    1-inch cubes
1 15-ounce can tomato sauce
2 teaspoons chili powder
2 teaspoons paprika
¼ cup packed light brown sugar

1 teaspoon salt
½ cup cider vinegar
½ cup light corn syrup
2 cups peeled and sliced carrots
2 cups chopped onions
1 green pepper, cut in 1-inch squares
1 4-ounce can pineapple chunks

Heat oil in a skillet and brown the round steak. Transfer meat to a crockpot or large kettle. Stir in remaining ingredients; cover and simmer for 6 hours or until meat is tender. Serve in individual bowls or hollowed out rounds of bread. Serve with tossed green salad and sourdough bread. Serves 6.

Lisa Master
Worldwide Challenge, FL

My soul will be satisfied as with the richest of foods; with singing lips my mouth will praise you (Psalm 63:5).

Tamale Bake Casserole

¾ pound ground beef
1 small onion, chopped
¾ teaspoon salt
1½ teaspoons chili powder
1 tablespoon Worcestershire sauce
1 tomato, diced

2 tablespoons flour
1 cup diced Monterey Jack cheese
Cornmeal Topping
1 tablespoon grated Parmesan
  cheese
sliced black olives (optional)

Preheat oven to 375 degrees. Sauté beef and onion in a skillet. Stir in salt, chili powder, Worcestershire sauce, tomato, and flour. Turn into a shallow 1½-quart baking dish. Sprinkle with Monterey Jack cheese and cover with *Cornmeal Topping*. Top with Parmesan cheese. Cover and bake for 25 minutes. Uncover and bake 10 minutes longer. Garnish with sliced black olives. Makes 4 servings.

Cornmeal Topping:

1 cup milk
¾ teaspoon salt
¼ teaspoon chili powder
2 tablespoons butter

⅓ cup yellow corn meal
1 egg
1 cup diced Monterey Jack cheese
¼ cup grated Parmesan cheese

Mix all ingredients.

Janice Gregory
ChurchLIFE, FL

Tamale Stew

1½ pounds ground beef
½ medium onion, diced
garlic or garlic salt to taste
1 package taco seasoning
1 16-ounce can tomato sauce
1 4-ounce can Ortega diced chilies

1 4-ounce can sliced black olives
1 16-ounce can whole kernel corn,
  drained
1 large can tamales
grated cheddar cheese

Preheat oven to 350 degrees. Brown ground beef, onion, and garlic; drain. Add dry taco seasoning, tomato sauce, chilies, olives, and corn. Mix well. Slice tamales and add to meat mixture. Pour into a 9×13-inch pan. Cover with grated cheese and bake for 30 minutes or until cheese melts. Serve with tortilla chips. *Tip:* Dish can be prepared in advance and refrigerated until ready to bake. *Variation:* Turkey can be used in place of beef.

Cheryl Henderson
Contributions and Postal Services, FL

BEEF

Tasty Brisket

½ teaspoon onion salt
½ teaspoon garlic powder
5–6 pounds brisket

2 tablespoons liquid smoke
½ cup Worcestershire sauce
½ cup barbecue sauce

Preheat oven to 300 degrees. Mix onion salt and garlic powder, and rub on the brisket. Combine liquid smoke and Worcestershire sauce. Pour over meat. Cover with foil and bake for 4½–5 hours. To make a sauce for serving, mix drippings with barbecue sauce.

Clara Nell Shirey
President's Office, FL

Tasty Taco Pie

1 pound ground beef
2 8-ounce cans tomato sauce
1 package taco seasoning mix
1 8-ounce tube crescent rolls
½ pound cheese, cubed

1 cup shredded lettuce
½ cup chopped tomato
¼ cup sliced olives (optional)
sour cream

Preheat oven to 375 degrees. Brown and drain meat. Stir in tomato sauce and seasoning mix. Simmer 5 minutes. Unroll dough, and press out onto the bottom and sides of an ungreased 12-inch pizza pan or cookie sheet. Prick the bottom and sides with a fork. Bake 10–12 minutes until golden brown. Cover crust with meat mixture and top with cheese. Continue baking until cheese begins to melt. Top with remaining ingredients and serve with sour cream.

Becky Rivera
Student LINC, FL

Tater Tot Casserole

1½ pounds ground beef
salt and pepper to taste
1 medium onion, chopped
1 can of any vegetable
1 32-ounce package tater tots

½ cup water
1 can cream of chicken soup
1 can cheddar cheese or any kind
  of soup

Preheat oven to 350 degrees. Brown ground beef slightly. Put in a 9×13-inch pan; salt and pepper. Layer onion, vegetable, then tater tots. Mix water with soups and pour on top. Bake for 1 hour. *Variation:* French fries can be substituted for tater tots.

Conda DeVries
International Ministry, FL

Texas Chili Con Carne

¼ cup vegetable oil
1 medium red onion, chopped
3 cloves garlic, minced
2½ pounds of beef chuck, cubed
⅓ cup chili powder
1 tablespoon ground cumin
2 teaspoons oregano
1 teaspoon paprika
2 cups canned beef broth or
  2 teaspoons beef bouillon

1 28-ounce can crushed tomatoes
1 teaspoon salt
⅓ cup yellow cornmeal
¼ cup water
2 15-ounce cans pinto beans,
  drained and rinsed
1 cup chopped scallions
  (about 5 medium)
1 cup shredded cheddar cheese

Sauté onion and garlic in oil until softened. Add beef and sauté until lightly cooked. Stir in seasonings. Add beef broth, tomatoes, and salt. Cover and simmer for about 1½ hours. Fifteen minutes before serving, combine cornmeal and water. Bring the chili back to a boil, and stir in the cornmeal mixture and pinto beans. Reduce heat to medium-low, cover and simmer until beans are heated and sauce thickens, about 5 minutes. Serve hot, sprinkled with scallions and cheese.

Cindy Mitchell
International Development, FL

BEEF

Vernasky
(Russian)

cooked potatoes	caraway seeds or dill, *divided*
chopped onion, *divided*	chopped beef (not ground beef)
butter	mushrooms
salt and pepper, *divided*	sour cream or cream of
egg yolk, beaten (optional)	mushroom soup
sauerkraut, drained	Worcestershire sauce (optional)
bacon grease	refrigerated biscuits

Preheat oven to 350 degrees. Prepare three different fillings for biscuits:

1. Mash the potatoes (do not add milk), and flavor with lots of chopped onion sautéed in butter, salt, and pepper. If potatoes are not holding shape, add a beaten egg yolk.

2. Sauté sauerkraut in bacon grease (or salt pork), and season with chopped onion, caraway seeds or dill, salt, and pepper.

3. Brown chopped beef with onion and mushrooms; season with dill and/or caraway seeds. Drain grease. Add sour cream or soup (or both) to desired consistency so filling is moist. Add Worcestershire sauce if desired.

Roll out each biscuit into a circle. Place a small portion of one of the three filling mixtures (potato, sauerkraut, or beef) on each biscuit. Fold in half, then pinch edges to seal. Place biscuits on a cookie sheet and bake until brown. This recipe is similar to the Polish dish Pierrogi.

Tip: If you freeze the Vernasky, they may be reheated by boiling for a few minutes then drizzling with butter (or boil for 1 minute, then sauté in butter and chopped onion). Or, they can be brushed with butter after they are thawed, and baked.

Variation: To make a dessert, use any pie filling, especially cherry.

Sus Schmitt
Computer Services, FL

Why spend money on what is not bread, and your labor on what does not satisfy? Listen, listen to me, and eat what is good, and your soul will delight in the richest of fare (Isaiah 55:2).

Yaksoba
(Japanese)

2 tablespoons oil
½–¾ pound round steak, sliced very thin
2 medium onions, cut into thin wedges
2 medium carrots, sliced very thin
¼ head cabbage, sliced into strips

2 cups fresh or 1 cup canned bean sprouts, drained
salt and pepper
1 cup thin noodles, cooked
soy sauce
rice (optional)

Heat oil in skillet; brown meat. Add vegetables in order, stir-frying each a few minutes, and adding salt and pepper with each addition. Vegetables should be crisp-tender. Add noodles and cook just long enough to heat through. Served with soy sauce, and on rice if desired.

Karen Horsey
International Ministry, FL

Fish & Seafood

Becky's Shrimp Delight

¼ cup chopped onion
1 4-ounce can sliced mushrooms, drained
¼ cup diced green pepper
2 tablespoons butter or margarine
1 10-ounce can frozen condensed cream of shrimp soup

½ cup milk
1 cup diced cooked shrimp (may use canned)
1 tablespoon chopped pimiento
¼ cup shredded cheddar cheese
3 cups cooked rice or 4 slices toast

Sauté onion, mushrooms, and green pepper in butter until tender. Add soup, milk, and shrimp. Heat until soup is thawed, stirring often. Add pimiento and cheese. Serve piping hot over rice or toast. Serves 4.

Becky Rieke
Crusade Family

FISH & SEAFOOD

Crab Patties

1 pound flaked crab or imitation
    crab meat
1 cup dried bread crumbs, *divided*
¼ cup low-fat mayonnaise

¼ cup egg substitute
2 teaspoons Dijon mustard
1 teaspoon thyme
1 tablespoon olive oil

In a large bowl, mix crab and ½ cup of bread crumbs. In a small bowl, combine mayonnaise, egg substitute, mustard, and thyme. Pour over the crab mixture and mix well. Form into 8 patties. Dip patties in remaining bread crumbs to coat well. In a large non-stick frying pan, warm oil over medium heat. Sauté the patties approximately 5 minutes on each side or until golden brown. *Variation:* Substitute salmon, tuna, or any other flaked fish for the crab.

Michelle Treiber
NewLife Publications, FL

Crawfish or Shrimp Etouffée

1 cup olive oil
¾ cup flour
1 large onion, chopped
½ bunch celery, chopped
1 large green pepper, chopped
¼ cup butter, softened
½ cup tomato paste
1 can chicken broth
3 cups water
2 chicken bouillon cubes

2 teaspoons salt
2 teaspoons black pepper
1 teaspoon Tabasco or more
1–2 teaspoons Tony Chachere's
    seasoning
1–2 teaspoons garlic powder
    or more
1–2 pounds raw shrimp or
    crawfish tails
rice

Heat olive oil and flour over medium heat until peanut color. Add onion, celery, and green pepper. Sauté until onion is clear. Mix butter and tomato paste until smooth and thick, and add to the onion mixture. Pour broth, water, and bouillon cubes into mixture. Stir in the remaining seasonings. Simmer at least 1 hour. Add crawfish or shrimp ½–1 hour before serving. Serve over rice with salad and French bread. Serves 4–6.

Jennifer Waddell
Campus Ministry, LA

Fish and Vegetable Bake

2 large potatoes, cubed
1 large carrot, sliced ¼-inch thick
1 medium onion, sliced ¼-inch thick
2 tablespoons butter, melted
1 teaspoon dill weed
1 teaspoon crushed basil
¼ teaspoon salt

¼ teaspoon pepper
1 16-ounce package frozen fish
    fillets, thawed and separated
1 small green or sweet red pepper,
    cut into rings
2 teaspoons lemon juice
1 large tomato, coarsely chopped

Preheat oven to 425 degrees. Place potatoes, carrot, and onion in a baking dish. Combine melted butter, dill weed, basil, salt, and pepper; spoon ½ of the butter mixture over vegetables. Cover and bake for 25 minutes. Place fish fillets, skin-side down, on top of vegetables; add pepper rings. Combine lemon juice and remaining butter mixture; spoon over fish. Cover; bake about 15 minutes or until fish flakes easily with a fork and vegetables are tender. Uncover; add chopped tomato. Bake about 5 minutes more or until tomato is hot. Serves 4.

Gayle Anne VanFulpen
NewLife Publications, FL

Grammy Sylvester's Salmon on Toast

1 14-ounce can red salmon (not pink)
¼ cup margarine
¼ cup flour

4 cups milk
1 cup frozen peas
whole-grain bread or saltines

Discard the dark salmon pieces and bones and set the red salmon aside. Make a medium white sauce by melting margarine over low heat in a large, heavy skillet. Add flour and stir until mixture is smooth and bubbly. Add milk while stirring over low heat. When white sauce is smooth and thickened, add salmon and peas. Allow to bubble just a little while stirring. When peas are hot, pour into a serving dish. Serve over saltines or toasted whole-grain bread.

Bob and Sandra Auer
International Ministry, FL

FISH & SEAFOOD

 "Which of you fathers, if your son asks for a fish, will give him a snake instead?" (Luke 11:11)

Korean Main Dish

A. ½ pound whole shrimp, dash salt, dash sugar, dash vinegar
B. 3 ounces beef, 2 teaspoons soy sauce, 1 teaspoon chopped green onion, ½ teaspoon chopped garlic or garlic powder (optional), 1 teaspoon sesame oil, ½ teaspoon salt, 1 teaspoon sugar
C. 6 dried brown oak mushrooms, 1 teaspoon soy sauce, ½ teaspoon sugar, sesame oil
D. 3 ounces carrot, ½ cucumber, 2 teaspoons salt, 2 teaspoons sesame oil
E. 3 ounces bamboo shoots, 1 teaspoon salt, 1 teaspoon sesame oil
F. 1 egg, dash salt
G. 3 ounces bellflower roots, 1 teaspoon salt, ½ teaspoon sesame oil, ½ teaspoon garlic powder (optional)
H. 1 cup flour, 1 cup water, salt
I. 1 tablespoon finely chopped pine nuts

This is a traditional 9-section dish. Prepare each section as follows, using the ingredients grouped above. As each section of the dish is done cooking, remove from pan; place in separate bowls and keep warm.

1. Remove the entrails from the shrimp. Insert toothpicks into the bodies, and scald them in boiling water; remove the shells. Cut the flesh into thin strips, and mix with the salt, sugar, and vinegar.

2. Cut the beef into thin strips. Season it with the B ingredients and stir-fry.

3. Soak the dried mushrooms in water, squeeze out water, and cut them into thin strips. Stir-fry with the C ingredients.

4. Cut the carrot and cucumber into thin strips, and sprinkle them with salt. Squeeze out the water and stir-fry.

5. Cut the bamboo shoots into thin strips and stir-fry.

6. Fry the beaten egg into a thin sheet and cut it into 2-inch strips.

7. Scald and finely shred the bellflower roots. Mix with the G ingredients and stir-fry.

8. Mix and beat the H ingredients until the batter is smooth. Drop the batter by spoonfuls into a hot, lightly oiled frying pan to make thin pancakes.

9. Layer the pancakes in the center of a 9-section dish, topping each one with a little pine nuts. Arrange the other prepared ingredients in the other sections.

Fill pancakes with the desired fillings and roll up like a burrito. Serve with soy sauce.

Hyang Sook Kim
Finance, FL

Lean and Mean Paella

2 cups defatted, reduced-sodium
   chicken stock
¼ teaspoon saffron, crushed
   or pinched
3 teaspoons olive oil, *divided*
½ pound medium shrimp, peeled
   and cleaned
½ pound boneless, skinless chicken
   breast, trimmed of fat and cut
   into ½-inch-thick strips
salt and ground black pepper to taste
1 onion, chopped

2 cloves garlic, minced
1–2 tablespoons water (optional)
1 14½-ounce can tomatoes
   with juice
⅛ teaspoon red pepper flakes
1 cup medium grain white rice
1 cup frozen artichoke hearts, thawed
1 cup frozen peas, thawed
⅓ cup bottled roasted peppers,
   cut into strips
½ cup (2 ounces) smoked mussels,
   not in oil (optional)

In a small saucepan, combine chicken stock and saffron, and bring to a simmer. Set aside. In a large non-stick skillet, heat 1 teaspoon oil over high heat. Add shrimp and sauté until pink and curled (about 3–4 minutes). Remove from skillet and set aside. Add another teaspoon oil to skillet. Add chicken and sauté until lightly browned on outside and opaque inside (about 3–4 minutes). Remove from skillet. Season shrimp and chicken with salt and pepper, and set aside. Reduce heat to medium and add 1 teaspoon oil to skillet. Stir in onions and garlic; sauté 3–5 minutes. Add 1–2 tablespoons water if they become dry. Stir in tomatoes and red pepper flakes. Simmer 3 minutes, breaking up tomatoes with a spoon. Add rice and stir to coat well. Stir in reserved stock and bring to a simmer. Cover and cook over low heat for 20 minutes. Gently stir artichokes, peas, peppers, mussels, and the reserved shrimp and chicken into the rice mixture. Cover and cook, stirring occasionally until rice is tender (about 5–10 minutes). Season with pepper and serve immediately. Serves 4. This dish is wonderful with *Green Salad Vinaigrette.*

Barbara Ball
ChurchLIFE, FL

FISH & SEAFOOD

Light Fish or Chicken Mexican Style

1 medium onion, sliced or chopped
1 clove garlic, minced
1–2 fresh or canned jalapeño
 peppers, chopped
3 medium tomatoes, peeled, seeded,
 and chopped, or 1 14½-ounce
 can low-sodium tomatoes
½ teaspoon sugar

1 bay leaf
dash cinnamon
⅔ cup long-grain rice
1 pound fresh or frozen skinless cod,
 red snapper, or orange roughy
 (3–5 pieces) or 3–5 skinless
 chicken breasts
1 cup water

Spray a medium saucepan with non-stick coating. For sauce, cook and stir onion and garlic until onion is tender, but not brown. Stir in jalapeño peppers, fresh or undrained tomatoes, sugar, bay leaf, and cinnamon. Bring to a boil; reduce heat and simmer uncovered 8–10 minutes or until slightly thickened. Remove and discard bay leaf. Cook rice according to package directions, but omit margarine or butter and salt. Keep warm.

For fish: Cut fish into equal portions; rinse and pat dry. In a large skillet, bring water to a boil and add fish. Return to a boil; cover and simmer just until fish begins to flake easily (allow 4–6 minutes per ½-inch thickness).

For chicken: Steam for about 20 minutes, or cook in a skillet with non-stick coating until cooked through (white in middle), about 10–15 minutes.

To serve, place rice on plates. Top with fish or chicken, then sauce. Serve immediately.

Stephanie Farris
Campus Ministry, KY

> *"Come, follow me," Jesus said, "and I will make you fishers of men" (Matt. 4:19).*

Okonomiyaki
(Japanese Pizza)

½ pound shrimp and/or sausage,
 sliced
½ cup milk
3 eggs
1 cup flour

1½ cups sliced red or green cabbage
spicy sauce (optional; available in
 Asian market)
ketchup (optional)
mayonnaise (optional)

Brown shrimp or sausage. Combine milk, eggs, and flour; beat well. Add cabbage. Pour mixture over shrimp or sausage, and form patties. Cover and cook over low heat until brown. Turn and brown second side. Serve with spicy sauce, ketchup, or mayonnaise.

Melissa Crabtree
Corporate Human Resources, FL

Salmon in a Blanket

prepared biscuit dough
2 cups flaked pink salmon
   (1-pound can) or other fish
¼ cup mayonnaise
1 tablespoon lemon juice

1 tablespoon minced onion
¾ teaspoon salt
dash of pepper
2 tablespoons finely chopped parsley
   or 1 tablespoon dried flakes

Preheat oven to 425 degrees. Roll dough into a 7×15-inch rectangle and transfer to a lightly greased baking sheet. Mix remaining ingredients and spread on dough to within 2 inches of ends. Fold edges lengthwise over salmon mixture to overlap. Turn over so seam is underneath, and tuck ends under. Make slashes along the top for steam to escape. Bake for 12–15 minutes. Serves 6.

Billie Thurman
Crusade Family

Seven Seas Casserole

1 cup cream of celery soup
1⅓ cups water
¼ teaspoon salt
¼ teaspoon pepper
¼ cup finely chopped onion

1½ cups uncooked rice
1½ cups cooked peas
1 can tuna, drained
½ cup grated cheddar cheese
pimiento strips

Preheat oven to 375 degrees. Combine soup, water, salt, pepper, and onion. Boil and stir. Pour ½ of mixture into a greased 1½-quart dish. Layer the rice, peas, and tuna, then cover with remaining soup mixture. Sprinkle with cheese. Cover and bake for 20–25 minutes. Let stand 10 minutes before cutting; garnish with pimientos.

Sherry Cumpstone
Worldwide Challenge, FL

FISH & SEAFOOD

Shrimp Creola

1 large onion, chopped
2 tablespoons salad oil
1 clove garlic, minced
4 stalks celery, chopped
1 green bell pepper, chopped
3 bay leaves
1 15¼-ounce can tomatoes

1 large can tomato sauce
¾ tablespoon chili powder
dash of hot sauce
2 tablespoons lemon juice
1½ pounds uncooked peeled shrimp
rice

Sauté onions in oil. Then add garlic, celery, and pepper, and lightly sauté. Add remaining ingredients except shrimp and rice, and simmer for 1 hour. Add shrimp and cook slowly until shrimp is very pink, approximately 12 minutes. Serve over rice. Makes 6 servings.

Betty Madison
ChurchLIFE, AL

Shrimp Newburg

6 tablespoons butter
2 tablespoons flour
1½ cups light cream
3 egg yolks, beaten
2 cups cooked shrimp
2 teaspoons lemon juice

3 tablespoons water or
   chicken broth
¼ teaspoon salt
paprika to taste
toast points

Blend butter and flour in a pan; add cream all at once. Heat over low heat and stir until thickened. Stir a small amount of hot mixture into yolks, and return to the pan. Cook, stirring until thick. Add shrimp, then add lemon juice, water or broth, salt, and paprika. Serve with toast points.

Liesl Buck
International Ministry, FL

Teriyaki Tuna With Fresh Pineapple

¼ cup low-sodium soy sauce
3 tablespoons honey
3 tablespoons sweet rice vinegar
2 teaspoons minced ginger root

½ teaspoon hot sauce
1 clove garlic, minced
1 small pineapple, pared and cored
6 4-ounce tuna steaks (¾-inch thick)

Combine the first 6 ingredients in a large baking dish. Cut pineapple lengthwise into 6 spears. Add pineapple and tuna to marinade, turning to coat. Cover and marinate in refrigerator 30 minutes, turning every 10 minutes. Remove tuna and pineapple from marinade, reserving marinade. Coat grill rack with cooking spray, and place tuna and pineapple on grill rack over medium-hot coals (350–400 degrees). Cook 4 minutes on each side for medium or longer for well-done. Baste occasionally with marinade. Makes 6 servings: 249 calories (22% from fat); 6.2 mg fat; 371 mg sodium.

Clara Thompson
JESUS Film Project, TX

Tuna Broccoli Casserole

5 tablespoons butter, *divided*
2 tablespoons flour
1 cup milk
2 teaspoons lemon juice
1 tablespoon prepared mustard
salt and pepper to taste

2 10-ounce packages frozen
  chopped broccoli
1 cup shredded cheddar cheese
1 medium can tuna
1 cup fresh bread crumbs

Preheat oven to 350 degrees. To make a mustard white sauce, melt 2 tablespoons butter in a small saucepan. Add flour and stir until it makes a smooth paste. Add milk and stir over medium heat until it begins to thicken. Once thickened, add lemon juice, mustard, and seasonings. Cook broccoli according to package directions, then drain. In a 2-quart casserole, layer ½ of the broccoli, mustard sauce, cheddar cheese, tuna, and remaining broccoli. Top with bread crumbs mixed with 3 tablespoons melted butter. Bake for 30 minutes.

Shawnlei Breeding
Corporate Human Resources, FL

FISH & SEAFOOD

Tuna Puff

1 large can flaked tuna in water
1½ teaspoons mustard
¼ teaspoon Worcestershire sauce
¾ cup mayonnaise, *divided*
1½ teaspoons grated onion

2 tablespoons chopped green pepper
English muffins
sliced tomato
¼ cup shredded yellow cheese

Blend tuna, mustard, Worcestershire sauce, ¼ cup mayonnaise, onion, and green pepper. Spread on English muffins. Top each with a tomato slice. Blend remaining mayonnaise and cheese; spread on top of tomato. Broil until cheese melts.

Linda Crone
Josh McDowell Ministry, CA

Tuna Rolls

baking powder biscuits
1 can tuna
½ cup chopped celery

1 egg, beaten
1 can cream of mushroom soup
milk

Preheat oven to 400 degrees. Prepare baking powder biscuits using your favorite recipe. Roll out onto a floured surface; cut into approximately 4-inch squares. Mix tuna, celery, and egg. Place filling on squares and roll up. Bake for 10–15 minutes. Thin one can cream of mushroom soup with milk and heat; pour over the baked rolls.

Karen Kuhne
Crusade Family

Ugandan Fish Dish

sliced raw white potatoes
sliced raw sweet potatoes
sliced onion
fish fillets (cod works well)

sliced ripe tomatoes
3 bay leaves
salt
1 cup vegetable oil

Layer ingredients in order in a large pot; pour vegetable oil over. Cook over low heat for 1 hour. Becomes stew-like with a delicious sauce. In Africa, we used talapia fish and African sweet potatoes.

Nan Green
International Ministry, FL

Lamb

Curried Lamb

1 pound ground lamb	1–1½ teaspoons curry powder
1 large onion, chopped	¾ teaspoon salt
1 clove garlic, minced	½ teaspoon ground ginger
2 tablespoons butter or margarine	1 tablespoon flour
2 tomatoes, peeled and chopped	½ cup water
¼ cold cup water	3 cups cooked rice

In a skillet, cook lamb, onion, and garlic in butter until onion is tender and meat is browned. Drain off excess fat. Add tomatoes, water, curry powder, salt, and ginger. Cover and simmer 30 minutes, stirring occasionally. Blend flour and water; add to meat mixture. Cook and stir until bubbly. Place over hot rice and serve with condiments of sliced green onion, shredded coconut, raisins, and peanuts. Serves 6.

Laurie Killingsworth
New Life Center, FL

Garlic and Rosemary Leg of Lamb

leg of lamb	flour
garlic cloves	dried rosemary
salt and pepper	water

Ask your butcher to bone and tie leg. Preheat oven to 350 degrees. Push garlic cloves into inside of lamb. Rub salt, pepper, and flour all over the lamb. Place into a pan and sprinkle with dried rosemary. Cook for 30 minutes per pound of meat. Add water to pan as needed. Remove cooked lamb and make gravy with drippings.

Mary Jane Morgan
Crusade Family

LAMB

"Worthy is the Lamb, who was slain, to receive power and wealth and wisdom and strength and honor and glory and praise!"
(Rev. 5:12)

Lamb Indienne

1½ pounds lamb, cut into
    1½-inch cubes
2 tablespoons shortening
1 can cream of chicken soup
½ cup water
1 Vidalia onion, chopped
1 large clove garlic, minced
1 tablespoon curry powder

pinch ground cardamon
pinch ground coriander
1 large apple, diced
3 cups cooked wild rice
chopped chutney
toasted coconut
raisins

In a large heavy pan, brown lamb cubes in shortening; pour off fat. Add soup, water, onion, garlic, and seasonings. Cover; cook over low heat for 1½ hours or until tender, stirring occasionally. Add apple the last 5 minutes. Serve with rice, and garnish with chutney, coconut, and raisins. Serves 4.

Laurie Killingsworth
New Life Center, FL

Lamb With Couscous and Minted Fruit Chutney

1 tablespoon olive oil
4 cloves garlic, minced
1 teaspoon packed, chopped fresh
    rosemary or ½ teaspoon dried
4 lamb loin chops (1¼-inch thick),
    trimmed
1¾ cups water

¼ cup dried tart cherries
¼ cup diced dried apricots
¼ cup dried cranberries
¼ cup chopped fresh mint
1 teaspoon balsamic vinegar
salt and pepper to taste
1 10-ounce box couscous

Mix oil, garlic, and rosemary in an 8-inch square glass baking dish. Add lamb and turn to coat. Cover and refrigerate 2–4 hours, turning occasionally. Mix water and dried fruit in a heavy medium saucepan. Bring to a boil; reduce heat and simmer until water is absorbed and fruits are tender (about 20 minutes), stirring occasionally. Remove from heat, and stir in mint and vinegar; season with salt and pepper. Cool chutney slightly. Prepare couscous according to package directions. Preheat broiler. Season lamb with salt and pepper, and broil to desired doneness (about 6 minutes per side for medium-rare). Top with chutney and serve with couscous. Makes 4 servings: 535 calories; 12 g fat; 3 g saturated fat; 81 mg cholesterol.

Barbara Ball
ChurchLIFE, FL

Rosemary Leg of Lamb

1 cup red grape juice
1 cup soy sauce
½ cup olive oil
5 cloves garlic, crushed
2 teaspoons ground pepper

2 tablespoons fresh rosemary or
  1 tablespoon dried rosemary
rice (optional)
leg of lamb

Thoroughly mix juice, soy sauce, oil, garlic, pepper, and rosemary; pour over lamb. Let meat marinate for 6 hours, then remove lamb and reserve marinade. For best results, roast lamb on an outdoor grill, roasting approximately 20 minutes on each side. Baste lamb with marinade while cooking to reduce dryness. Bring remaining marinade to a boil (heating eliminates any bacteria that might have been present on the raw meat while soaking). Serve the lamb on a bed of rice, with the marinade as a sauce for individual servings. *Tip:* When buying the leg of lamb, ask the butcher to "butterfly" it, removing the bone and excess fat. USA domestic lamb is recommended, since these are usually larger and milder than the leaner, more gamy-tasting imports.

Lori Burns
Staff & Ministry Opportunities, FL

> "Look, the Lamb of God, who takes away
> the sin of the world!" (John 1:29)

Sesame Lamb Meatballs

⅓ cup minced onion
1 large clove garlic, minced
1½ teaspoons olive oil
½ teaspoon dried mint, crumbled
½ teaspoon salt
¼ teaspoon ground allspice
pinch of cinnamon
1 pound ground lamb (10% fat)

1 cup fine fresh bread crumbs
1 large egg, slightly beaten
2 tablespoons dried currants
¼ cup black sesame seeds
¼ cup white sesame seeds, toasted
  lightly
Minted Yogurt Dip

LAMB

Preheat oven to 450 degrees. In a small non-stick skillet, cook onion and garlic in oil over moderately low heat, stirring until softened. Place mixture in a bowl and stir in mint, salt, allspice, and cinnamon. Add lamb, bread crumbs, egg, and currants; combine well. Form 1¼-inch meatballs and set them on a tray. Put black sesame seeds in a small bowl. Roll ½ of the meatballs in seeds, then place them on a rack set in a shallow baking pan. Put white sesame seeds into a separate bowl, and coat remaining meatballs with white sesame seeds in the same manner. Meatballs may be prepared a day ahead, covered loosely, and refrigerated. Bake meatballs in the upper third of the oven for 8–10 minutes or until golden and just cooked through. Serve meatballs with *Minted Yogurt Dip*. Makes about 32 meatballs. *Tip:* Black sesame seeds are available as Asian markets and some specialty food shops.

Minted Yogurt Dip:

¼ cup packed chopped fresh mint leaves	2 cups plain yogurt
	½ teaspoon salt

To make yogurt cheese, place yogurt in a fine sieve, and set over a bowl to drain. Cover and chill for 3 hours. Then discard whey and transfer yogurt into a bowl. Yogurt cheese may be made 2 days ahead, covered, and refrigerated. Stir mint and salt into yogurt cheese. Makes about 1½ cups.

Barbara Ball
ChurchLIFE, FL

Pork

Barbecued Frankfurters

1 onion, chopped	¼ cup vinegar
3 tablespoons cooking oil	½ cup water
1½ teaspoons sugar	1 tablespoon Worcestershire sauce
1 teaspoon dry mustard	1 tablespoon chili powder (optional)
dash salt	1 dash Tabasco (optional)
dash pepper	1 pound frankfurters, nearly split
1 teaspoon paprika	through lengthwise
½ cup ketchup	1 package frankfurter buns

Preheat oven to 450 degrees. Brown onion in oil. In a bowl, mix remaining ingredients except frankfurters. and buns; add onion. Place frankfurters in a baking pan and cover with sauce. Bake for 20 minutes, turning franks once while baking. Serve on frankfurter buns.

Dorothy Brooks
Here's Life America, MA

Caribbean Pork Roast

3–4 large cloves garlic, peeled
6 peppercorns or ⅓ teaspoon
   black pepper
2–3 teaspoons oregano
¼ cup olive oil

½ teaspoon salt for each pound
   of meat (optional)
2 teaspoons vinegar
6–7 pounds leg of pork or pork loin

Several days before roasting, mix the garlic, peppercorns, oregano, olive oil, salt, and vinegar. Blend well with a pestle and refrigerate. To prepare meat, place fat-side up in a roasting pan. With a sharp knife, make deep stabs 3–4 inches in length about 2–3 inches apart over the entire roast. Stuff each incision with the seasoning mixture. Cover and refrigerate until ready to bake. (Roast can be frozen after it has been seasoned.) Remove meat from refrigerator at least 30 minutes before cooking. Drain liquid that may have seeped from meat and pour over meat. Bake at 450 degrees for the first 30 minutes, then bake at 325 degrees for 1 hour. Served with rice and a salad, this makes a great dish for company.

Barbara Ball
ChurchLIFE, FL

Chop Suey

2 cups carrots
2 cups cabbage
2 cups string beans
1 cup onions, chopped
1 package or can bean sprouts
1 pound pork or beef
2 tablespoons salad oil

1 piece ginger root, minced, or
   1 teaspoon ground ginger
6 tablespoons soy sauce
2 tablespoons sugar
3 tablespoons flour
⅔ cup water
1 teaspoon salt

Cut vegetables in strips lengthwise. Slice beef or pork across the grain. Heat a frying pan or pot, and add oil. Brown ginger in oil and add meat. Cook for 2–3 minutes. Add vegetables and cook for 5 minutes. Prepare gravy by mixing remaining ingredients; add to vegetables and meat. Cook for 5 minutes. Serve hot. *Optional:* To make *Chow Fun*, add boiled noodles.

Eloise Knippers
Crusade Family

PORK

Crown Roast of Pork
With Savory Stuffing

1 16-rib crown roast of pork   salt and pepper to taste
    (7–8 pounds)   *Savory Stuffing*
1 tablespoon salad oil

Preheat oven to 475 degrees. Brush roast with oil, sprinkle with salt and pepper. Wrap bones with foil to prevent burning. Insert meat thermometer into center of loin, being careful not to touch the bone. Place in a shallow roasting pan. Roast 45 minutes, then reduce temperature to 325 degrees and roast 1½ hours longer. Remove roast from oven. Fill the center with *Crown Roast Stuffing*, mounding it lightly. (Wrap extra stuffing in heavy foil or place in a baking dish, and bake with roast.) Roast for 50 minutes to 1 hour, or until thermometer reaches 170 degrees. Transfer roast to serving platter and serve with stuffing. Makes 12–16 servings. *Optional:* Decorate the bones with colored covers from the meat market.

Savory Stuffing:

1 pound sweet Italian sausage   2 cloves garlic, minced
½ cup water   7 medium potatoes (about
2 tablespoons salad oil   2 pounds), peeled and diced
4 cups finely chopped onion   1¼ tablespoons salt, *divided*
2 cups finely chopped carrots   ⅓ cup parsley, chopped
2 cups finely chopped celery   1 tablespoon fennel seed

Cut sausage in half and remove casing. In a heavy skillet over medium heat, cook sausage with water, breaking it up with a wooden spoon. Cook until water has evaporated and sausage is browned. Remove with a slotted spoon, drain on paper towels, and chop into fine pieces. Add oil to drippings in skillet. Sauté onions, carrots, celery, and garlic over medium heat until carrots are tender (about 15–20 minutes). Place potatoes in a medium saucepan and add ½ teaspoon salt and enough water to cover. Boil over high heat until tender (20 minutes); drain. In a large bowl, combine sausage, sautéed vegetables, potatoes, parsley, fennel, remaining salt, and pepper. Mix. Makes 9 ½-cup servings: 180 calories per serving.

This recipe has become our new Christmas favorite since we "moved" our family Christmas from our house to our daughter, Robbyn's, cabin in Truckee, California.

Barbara Ball
ChurchLIFE, FL

Dinner Crepes
(Brittany, France)

½ cup wheat flour
1 cup all-purpose flour
½ teaspoon salt
1 cup water
4 large eggs

1 cup apple cider
1 cup milk
⅓ cup unsalted butter, melted
Gruyère cheese, thinly sliced
ham, thinly sliced

In a blender or food processor, quickly combine flours and salt. Add water, eggs, cider, milk, and melted butter. Blend until smooth. Cover and let mixture stand for 1 hour. Blend briefly before using. Spray a 12-inch non-stick frying pan with vegetable spray, and heat over moderately high heat. Pour in ⅓ cup batter (for a 10-inch pan, use ¼ cup batter). Quickly swirl pan to spread batter thinly over entire bottom surface and halfway up sides of pan. Cook until browned around edges and set in the middle. Top uncooked side with a thin slice of ham and cheese. Fold crepe in half and remove from pan. Serve on warm plates and eat immediately. Makes 15 12-inch crepes.
Tip: Batter may be made a day ahead and refrigerated. Crepes are best suited to informal kitchen dinners.

Nancy Austin
JESUS Video Master Studio, FL

The Lord delights in those who fear him, who put their hope in his unfailing love (Psalm 147:11).

Donna's Ham Delights

¼ cup diced onions
¼ cup butter
¼ cup flour
2 cups milk

1½ pounds canned ham, thinly sliced
12 ounces sliced Swiss cheese
1 or more boxes frozen chopped
   broccoli, cooked

Preheat oven to 350 degrees. Sauté onions in butter until tender. Stir in flour to make a paste. Add milk; heat sauce while stirring until thick and creamy. In a shallow pan, alternate layers of ham, cheese, and broccoli. Cover with sauce. Bake for 45 minutes. Serves 6–7. *Variation:* Instead of milk and flour, use 1 package instant chicken gravy, prepared according to package directions.

Kathie Brooks
Campus Ministry, MO

PORK

Indonesian Pork Roast

5–6 pounds fresh pork
   shoulder butt
1 clove garlic, minced
1 chicken bouillon cube
¼ cup sugar

1 cup water
½ cup soy sauce
plain or curried rice
applesauce or chutney

Brown pork in its own fat in a Dutch oven or heavy kettle. Combine remaining ingredients; pour over meat and cover. Simmer, turning 2–3 times, for 2–2½ hours or until tender. Place meat on a heated platter; slice and serve with rice and applesauce or chutney. Serves 8. *Tip:* To use leftover meat, arrange slices on broiler rack and brush with liquid saved from roast. Broil about 4 inches from heat, basting often with liquid, 5 minutes on each side or until brown and crisp. Arrange slices in a ring on top of *Chinese Vegetable Bowl* and serve with hot, buttered rice.

Dorothy Brooks
Here's Life America, MA

Maple-Glazed Ham

3–4 pounds fully cooked ham
1 cup maple syrup
1 tablespoon prepared mustard
1 tablespoon Worcestershire sauce

3 tablespoons undiluted orange
   juice concentrate
dash of ground cloves
orange slices (optional)

Preheat oven to 325 degrees. Place ham in a shallow roasting pan and bake 14–16 minutes per pound. While cooking, make a glaze by combining the remaining ingredients except orange slices and boiling for 5 minutes or until the liquid is thickened. During the last 30 minutes of baking, use a pastry brush to brush ham often with glaze. To serve, spoon the glaze from the bottom of the pan over the ham, and decorate with orange slices.

Joette Whims
NewLife Publications, CA

 He who eats meat, eats to the Lord, for
he gives thanks to God (Rom. 14:6).

Marinated Pork Tenderloin

1 cup mayonnaise
½ cup sour cream
⅓ teaspoon salt
½ teaspoon garlic powder
1 tablespoon Dijon mustard
½ teaspoon Worcestershire sauce
2 cups oil

⅓ cup soy sauce
½ cup honey
1 teaspoon onion powder
1 teaspoon garlic powder
salt and pepper
pork tenderloins or pork steaks

Make a dipping sauce by mixing the first 6 ingredients; chill. Bring to room temperature before serving. To make marinade, mix oil, soy sauce, honey, onion powder, and garlic powder. Pour over pork and marinate at least 6 hours. Remove pork and season with salt and pepper. Broil for about 15 minutes, turning over halfway through cooking time. Serve with dipping sauce. *Variation:* For a lower-fat version, substitute chicken broth for at least ½ of the oil, and use fat-free mayonnaise and sour cream.

Cathy Hertzler
Computer Services, FL

Let your light shine before men, that they may see your good deeds and praise your Father in heaven (Matt. 5:16).

Peachy Pork Surprise

1 pound boneless pork, cut
    into ¾-inch cubes
2 tablespoons taco seasoning mix

2 teaspoons vegetable oil
1 8-ounce bottle chunky-style salsa
½ cup peach preserves

Coat pork cubes with taco seasoning. Heat oil in a large non-stick skillet over medium heat; add pork and brown, stirring occasionally. Add salsa and preserves to pan and lower heat. Cover and simmer for 15–20 minutes. Serves 4. Serve with rice and three-bean salad.

Mary Canada
President's Office, FL

PORK

Pork Chop Supper

4 pork chops	6–8 small potatoes or 3 medium,
1 can tomato soup or juice	quartered
½ cup water	4 small carrots, split lengthwise and
1 teaspoon Worcestershire sauce	cut into 2-inch pieces
½ teaspoon salt	chopped green pepper (optional)
½ teaspoon caraway seeds or oregano	quartered onions (optional)

Brown chops in a skillet or Dutch oven. Pour off fat and add remaining ingredients. Add green pepper or onion quarters if desired. Cover and simmer 45 minutes or until tender.

Dorothy Brooks
Here's Life America, MA

Pork Chops and Rice Supper

water for rice	oil
2–3 beef bouillon cubes	1–2 stalks celery, chopped
3–4 dashes soy sauce	4–5 green onions, chopped
1 small box Minute Rice	1 small package fresh mushrooms,
3–5 pork chops, diced small	sliced

Boil water for rice. Add bouillon cubes and soy sauce. Add rice; cover and let stand. While rice is sitting, fry pork in a small amount of oil. When meat is done, add celery, onions, and mushrooms. Simmer for 10 minutes. Add rice and simmer until all the flavors are mixed well and vegetables are done.

Cindy Bogan
JESUS Film Project, FL

Pork Chops or Chicken With Rice

1⅓ cups water	butter
1 cup uncooked rice	salt and pepper
5–6 pork chops or chicken pieces	1 can chicken with rice soup

Preheat oven to 350 degrees. Place water and rice in a casserole dish. Brown chops in butter and season with salt and pepper. Arrange in casserole over rice, then pour soup over all. Cover and bake for 45 minutes. Remove cover and cook a few minutes longer. Serve with black-eyed peas.

Janice Gregory
ChurchLIFE, FL

Quick and Easy Pizza

1 package dry yeast
1 cup plus 2 tablespoons warm water
3 cups flour
1 teaspoon salt
2 tablespoons cornmeal
   (not self-rising)
1½ teaspoons oil

1 8-ounce can tomato juice
dash of garlic powder
¼ teaspoon oregano (or ½ teaspoon store-bought pizza seasoning)
1¼ pound grated mozzarella cheese
sausage, pepperoni, or other toppings

Preheat oven to 475 degrees. Add yeast to warm water. Let stand a few minutes to soften, then stir until completely dissolved. In a separate bowl, mix flour, salt, and cornmeal. Add about ½ of the flour mixture to the yeast mixture; beat until smooth. Add oil and mix well, then add remaining flour mixture. Mix thoroughly with a spoon until the dough begins to clean the sides of the bowl, then beat hard. Grease two pizza pans lightly with oil. Divide the dough in ½ and place on each pan. Cover the dough with bowls and let it rest for 5 minutes. Rub oil on your hands to handle the dough with ease, then gently pat and spread dough with your hands until it covers the pizza pan. Build up the edges to hold the filling. Bake the dough for 3 minutes or less. To make sauce, stir tomato juice in can until blended; add seasonings to taste. Spread sauce over the partially cooked dough until it covers the crust. Place ½ of the mozzarella cheese on each pizza. Add desired meat or other toppings. If using sausage or pepperoni, cook meat and blot the grease between paper towels before putting meat on pizzas. Bake on the lowest rack of the oven for 15 minutes or until crust is nicely browned. Yields 2 12-inch round crusts.

Carolyn Justice
Single Life Resources, NC

PORK

Roberta's Fantastic Fajitas

1 pound lean boneless pork or
    boneless chicken breasts
2 cloves garlic, minced
1 teaspoon dried oregano
½ teaspoon cumin
1 teaspoon seasoned salt
2 tablespoons orange juice
2 tablespoons vinegar
dash of Tabasco

1 tablespoon oil
1 onion, sliced
1 jalapeño pepper, seeded and sliced
6–8 flour tortillas
sliced green onions
sour cream
shredded lettuce
bottled salsa

Slice meat into ⅛-inch strips. Marinate in a mixture of garlic, oregano, cumin, salt, orange juice, vinegar, and Tabasco for 10 minutes. Heat skillet over medium-high heat (400 degrees for an electric skillet). Add oil, onion, pepper, and meat. Stir fry until meat is no longer pink. Serve with flour tortillas and accompany with green onions, sour cream, lettuce, and salsa. Serves 4.

Jennifer Segalini
Corporate Human Resources, FL

Rob Isham's Famous Pizza

6 cups flour, *divided*
1 tablespoon salt
2 tablespoons yeast
2 cups lukewarm water
1 medium onion, diced
1 green bell pepper, diced
1 carton mushrooms, diced

olive oil
basil (fresh is best)
1 8-ounce jar spaghetti sauce
3 cups shredded mozzarella
    cheese, *divided*
1 package sliced pepperoni or
    other cooked meat

Begin preparing dough in the morning for an evening meal since it takes 4 hours to rise. Evenly mix 4 cups flour, salt, yeast, and water. Spread out 1 cup flour on the counter, then flour your hands and knead dough until even. (Pull all the dough's edges into the center and press down, kneading until the flour and water are evenly distributed and the dough is no longer sticky.) Place the dough in a bowl; let rise to twice its size. Punch the dough so that all the air is released; let rise again to twice the size.

While the dough is rising, place vegetables in a bowl with some olive oil and basil, and set aside. Put 2–3 tablespoons olive oil on a cookie sheet and spread evenly. Next, spread out 1 cup flour on the counter and roll out the dough to the approximate shape of the cookie sheet. Place dough on the cookie sheet. Cover with spaghetti sauce to within 1 inch of the edges. Spread on 1 cup mozzarella cheese, then add pepperoni. (Whatever topping you use, always add the meat immediately after the cheese.) Then add the vegetable mixture and top with remaining cheese. Bake at 425 degrees for 25 minutes. Check after 15 minutes; pizza is done when the cheese is slightly golden brown.

Rob Isham
International Ministry, FL

Stuffed Chops and Yams

1 large apple, diced
⅓ cup chopped celery
¼ cup raisins
½ teaspoon paprika, *divided*
2 tablespoons butter
4 thick pork chops (about
    1½ pounds)

1 can cream of mushroom soup
½ cup sour cream
¼ cup water
1 16-ounce can sweet potatoes,
    drained

In a saucepan, cook the apple, celery, raisins, and ¼ teaspoon paprika in butter until celery is tender. Trim excess fat from chops. Slit each chop horizontally from the outer edge toward the bone, making a pocket; stuff with apple mixture. Fasten with skewers or toothpicks. In a skillet, brown chops and pour off fat. Stir in soup, sour cream, water, and remaining paprika. Cover and cook over low heat approximately 5 hours or under tender. Add sweet potatoes and heat 10 more minutes. Serves 4.

Laurie Killingsworth
New Life Center, FL

PORK

Kitchen Prayer

Bless my little kitchen, Lord
And the food Thou dost afford;
May joy and happiness abound;
As in Thy service we are found.

Swedish Ham and Cheese Casserole

1 cup rice
2 cups water
¼ cup flour
½ teaspoon seasoned salt
¼ teaspoon black pepper
⅛ teaspoon nutmeg
1 12-ounce can evaporated milk
    (not condensed)

½ cup chili sauce
½ cup mayonnaise
5–6 green onions including tops,
    chopped
1–2 cups chopped cooked ham or
    2 5-ounce cans chunk ham,
    drained and flaked
2 cups shredded cheddar cheese

Preheat oven to 350 degrees. Cook rice in water according to package directions. Whisk together flour and seasonings in a saucepan. Slowly whisk in evaporated milk until smooth. Bring to a boil, stirring continuously. Boil over medium heat 3–4 minutes until thick and bubbly. Remove from heat; whisk in chili sauce, then mayonnaise. Stir in green onions and set aside. Spray a 2-quart casserole dish with non-stick spray. Press cooked rice into the bottom of the dish, then add ham. Pour sauce mixture over ham layer, and smooth the surface. Cover with cheese and bake 30 minutes. Let stand 10 minutes before serving. Makes 6 servings. This recipe is from my sister, Kari Apted, and it really is Swedish.

Cherie Allen
CoMission, FL

*Whatever you do, work at it with all your heart, as working
for the Lord, not for men (Col. 3:23).*

Sweet and Sour Pork

¾ pound boneless pork, cut into
    1-inch cubes
1 tablespoon cooking oil
1 large green pepper, seeded and
    chopped into ¾-inch pieces
2 medium carrots, sliced diagonally
1 clove garlic, minced
1¼ cups water

¼ cup sugar
¼ cup red wine vinegar
1 tablespoon soy sauce
1¼ teaspoons instant chicken
    bouillon
¼ cup cold water
2 tablespoons cornstarch
rice

In a skillet over high heat, cook pork in oil for 4 minutes. Remove pork and drain on paper towels. Add green pepper, carrots, and garlic to skillet; cook for 4 minutes. Drain any fat from the skillet. Stir in 1¼ cups water, sugar, red wine vinegar, soy sauce, and bouillon, along with pork. Bring to a boil for 1 minute. Blend ¼ cup cold water with cornstarch and add to skillet. Cook and stir until thick. Serve over rice.

Shawnlei Breeding
Corporate Human Resources, FL

Swiss Ham Ring

¼ cup chopped parsley or
   2 tablespoons parsley flakes
2 tablespoons finely chopped onion
2 tablespoons prepared mustard
1 tablespoon margarine or butter,
   softened
1 teaspoon lemon juice

¾ cup (3 ounces) shredded Swiss
   cheese
1 cup fresh or frozen chopped
   broccoli, cooked
1 can chunk ham, drained and flaked
1 can refrigerated crescent rolls
grated Parmesan cheese

Preheat oven to 350 degrees. In a large mixing bowl, combine parsley, onion, mustard, margarine, and lemon juice; blend well. Add cheese, broccoli, and ham. Mix lightly and set aside. Separate crescent dough into 8 triangles. On a greased cookie sheet, arrange triangles in a circle, with points toward the outside and bases overlapping. The center opening should be about 3 inches in diameter. Spoon ham filling evenly in a ring over bases of triangles. Fold points of triangles over filling and tuck under bases of triangles at center of circle. Sprinkle with Parmesan cheese. Bake for 25–30 minutes or until golden brown. Serve hot. Makes 6 servings. *Tip:* Dish can be made ahead, covered and refrigerated for up to 3 hours, then baked for 30–35 minutes.

Crystal Keller
Computer Services, FL

PORK

Poultry

Apricot Chicken

1 whole chicken, cut and cleaned,
    or 6 boneless chicken breasts
1 jar apricot preserves
1 bottle Catalina salad dressing
1 packet Lipton onion soup mix
white rice

Preheat oven to 350 degrees. Place chicken in a 9×13-inch baking dish. Combine apricot preserves, Catalina dressing, and dry onion soup mix. Pour mixture over chicken. Cover and bake for 1 hour. Uncover and bake 30 more minutes or until bubbly. Serve with rice. *Variations:* Ginni Christopher (Executive Ministry, FL) substitutes peach jelly for the apricot preserves. Juli Emory (Military Ministry, VA) substitutes 1 can whole berry cranberry sauce for the preserves.

Lisa Randle
Campus Ministry, KY

Bacon Chicken Dish

1½ pounds bacon
12 boneless, skinless chicken
    breasts, flattened
lemon pepper
salt
thyme
4 ounces pimientos
4 ounces mushrooms, sliced and
    broiled
4 ounces pitted ripe olives, sliced
4 ounces stuffed green olives, sliced
chopped fresh celery leaves
Cheese Sauce or *Simple Hollandaise
    Sauce*

Preheat oven to 375 degrees. Lay half the bacon strips diagonally on a flat surface with sides overlapping ¼ inch. Place 3 pieces of chicken end-to-end across bacon strips. Sprinkle chicken with lemon pepper, salt, and thyme. Combine the vegetables and put half on top of chicken. Place 3 more chicken pieces on top of vegetable mixture. Fold bacon slices over the top of chicken to prevent vegetables from falling out; secure with toothpicks. Repeat with the other 6 chicken breasts. Bake loaves in a 10×12-inch pan for 45 minutes. Cut each loaf into 6 serving pieces. Remove toothpicks and cover with *Cheese Sauce* or *Simple Hollandaise Sauce*.

Cheese Sauce:

6 tablespoons margarine	½ teaspoon salt
6 tablespoons flour	¼ teaspoon pepper
1½ cups milk or chicken broth	1 cup grated Longhorn cheese

Melt margarine in top of double boiler. Blend in flour until smooth. Add milk or chicken broth slowly and stir until thick. Add other ingredients, stirring constantly. If too thick, add a little milk. Serves 6.

Simple Hollandaise Sauce:

¼ cup lemon juice	1 cup melted margarine
1 teaspoon salt	6 egg yolks, beaten

Add lemon juice and salt to margarine. Cook and stir over low heat. Slowly add egg yolks, stirring continuously until heated through. Serves 6.

Mary Jane and Jim Morgan
Crusade Family

Bacon-Wrapped Chicken

salt and pepper to taste	6–8 thin slices roast beef
6–8 chicken breasts	1 can cream of chicken soup
6–8 bacon slices	1 can cream of mushroom soup

Preheat oven to 350 degrees. Salt and pepper the chicken. Lay chicken in a glass baking dish. Place one slice of beef on each, then wrap one slice of bacon around each piece. Combine the soups in a bowl and pour over chicken. Cook for about 40 minutes. The soups also make good gravy.

Kelly Richards
Athletes in Action, OH

POULTRY

Baked Lemon Chicken With Soy Sauce

3 pounds chicken, cut into pieces	¼ cup butter, melted
¼ cup soy sauce	1 cup water
3 lemons, cut in wedges	1 teaspoon paprika
¼ teaspoon onion salt	1 cup cooked rice

Place chicken pieces in a baking dish. Combine soy sauce, onion salt, butter, water, and paprika. Coat chicken with this mixture and top with lemon wedges. Cover and cook on high 18 minutes in a microwave, turning dish once or twice. Let stand 10 minutes. Serve over rice.

Jennifer Clark
Corporate Human Resources, FL

Barbecue Chicken

1 frying chicken, cut up	2 tablespoons Worcestershire sauce
shortening	2 tablespoons brown sugar
2 tablespoons butter	2 tablespoons lemon juice
1 can tomato soup	2 teaspoons mustard
⅓ cup chopped onion	2–4 drops Tabasco
⅓ cup chopped celery	rice
1 small clove garlic, minced	lemon slices (optional)

In a skillet, brown chicken in shortening and butter. Mix remaining ingredients except rice and lemon slices. Pour over chicken; cover and simmer 45 minutes. Serve with rice and garnish with lemon slices.

Dorothy Brooks
Here's Life America, MA

Barbecue Chicken Marinade

1 cup oil	⅓ cup wine vinegar
½ cup soy sauce	1 tablespoon chopped parsley
⅙ cup Worcestershire sauce	1 clove garlic, crushed
1½ tablespoons dry mustard	¼ cup lemon juice
½ teaspoon salt	2 pounds boneless, skinless
2 teaspoons pepper	chicken breasts

Mix all ingredients except chicken. Marinate chicken in mixture for several hours. Cook on grill, basting occasionally while barbecuing. *Tip:* Chicken breasts can be frozen with marinade in a ziplock bag, then thawed and grilled.

Denise Dahlberg/Debbie McGoldrick
Campus Ministry, NH/Student Venture, GA

Black Raspberry Glazed Chicken Breasts With Wild Rice and Almond Stuffing

8 boneless, skinless chicken breasts
    (6–8 ounces each), flattened
salt
paprika
garlic powder

Wild Rice and Almond Stuffing
Black Raspberry Honey Glaze
flour
½ cup butter

Preheat oven to 325 degrees. Sprinkle chicken with salt, paprika, and garlic powder. Make *Wild Rice and Almond Stuffing* and *Black Raspberry Honey Glaze*. Place 1 part stuffing in the center of each breast half. Roll and secure with a wooden toothpick, then dust lightly with flour. Melt butter in a 9×13-inch baking pan and roll stuffed breasts in melted butter. Bake for 40 minutes. Baste with honey glaze, and continue baking and basting until chicken is tender and highly glazed (about 30 more minutes). Serve with additional wild rice, a simple buttered vegetable, or spiced fruit. Carrots glazed with raisins are especially nice. Serves 8.

Wild Rice and Almond Stuffing:

1 7-ounce package Herb Seasoned
    Wild and Long Grain Rice

2 cups chicken broth
½ cup slivered almonds, toasted

Cook rice according to the directions on the package, substituting chicken broth for the water. When rice is tender and all the liquid is absorbed, stir in almonds.

Black Raspberry Honey Glaze:

½ cup seedless black raspberry jam
2 tablespoons frozen orange juice
    concentrate

½ cup honey
1 teaspoon finely grated orange peel

In a saucepan, heat all the ingredients and stir until blended.

Barbara Ball
ChurchLIFE, FL

POULTRY

From the fruit of his lips a man is filled with good things
as surely as the work of his hands rewards him
(Prov. 12:14).

Buttermilk Chicken Casserole

1 2–3 pound chicken	1 small onion, chopped
water	½ cup (or less) margarine, melted
1 can cream of celery soup	1 cup buttermilk
1 can cream of chicken soup	1 cup self-rising flour

Preheat oven to 425 degrees. In a large pot, place chicken with enough water to cover. Boil until tender. When cooled, cut chicken into bite-size pieces and place in a large casserole dish. Reserve the broth. Add soups and mix well, then add onion. Pour reserved broth into chicken mixture and stir until it reaches a soup consistency. Mix margarine with buttermilk and flour (mixture will be runny), and pour over the chicken. *Do not stir.* Bake for 15–20 minutes until browned. *Tip:* For a darker brown crust, broil dish for a minute or so.

Brenda Morrow
ChurchLIFE, NC

Chicken Almond Casserole

3–4 cups diced cooked chicken	1 cup sour cream
1 cup chopped celery	1 cup mayonnaise
2 cans cream of chicken soup	1 cup slivered almonds

Preheat oven to 350 degrees. Combine all ingredients and place in a 9×13-inch pan. Bake until bubbly (about 30 minutes). *Tip:* Instead of buying slivered almonds, chop whole almonds in a blender.

Laurie Killingsworth
New Life Center, FL

Chicken Almond Noodle Casserole

2 tablespoons butter or margarine	1 can cream of chicken soup
1 small clove garlic, minced	⅓ cup milk
¼ cup chopped onions	1 cup diced chicken
¼ cup slivered almonds	4 ounces noodles, cooked
½ teaspoon salt	buttered bread crumbs
¼ teaspoon pepper	grated Parmesan cheese

Preheat oven to 350 degrees. Melt butter in a skillet; add garlic, onion, and almonds, and brown lightly. Add salt and pepper; stir in soup, milk, and chicken. Fold in noodles. Pour into a greased casserole, and sprinkle with crumbs and cheese. Bake for 25–30 minutes. Serves 6–8.

Jerri Younkman
International School of Theology, CA

Chicken and Dressing Casserole

½ cup butter or margarine
1 small box Pepperidge Farm
    cornbread dressing crumbs
1 can cream of celery soup

1 can cream of chicken soup
1 can chicken broth
2–3 cups cooked cut-up chicken

Preheat oven to 350 degrees. Melt margarine and stir in dressing. Dilute soups with chicken broth. In a casserole, place a layer of dressing, a layer of chicken, and ½ the soup mixture. Add another layer of chicken, then the remaining soup mixture, and top with the remaining dressing. Bake for 45 minutes or until casserole is a little firm. *Variation:* Turkey is great to use, too.

Rachael Garland
Corporate Human Resources, FL

Chicken and Ham Supreme

8 boneless chicken breasts
8 ¼-inch slices cooked ham
1 cup sour cream
½–1 cup milk
1 can cream of mushroom soup

pinch salt
dash pepper
⅛ teaspoon garlic salt
1 cup grated sharp cheese
1 cup crushed corn flakes

Preheat oven to 350 degrees. Place ham slices in a baking pan and top with chicken. Combine remaining ingredients and pour over chicken and ham. Cover and bake for 1 hour. Sprinkle with cheese and crushed corn flakes. Bake for 10 more minutes.

Barbara Ball
ChurchLIFE, FL

Chicken and Mushroom in Parmesan Cream

2 chicken cutlets (¼ pound) or
   2 chicken breasts
2 tablespoons flour
1 teaspoon margarine
1 teaspoon olive oil
1 cup sliced mushrooms
⅓ cup evaporated skimmed milk
1 tablespoon cornstarch
½ cup cold water
1 tablespoon grated Parmesan cheese
1 tablespoon chopped fresh parsley
dash white pepper

Lightly dredge chicken in flour. In a 10-inch non-stick skillet, combine margarine and oil; heat until margarine is melted. Add chicken and cook over medium-high heat, turning once, until lightly browned (about 2–3 minutes per side). Transfer chicken to a plate and set aside.

In the same skillet, sauté mushrooms over high heat, stirring every 1–2 minutes. Stir in milk and reduce heat to medium-low. Mix cornstarch with cold water until dissolved and add to mixture. Stir frequently until heated through (about 1–2 minutes). Stir in remaining ingredients and cook until cheese is melted. Return chicken to skillet and cook until heated through (about 1–2 minutes). Makes 2 servings.

Stacie Unruh
Headquarters Development Office, FL

Chicken and Rice

2 pounds boneless chicken breast
   or pieces
Minute Rice to serve 6–8
1 cup milk
1 egg
½ cup flour
1 teaspoon garlic powder
½ teaspoon salt
¼ teaspoon pepper
1 can cream of celery, broccoli,
   chicken, or mushroom soup
fresh or frozen vegetables (optional)

Preheat oven to 350 degrees. Wash chicken. Cook Minute Rice according to directions. Combine milk and egg, then combine flour with garlic powder, salt, and pepper. Dip chicken pieces in milk mixture, then into flour. Fry until slightly browned (not very long). Put rice into a 9×13-inch glass casserole dish. Layer chicken on top of rice. Combine soup with the remaining milk mixture, and pour over chicken and rice. (Vegetables can be mixed in or cooked separately.) Bake for 1 hour.

Bob MacLeod
Finance, FL

Chicken and Rice All-in-One Dish

4 chicken breasts
⅓ cup Italian salad dressing
⅔ cup uncooked Minute Rice
1 bag frozen vegetables

1 2.8-ounce can Durkee French-
  fried onions, *divided*
1¾ cups chicken stock
½ teaspoon Italian seasoning

Preheat oven to 400 degrees. Place chicken in an 8×12-inch baking dish. Pour dressing over them, and bake uncovered for 20 minutes. Layer rice, vegetables, and ½ cup onions around chicken. Combine stock and Italian seasoning and pour over all. Reduce temperature to 375 degrees and bake uncovered for 25 minutes. Top with remaining onions and cook 5 more minutes.

Sherry Cumpstone
Worldwide Challenge, FL

Chicken Au Gratin

3–3½ pounds chicken pieces
¼ cup flour
10 tablespoons butter, melted
1 large onion, diced
1 4-ounce can sliced mushrooms

1 cup evaporated milk
1 can cream of mushroom soup
1 cup grated cheese
¾ teaspoon salt
⅛ teaspoon pepper

Preheat oven to 425 degrees. Dip chicken in flour; place skin-side down in 8 tablespoons melted butter in a shallow 2-quart baking dish. Bake uncovered for 30 minutes. Turn chicken and bake an additional 15–20 minutes. Pour off excess fat. While chicken is baking, sauté onion in 2 tablespoons butter until soft. Combine sautéed onions with remaining ingredients and pour over chicken. Reduce temperature to 325 degrees; cover and bake for 15–20 minutes.

Laura Staudt
Women Today International, FL

POULTRY

When your words came, I ate them; they were my joy and my heart's delight, for I bear your name (Jer. 15:16).

Chicken Breast and Broccoli

6 boneless chicken breasts, cooked
1 10-ounce package frozen chopped
    broccoli, cooked
¼ cup butter
¼ cup flour

½ teaspoon pepper
1 teaspoon dry mustard
2 cups milk
2 cups grated Old English cheese
1 teaspoon Worcestershire sauce

Prepare individual servings by placing chicken breasts in a baking dish and
topping with broccoli. Combine remaining ingredients to make a sauce and
pour over chicken mounds. Broil until sauce bubbles.

Betty Van Tuinen
History's Handful, FL

Chicken Breast Supreme

1 cup plain yogurt
2 tablespoons lemon juice
2 cloves garlic, minced
1½ teaspoons celery seeds
1 teaspoon paprika

¼ teaspoon cayenne pepper
1 teaspoon salt (optional)
6–8 boneless, skinless chicken breasts
3 rye crackers, crumbled
2 tablespoons butter, melted

Combine yogurt, lemon juice, and seasonings. Add chicken to yogurt mixture, coating each piece. Cover and refrigerate overnight. When ready to
bake, preheat oven to 350 degrees. Arrange chicken with yogurt mixture in a
single layer in a baking dish. Sprinkle crumbs over chicken and spoon melted
butter over crumbs. Bake uncovered for 35–40 minutes.

Jennie Mitchell
Josh McDowell Ministries, CA

Chicken Casserole

2 cups cooked chicken, cut into
    pieces
2 cans cream of mushroom soup
¼ cup water

¼ cup chopped onion
2 cups chopped celery
4 ounces cashew nuts
chow mein noodles

Preheat oven to 325 degrees. Combine all ingredients and bake for 40 minutes. Serve over chow mein noodles.

Marilyn Klein
Crusade Family

Chicken Casserole With White Sauce

cooked chicken
cut-up carrots
cut-up broccoli
sliced mushrooms
peeled and chopped tomatoes
chopped onions

cauliflowerettes
Basic White Sauce (see
   Accompaniments)
grated cheese
toasted bread crumbs

Preheat oven to 350 degrees. Heat the first 8 ingredients in a saucepan. (Sauce should be slightly thick.) Pour into a casserole dish; cover with cheese and bread crumbs. Bake for 30–40 minutes until bubbly hot.

Sue Patterson
International Ministry, Zimbabwe

Chicken Continental

3–4 pounds frying chicken pieces
⅓ cup seasoned flour
¼ cup butter
1 can cream of chicken soup
2½ tablespoons grated onion
1 tablespoon chopped parsley

1 teaspoon salt
⅛ teaspoon thyme
½ teaspoon celery flakes
1⅓ cups water
1⅓ cups Minute Rice
½ teaspoon paprika

Preheat oven to 375 degrees. Roll chicken in flour and sauté in butter until golden brown. Mix soup, onion, parsley, salt, thyme, and celery flakes in a saucepan. Gradually stir in water. Bring to a boil, stirring constantly. Pour rice into a shallow 2-quart casserole. Stir all except ⅓ cup soup mixture into the rice. Add chicken and top with remaining soup mixture. Cover and bake for 30 minutes or until chicken is tender. Sprinkle with paprika.

Karen Dace
International Ministry, Kenya

Chicken Fajitas

boneless, skinless chicken
prepared bouillon
brown sugar
soy sauce
bell pepper
onion

1 tablespoon oil
flour tortillas
guacamole
salsa
sour cream

Slice chicken into small strips. Make enough marinade of equal parts bouillon, brown sugar, and soy sauce to cover the meat. Marinate chicken in refrigerator for at least 3 hours. Slice bell pepper into strips and onion into thin rings. Sauté chicken in oil and remove. Sauté onion and pepper, then add chicken to warm it. Serve in warm tortillas with guacamole, salsa, and sour cream. *Variation:* Strips of beef can be used instead of chicken. The marinade is what tenderizes and flavors the meat.

Terry Morgan
Campus Ministry, Mexico

Chicken la France

4 boneless, skinless chicken breasts
6–8 mushrooms, sliced
4 slices Alpine Lace low-fat
    Swiss cheese
⅓ cup water or broth

1 can Healthy Request cream of
    chicken soup
1 cup crushed seasoned croutons
4 servings rice or couscous

Preheat oven to 350 degrees. Place a layer of chicken breasts in a 9×12-inch baking dish. Cover each breast with sliced mushrooms and top with a slice of cheese. In a medium bowl, mix water or broth and soup with a wire whisk, and pour over chicken breasts. (Double this portion if you prefer more gravy.) Sprinkle crushed croutons over the top. Cover with foil and bake for 45 minutes. Serve over rice or couscous.

Carolyn Murphy
Church Dynamics, CO

 The lions may grow weak and hungry, but those who seek the Lord lack no good thing (Psalm 34:10).

Chicken Marengo

3–4 pounds chicken, cut up
3 tablespoons vegetable oil
1 15½-ounce jar spaghetti sauce
  with meat

1 8-ounce can boiled onions, drained
1 4-ounce can sliced mushrooms,
  drained
cooked noodles (optional)

Preheat oven to 375 degrees. Wash chicken pieces and pat dry. Heat oil in a
skillet over moderately high heat (about 350 degrees). Add chicken and
brown well on all sides. Arrange in an ungreased shallow 3-quart casserole;
top with spaghetti sauce. Cover with aluminum foil and bake for 45 minutes. Add onions and mushrooms to casserole and bake uncovered for
15 more minutes. Serve with cooked noodles, if desired. Makes 4–6 servings.

Laurie Killingsworth
New Life Center, FL

Chicken Orange

1 chicken, cut into pieces
Fines herbs
½ cup butter, melted

1 small can frozen orange juice
  concentrate

Preheat oven to 325–350 degrees. Remove skin from chicken and arrange
pieces in a baking dish. Sprinkle with herbs. Combine melted butter and
undiluted orange juice. Pour mixture over chicken and bake uncovered for
1 hour.

Anne Lawrence
World Changers Radio, FL

Chicken-Pineapple Skillet

2–3 boneless, skinless chicken breasts
2 tablespoons margarine or oil
salt to taste
1 onion, halved and sliced
1 cup celery, sliced diagonally
1 green pepper, cut into strips

2 cups pineapple chunks with juice
½ teaspoon cinnamon
2 teaspoons cornstarch
1½ teaspoons soy sauce
1 cup cooked rice

POULTRY

Cut each breast half into 10–12 strips. Over high heat, sauté strips of chicken in margarine. Sprinkle with salt and stir constantly for 3 minutes. Add onion, celery, and green pepper. Continue to cook, stirring constantly for 2 minutes. Drain pineapple chunks and reserve the juice. Combine pineapple juice, cinnamon, cornstarch, and soy sauce in a bowl. Add pineapple to chicken, then juice mixture. Stir and bring to a boil. Reduce heat and cook until clear. Serve over hot rice. Makes 6 servings. *Tip:* Cook bones and skin of chicken to make broth to use in another dish. *Optional:* Leftover cooked chicken can also be used.

Karen Horsey
International Ministry, FL

Chicken Pot Pie

1 can cream of celery soup
1¼ cups chicken broth
1 frying chicken, cooked and shredded
onion (optional)
salt and pepper to taste

peas, carrots, chopped onion, diced potatoes, mushrooms (optional)
1 cup milk
1 cup Bisquick
½ cup margarine

Preheat oven to 375 degrees. Mix soup and chicken broth, and combine with chicken. Add a little onion if desired and salt and pepper to taste. Add any desired vegetables. Put mixture in an 8-inch square baking dish. Mix milk, Bisquick, and margarine to make topping, and pour over chicken mixture. Bake for 30–45 minutes.

Stephanie Ramirez
Student Venture, FL

Chicken Pot Pie With Flaky Pastry

3 tablespoons butter or margarine
¼ cup all-purpose flour
1¼ cups chicken broth
1 cup milk
2 cups cubed chicken
2 cups peas and carrots, cooked

1 hard-boiled egg, sliced
½ teaspoon salt
¼ teaspoon poultry seasoning
⅛ teaspoon pepper
Flaky Pastry

Preheat oven to 400 degrees. Melt butter in saucepan; add flour, stirring and cooking 1 minute. Gradually add broth and milk. Cook and stir over medium heat until thickened and bubbly. Stir in the next 6 ingredients. Pour chicken mixture into a deep 1½-quart casserole. Top with *Flaky Pastry*. Bake for 25–30 minutes or until crust is golden brown. Makes 6 servings.

Flaky Pastry:

1 cup flour
¾ teaspoon baking powder
½ teaspoon salt

⅓ cup shortening
3 tablespoons ice water

Combine flour, baking powder, and salt in a mixing bowl. Cut in shortening with a pastry blender. Sprinkle cold water evenly over the surface; stir together and knead a few times. Roll out on a floured surface and shape to fit casserole dish.

Sarah Willis
International Ministry, FL

Chicken, Rice, Broccoli Casserole with Cheese

½ cup margarine
1 pound Velveeta cheese
½ cup milk
1 can cream of chicken soup

8 cooked chicken thighs
3 cups cooked rice
2 boxes frozen chopped broccoli, cooked and drained

Preheat oven to 350 degrees. In a saucepan (or microwave pan), melt margarine and cheese. Add milk and soup, then heat. Cut chicken into bite-size pieces, then stir into mixture. In a lightly greased baking dish, place a small layer of mixture; add rice and top with broccoli. Pour remaining mixture over all. Bake for 30 minutes. Serves 4. *Optional:* A topping of shredded cheese and sliced almonds added the last 10 minutes of baking is delicious. Serve with a garnish of sliced or baby beets, rolls and jelly, and ice cream pie. *Tip:* Prepare the casserole ahead of time and refrigerate. Bring to room temperature before baking. This is a good dish to take to a family in times of death or illness.

Mary Canada
President's Office, FL

POULTRY

Chicken Ruby

1 2½–3 pound chicken, cut-up
⅓ cup flour
1 teaspoon salt
¼ cup melted butter
1½ cups fresh or frozen cranberries
¾ cup sugar

¼ cup chopped onion
1 teaspoon grated orange peel
¾ cup orange juice
¼ teaspoon cinnamon
¼ teaspoon ginger

Coat chicken pieces with a mixture of flour and salt. Brown in butter in a skillet, turning once. Meanwhile, combine remaining ingredients in a saucepan and bring to a boil. Pour over chicken. Cover and cook on low for 35–40 minutes or until chicken is tender. Makes 4 servings.

Helen Koopman
JESUS Film Project, FL

Chicken Wild Rice Casserole

½ cup chopped celery
½ cup chopped green pepper
1 chicken or 6 chicken breasts
1 package Uncle Ben's Wild Rice
1 can cream of mushroom soup

1 can mushrooms
1 package slivered almonds
8 ounces shredded cheddar cheese,
   divided

Preheat oven to 350 degrees. Sauté celery and green pepper. Boil chicken until tender and remove from broth; cube or chop the chicken. Using the chicken broth as the liquid, prepare the rice according to package directions. Mix the remaining ingredients with the chicken and rice, reserving some of the cheese for a topping. Place into a casserole dish and bake for 30 minutes. Melt reserved cheese on top of casserole and serve.

Laura Callaway
Finance, FL

Godliness with contentment is great gain. For we brought nothing into the world, and we can take nothing our of it. But if we have food and clothing, we will be content with that (1 Tim. 6:6).

Chicken With Pineapple and Nuts

1 pound boneless chicken breasts
1 piece minced ginger root or
   1 teaspoon ground ginger
1 tablespoon soy sauce
1 tablespoon water

1 teaspoon cornstarch
2 tablespoons oil
4 ounces nuts
1 8-ounce can pineapple tidbits,
   drained

Cut chicken into small cubes. Place chicken and ginger in a small bag and shake. To make sauce, combine soy sauce, water, and cornstarch. (You may want to double the amount of sauce.) Set wok to 420 degrees. Heat oil and stir-fry chicken for 3 minutes; push to the side. Add sauce to wok and stir until thickened. Add pineapple and nuts; stir and cook for 1 more minute.

Mike and Lori Burns
Staff & Ministry Opportunities, FL

Chinese Chicken Chow Mein

2½ tablespoons water plus ½ cup,
   divided
2 tablespoons soy sauce, *divided*
3 teaspoons cornstarch, *divided*
2 boneless, skinless chicken breasts,
   cut into 1-inch pieces
8 ounces lean pork, cut into
   1-inch pieces
2 teaspoons instant chicken bouillon
2 tablespoons vegetable oil

1 piece fresh ginger, finely chopped
3 cloves garlic, crushed
8 ounces shelled shrimp
2 medium yellow onions, chopped
1 red or green bell pepper, sliced
2 stalks celery, cut 1-inch diagonally
8 green onions, chopped
4 ounces cabbage, shredded
Fried Noodles

Blend 2½ tablespoons water, ½ tablespoon soy sauce, and 1 teaspoon cornstarch in a large bowl. Add chicken and pork; toss to coat well. Cover and refrigerate 1 hour. Combine ½ cup water, bouillon, 2 teaspoons cornstarch, and 1½ tablespoons soy sauce in a small bowl. Set aside. Heat oil in a wok or large skillet over high heat. Add ginger and garlic, and stir-fry 1 minute while stirring with a spatula. Add chicken and pork; stir-fry until pork is no longer pink (about 5 minutes). Add shrimp and stir-fry until shrimp turns pink (about 3 minutes). Add all vegetables to wok. Stir-fry until vegetables are crisp and tender (about 3 minutes). Add reserved bouillon/soy sauce mixture to wok. Cook and stir until sauce boils and thickens. Serve over rice or fried noodles. Serves 4–6.

POULTRY

Fried Noodles:

3 packages Ramen noodles   ⅓ cup oil
salt

Cook Ramen noodles and salt according to package directions. (Do not use
seasoning packet.) Drain. Lay noodles flat on a cookie sheet lined with paper
towels, and allow to dry completely. Heat oil in a skillet and fry dried
noodles. This is a great dish to serve company. Our children also enjoy it.

Yvonne Bibby
International Ministry, FL

Congealed Chicken Loaf

1 envelope Knox plain gelatin   ½ cup sliced almonds
1 cup hot chicken stock, *divided*   ¾ cup diced celery
2 cups diced chicken   1 cup Hellman's mayonnaise
½ can Le Suer English peas   seasoned salt
2 hard-boiled eggs, chopped   minced onion

Dissolve gelatin in ½ cup of hot stock, then add the other ½ cup. Add
remaining ingredients. Mix well, place in a loaf pan, and chill until set.
Serves 6–8.

Sherry Cumpstone
Worldwide Challenge, FL

Country Kiev Chicken

½ cup bread crumbs   4–6 boneless, skinless chicken breasts
¼ cup grated Parmesan cheese   ⅓ cup butter, melted
1 teaspoon oregano   ¼ cup apple juice
1 teaspoon basil   ½ cup sliced green onions
½ teaspoon garlic salt   ¼ cup parsley

Preheat oven to 400 degrees. Mix bread crumbs, cheese, and seasonings. Dip
chicken breasts into melted butter, then into bread crumb mixture to coat.
Place in a pan and bake for 20 minutes. Mix remaining butter with apple
juice, onions, and parsley. Pour mixture over cooked breasts and bake an
additional 5–10 minutes.

Brenda Stewart
Church Dynamics, WA

Cream Cheese Chicken Enchiladas

1 onion, diced or puréed
½ cup butter
1 8-ounce package cream cheese
3 chicken breasts, boiled and cut
    into small pieces

flour tortillas
8 ounces Monterey Jack cheese,
    grated
1 small can Carnation milk
hot sauce (optional)

Preheat oven to 350 degrees. Sauté onions in butter. Add cream cheese and chicken. Put a few spoonfuls in each flour tortilla and roll up. Place seam-side down in a greased 9×13-inch pan. Sprinkle with grated cheese and top with milk. Bake for 20 minutes. Serve with hot sauce on top.

Barbara Calwell
Campus Ministry, TX

Creamy Chicken Casserole

½ cup uncooked rice
2 hard-boiled eggs, diced
1 cup grated cheddar cheese
1 tablespoon Worcestershire sauce
½ cup green olives, sliced
½ cup mayonnaise

2 cups chicken, cubed
1 cup chicken stock
½ onion, grated
1 can cream of chicken soup
1 cup Ritz cracker crumbs

Preheat oven to 350 degrees. Combine all ingredients except cracker crumbs, and place in a buttered casserole dish. Sprinkle crumbs on top. Bake for 30 minutes.

Laurie Killingsworth
New Life Center, FL

POULTRY

Come in the evening, come in the morning,
Come when expected, come without warning;
Thousands of welcomes you'll find here before you,
And the oftener you come, the more we'll adore you.

— Irish Rhyme

Creamy Mushroom Baked Chicken Breasts

8 whole chicken breasts
vegetable oil
1 can cream of mushroom soup

2 small cans mushrooms
1 pint whipping cream

Preheat oven to 350 degrees. Heat oil in a skillet and brown chicken breasts on all sides. Place in a single layer in a shallow baking pan. Add soup, mushrooms, and whipping cream to the skillet. Simmer until well mixed, stirring thoroughly to loosen drippings from the chicken. Pour mixture over the chicken breasts. Cover and bake for 1 hour. Serve with baked potatoes smothered in creamy gravy from the chicken.

Joette Whims
NewLife Publications, CA

Delicious Chicken

1 can cream of mushroom soup
8 ounces light sour cream
¼ pound sliced bacon

2–3 boneless chicken breasts
1 jar thin-sliced dried beef

Preheat oven to 350 degrees. Mix soup and sour cream; set aside. Line the bottom of a casserole dish with bacon. Add chicken, then add dried beef. Top with soup mixture. Bake covered for 45 minutes to 1 hour. Uncover and cook until brown. Serve with corn and rice or mashed potatoes.

Fran Williams
Executive Ministry, SC

Delicious Turkey Chili

2 medium onions, finely chopped
1 green pepper, finely chopped
1 stalk celery, finely chopped
2 cloves garlic, minced

2 14½-ounce cans stewed tomatoes, undrained
1 15-ounce can tomato sauce
1 6-ounce can tomato paste

2 teaspoons oil
4 pounds lean ground turkey
1 package McCormick's Chili mix

½ cup water
garlic salt
pepper

In a large skillet, sauté the first 4 ingredients in oil. Add meat, 1 pound at a time, stirring until brown. Drain off grease. Place cooked vegetables and turkey in a large pot. Add remaining ingredients, stirring after each addition. Simmer 2½–3 hours, stirring frequently. Season to taste with garlic salt and pepper. Makes 8 servings. Great with bread sticks or cornbread. *Variation:* For spicier chili, add ¼ cup green chili salsa; 1 whole jalapeño, finely chopped; and 1 4-ounce can diced green chilies, undrained.

Robyn Skur
Worldwide Challenge, FL

Easy-Cheesy Chicken Pot Pie

½ cup milk
½ cup picante sauce
1 tablespoon cornstarch
2 tablespoons butter
¼ teaspoon salt
1 large onion, cut into large pieces
1 cup grated mild cheddar cheese

2 cups cooked chicken, cut into bite-size pieces
1 cup sliced carrots, cooked
1 cup peas or green beans, cooked
1 9-inch pie crust
1 2.8-ounce can Durkee French-fried onions

Preheat oven to 350 degrees. Combine milk, picante sauce, and cornstarch in a medium saucepan; stir until smooth. Add butter, salt, and onion. Bring to a boil over medium heat; boil one minute, stirring constantly. Remove from heat and stir in cheese until melted. Add chicken, carrots, and peas. Spoon into pastry crust and bake for 35 minutes. Sprinkle with French-fried onions and bake for 5 more minutes. Serves 6–8.

Terry Morgan
Campus Ministry, Mexico

POULTRY

Easy Chicken and Rice

1 package dry onion soup mix
3½ cups water
1½ cups regular rice

8–12 pieces of chicken
margarine

Preheat oven to 350 degrees. Mix soup, water, and rice, and pour into a
9×13-inch buttered casserole. Dot chicken with margarine and place on top
of rice. Bake for 30 minutes.

Debbie McGoldrick
Student Venture, GA

Easy Chicken-Broccoli Dinner

½ onion, chopped
1 cup sliced mushrooms
olive oil
2 cups chopped broccoli
1–2 cooked chicken breasts, cut up
salt and pepper to taste

basil
beau monde
1 can cream of mushroom soup
½ cup milk
rice or noodles, cooked

Stir-fry onion and mushrooms in oil. As they begin to get tender, add the
broccoli and chicken pieces. Continue stir-frying until broccoli is crisp and
tender. Season with salt, pepper, basil, and beau monde. Mix soup and milk,
and add to chicken. Heat through and serve immediately over rice or
noodles. Makes 4 servings.

Joanne Austin
International Resource Ministries, FL

Egyptian Curry Chicken

1 chicken, cut up
¼ cup butter
2 teaspoons curry powder
3½ cups unsweetened pineapple
    juice, *divided*
¾ cup honey
¾ cup ketchup

1 teaspoon garlic powder
2 or more strips of bacon, chopped
1½–2 tablespoons cornstarch
1 medium green pepper, chopped
1 cup halved cherry tomatoes
onions

Sauté chicken in butter, browning on both sides; drain butter. Mix curry
powder, 2½ cups pineapple juice, honey, ketchup, and garlic powder; pour
over chicken. Simmer for 35 minutes. Meanwhile, fry bacon pieces. Remove
chicken from sauce. To thicken sauce, mix 1 cup pineapple juice with cornstarch, then stir into sauce. Heat and stir to desired consistency; add green

pepper and tomatoes. Coat chicken with sauce. Garnish with bacon and onion. *Variation:* Add more curry for a "hotter" dish.

Lynn Rustulka
Church Dynamics International, CA

Elaine Beeber's Curry Chicken Divan

2 10-ounce packages frozen broccoli
6 whole chicken breasts, cooked and cut into large pieces
1 can cream of chicken soup
⅓ cup water
½ cup mayonnaise
1 tablespoon lemon juice
1 teaspoon curry powder
4 ounces cheddar cheese, shredded
1 cup cornflake crumbs
¼ cup butter, melted

Preheat oven to 350 degrees. Boil broccoli in salted water; drain. Arrange broccoli in a greased casserole. Place chicken pieces on top. Combine soup, water, mayonnaise, lemon juice, and curry powder. Pour over chicken and top with cheese. Combine crumbs with melted butter, and sprinkle on top. Bake for 30 minutes.

Allan Beeber
National Ministry, FL

Delight yourself in the Lord and he will give you the desires of your heart (Psalm 37:4).

Gourmet Chicken Delight

1 2½–3 pounds fryer cut into pieces or 4 whole chicken breasts
¼ cup butter or oil
1 medium onion, chopped (½ cup)
½ pound fresh mushrooms, sliced, or 1 4-ounce can, drained
1 can cream of mushroom soup
½ soup can water
1 tablespoon chopped parsley
1 teaspoon salt
1 teaspoon paprika
dash of pepper
2 lemon slices

Preheat oven to 350 degrees. In a skillet, brown chicken slowly in butter or oil. Place in a single layer in a 7×11-inch shallow baking dish. Add onion

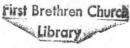
POULTRY

and mushrooms to butter remaining in the skillet, and cook until tender, not brown. Add soup, water, seasonings, and lemon slices. Blend thoroughly and pour over chicken. Bake uncovered for 1 hour or until chicken is fork-tender. Serves 4.

Cinny Hicks
Crusade Family

Grilled Chicken Marinade

½ cup canola oil
1 cup apple cider vinegar
1½ tablespoons salt
¼ teaspoon pepper

1 tablespoon poultry seasoning
1 egg
24 skinless chicken thighs
　(or other pieces)

To make sauce, mix all ingredients except chicken. Marinate chicken in sauce overnight or brush sauce over chicken while grilling.

Ann Tormanen
International Ministry, FL

Grilled Tropical Chicken Delight

⅓ cup fresh orange juice
¼ cup fresh lemon juice
¼ cup olive oil
¼ cup honey
¼ cup frozen lemonade concentrate
3 tablespoons fresh lime juice
3 tablespoons fresh mint
1 tablespoon orange peel

1 teaspoon lime peel
1 teaspoon lemon peel
4 teaspoons cumin
4 teaspoons cinnamon
¼ red onion, thinly sliced
salt and pepper
3 pounds boneless, skinless
　chicken pieces

To make marinade, mix all ingredients except chicken. Pour over chicken pieces; cover and refrigerate overnight. Remove chicken, reserving marinade. Grill chicken over hot coals. While chicken is cooking, place marinade in a small saucepan and cook over medium-high heat until thickened. Serve as sauce for chicken. This recipe is from my sister, Pat.

Sue McDaniel
International Ministry, FL

Homemade Chicken Pot Pie

1 whole chicken, cooked and cut up
1 cup carrots
1 cup peas
⅔ cup chicken broth
1 can cream of celery soup
1 can cream of chicken soup
salt and pepper to taste
1 cup self-rising flour
1 teaspoon baking powder
1 cup milk
½ cup margarine, melted

Preheat oven to 425 degrees. Place chicken pieces in a casserole dish. Add carrots and peas. Mix broth with soups and pour over chicken. In a separate bowl, mix remaining ingredients to make a crust, and spread over chicken mixture. Bake for 35 minutes.

Cindy Brogan
JESUS Film Project, FL

Hot Chicken Salad Casserole

2 cups cubed cooked chicken
2 cups thinly sliced celery
1 cup mayonnaise
½ cup slivered almonds
2 tablespoons lemon juice
2 teaspoons instant minced onion
½ teaspoon salt
2 cups croutons, *divided*
1 cup shredded cheddar cheese

Preheat oven to 350 degrees. Mix all ingredients except 1 cup croutons and cheese. Spoon into a 9×13-inch baking dish, and top with remaining croutons and cheese. Bake for 15–20 minutes until bubbly.

Stephanie Ramirez
Student Venture, FL

Huntington Chicken Casserole

3 cups or more cut-up chicken
28 ounces noodles
6 tablespoons butter
6 tablespoons flour
salt and pepper
3 cups milk or broth (or combined)
1 tablespoon celery seed
1 can cream of chicken soup
1 can cream of mushroom soup
3 hard-boiled eggs, chopped
8 ounces cheddar cheese, diced
1 2-ounce jar pimientos
½ package Pepperidge Farm
    dressing crumbs

POULTRY

Preheat oven to 300 degrees. Cook chicken, reserving broth. Cook noodles in chicken broth, then drain. Prepare a white sauce: melt the butter, then mix in flour and cook until bubbly. Slowly stir in milk or broth, then add seasonings. Add soups, eggs, cheese, and pimientos. Place a layer of noodles, sauce, then chicken in a greased casserole. Top with dressing crumbs. Bake until bubbly (about 20 minutes). Serves 12.

Charlotte Day
Crusade Family

Impossible Chicken Vegetable Pie

1 cup cubed cooked chicken
1 cup chopped zucchini
1 cup chopped tomato
½ cup chopped onion
⅓ cup grated Parmesan cheese
2 eggs

¼ teaspoon pepper
½ cup Bisquick
1 cup milk
tomato slices (optional)
zucchini slices (optional)

Preheat oven to 400 degrees. Grease a 9-inch pie plate (for high altitudes, use a 10-inch pie plate). Mix chicken, zucchini, tomato, onion, and cheese. Spoon evenly into pie plate. Beat eggs, pepper, Bisquick, and milk 15 seconds in blender on high speed, 1 minute with wire whisk, or hand beater until smooth. Pour evenly over chicken mixture. Bake about 35 minutes or until knife inserted in center comes out clean. Let stand 5 minutes before cutting. Garnish with tomato and zucchini slices if desired. Serves 6.

Lila Kremer
ChurchLIFE, NE

Impossible Turkey Pie

2 cups cubed cooked turkey
1 4½-ounce jar sliced mushrooms,
    drained
½ cup sliced green onions
½ teaspoon salt

1 cup shredded Swiss cheese
1½ cups milk
3 eggs
¾ cup Bisquick

Preheat oven to 400 degrees. Grease a 10-inch pie plate. Sprinkle turkey, mushrooms, onions, salt, and cheese in pie plate. Beat remaining ingredients for about 15 seconds in blender until smooth. Pour into plate. Bake until knife inserted comes out clean (about 30–35 minutes). Cool 5 minutes. Serves 6–8.

Doris Maugle
Contributions and Postal Services, FL

Individual Chicken Pot Pies

¾ cup plus 1½ tablespoons flour,
   divided
¼ cup shortening
up to 3 tablespoons water
2 tablespoons margarine
1 medium onion, chopped
6 medium mushrooms, sliced
½ teaspoon salt

⅛ teaspoon pepper
⅛ teaspoon rosemary
1 beef bouillon cube
¾ cup hot water
¼ cup milk
½ package frozen peas and carrots
1¼ cup cubed cooked chicken
   breasts

Preheat oven to 425 degrees. To make pastry dough, use a pastry blender or spoon to combine ¾ cup flour and shortening. Add water until manageable. Refrigerate until ready to use. To make chicken mixture, melt margarine in a frying pan over medium heat. Add onion and mushrooms, and sauté until onions are limp. Stir in 1½ tablespoons flour, salt, pepper, and rosemary. Dissolve boullion cube in hot water to make broth. Blend broth and milk into onion mixture until it boils and thickens. Stir in the vegetables and chicken. Spoon into individual casserole dishes. Divide dough in half. Roll out into circles 2 inches larger than the diameter of the casserole dishes. Use a small cookie cutter to cut a design in the center if desired. Fit dough over chicken mixture, and pinch edges to seal. Brush with milk and bake for 20 minutes. Makes 2 servings.

Melissa Crabtree
Corporate Human Resources, FL

POULTRY

Do not set your heart on what you will eat or drink;
do not worry about it…but seek his kingdom, and these
things will be given to you as well (Luke 12:29,31).

Italian Baked Chicken

½ cup butter or margarine
½ cup Italian salad dressing
¼ cup lemon juice
¼ cup Worcestershire sauce

2 cloves garlic, crushed
2 whole chicken breasts, split
salt and pepper

Preheat oven to 325 degrees. Combine the first 5 ingredients in a medium saucepan; cook over medium heat until butter melts. Place chicken in a 12×8×2-inch baking dish, and sprinkle with salt and pepper. Pour sauce over chicken. Bake uncovered for 1 hour or until tender. Makes 4 servings.

Juli Emory
Military Ministry, VA

Italian Chicken and Rice

2½ pounds chicken pieces
2 teaspoons olive oil
salt and pepper
2 onions, chopped or sliced
½ pound mushrooms, sliced
   (optional)
2 small sliced zucchini, 1 bunch
   broccoli, or ½ pound green beans
1 cup uncooked rice

5 sliced tomatoes and 1 cup water,
   or 1 28-ounce can undrained
   tomatoes
1 cup chicken stock or broth
2 teaspoons vinegar
1 teaspoon basil
1 teaspoon oregano
½ teaspoon thyme
½ teaspoon garlic powder

Brown chicken in oil in a skillet. Sprinkle with salt and pepper, and set aside when cooked. Sauté onions, mushrooms, and green vegetable for 3 minutes. Add rice to vegetables and cook for 1 minute, stirring frequently. Add tomatoes to vegetables and rice. If using canned tomatoes, break up while stirring. Stir in chicken stock, vinegar, and seasonings. Bring to a boil. Place chicken on top of mixture; cover and simmer for 20 minutes or until rice and chicken are tender.

Jeannette Entz
Campus Ministry, TX

 Taste and see that the Lord is good; blessed is the man who takes refuge in him (Psalm 34:8).

Javanese Dinner

steamed rice to serve 40	2 cups chopped yellow onions
5 stewing chickens	3 cups chopped celery
bouillon	5 cups grated Monterey Jack or
cream of celery soup or cream of	cheddar cheese
mushroom soup	5 cups shredded coconut
curry powder	5 cups crushed pineapple, drained
1¼ gallon chow mein noodles	5 cups blanched almonds, cut
(optional)	into large pieces

Cover chickens with water and simmer until done. Bone and cut meat into chunks. Make a clear gravy with the chicken broth by adding bouillon, soup, and curry powder. Put ½ of the gravy into a serving bowl and mix the other ½ with the chicken pieces. Set out ingredients on a buffet table, and have guests help themselves to these approximate amounts, in the order given:

a large serving of rice, patted down	2 tablespoons cheese
2 tablespoons chicken in gravy	2 tablespoons coconut
1 heaping tablespoon chow mein	2 tablespoons pineapple
noodles, if desired	2 tablespoons almonds
1 tablespoon onion	chicken gravy to cover
1 tablespoon celery	

Makes 40 servings. Serve with tea; no salad or bread is needed. For dessert, serve Chinese cookies with pineapple sherbet, coconut ice cream, or *Frosted Fruit Cocktail*. This recipe is a Campus Crusade family favorite from early ministry days. It's excellent for serving a crowd or for a shared meal with everyone bringing the ingredients.

Vonette Bright
Co-founder, Campus Crusade for Christ
Executive Director, Women Today International, FL

Lemon Chicken

1 tablespoon thyme leaves	1 cup lemon juice
1 tablespoon salt	7 chicken breasts
½ teaspoon pepper	rice
3 cloves garlic, minced	

Preheat oven to 350 degrees. Mix spices and lemon juice in a 1-gallon bag. Add chicken pieces and shake. Arrange pieces skin-side down in a pan. Pour

POULTRY

liquid over chicken and bake for 20 minutes; turn chicken over and baste it. Bake until done, basting every 20 minutes. Serve chicken over rice.

Becky Leppard
International Ministry, FL

Mandarin Orange Chicken

1 pound boneless chicken breasts,
    cut into 1-inch chunks (2 cups)
1 tablespoon vegetable oil
2 cups sliced fresh mushrooms
2 teaspoons all-purpose flour
1 6-ounce can frozen orange juice
    concentrate, thawed

⅔ cup water
½ cup thinly sliced green onion
    (tops only)
2 chicken bouillon cubes
1 cup uncooked rice
1 11-ounce can mandarin oranges

Cook chicken chunks in oil on medium-high until browned on both sides. Remove and set aside. Cook mushrooms over medium-high, stirring constantly. Sprinkle flour over mushrooms, stirring quickly to combine. Gradually stir in orange juice concentrate, water, green onion tops, and bouillon cubes. Bring to a boil, stirring constantly. Reduce heat and add chicken; simmer 3–4 minutes. *Cool and freeze.* To serve, cook rice according to package directions. Thaw chicken mixture and heat until bubbly. Stir in orange segments and heat through. Makes 4 servings. Serve over rice with French-cut green beans and biscuits.

Lorraine Pettijohn
Military Ministry, VA

Mediterranean Meatball Pitas

1 pound ground turkey
¼ cup chopped onion
1½ teaspoons dried oregano
½ teaspoon dried mint
½ teaspoon parsley
½ teaspoon lemon pepper
1 clove garlic, minced
2½ teaspoons lemon juice, *divided*

½ cup non-fat sour cream
½ medium cucumber, peeled and
    finely chopped
⅛ teaspoon black pepper
3 6-inch pita breads, cut in half
lettuce
tomato

Mix the first 7 ingredients and 1 teaspoon lemon juice in a bowl. Form approximately 18 small meatballs. Cook 8–10 minutes in a skillet coated with cooking spray. Make sauce by mixing sour cream, cucumber, 1½ teaspoons lemon juice, and pepper. Serve 3 meatballs in each ½ pita with lettuce, tomato, and sauce.

Karen T. Clemente
Campus Ministry, New England

Mexican Casserole

1 8-ounce package Mexican rice (Vigo)
1 pound ground turkey
2 cloves garlic, minced
1 medium onion, chopped

1 can Ortega refried beans
1 4-ounce can chopped green chilies
1 jar ChiChi chunky salsa
1 package grated Mexico 4 cheese

Preheat oven to 350 degrees. Cook rice according to directions. Brown turkey with garlic and onion. Spread beans in the bottom of a shallow dish; add browned turkey mixture. Layer green chilies, rice, and salsa in order. Bake about 30 minutes. Add cheese and bake until cheese is melted (about 5 minutes).

Frances Thomas
Crusade Family

Mexican Chicken

8 chicken breasts, cooked and cut up
1 can cream of mushroom soup
1 can Ortega diced green chilies
3 cups sour cream
6 green onion tops, chopped

½ cup milk
garlic salt to taste
1 10-ounce package tortilla chips
½ pound Monterey Jack cheese, grated
½ pound cheddar cheese, grated

POULTRY

Preheat oven to 350 degrees. Mix all ingredients except chips and cheeses. Put tortilla chips on the bottom of a 9×13-inch baking dish. Pour chicken mix over chips and top with cheeses. Bake for 30 minutes or until hot and bubbly.

Belle McAdams
Church Dynamics International, CA

Mexican Chicken Casserole

4 whole chicken breasts
12 corn tortillas
1 can cream of chicken soup
1 can cream of mushroom soup

1 cup milk
1 onion, grated
1–1½ cans green chili salsa
1 pound cheddar cheese, grated

Preheat oven to 400 degrees. Cook chicken breasts and cut into large pieces. Reserve 1 tablespoon chicken juice. Cut tortillas into 1-inch strips or squares. Mix soups, milk, onion, and salsa. Butter a large, shallow baking dish, and put juice from chicken in dish. Layer ½ of the tortillas in the dish, then ½ of the chicken, and ½ of the soup mixture. Layer once more and top with cheese. *Refrigerate 24 hours.* Bake at 300 degrees for 1–1½ hours. Serves 8 generously.

Carol Herron
Church Dynamics International

Mexican Chicken in Orange Juice

1 large fryer, cut into pieces
salt and pepper
3 tablespoons margarine
½ cup sliced almonds
⅓ cup golden raisins
1 8-ounce can crushed pineapple
    with liquid

⅛ teaspoon ground cinnamon
⅛ teaspoon ground cloves
2 cups orange juice
1 tablespoon flour
2 tablespoons cold water
avocado slices (optional)
cooked rice

Sprinkle the chicken with salt and pepper. Melt margarine in a large skillet; sauté chicken until brown on all sides. Add almonds, raisins, pineapple, cinnamon, cloves, and orange juice. Cover the skillet tightly, and simmer for 45 minutes or until the chicken is fork tender. Remove chicken to a warmed platter. Mix the flour with cold water to make a smooth paste, and stir into drippings remaining in skillet. Pour a little of the sauce over the chicken, and serve the remainder in a gravy bowl. Garnish the chicken platter with slices of avocado and serve with fluffy rice. Serves 4. *Tip:* This is a very simple recipe to quadruple for a buffet supper; use a dutch oven instead of a skillet.

Carol Williams
Crusade Family

Mexican Meatloaf

1 pound ground turkey or beef
1 15-ounce can tomato sauce, *divided*
½ cup crushed tortilla chips
¼ cup chopped onion
2 tablespoons diced green pepper
1 package taco seasoning mix

Preheat oven to 350 degrees. Combine all ingredients, reserving 1 cup of the tomato sauce. Spoon into a 9×5-inch loaf pan. Bake for 45–50 minutes. Heat remaining sauce and serve over loaf. Makes 4 servings.

Cherie Allen
CoMission, FL

Mexican Olé Dish

4–6 cups cooked rice
1–2 jars salsa
2–3 chicken breasts, cooked and cubed
1–1½ cups shredded cheddar cheese
chips
extra salsa

Preheat oven to 300 degrees. Combine the first 3 ingredients in a casserole dish. (Rice and chicken should still be warm from cooking.) Thoroughly stir in salsa to moisten all the rice and chicken. Top with cheese and bake until cheese is melted. Serve with chips and salsa on the side.

Laura Hudson
Finance, FL

One-Pot Chicken Couscous

¼ cup olive oil
2 pounds boneless, skinless chicken
 breasts, cut into 1-inch pieces
4 large carrots, peeled and sliced
2 medium onions, diced
1 large clove garlic, minced
2 14-ounce cans chicken broth
2 cups cooked couscous
2 teaspoons Tabasco
½ teaspoon salt
1 cup raisins or currants
1 cup slivered almonds, toasted
¼ cup fresh chopped parsley
 or mint

Heat oil in a 12-inch skillet over medium-high heat. Add chicken and cook until well browned on all sides. With a slotted spoon, remove chicken and place on a plate. Reduce heat to medium. In drippings remaining in skillet,

POULTRY

cook carrots and onion for 5 minutes. Add garlic; cook 2 minutes longer, stirring frequently. Add chicken broth, couscous, Tabasco, salt, and chicken. Bring to a boil, then reduce heat to low; cover and simmer 5 minutes. Stir in raisins or currants, almonds, and parsley or mint. Makes 8 servings.

Crystal Keller
Computer Services, FL

Oven-Fried Chicken

chicken breasts, halved
flour
Dixie Fry or Shake 'n Bake mix
salt and pepper
¼ cup melted margarine

paprika
1 can cream of mushroom soup
1 can cream of chicken soup
½–1 soup can of half & half or milk
rice

Preheat oven to 325 degrees. Combine equal amounts of flour and Dixie Fry, and season with salt and pepper. Dip washed chicken into flour mixture and place on a greased cookie sheet. Brush with melted margarine, then sprinkle with paprika. Bake for 1 hour. Combine and heat the remaining ingredients to make a quick gravy. Serve chicken with rice and gravy.

Vonette Bright
Co-founder, Campus Crusade for Christ
Executive Director, Women Today International, FL

Oven-Fried Dijon Chicken

½ cup mayonnaise
½ cup sour cream
2 tablespoons Dijon mustard

6 boneless, skinless chicken breasts
½ teaspoon garlic powder
1 cup bread crumbs

Preheat oven to 400 degrees. Combine mayonnaise, sour cream, and mustard. In a separate bowl, combine garlic powder and bread crumbs. Coat chicken with mayonnaise mixture, then roll in bread crumbs. Place in a 9×13-inch pan and bake for 45 minutes. *Variation:* Use low-fat mayonnaise and sour cream if desired.

Nancy Austin
JESUS Video Master Studio, FL

Oyako-Domburi
(Japanese)

½ pound boneless chicken
5 eggs, beaten
hot oil
1 cup water
3 mushrooms, finely chopped

3 tablespoons sugar
⅓ cup soy sauce
2 scallions or 1 onion, sliced
4 cups cooked rice

Cut chicken into small servings. Dust chicken pieces with flour, dip in beaten egg (reserve extra), and fry on both sides in hot oil until brown. Drain excess oil, then add remaining ingredients. Simmer 10 minutes. Add reserved beaten eggs to skillet and cover until eggs are set. Ladle over individual rice servings in bowls. Serves 4. In this "Parent-Child" dish, the chicken is the parent; the egg is the child.

Sarah Willis
International Ministry, FL

Parmesan Breaded Chicken

¼ cup seasoned bread crumbs
¼ cup grated Parmesan cheese
½ teaspoon oregano
¼ teaspoon rosemary

¼ teaspoon basil
¼ teaspoon pepper
4 skinless chicken breasts
½ cup buttermilk

Preheat oven to 350 degrees. Combine the first 6 ingredients in a shallow bowl. Dip chicken in buttermilk, and roll in bread crumb mixture. Coat a baking pan with cooking spray, and place chicken bone-side down in pan. Bake covered for 25 minutes, then uncover and bake for another 20 minutes or until done. Makes 4 servings.

Vonette Bright
Co-founder, Campus Crusade for Christ
Executive Director, Women Today International, FL

POULTRY

Just as my mouth can taste good food, so my mind
tastes truth when I hear it (Job 12:11).

Pat's Cassoulet

3½ cups dry navy beans
4½ cups cold water
6 medium onions
4 whole cloves
3 cups chicken broth
½ cups chopped celery with leaves
2 bay leaves
3 peppercorns
3 cloves garlic, crushed
1½ teaspoons thyme

1 teaspoon marjoram
1 teaspoon sage
½ teaspoon pepper
5 carrots, peeled and quartered, *divided*
4 pounds boneless chicken pieces
2 tablespoons butter
½ pound thick-sliced bacon, fried
1 16-ounce can tomatoes with liquid
1 pound Polish sausage, sliced
2 tablespoons parsley

Soak beans in cold water for two hours; do not drain. Stick cloves into one peeled onion, and chop the other five onions. To the beans, add chicken broth, celery, and spices, including the "cloved" onion, the chopped onions, and ¼ of the carrots. Bring to a boil and simmer for 1 hour. Add remaining carrots. Brown chicken pieces in butter. Add chicken, bacon, tomatoes, sausage, and parsley to bean and vegetable mixture. Bake covered at 350 degrees until meats are tender (about 1 hour). This is a recipe from my sister, Pat.

Sue McDaniel
International Ministry, FL

Peach-Broccoli Chicken

2 cups cubed cooked chicken
1 cup sour cream
¼ cup mayonnaise

¼ cup grated Parmesan cheese
1 bunch broccoli, cut up and cooked
4 canned peach halves, chopped

Heat all ingredients together in a saucepan. Serve alone or over noodles or baked potatoes.

Sus Schmitt
Computer Services, FL

In everything you do, put God first, and he will direct you and crown your efforts with success (Prov. 3:6).

Poppy Seed Chicken

4 whole cooked chicken breasts,
   cut into pieces
2 cans cream of chicken soup
2 cups sour cream

¾ cup margarine
2 sleeves Ritz or Townhouse crackers
   (55 crackers), crushed
2 tablespoons poppy seeds

Preheat oven to 350 degrees. Mix chicken with soup and sour cream; set aside. Melt margarine in a saucepan. Remove from heat and add crushed crackers and poppy seeds. Place ½ of cracker mixture in a 9×13-inch pan or casserole dish. Add chicken mixture and sprinkle with remaining cracker mixture. Bake uncovered 30–45 minutes or until heated through. Serve with rice and a green vegetable or salad. Serves 10–12. Recipe can easily be halved.

Karen Cunningham
Campus Ministry, PA

For you have been born again, not of perishable seed,
but of imperishable, through the living and
enduring word of God (1 Peter 1:23).

Poulet Yasa
(West African Chicken)

2 chicken bouillon cubes
1 medium onion, thinly sliced
4 teaspoons dry mustard
juice of 1 lemon
2 cloves garlic, crushed
1 teaspoon salt

¼ teaspoon pepper
½ cup water
1 chicken, cut up
thin slices lemon
rice

To make marinade, combine the first 8 ingredients. In a 9×13-inch glass baking dish, marinate chicken for 2 hours. When ready to bake, arrange thin slices of lemon on top. Add additional salt and pepper if desired. Bake covered at 350 degrees for 1 hour, basting occasionally. Serve over rice.

Nancy Austin
JESUS Video Master Studio, FL

POULTRY

Rebecca's Chicken

½ cup butter
1 frying chicken, cut into pieces
flour
seasonings
1 green pepper, sliced in strips
2 medium tomatoes, sliced in wedges
    (or 2 cups canned tomatoes)

1 medium onion, sliced in thin
    wedges
1 teaspoon rosemary
salt and pepper to taste
1 cup hot water or more
mozzarella cheese (optional)
rice

Melt butter in an electric skillet at about 325 degrees. Mix flour and your choice of seasonings; coat chicken pieces with seasoned flour and brown in skillet. Reduce heat to about 250 degrees, and add green pepper, tomatoes, onion, and seasonings. Add hot water; cover and cook for 2 hours. Serve over rice. *Optional:* Immediately before serving, top with sliced mozzarella and allow to melt.

Lori Burns
Staff & Ministry Opportunities, FL

Savory Crust Chicken Squares

1 3-ounce package cream cheese,
    softened
3 tablespoons melted margarine,
    divided
2 cups cooked chicken
¼ teaspoon salt
⅛ teaspoon pepper
2 tablespoons milk

1 tablespoon chopped chives or onion
1 tablespoon chopped pimiento
    (optional)
1 8-ounce can Pillsbury refrigerated
    quick crescent dinner rolls
¾ cup seasoned crushed croutons
    or bread crumbs

Preheat oven to 350 degrees. In a medium bowl, blend cream cheese and 2 tablespoons margarine until smooth. Add the next 6 ingredients and mix well. Separate dough into 4 rectangles; firmly press perforations to seal. Spoon ½ cup mixture into the center of each rectangle. Pull the 4 corners of dough to center of mixture. Twist slightly and seal edges. Brush the top with 1 tablespoon melted margarine and dip in bread crumbs (I usually just dip the top). Place on an ungreased cookie sheet and bake for 20–25 minutes or until golden brown. Serves 4. *Tip:* The filling can be made the night before, the squares assembled in the morning, and cooked that evening. It makes a great dinner for company since it is attractive and the work can be done ahead of time.

Linda Painton
Travel Department, FL

Sesame Chicken

8 boneless chicken breasts
1 can cream of chicken soup
1 cup sour cream

1½ cups crumbled Ritz crackers
½ cup butter, melted
1 tablespoon sesame or poppy seeds

Preheat oven to 350 degrees. Bake chicken for 20 minutes in a 9×13-inch pan. Drain fat if necessary. Mix soup and sour cream. In separate bowl, mix crackers, butter, and seeds. Pour soup mixture over chicken and top with cracker mixture. Bake an additional 45 minutes.

Cheryl Greenwald
Finance, FL

 If you belong to Christ, then you are Abraham's seed, and heirs according to the promise (Gal. 3:29).

Slow-Roasted Chicken

1½ teaspoons salt
1 teaspoon paprika
¼ teaspoon black pepper
¼ teaspoon white pepper
¼ teaspoon thyme

¼ teaspoon garlic
1½–2 tablespoons olive oil
roasting chicken
1 onion, cut up

Mix all ingredients together, except chicken and onion. Rub mixture onto chicken skin and into cavity of chicken. (If time allows, place chicken in plastic wrap and marinate in refrigerator overnight.) When ready to bake, put the onion into the cavity. Place chicken in a baking dish and bake at 250 degrees for 5 hours. *Variation:* Substitute lemon juice for the oil and add 1–1½ tablespoons brown sugar.

Cathy Hertzler
Computer Services, FL

POULTRY

Smoked Game Hens

grated rind of lemon and orange
½ cup plus 1 tablespoon soy sauce
½ cup oyster sauce
½ teaspoon ginger, chopped
3 cloves garlic, *divided*
1 tablespoon cilantro
¼ teaspoon black pepper
1 bay leaf
2 tablespoons honey

3 game hens, halved with backbones removed
2 teaspoons vegetable oil
¼ teaspoon hot pepper flakes
3 shallots, minced
1 teaspoon red wine vinegar
2 tablespoons brown sugar
1½ tablespoons water
2 teaspoons sesame oil

To make marinade, blend grated rind, soy sauce, oyster sauce, ginger, 2 cloves garlic, cilantro, pepper, bay leaf, and honey in a food processor. Marinate hens overnight. In a kettle, barbecue/smoke hens for 1 hour with vents closed. The last 15 minutes, baste several times with marinade. Mince the remaining garlic clove. For the sauce, place remaining ingredients except sesame oil in a saucepan. Bring to a boil and simmer for 5 minutes. Let cool, then add oil and brush hens with sauce. Serve hot or cold. These are excellent! The recipe is from my daughter, Robbyn.

Barbara Ball
ChurchLIFE, FL

Sour Cream Chicken Enchiladas

2 cups diced cooked chicken
1 cup diced onion
1 cup diced green pepper
5 tablespoons melted butter, *divided*
¼ cup flour
½ cup green chilies, diced

2½ cups chicken broth
1 cup sour cream
1½ cup shredded cheese, *divided*
½ cup black olives, sliced (optional)
flour tortillas

Preheat oven to 350 degrees. Mix chicken, onion, pepper, and 2 tablespoons butter. In a medium saucepan, cook the remaining 3 tablespoons butter, flour, chilies, and broth until thick. Add sour cream, ½ cup cheese, and olives to sauce. Mix ½ cup sauce with chicken. Dip tortillas in sauce and fill with 2–3 tablespoons chicken mixture. Roll up and place in a pan. Top tortillas with remaining sauce and 1 cup shredded cheese. Bake for 25 minutes.

Terry Morgan
Campus Ministry, Mexico

Stephanie's Chicken Casserole

2 cups cubed cooked chicken
2 cups cream of chicken or
    mushroom soup
¼ cup minced onion
1 can sliced water chestnuts
1¼ cups mayonnaise

1 teaspoon salt
2 tablespoons lemon juice
2 cups cooked flat noodles
1 box Pepperidge Farm Herb
    Dressing
¾ cup margarine, melted

Preheat oven to 400 degrees. Mix the first 8 ingredients and place in a baking dish. Mix dressing and margarine, and sprinkle over casserole. Bake for 15 minutes. If made ahead and frozen, omit dressing mixture until ready to cook.

Judy Kifer
Christian Leadership, Washington, D.C.

"My food," said Jesus, "is to do the will of him who sent me and to finish his work" (John 4:34).

Stuffed Chicken Breasts Italiano

4 large boneless, skinless chicken
    breasts
salt and pepper
8 ounces Ricotta cheese
2 tablespoons chopped ripe olives
2 tablespoons chopped Italian parsley

2 tablespoons chopped onion
¼ teaspoon garlic salt
1 can diced Italian tomatoes
1 cup shredded mozzarella cheese
12 ounces fettuccine, cooked
    and drained

Preheat oven to 350 degrees. Carefully slit a lengthwise "pocket" in each chicken breast, starting at the thick side and cutting approximately ¾ of the way through the width of each breast. Season the inside and outside of each breast with salt and pepper. Combine Ricotta cheese with olives, parsley, onion, and garlic salt. Place approximately ¼ cup filling into the "pocket" of each chicken breast. Arrange stuffed chicken breasts in a 9×13-inch baking pan and cover with tomatoes. Bake for 35–40 minutes or until chicken is done. Sprinkle mozzarella cheese on top, and return to oven for 2–3 minutes or until cheese melts. Serve over fettuccine.

Stephanie Ramirez
Student Venture, FL

POULTRY

Swiss and Chicken Casserole

4 cups chopped cooked chicken
2 cups sliced celery
2 cups croutons
2 cups (8 ounces) shredded
    Swiss cheese
½ cup milk

1 cup Miracle Whip or Miracle
    Whip Light
¼ cup chopped onion
1 teaspoon salt
⅛ teaspoon pepper
¼ cup chopped walnuts, toasted

Heat oven to 350 degrees. Mix all ingredients except walnuts. Spoon into a 2-quart casserole; sprinkle with walnuts. Bake 40 minutes or until thoroughly heated. Makes 6 servings.

Stacie Unruh
Headquarters Development Office, FL

Szechuan Chicken

1–2 tablespoons oil
½–1 pound boneless chicken
    breast, sliced
1 medium onion, chopped into
    chunks
¼–½ green bell pepper, chopped
1 clove garlic, minced
½ cup sliced carrots
1 cup broccoli florets

1 cup chicken broth or bouillon
½ teaspoon ground ginger
½ teaspoon red pepper flakes
2 tablespoons cornstarch
2 tablespoons soy sauce
2 tablespoons orange juice
¼ cup honey
cooked rice

Heat oil in a skillet or wok over high heat. Add chicken pieces and stir-fry for 3–4 minutes or until done; remove from pan. Stir-fry onion, bell pepper, garlic, carrots, and broccoli for 3–5 minutes or until crisp and tender. (If necessary, add a few tablespoons water to keep the vegetables from sticking.) Return chicken to skillet. Make a sauce by mixing broth, ginger, pepper flakes, cornstarch, soy sauce, orange juice, and honey. Pour over meat and vegetables. Stir constantly and bring to a boil. Cook for 2–3 minutes, until thickened. Serve over rice. Makes 4 servings. *Variation:* In place of chicken and chicken broth, substitute flank steak, thinly sliced against the grain, and beef broth or bouillon.

Cherie Allen
CoMission, FL

Taco Bake

1 pound ground turkey
½ cup chopped onions
½ cup chopped green peppers

½ package taco seasoning mix
1 16-ounce can diced tomatoes
1 box Jiffy cornbread mix

Preheat oven to 450 degrees. In a skillet, cook together ground turkey, onions, green peppers, and taco seasoning until meat is brown. Add diced tomatoes and simmer for 10 minutes; remove from heat. Prepare cornbread according to package directions; spread over the meat in the skillet. Bake for 20 minutes or until cornbread is brown.

Trena Jones
Finance, FL

Taco Casserole

1 pound ground turkey
2 packages taco seasoning mix
1 12-ounce can tomato sauce

1 24-ounce can Mexican-style
   stewed tomatoes
3 cups crushed tortilla chips

Preheat oven to 400 degrees. Brown ground turkey in a large skillet; drain. Stir in taco seasoning, tomato sauce, and tomatoes. Bring to a boil; reduce heat and simmer 10 minutes, stirring occasionally. Gently mix in tortilla chips. Spoon into a 9×13-inch dish. Bake for 15 minutes. Makes 8 1-cup servings.

Angela Rosa
Sunport Ministry Office, FL

Tasty Sweet and Sour Chicken

6 chicken breasts or 1 chicken,
   cut-up

1 package onion soup mix
1 can whole berry cranberry sauce

Preheat oven to 325 degrees. Place chicken in a 9×13-inch pan. Mix together dry soup mix and cranberry sauce. Pour over chicken. Cover and bake for 1 hour; uncover and bake for 30 more minutes.

Debbie McGoldrick
Student Venture, GA

POULTRY

Top-Notch Turkey Loaf

2 eggs, beaten
1 6-ounce can evaporated milk
⅓ cup chicken broth
1½ cups soft bread crumbs
   (about 2 slices bread)
¾ cup finely chopped celery
¾ teaspoon salt
pinch ground nutmeg

pinch dried rosemary leaves,
   crushed
pinch dried marjoram leaves,
   crushed
4 cups coarsely ground cooked
   turkey
Pimiento Sauce

Preheat oven to 350 degrees. Combine eggs, milk, broth, bread crumbs, celery, and seasonings. Add turkey and mix well. Line the bottom of a greased 8½×4½×2½-inch loaf pan with foil, then grease the foil. Pat in the turkey mixture. Bake for 45 minutes or until center of loaf is firm. Invert onto a serving platter and remove foil. Serve with *Pimiento Sauce*. Makes 6 servings.

Pimiento Sauce:

1 can cream of chicken soup
⅓ cup milk

2 tablespoons chopped pimientos

Heat together soup, milk, and pimientos.

Laurie Killingsworth
New Life Center, FL

Turkey Curry

4 slices bacon
¼ cup chopped celery
¼ cup chopped onion
1 clove garlic, chopped
2 tablespoons flour
1 cup milk
1 cup water
½ cup applesauce
3 tablespoons tomato paste

3 tablespoons curry powder
2 chicken bouillon cubes
3 cups cooked turkey
cooked rice
raisins
toasted coconut
diced green pepper
peanuts
chutney

Cook bacon until crisp; set aside. Drain all but 1 tablespoon drippings. Sauté celery, onion, and garlic in drippings. Blend in flour. Slowly stir in milk, then water, applesauce, tomato paste, curry powder, and bouillon cubes. Cook until thickened and bubbly. Stir in turkey and bacon; heat through. Serve over rice with small bowls of raisins, toasted coconut, green pepper, peanuts, and chutney as condiments.

Stephanie Reeves
Worldwide Challenge, FL

Turkey Marinara

1 pound turkey cutlets, ¼-inch thick	½ teaspoon pepper
1 tablespoon flour	½ teaspoon dried thyme
1 teaspoon olive oil	¼ teaspoon dried basil
½ cup diced onions	2 cups low-sodium tomato sauce
1 clove garlic, minced	

Dredge turkey in flour to coat lightly on both sides. Coat a non-stick pan with spray and place over medium-high heat. Add turkey in a single layer, and cook for 2 minutes per side or until lightly browned. Remove from pan and set aside. Add the oil, onions, garlic, pepper, thyme, and basil to pan. Cook over medium heat, stirring constantly for 5 minutes or until onions are tender. Add tomato sauce and turkey; cover and heat for 5 minutes. Makes 4 servings: 3.5 g fat per serving.

Critty Fairback
Christian Embassy, VA

Little children, let us stop just saying we love people; let us really love them, and show it by our actions (1 John 3:18).

Turkey Parmesan

2 tablespoons flour	¼ cup grated Parmesan cheese
¼ teaspoon ground black pepper	1 pound turkey breast cutlets,
½ cup fat-free egg substitute	¼-inch thick
¾ cup dry bread crumbs	1 cup tomato sauce, heated

Preheat oven to 400 degrees. Combine flour and pepper on a sheet of wax paper. Place the egg substitute in a shallow bowl. Combine the bread crumbs and Parmesan cheese in a flat dish. Dredge the turkey in flour mixture to coat both sides. Dip each cutlet into egg, then into the Parmesan mixture to coat well. Coat a large baking sheet with non-stick spray. Place cutlets on the sheet and bake for 5 minutes. Flip pieces and bake another 5 minutes or until cutlets are golden and crisp. Serve topped with tomato sauce. Makes 4 servings: 5.7 g fat per serving.

Critty Fairback
Christian Embassy, VA

Turkey Stroganoff

1 pound ground turkey	1 jar fat-free turkey gravy
1 medium onion, sliced	dash Worcestershire sauce
2 tablespoons garlic powder	1 package egg noodles, cooked
dash salt and pepper	

In a skillet, cook turkey with onion and seasonings until done. Drain and add gravy; bring to a low boil. Spoon noodles onto plates and top with turkey and gravy.

Kelly Hall
Corporate Human Resources, FL

Viva Chicken

1 can cream of chicken soup	½ cup milk
1 can cream of mushroom soup	12 corn tortillas
1 16-ounce can Hormel chili	4 cups cubed cooked chicken
without beans	¼ cup chopped onion
2 4-ounce cans Ortega green salsa	1½ cups shredded cheddar cheese

Preheat oven to 350 degrees. Mix soups, chili, salsa, and milk. Cut or tear up corn tortillas. Layer tortillas, soup mixture, chicken, onion, and cheese. If time allows, it's best if refrigerated overnight. Bake covered for 1 hour.

Becky Leppard
International Ministry, FL

White Chili

1 pound ground turkey
1 onion, chopped
crushed or dried garlic
2 tablespoons flour
3 cans chicken stock

½ can green chilies
¼ cup salsa
1 teaspoon cumin
2 cans white beans, undrained

Brown ground turkey with onion; add garlic. When browned, drain. Stir in flour, then add chicken stock, green chilies, salsa, and cumin. Let simmer for 30 minutes. Add beans; stir and bring to a boil.

Cathy Emmans
Contributions and Postal Services, FL

Yogurt-Broiled Chicken

½ cup plain low-fat yogurt
1 green onion, chopped
1 teaspoon dried crushed oregano
1 tablespoon olive or salad oil
1 tablespoon white wine vinegar

1 teaspoon salt
⅛ teaspoon pepper
4 large boneless, skinless chicken
   breasts

In a large bowl, mix yogurt, onion, oregano, oil, vinegar, salt, and pepper. Add chicken; toss well. Let stand 10–15 minutes, turning chicken occasionally. Place on a rack in a broiling pan. Broil at position closest to heat for 4 minutes. Turn chicken; brush with remaining yogurt mixture, and broil 5–6 minutes or until chicken is fork-tender and lightly browned. Makes 4 servings: 190 calories; 7 g fat; 74 mg cholesterol; 615 mg sodium.

Kristen Warren
Campus Ministry, FL

POULTRY

Don't be selfish; don't live to make a good impression on others.
Be humble, thinking of others as better than yourself (Phil. 2:3).

Veal

Osso Buco

¼ cup butter
6 tablespoons olive oil, *divided*
2 cups chopped onions
1 cup chopped carrots
1 cup chopped celery
4 large cloves garlic, chopped
12 center-cut pieces veal shank
   (1½-inches thick)
salt and pepper
flour
1 cup water

4 cups beef broth
1¾ cups canned chopped Italian-
   style tomatoes with juice
2 bay leaves
2 3-inch strips lemon peel (yellow
   part only)
1 teaspoon dried thyme
1 teaspoon dried basil
⅛ teaspoon nutmeg
Gremolata

Melt butter with 2 tablespoons olive oil in a heavy, large Dutch oven over medium-high heat. Add onions, carrots, celery, and garlic. Sauté until vegetables are tender and golden brown (about 15 minutes); remove from heat. Season veal with salt and pepper. Coat with flour and shake off excess. Heat 4 tablespoons oil in a large, heavy skillet over high heat. Working in batches, add veal to skillet and brown on all sides (about 4 minutes per side). Arrange veal on vegetables in Dutch oven. Pour off fat from skillet. Add water and boil 3 minutes, scraping up any browned bits. Add broth, tomatoes with juice, bay leaves, lemon peel, thyme, basil, and nutmeg to Dutch oven. Bring to a boil. Reduce heat; cover and simmer until veal is very tender (about 1 hour and 40 minutes). Spoon *Gremolata* over meat before serving. Makes 12 servings.

Gremolata:

½ cup chopped Italian parsley
2 tablespoons grated lemon peel

4 large cloves garlic, minced

Mix ingredients in a small bowl.

Barbara Ball
ChurchLIFE, FL

 Don't just think about your own affairs, but be interested in others, too, and in what they are doing (Phil. 2:4).

Veal à la Basil

8 ounces veal cutlets
½ teaspoon salt
⅛ teaspoon pepper
2 tablespoons lemon juice

½ teaspoon basil leaves
2 tablespoons vinegar
1 tablespoon parsley flakes

Season veal with salt and pepper. Brown meat in pan over high heat, using no fat. Add remaining ingredients. Cover; simmer over low heat until meat is tender, about 6 minutes.

Evelyn Bromberg
Crusade Family

Christ has given each of us special abilities—whatever he wants us to have out of his rich storehouse of gifts (Eph. 4:7).

Veal Parmigiana

1 egg
milk
4–6 veal chops (or thinly sliced veal)
bread crumbs
1 tablespoon oil

Napolitana Sauce
4 thin strips Monterey Jack cheese
1 tablespoon grated cheddar
1 tablespoon grated Parmesan

Preheat oven to 350 degrees. Beat egg with a little milk. Dredge chops through egg mixture and crumbs. Fry in oil 10 minutes on each side (or less if very thin). Place in a baking pan and bake for 10–15 minutes. Remove. Pour ¼ cup *Napolitana Sauce* over veal, then layer cheeses in order. Broil until cheese bubbles.

Napolitana Sauce:

1 can tomato sauce
pinch oregano
pinch basil

2 cloves garlic, minced
dash or two Worcestershire sauce

Mix ingredients and simmer for 10 minutes. *Tip:* Save leftover sauce for use on other dishes; it goes well with eggplant, too.

Joanne Austin
International Resource Ministry, FL

VEAL

Vegetarian

Black Bean Tortilla Casserole

2 cups chopped onion
1½ cups chopped green pepper
1 14½-ounce can diced tomatoes
¾ cup picante sauce
2 cloves garlic, minced
2 teaspoons ground cumin
2 15-ounce cans black beans, drained
12 6-inch corn tortillas

2 cups shredded low-fat Monterey
    Jack cheese (8 ounces)
2 medium tomatoes, chopped
2 cups shredded lettuce
sliced green onions
sliced pitted ripe olives
1 cup reduced-calorie or low-fat
    sour cream

Preheat oven to 350 degrees. In a large skillet, combine onion, green pepper, undrained tomatoes, picante sauce, garlic, and cumin. Bring to boiling; reduce heat, then simmer uncovered for 10 minutes. Stir in beans. Spread ⅓ of the bean mixture in a 9×13-inch baking dish. Top with ½ of the tortillas, overlapping as necessary, and ½ of the cheese. Add another ⅓ of the bean mixture, then remaining tortillas and bean mixture. Cover and bake for 30–35 minutes or until heated through. Sprinkle with remaining cheese. Let stand for 10 minutes. Garnish with tomatoes, lettuce, green onions, olives, and sour cream. Makes 8 servings.

Iris Cutshall
International Ministry, FL

Calzone

1½ teaspoons dry yeast
1 tablespoon honey
1 cup warm water
1½ teaspoons salt
2½–3 cups flour
1 pound fresh or 10 ounces
    frozen spinach
½ cup minced onions
2 cloves garlic, minced

1 pint ricotta or cottage cheese
2 cups (8–10 ounces) packed grated
    mozzarella cheese
½ cup freshly grated Parmesan
    cheese
2 tablespoons butter
dash nutmeg
salt and pepper to taste

Soften together the yeast, honey, and water. Add salt and flour; knead for 10–15 minutes. Cover and set in a warm place to rise until double in bulk (about 1 hour). While dough rises, steam spinach without adding water. When wilted, drain and place in a mixing bowl. Sauté onion and garlic in butter until soft. Combine spinach, onion mixture, cheeses, butter, and nutmeg; mix well. Salt and pepper to taste. When dough is doubled, punch it down. Divide into 6 sections and roll out in rounds ¼-inch thick. Fill with ½–¾ cups filling per round. Place filling on ½ of circle leaving a ½-inch rim. Moisten rim with water; fold over and crimp edges with a fork. Prick a couple of times for steam to escape. Bake on an oiled tray at 450 degrees for 15–20 minutes or until crisp and lightly browned. Brush each round with butter when removed from oven. Serves 6.

Helen Koopman
JESUS Film Project, FL

Corn, Cheese, and Chili Pie

3 large eggs
1 8½-ounce can cream corn
1 10-ounce package frozen corn, thawed and drained
½ cup butter or margarine, melted
½ cup yellow cornmeal
1 cup sour cream
4 ounces Monterey Jack cheese, shredded

4 ounces sharp cheddar cheese, shredded
1 4-ounce can diced green chilies
¼ teaspoon Worcestershire sauce
1 teaspoon salt
sour cream
chopped tomatoes
shredded cheese
chopped green onion

Preheat oven to 350 degrees. Grease a 9-inch pie plate or 8-inch square glass dish with shortening. Beat eggs in a large bowl. Add the next 10 ingredients and stir until blended. Pour mixture in the pie plate and bake 1 hour or until firm when pressed in the center. Let stand 10 minutes before cutting. Garnish each piece with a dollop of sour cream, tomatoes, cheese, and green onion.

Debbie McGoldrick
Student Venture, GA

VEGETARIAN

Charm is deceptive, and beauty is fleeting; but a woman who fears the Lord is to be praised (Prov. 31:30).

Cornmeal Quiche

½ cup cornmeal
¾ cup sifted flour
1½ teaspoons salt, *divided*
⅛ teaspoon pepper
⅓ cup shortening
3 tablespoons cold water

6 slices or 1¼ cups shredded cheese
2 cups whole kernel corn, well
   drained
5 eggs
¾ cup light cream or evaporated milk
¼ teaspoon cayenne pepper

Preheat oven to 425 degrees. To make crust, combine cornmeal, flour, ½ teaspoon salt, and pepper in a bowl. Cut in shortening. Sprinkle cold water over mixture while stirring with a fork. Stir gently until mixture forms a ball. Roll out on a lightly floured board. Fit loosely into a 9-inch pie plate; fold edge under and flute. For filling, lay cheese on the bottom, and cover with corn. Combine eggs, cream, 1 teaspoon salt, and cayenne in a bowl. Beat until well blended and pour over corn. Place on bottom rack of oven and bake for 15 minutes. Reduce temperature to 350 degrees and continue baking 25–30 minutes. Let stand 10 minutes before cutting. Serves 6.

Karen Horsey
International Ministry, FL

Creamy Cheese Enchiladas

6 flour tortillas
3 cups shredded Monterey Jack
   cheese, *divided*
6 tablespoons chopped green onion,
   divided

¼ cup butter
¼ cup flour
2 cups chicken broth
1 cup sour cream
1 4-ounce can chopped green chilies

Preheat oven to 350 degrees. Fill each tortilla with ½ cup cheese and 1 tablespoon green onion. Roll and place in an 8-inch square baking dish. Melt butter in a saucepan; add flour and stir to blend. Add chicken broth and cook until sauce is thickened. Remove from heat and add sour cream and chilies. Stir until smooth. Pour sauce over tortillas and bake for 25 minutes, or heat in microwave 5–6 minutes. *Variation:* Finely chopped chicken can be added to tortillas before rolling.

Cathy Emmans
Contributions and Postal Services, FL

Fresh Corn Casserole

2 cups fresh corn kernels (about
    5 ears), *divided*
½ cup butter, melted
2 eggs
1 cup sour cream

1 cup diced Monterey Jack cheese
½ cup cornmeal
1 4-ounce can diced green chilies
1½ teaspoons salt

Preheat oven to 350 degrees. Generously butter a 2-quart casserole. In a
blender or food processor, purée 1 cup corn with butter and eggs. Mix
remaining ingredients in a medium bowl. Add puréed mixture and blend
well. Pour into a greased pan and bake uncovered for 50–60 minutes. Serves
6. It's a delicious, informal supper when served hot. Also great cold for
lunch. May be prepared a day ahead and reheated before serving. It also
freezes beautifully; defrost before reheating.

Debra Brady
Staff & Ministry Opportunities, FL

Fresh Corn Tamales

4 ears corn in husks
water
2 tablespoons finely chopped garlic
½ cup finely chopped onion
¼ cup chopped red pepper
¼ cup chopped yellow pepper
2 cups Masa Harina (Mexican flour)

¾ teaspoon baking powder
1 teaspoon chili powder
½ teaspoon ground cumin
1 teaspoon oregano, crushed
½ cup finely chopped cilantro
2 cups chicken broth or more
salsa (optional)

Carefully remove corn husks from cobs, and discard silk. Sprinkle husks with
water and place in a plastic bag. Remove kernels from cobs; sauté a little
then set aside. Spray a heavy-bottomed saucepan with cooking spray and
heat until very hot. Add garlic, onion, and peppers; reduce heat and sauté
until onions are golden. Stir in corn and continue to cook for 2 minutes,
adding small amounts of water if necessary to keep vegetables from sticking.
Set aside to cool. In a large bowl, mix Masa, baking powder, chili powder,
cumin, oregano, and cilantro. Add chicken broth, slowly mixing with a
wooden spoon until mixture holds together like a soft dough. Stir in corn
mixture. Spread onto each reserved corn husk, smoothing out to edges
(covering the entire husk). Tie each end with a strip of corn husk. Cook in a
steamer for approximately 1 hour. Remove carefully and cool for 10 minutes.

VEGETARIAN

Serve with salsa if desired. Goes well with seared swordfish (cook 10 minutes per inch) and a green salad. Makes approximately 20 tamales: 99 calories (21% from fat); 2 g fat; 132 mg sodium.

Lois Mackey
CoMission, CA

Fresh Veggies and Noodles

½ pound broccoli florets and stalks
1 cup sliced cauliflower florets
½ cup fennel, cut into 2×½-inch
    sticks (optional)
1 medium zucchini or yellow squash,
    sliced ½-inch thick
½ cup chopped onion
3 tablespoons butter

1 teaspoon light cream
1 teaspoon crushed basil
dash ground nutmeg
½ teaspoon salt
⅛ teaspoon pepper
½ cup (2 ounces) grated Gruyère
    or Parmesan cheese
8 ounces pasta, cooked

Cut off broccoli florets and set aside. Cut stalks crosswise into ½-inch slices. In a large saucepan, cook broccoli stalks, cauliflower, and fennel in a small amount of boiling, salted water for 5 minutes. Add broccoli florets and squash; return to a boil. Reduce heat and simmer until tender and crisp (about 5 minutes). Drain and set aside. In a medium saucepan, cook onion in 1 tablespoon butter until tender but not brown. Stir in cream, basil, nutmeg, salt, and pepper. Boil gently until slightly thickened (about 4 minutes). Stir about ½ cup hot mixture into cheese. Return to pan and heat until cheese is melted. Stir in vegetables. Toss cooked pasta with 2 tablespoons butter. Pour vegetable sauce over pasta and toss until coated. Serve with additional cheese if desired.

Helen Koopman
JESUS Film Project, FL

We try to live in such a way that no one will ever be offended or kept back from finding the Lord by the way we act, so that no one can find fault with us and blame it on the Lord (2 Cor. 6:3).

Green Chili Burritos

4 cups sliced mushrooms
2 tablespoons butter
3 10-ounce packages frozen chopped spinach, thawed, drained, and squeezed dry
4 medium flour tortillas
5 7-ounce cans diced mild green chilies

2 7-ounce cans diced hot green chilies
1 clove garlic, minced
3 cups water
salt to taste
½ cup vegetable oil
½ cup flour
1 cup grated Monterey Jack cheese

Sauté mushrooms in butter until barely cooked. Add spinach and cook until mixture is hot. Spread each tortilla evenly with the mushroom/spinach mixture. Roll the tortillas tightly and place them seam-side down in a buttered, shallow baking dish. Place the mild and hot chilies and their liquid in a saucepan with the garlic, water, and salt. Bring to a boil, then remove from heat. In a separate small pan, heat the oil, then slowly add flour, stirring to make a paste. Reheat the chili mixture until it simmers and slowly add the flour paste, stirring constantly until it thickens. If it's too thick, add more water. Spread sauce over the top of the tortillas and sprinkle with grated cheese. Bake for about 5 minutes until cheese has melted. These are also excellent for brunch.

Barbara Ball
ChurchLIFE, FL

Kara's Veggie Stir-Fry
(With Lentils and Fettucine)

lentils, cooked
fettuccine, cooked
2 tablespoons olive oil
½ onion, chopped
1 large carrot, sliced
2 medium zucchini, sliced

fresh mushrooms, sliced
salt and pepper to taste
basil to taste
beau monde to taste
1 can stewed tomatoes

Stir-fry the onion and carrot in olive oil. As they begin to get tender, add zucchini and mushrooms. Add seasonings to taste while stir-frying. When zucchini and mushrooms begin to get tender, add stewed tomatoes. Heat through; add more seasonings if desired. Immediately serve the veggies over the cooked fettucine, with the lentils alongside. Or, add the cooked lentils to the veggies after adding the stewed tomatoes, and serve over fettucine. Serves 4.

Joanne Austin
International Ministry, FL

Mediterranean Quiche

1 9-inch uncooked pie shell
¼ cup chopped onion
2 cups eggplant, cubed
¼ cup oil
2 medium tomatoes, diced
2 tablespoons chopped parsley

½ teaspoon basil
¾ cup milk
4 eggs
3 tablespoons grated Parmesan
   cheese
¾ teaspoon salt

Preheat oven to 400 degrees. Bake the pie shell until slightly browned. Sauté onion and eggplant in oil until just tender. Add tomatoes, parsley, and basil, and cook an additional 5 minutes. Spoon into pie shell. Using a blender or whisk, blend together milk, eggs, Parmesan, and salt. Pour over vegetable mixture in shell and bake for 30 minutes.

Sue Imbrock
International Ministry, Africa

Mixed Roasted Peppers Vinaigrette

1 medium green bell pepper
   (about 6 ounces)
1 medium red bell pepper
1 medium yellow bell pepper
1 medium orange bell pepper
2 teaspoons plus 2 tablespoons
   balsamic vinegar, or a good-
   quality red wine vinegar, *divided*

4 tablespoons olive oil, *divided*
2 medium cloves garlic,
   finely chopped
1 tablespoon finely shredded
   fresh basil
1 tablespoon finely chopped fresh
   Italian parsley

You may or may not choose to use different colored peppers. To roast peppers, slice them in half and broil until black. Place immediately into a closed

Tupperware container and let cool. Peel off skin. Mix 2 teaspoons balsamic vinegar and 2 tablespoons olive oil, and marinate peppers. Save marinade. Slice marinated peppers ¼–½ inch wide. In a large skillet, heat 2 tablespoons olive oil with garlic over moderate heat. When the garlic sizzles, add the pepper strips and the marinade. As soon as the liquid sizzles, stir in 2 tablespoons vinegar. Stir in basil and parsley, and spoon the sauce over cooked pasta. Excellent!

Veronica Ventrice
JusticeLINC, WI

Nancy Norwood's Italian Zucchini Crescent Pie

2 cups coarsely chopped zucchini	¼ teaspoon sweet basil
2 cups coarsely chopped onion	2 eggs, well beaten
½ cup margarine	8 ounces Muenster or mozzarella
½ cup chopped parsley	cheese, shredded
¼ teaspoon oregano	1 pie crust
½ teaspoon salt	2 teaspoons Dijon or prepared
½ teaspoon pepper	mustard

Preheat oven to 375 degrees. Cook zucchini and onion in margarine until tender (about 10 minutes). Stir in parsley and seasonings. In a large bowl, blend eggs and cheese; add vegetable mixture. Spread mustard over pie crust, then distribute cheese mixture evenly into crust. Bake for 18–20 minutes or until knife comes out clean. If crust becomes too brown, cover with foil during the last 10 minutes of baking.

Judy Kifer
Christian Leadership Ministries, Washington, D.C.

VEGETARIAN

"When you give a banquet, invite the poor, the crippled, the lame, the blind, and you will be blessed. Although they cannot repay you, you will be repaid at the resurrection of the righteous"
(Luke 14:13,14).

Roasted Pepper and Mozzarella Sandwich

3 medium red peppers
⅓ cup olive oil
2 cups packed basil or watercress
    leaves

½ teaspoon salt
1 12-ounce loaf French bread
1 pound mozzarella cheese, cut into
    ¼-inch slices

Cut each pepper in half lengthwise; discard stem and seeds. Arrange peppers cut-side down in a jelly roll pan. Place pan in broiler at closest position to heat, and broil peppers for 15 minutes or until charred and blistered. Turn peppers and broil 5 minutes longer. Place peppers in a clean brown bag; fold top of bag to seal and let stand at room temperature for 15 minutes. (Peppers will steam, which will make them easier to peel.) Remove peppers from bag; peel off skin and cut each into thirds lengthwise. In a blender or food processor, blend olive oil, basil, and salt until almost smooth. Cut French bread in half horizontally. Remove and discard some soft bread from each half. Evenly spread basil mixture on the cut side of both halves. Arrange mozzarella slices on the bottom half of loaf; top with roasted peppers. Replace top half of loaf. Makes 16 servings: 175 calories; 7 g protein; 12 g carbohydrates; 11 g fat (4 g saturated); 22 mg cholesterol; 200 mg sodium.

Barbara Ball
ChurchLIFE, FL

Rolled Tortillas With Sour Cream

6 corn tortillas
butter or margarine
½ pound Monterey Jack cheese, cubed
2 green chilies, peeled and cut in strips

1½ cups tomato purée
salt and pepper
1 pint sour cream

Preheat oven to 350 degrees. Fry tortillas in butter or margarine. Place cheese cubes, chili strips, and ¼ cup of tomato purée on each tortilla. Sprinkle with salt and pepper. Roll and place in a shallow baking dish. Cover with sour cream and bake for 30 minutes. Serves 6.

Barbara Ball
ChurchLIFE, FL

Skillet Rice Dinner

½ cup chopped scallions
1 cup chopped celery
10 mushrooms, sliced
½ large green pepper, chopped
¼ cup butter
3 cups cooked brown rice

½ cup raw sunflower seeds
½ cup sliced almonds
2 teaspoons coriander (optional)
½ pound cheddar cheese, grated
2 ripe tomatoes, cut into wedges

Sauté scallions, celery, mushrooms, and pepper in butter. Add rice, sunflower seeds, almonds, and coriander. Top with cheese and tomatoes. Heat until cheese is melted. *Variation:* Cooked macaroni can be used instead of rice.

Sus Schmitt
Computer Services, FL

The people of Israel called the bread manna. It was white like coriander seed and tasted like wafers made with honey (Exodus 16:31).

Spinach and Brown Rice Quiche

3 eggs, *divided*
1½ cups hot cooked brown rice
3 ounces sharp cheddar cheese, grated
¾ cup sliced mushrooms

2 10-ounce packages frozen chopped
   spinach, cooked and well drained
6 tablespoons skim milk
⅛ teaspoon pepper

Preheat oven to 375 degrees. To form the crust, beat 1 egg, rice, and half the cheese. Press mixture into pie pan. Combine remaining ingredients and mix well. Pour over crust and bake for 30 minutes. Cool 15 minutes before serving.

Doris Maugle
Contributions and Postal Services, FL

VEGETARIAN

Vidalia Onion Pie

3 cups sliced Vidalia onions   ½ cup milk
3 tablespoons butter   3 tablespoons flour
1 pie crust   1 teaspoon salt
1½ cups sour cream   2 eggs

Preheat oven to 350 degrees. Sauté onions in butter and place in pie crust. Mix remaining ingredients and pour over onions. Bake for 20–30 minutes or until knife comes out clean.

Debbie McGoldrick
Student Venture, GA

Zucchini Skillet Supper

4 cups zucchini, thinly sliced   2 cups canned tomatoes with juice
1 onion, sliced   salt and pepper to taste
¾ cup canned sliced mushrooms,   oregano to taste
   drained (optional)   grated Parmesan cheese

Sauté zucchini and onion in a skillet with a small amount of fat. Add mushrooms, tomatoes with juice, and seasonings. Simmer just until heated through. Serve in soup bowls and sprinkle with Parmesan cheese. Serves 4–5. *Variations:* Use fresh sliced mushrooms and sauté with zucchini; use fresh tomatoes in season and add tomato juice for liquid; add cubed cooked chicken, beef, ham, or browned ground beef and serve over noodles or rice.

Karen Horsey
International Ministry, FL

As the Scripture says, "Anyone who trusts in him will never be put to shame" (Rom. 10:11).

Vegetables

Baked Corn Casserole

2 eggs, slightly beaten
1 cup sour cream
½ cup margarine, melted
1 16-ounce can cream-style corn

1 16-ounce can whole kernel
   corn, drained
1 package corn muffin mix
1 tablespoon sugar

Preheat oven to 350 degrees. Combine all ingredients in a bowl and mix well. Spoon into a greased 9×13-inch baking dish. Bake for 35–40 minutes or until golden brown.

Grace Swartz/Laura Callaway
NewLife Resources, GA/Finance, FL

Broccoli and Corn Bake

1 10-ounce package frozen
   chopped broccoli, cooked
2 eggs, beaten
1 16-ounce can cream-style corn

2 cups herb-seasoned stuffing mix
¼ cup finely chopped onion
3 tablespoons margarine, melted
salt and pepper to taste

Preheat oven to 350 degrees. Combine all ingredients and mix well. Spoon into a 1½-quart baking dish. Bake for 40 minutes. Serves 8.

Grace Swartz
NewLife Resources, GA

Broccoli Casserole

¼ cup finely chopped onion
6 tablespoons butter, *divided*
2 tablespoons flour
1 cup water
¾ cup grated Parmesan cheese

salt and pepper to taste
2 packages frozen broccoli,
   thawed and drained
3 eggs, well beaten
½ cup cracker crumbs

279

VEGETABLES

Preheat oven to 325 degrees. Sauté onion in 4 tablespoons butter. Stir in flour, then add water. Cook slowly over low heat until mixture thickens and comes to a boil. Blend in cheese. Season with salt and pepper. Combine sauce and broccoli. Add eggs and gently blend. Pour into a greased casserole dish. Cover with crumbs and dot with remaining butter. Bake for 45 minutes. Serves 8.

Cinny Hicks
Crusade Family

My brothers, as believers in our glorious Lord Jesus Christ, don't show favoritism (James 2:1).

Broccoli Onion

2 10-ounce packages frozen cut
  broccoli
2 cups frozen whole small onions or
  2 cans York country onions
4 tablespoons butter or margarine,
  divided
2 tablespoons flour

¼ teaspoon salt
dash pepper
1 cup milk
1 3-ounce package cream cheese
1 cup soft bread crumbs
¼ cup grated Parmesan cheese

Preheat oven to 350 degrees. Cook onions, if frozen, in boiling salted water until tender (about 10 minutes); drain. In a saucepan, melt 2 tablespoons butter; blend in flour, salt, and pepper. Add milk all at once. Cook and stir until thick and bubbly. Reduce heat; blend in cream cheese until smooth. Stir in broccoli and onions, and place in a 1½-quart casserole. Bake for 20 minutes. While baking, melt remaining butter; toss with bread crumbs and Parmesan cheese. Sprinkle crumbs over casserole and bake for another 15–20 minutes.

Marlyse Milburn
Milburn Projects, CA

Broccoli Rice Casserole

1 cup chopped celery
1 onion, chopped
½ cup margarine
2 10-ounce packages frozen
    chopped broccoli

1 cup uncooked Minute Rice
1 8-ounce jar Cheez Whiz
1 can cream of chicken soup
1 can cream of mushroom soup
1 small can sliced mushrooms

Preheat oven to 350 degrees. Sauté onion and celery in margarine. Cook broccoli according to package directions; drain. Combine all ingredients and place in a large casserole dish. Bake for 1 hour.

Lynn Copeland
NewLife Publications, OK

Buttered Split Peas

1 cup split peas
2½ cups chicken broth
1 cup sliced green onions

¼ tablespoon thyme
¾ teaspoon salt
2 tablespoons butter

Combine the first 4 ingredients in a saucepan and bring to a boil. Simmer for 30 minutes. Add salt and butter. Serves 4–6. Goes well with cornbread or muffins.

René Brygger
JusticeLINC, WI

Cabbage Supreme

1 medium head green cabbage,
    cored and cut into 8 wedges
¼ cup chopped sweet onion
¼ cup chopped sweet red or
    green pepper
3 tablespoons butter, *divided*

1 tablespoon cornstarch
1 cup skim milk
salt to taste
dash red or black pepper
⅓ cup plain yogurt
¼ cup shredded cheddar cheese

In a large skillet, cook cabbage in a small amount of boiling, lightly salted water for 3 minutes. Cover and cook 10–12 minutes longer until tender. Meanwhile, sauté onion and pepper in 2 tablespoons butter until tender.

Add cornstarch and mix well. Stir in skim milk, salt, and pepper. Cook, stirring until thick and bubbly, then cook 1–2 minutes more. Stir in yogurt, 1 tablespoon butter, and cheese until cheese melts. Pour over drained cabbage and serve.

Gayle Anne VanFulpen
NewLife Publications, FL

Cajun Stuffed Tomatoes

4 large fully ripe tomatoes (about   ½ cup chopped green pepper
    2 pounds), at room temperature   ½ cup chopped celery
1 pound andouille or sweet sausage,   2 teaspoons minced garlic
    casing removed and coarsely   2 teaspoons crushed thyme
    chopped (or shrimp or other meat)   2 eggs, slightly beaten

Preheat oven to 350 degrees. Cut off the stem end of each tomato. Scoop out pulp (save for stews or soups), leaving ¼-inch-thick shells. Turn tomatoes upside down to drain; set aside. Heat a large skillet; add sausage. Cook and stir until sausage is browned (about 3 minutes). Add green pepper, celery, garlic, and thyme. Cook and stir until vegetables are tender (about 2 minutes). Remove from heat and stir in eggs. Spoon meat mixture into tomato shells. Place in a shallow baking pan with ½ inch of water. Cover and bake until tomatoes are tender (20–25 minutes). Makes 4 servings.

Lois Mackey
CoMission, CA

Can Do Cabbage

4½ cups shredded cabbage   ⅓ cup red wine vinegar
    (can mix red and green)   ⅓ cup water
2 tablespoons light brown sugar   ½ teaspoon ground nutmeg
3 medium Granny Smith's apples,   ½ teaspoon cinnamon
    unpared and chopped

Warm all ingredients except nutmeg and cinnamon over medium heat in a large pan or wok. Cover and simmer until cabbage becomes slightly tender but is still snappy (about 12–14 minutes). Combine nutmeg and cinnamon and stir in. A side of fat-free yogurt (such as Dannon Light Vanilla or Lemon) is a nice complement, especially partially frozen.

Gayle Anne VanFulpen
NewLife Publications, FL

Cauliflower Au Gratin

1 medium head cauliflower	1 cup grated sharp cheddar cheese, *divided*
salt and pepper to taste	
1 cup sour cream, *divided*	1 tablespoon toasted sesame seeds

Preheat oven to 350 degrees. Break cauliflower into florets. Cook uncovered in a small amount of boiling salted water until tender (10–15 minutes); drain well. Place ½ of the florets in a 1-quart casserole and season with salt and pepper. Spread with ½ cup sour cream and ½ cup cheese. Top with ½ of the sesame seeds. Repeat layers. Bake uncovered until cheese melts and sour cream is heated through (about 10 minutes). Serves 4.

Lisa Master
Worldwide Challenge, FL

Company Carrots

1 cup orange juice	1 teaspoon cornstarch
¼ cup sugar	1 pound tiny carrots

Combine orange juice, sugar, and cornstarch in a saucepan. Bring to a boil, then add carrots. Bring to a boil again. Reduce heat and simmer until carrots are tender (15–20 minutes). Serve warm or cold.

Georgia Crawley
JESUS Film Project, AL

In everything you do, put God first, and he will direct you and crown your efforts with success (Prov. 3:6).

Corn Pudding

2 tablespoons butter or margarine   1 tablespoon sugar
2 tablespoons flour   1 teaspoon salt
1 cup milk   ¼ teaspoon pepper
3 cups frozen or canned corn   2 eggs, well beaten

Preheat oven to 350 degrees. Melt butter, then stir in flour. Add milk gradually and bring to a boil, stirring constantly. Add corn, sugar, salt, and pepper. Heat well. Remove from heat and stir in eggs. Pour into a greased baking dish and bake for 25 minutes.

Judy Douglass
U.S. Staff Women, FL

Corn With Cream Cheese

¼ cup milk   dash pepper
1 3-ounce package light cream cheese   2 cans whole kernel corn or
1 tablespoon butter   16 ounces frozen or fresh corn
½ teaspoon salt

Combine milk, cream cheese, butter, salt, and pepper in a saucepan. Cook on low heat, stirring constantly until cheese melts and is blended. Thaw corn if frozen. Add corn and heat. Serves 6.

René Brygger
JusticeLINC, WI

Cream-Style Corn Pudding

2 cans Del Monte cream-style corn   2 heaping tablespoons flour
4 eggs, beaten   dash cinnamon
½ cup butter, melted   dash nutmeg
½ cup sugar

Preheat oven to 350 degrees. Mix all ingredients except cinnamon and nutmeg. Sprinkle those 2 ingredients on top. Bake for approximately 1 hour or until puffed up in the center.

Beverly Estorge
Campus Ministry, FL

Crescent Zucchini

1 8-ounce can refrigerated
   crescent rolls
2 teaspoons mustard
4 cups thinly sliced zucchini
1 cup chopped onion
butter
2 tablespoons parsley flakes

½ teaspoon salt
½ teaspoon pepper
¼ teaspoon garlic powder
½ cup mayonnaise
¼ teaspoon oregano
2 eggs, beaten
8 ounces mozzarella cheese, shredded

Preheat oven to 375 degrees. Place crescent rolls in the bottom of an 8×10-inch baking dish. Spread mustard on the rolls. Sauté zucchini and onion in butter until tender but crisp. Layer over the rolls. Combine the remaining ingredients and pour over the zucchini. Bake for 20 minutes.

Rachael Garland
Corporate Human Resources, FL

Crunch and Munch Onion Hoops

4 large Vidalia onions
2 cups plus 3 tablespoons skim
   milk, *divided*
2 cups whole wheat flour

3 egg whites
6 tablespoons Progresso bread
   crumbs or dried whole wheat
   bread crumbs

Preheat oven to 375 degrees. Cut onions into ¼-inch slices and separate "hoops." Place remaining ingredients in 4 bowls: 2 cups skim milk; whole wheat flour; egg whites beaten with 3 tablespoons skim milk; and bread crumbs. Dip hoops into bowls in the order given. Place on a non-stick baking sheet and bake for approximately 15 minutes. These are great for you.

Gayle Anne VanFulpen
NewLife Publications, FL

Curried Potatoes

1 pound new potatoes
1 small sweet onion, sliced
1 clove garlic, minced
¼–½ teaspoon curry powder
2 tablespoons butter

1 tablespoon snipped parsley
1 teaspoon lemon juice
¼ teaspoon salt
dash ground red pepper

In a covered saucepan, boil unpeeled potatoes and sliced onions for 15 minutes or until potatoes are tender; drain. Meanwhile, sauté garlic and curry powder in butter for about 1 minute. Stir in parsley, lemon juice, salt, and red pepper. Gently toss into potatoes and onions.

Gayle Anne VanFulpen
NewLife Publications, FL

Dutch Green Beans

1 pound bacon
1 medium onion, chopped
½ cup sugar
½ cup vinegar

¼ cup mustard
4 cans Blue Lake whole green beans,
    drained

Cook bacon; drain all but 2 tablespoons grease. Crumble bacon and set aside. Sauté onion in bacon grease. Add sugar, vinegar, mustard, and beans. Simmer for 2 hours, then add bacon.

Juli Emory
Military Ministry, VA

English Broccoli Walnut

2 boxes frozen broccoli
    (or equivalent fresh broccoli)
14 tablespoons butter, *divided*
¼ cup flour
4 chicken bouillon cubes

2 cups milk
⅔ cup water
2 cups Pepperidge Farm dressing
⅔ cup chopped walnuts

Preheat oven to 350 degrees. Cook broccoli as directed on package. Place into a 2½-quart baking dish. Melt 8 tablespoons butter in a frying pan;

blend in flour and bouillon cubes. Gradually add milk, stirring constantly.
Cook until thick and smooth. Pour over broccoli. To make topping, heat
6 tablespoons butter in water until melted. Pour over stuffing; mix together.
Add nuts and toss. Pour over broccoli and bake 30 minutes. Serves 8.

Laurie Horvath
National Ministry, MI

Gala Glazers

1 bag carrots, peeled, thinly sliced
2 tablespoons butter

2 tablespoons brown sugar
½ cup water

Place all ingredients in a frying pan and stir together. Cover and cook slowly,
stirring occasionally, until carrots are tender.

Gayle Anne VanFulpen
NewLife Publications, FL

All of you serve each other with humble spirits, for God gives
special blessings to those who are humble, but sets himself
against those who are proud (1 Peter 5:5).

Green Bean Bundles

1 16-ounce can whole green beans,
   drained
2 slices bacon, halved

¼ cup margarine, melted
1 clove garlic, pressed
½ cup firmly packed brown sugar

Preheat oven to 350 degrees. Divide beans into 4 portions. Wrap each portion with ½ strip bacon; secure with a toothpick, forming 4 bundles. Place in a baking dish. Combine remaining ingredients; blend well and pour over beans. Bake for 35 minutes. Serves 4.

Juli Emory
Military Ministry, VA

Herbed Mashed Potatoes

6 medium potatoes, peeled and cooked ½ teaspoon garlic salt
milk   1 tablespoon dill weed
butter   1 tablespoon chives (fresh, if possible)

Mash potatoes with milk and butter. Add herbs to taste.

Alison Druckemiller
Keynote Communications, IN

Hot Carrots

2 pounds carrots, sliced   ½ cup margarine
1 cup sugar   1 can tomato soup
¼ cup vinegar   1 bell pepper, sliced
1 teaspoon mustard   1 onion, sliced

Cook carrots and drain. Combine sugar, vinegar, mustard, margarine, and
soup with carrots. Add bell pepper and onion. Refrigerate overnight. Serve
hot or cold.

Doris Maugle
Contributions and Postal Services, FL

*If it is possible, as far as it depends on you,
live at peace with everyone (Rom. 12:18).*

Italian Green Beans Amandine

3 tablespoons butter   2 9-ounce packages frozen Italian
¼ cup blanched slivered almonds   green beans
½ teaspoon seasoned salt

Melt butter in a skillet over low heat. Add almonds and stir until browned.
Add frozen beans and salt; cover and cook for 5 minutes, separating beans
with a fork as soon as possible. Heat and stir uncovered for 8–10 minutes or
until water is evaporated and beans are tender and crisp.

Lois Mackey
CoMission, CA

Laura's Sweet Potato Souffle

4 cups cooked mashed sweet potatoes
    or 2 29-ounce cans, well drained
1 cup sugar
½ teaspoon salt
2 eggs, slightly beaten

¼ cup margarine, melted
½ cup milk
2 teaspoons vanilla
Topping

Preheat oven to 350 degrees. In a large mixing bowl, blend all ingredients except *Topping* on low speed with mixer. Whip at high speed until smooth. Pour into a greased 2-quart casserole. Prepare *Topping* and spread over sweet potato mixture. Bake uncovered for 40 minutes. Can be mixed ahead and refrigerated before baking; add 20–30 minutes to cooking time.

Topping:

¼ cup margarine, melted
1 cup chopped pecans
⅓ cup flour

1 cup dark brown sugar
½ cup flaked coconut (optional)

Stir ingredients together until well blended.

Laura Staudt
Women Today International, FL

Marty's Carrot Souffle

1 pound carrots, cooked and chopped
⅓ cup sugar
½ cup butter

3 tablespoons flour
3 eggs
2½ tablespoons vanilla

Preheat oven to 350 degrees. Mix all ingredients in a blender until well mixed. Bake for 45 minutes. *Variation:* Serve as a great dessert by using ¾ cup sugar and topping with a dab of whipped cream.

Peggy Hawkins
JESUS Video Project, FL

The whole Law can be summed up in this one command:
"Love others as you love yourself" (Gal. 5:14).

Mashed Potatoes With Leeks

2 pounds baking potatoes
3 leeks
½ cup milk

¼ cup unsalted butter, softened
freshly ground black pepper
to taste

Prick potatoes with a fork. Place in oven and cook for 1 hour or until fork-tender. Trim and discard root ends and all but 1 inch of green tops on leeks. Cut each in half lengthwise, and rinse under running water to remove sand. Cut into ½-inch slices; place in a saucepan with enough lightly salted water to cover. Simmer until tender (about 15 minutes); drain. Peel the potatoes and add to leeks. Mash together with a wooden spoon or masher until fairly smooth. Add milk and butter, and beat with a fork or wire whisk until light and fluffy. (Do not try to remove all lumps.) Season with pepper to taste. Makes 6 servings.

Barbara Ball
ChurchLIFE, FL

Minted Peas

20 ounces frozen peas or 2 pounds
    fresh peas, shelled

½ teaspoon dried mint
½ teaspoon dried grated lemon rind

Place peas in a saucepan with a little water. Add mint and lemon rind. Cover and cook until peas are tender; drain. Makes 4 servings.

Lisa Master
Worldwide Challenge, FL

Momma Green's Vegetable Dish

2 packages frozen chopped broccoli
2 packages frozen chopped spinach
1 cup sour cream

1 package dry onion soup mix
grated cheddar cheese or croutons

Preheat oven to 350 degrees. Heat broccoli and spinach until thawed, then drain. In a separate bowl, combine sour cream and soup mix. Add vegetables and place in a greased casserole. Sprinkle cheddar cheese and/or croutons on top. Bake for 20–30 minutes.

Debbie McGoldrick
Student Venture, GA

Oven-Steamed Asparagus

2 pounds asparagus, trimmed
¼ cup butter, cut up
½ teaspoon salt

½ teaspoon pepper
1 tablespoon water

Preheat oven to 350 degrees. In a 9×13-inch glass baking dish, arrange asparagus evenly in a single layer. Add remaining ingredients and cover lightly with foil. Bake 15 minutes for thin stalks and 25–30 minutes for medium stalks. Serves 8–10.

Barbara Ball
ChurchLIFE, FL

Potato Casserole

6 large or 8–10 small potatoes,
    with or without skin
1 pint sour cream
1 can cream of mushroom soup
1 small onion, minced

1½ cups shredded cheddar cheese
salt and pepper to taste
1 cup crushed corn flakes
2 tablespoons butter, melted

Preheat oven to 350 degrees. Boil potatoes until tender. While potatoes are cooking, combine all other ingredients except corn flakes and butter. Cool potatoes, then grate and combine with soup mixture. Place in an oblong baking dish. Mix corn flakes with butter and sprinkle over casserole. Bake for 45 minutes. May be prepared a day ahead and refrigerated until ready to bake. *Variation:* Barbara Nigh (Contributions and Postal Services, FL) uses 32 ounces Southern-style frozen hash browns and 28 ounces O'Brien-style frozen hash browns.

Sabrina Genasci
World Changers Radio, FL

VEGETABLES

Sautéed Green Beans With
Shallots, Rosemary, and Hazelnuts

2 pounds green beans, trimmed
butter
1 teaspoon chopped fresh or
   dried rosemary

¼ cup chopped shallots (about
   3 large)
salt and pepper to taste
½ cup hazelnuts, toasted and chopped

Cook green beans in a large pot of boiling, salted water until tender and crisp (about 5 minutes). Drain. Rinse green beans with cold water; drain well and pat dry with paper towels. (Green beans can be prepared a day ahead, covered and refrigerated.) Melt butter in a large, heavy skillet over medium-high heat. Add rosemary and shallots; sauté until shallots are tender (about 5 minutes). Add green beans and toss until heated through (about 5 minutes). Season to taste with salt and pepper. Add hazelnuts and toss. Serves 10.

Barbara Ball
ChurchLIFE, FL

Serve wholeheartedly, as if you were serving the Lord, not men (Eph. 6:7).

Scalloped Cheesy Potatoes

6 tablespoons light margarine
¼ cup flour
garlic powder to taste
3 cups low-fat milk

1 pound Chedarella cheese, grated
3 pounds unpeeled white potatoes,
   thinly sliced
2 large Vidalia onions, sliced

Preheat oven to 350 degrees. Melt margarine in a saucepan over medium-high heat. Mix in flour and garlic; cook for 1 minute, stirring until it bubbles. Remove from heat and stir in milk. Return sauce to heat and cook, stirring constantly for 4–5 minutes until sauce thickens and comes to a boil. Reduce heat to low and add ¾ of cheese. Cook and stir until cheese is melted. Pour ½ of sauce into an oblong baking dish, then add potatoes and onions. Pour remaining sauce over potatoes and sprinkle with remaining cheese. Bake for 30 minutes.

Holly Weber
World Changers Radio, FL

Scalloped Corn

¼ cup flour
1 can cream-style corn
2 eggs, beaten
1 cup milk

salt to taste
½ cup sharp cheddar cheese, or
⅛ cup more milk if preferred

Mix flour with corn in a medium casserole; add eggs, blending into mixture. Stir in milk, salt, and cheese, reserving a little cheese to sprinkle on top. Bake for 1¼ hours or until a knife inserted in middle comes out clean. When cooked, this dish is like a custard.

Vonette Bright
Co-founder, Campus Crusade for Christ
Executive Director, Women Today International, FL

Sesame Green Beans

½ pound fresh or 9 ounces frozen
    French-style green beans
1 tablespoon butter
1 tablespoon sesame seeds

¼ cup thinly sliced celery
1 small sweet onion, diced
¼ teaspoon salt or salt substitute

Boil green beans in a small amount of water for 12 minutes or just until tender; drain. Meanwhile, melt butter in a saucepan and add sesame seeds; cook over low heat, stirring constantly, for approximately 5 minutes or until seeds are golden brown. Add celery, onion, and salt. Cook until vegetables are tender. Pour over hot beans; toss and serve immediately.

Gayle Anne VanFulpen
NewLife Publications, FL

Soufflé de Broccoli

2½ cups cooked bite-size broccoli
¼ teaspoon nutmeg
dash red pepper

3 large egg whites, beaten
¼ cup evaporated skim milk

Preheat oven to 400 degrees. Season broccoli with nutmeg and pepper. Pour in egg whites and milk while stirring. Bake for 25 minutes.

Gayle Anne VanFulpen
NewLife Publications, FL

Spinach and Cottage Cheese Casserole

1 pint cottage cheese
1 16-ounce package frozen spinach, defrosted and squeezed to drain

3 eggs, beaten
¼ cup margarine, melted
3 tablespoons flour

Preheat oven to 350 degrees. Mix ingredients and place in a buttered 9-inch square pan. Bake for 1 hour or until knife comes out clean.

Sus Schmitt
Computer Services, FL

Spinach Casserole

3 packages frozen chopped spinach
1½ cups medium *White Sauce*
3 tablespoons water or broth
salt and pepper to taste
8 ounces noodles, cooked

1 pound grated Swiss cheese
 (can use part mozzarella)
butter
grated Parmesan cheese

Preheat oven to 350 degrees. Cook spinach; drain well. Prepare *White Sauce*; mix with spinach and water; salt and pepper to taste. Place ½ of the noodles in a greased 9x13-inch pan. Layer with ½ of the Swiss cheese and all of the spinach mixture. Top with the remaining noodles and Swiss cheese. Dot with butter and sprinkle with Parmesan cheese. Bake for 30 minutes. Serves 8–10.

White Sauce:
¼ cup butter
¼ cup flour

1½ cups milk
1 teaspoon salt

Melt butter in a saucepan. Add flour and heat until bubbly. Gradually mix in milk and cook, stirring constantly until thickened. Add salt. Makes 1½ cups.

Rose Sutherland
ChurchLIFE, IL

*Better a meal of vegetables where there is love
than a fattened calf with hatred (Prov. 15:17).*

Spinach-Stuffed Tomatoes

1 package frozen chopped spinach
¼ cup water
¼ cup mayonnaise
1 tablespoon dried minced onion
⅛ teaspoon nutmeg
salt and pepper to taste
6 small whole tomatoes

Preheat oven to 350 degrees. Cook spinach in water for 3 minutes, stirring to defrost; drain thoroughly. Combine spinach with mayonnaise, onion, nutmeg, salt, and pepper. Cut a thin slice off the top of tomatoes and scoop out the center; drain upside down. Sprinkle inside of tomatoes with salt and fill with spinach mixture. Place tomatoes in a baking dish and pour hot water ¼-inch deep around tomatoes. Bake for 12–15 minutes. Serves 6. *Tip:* For faster preparation, cook spinach in a microwave.

Nina Locke
Crusade Family

Stuffed Baked Tomatoes

4 large pink or lightly green tomatoes
4 sprigs parsley
1 medium onion
1 clove garlic
4 tablespoons margarine, *divided*
ham, shrimp, or crab meat
¾ cup seasoned bread crumbs, *divided*

Preheat oven to 350 degrees. Scoop out center of tomatoes; save the filling. Finely chop all ingredients, including any meat or seafood and the tomato filling. Sauté parsley, onion, and garlic in 2 tablespoons margarine, then add meat or seafood; cook until well blended. Add tomato pulp and ½ cup bread crumbs. Fill tomatoes; sprinkle remaining bread crumbs on top and dot with remaining margarine. Bake until browned.

Lois Mackey
CoMission, CA

Stuffed Cauliflower
(Puerto Rican)

2 pounds lean ground beef
seasonings of your choice
adobo (Spanish seasoning) to taste
Sazon seasoning (natural coloring
    with achoite and cilantro) to taste

Goya seasoning to taste
whole cauliflower
2 slices smoked ham or Canadian
    bacon
2 slices Swiss cheese

Preheat oven to 350 degrees. Fry ground beef and drain. Season beef to your taste with ingredients that you would put into meatloaf, such as onion, pepper, garlic, salt, egg, or ketchup. To make this a genuine Puerto Rican dish, add adobo. Also season with Sazon and Goya. Steam cauliflower for 1–2 minutes to keep firm; set aside to cool. When cooled, turn upside down in a baking dish and fill open areas of cauliflower with meat mixture. Cover with ham or Canadian bacon. Bake for 15–20 minutes, basting every 3–4 minutes. Add slices of cheese over ham and cook another 3–5 minutes. Slice and serve by itself or with any pasta or rice.

Lucy Capetillo
NewLife Publications, FL

Summer Garden Casserole

1 cup Italian seasoned bread crumbs
2 medium zucchini, unpeeled
2 medium cucumbers, unpeeled
1 sweet Burmuda onion, peeled

¾ cup grated cheddar cheese
¾ cup grated Monterey Jack cheese
½ teaspoon Italian seasoning

Preheat oven to 350 degrees. Butter a 2-quart casserole and sprinkle with a thin layer of bread crumbs. Slice vegetables ¼-inch thick. Place a layer of squash in the casserole; sprinkle lightly with crumbs and dot with butter. Add a layer of cucumbers; add more crumbs and butter, then a layer of onions, and more crumbs and butter. Top with ½ of cheeses and seasoning, then repeat layering. Bake for 1 hour. *Variation:* Substitute any other vegetables that you prefer.

Marlyse Milburn
Milburn Projects, CA

Sweet and Sour Green Beans

1 tablespoon brown sugar
½ teaspoon salt
dash white or black pepper
¼ teaspoon paprika
¼ teaspoon dry mustard
2 strips bacon, fried and crumbled

3 tablespoons cider vinegar
1 tablespoon water
1 package frozen French-style green beans (or an equivalent amount canned or fresh)

Combine the dry ingredients and mix with the bacon. Add vinegar and water, and stir thoroughly to dissolve dry ingredients. Cook beans until tender, then drain. Add the vinegar mixture to the beans and heat until liquid is just boiling. *Tip:* This recipe can be made ahead of time and kept almost indefinitely; leftovers are easily reheated. If recipe is doubled, use 5 tablespoons vinegar instead of 6. This recipe is also good using cooked cabbage, spinach, and wilted lettuce.

Ronnie Lesher
Military Ministry, VA

Sweet Potato and Carrot Purée

4 large sweet potatoes (about 2 pounds)
1 pound carrots
2½ cups water
1 tablespoon sugar
¾ cup sweet butter, softened

salt and freshly ground pepper
to taste
½ cup *Creme Fraiche*
½ teaspoon freshly grated nutmeg
dash cayenne pepper

Preheat oven to 375 degrees. Scrub sweet potatoes and cut a small, deep slit in the top of each. Set on the center rack of the oven; bake for about 1 hour or until potatoes are tender when pierced with a fork. Meanwhile, peel and trim the carrots; cut into 1-inch lengths. Put them in a saucepan and add water, sugar, 2 tablespoons butter, salt, and pepper. Place over medium heat; bring to a boil, and cook uncovered until water has evaporated and carrots begin to sizzle in the butter (about 30 minutes). The carrots should be tender. If not, add a little water, and cook until carrots are done and water has evaporated. Scrape out the flesh of the sweet potatoes, and combine with carrots in a food processor fitted with a steel blade. (If you use a blender, purée ½ of the recipe at a time.) Add remaining butter and *Creme Fraiche*, and process until very smooth. Add nutmeg, and season with salt and pepper. Add cayenne and process briefly to blend. Serves 6.

Creme Fraiche:

¼ cup heavy cream   ¼ cup sour cream

Whisk together cream and sour cream. Allow to thicken for at least 4 hours.

Mary Graham
Women Today International, FL

Sweet Potato Casserole

1 40-ounce can sweet potatoes
1–2 teaspoons salt
cinnamon to taste
nutmeg to taste
allspice to taste

ground cloves to taste
1 8-ounce can frozen orange
    juice concentrate
marshmallows (optional)
pecans (optional)

Preheat oven to 350 degrees. Beat potatoes with seasonings. Add orange juice and beat well. Pour into a buttered dish and bake for 30 minutes. For special occasions, sprinkle marshmallows and pecans on top and bake for another 1–2 minutes or until lightly browned. This recipe contains no fat or sugar.

Vonette Bright
Co-founder, Campus Crusade for Christ
Executive Director, Women Today International, FL

Three-Vegetable Casserole

1 10-ounce package frozen
    green beans
1 10-ounce package frozen
    Foodhook lima beans
1 10-ounce package frozen peas

½ cup sour cream
½ cup mayonnaise
⅓ cup grated Parmesan cheese
paprika

Preheat oven to 325 degrees. Cook vegetables separately as directed on packages; drain. Combine sour cream and mayonnaise; mix with vegetables. Put into a shallow 2-quart baking dish, and sprinkle with cheese and paprika. Bake for 20 minutes.

Cheryl Hile
Computer Services, FL

Vegetable Casserole Supreme

2 cups frozen cut green beans
1 large can stewed tomatoes
1½ cups carrot strips
2 cups sliced celery
¾ cup green pepper strips
1 small onion, chopped

2 teaspoons salt
¾ teaspoon pepper
¼ cup butter chunks
1 tablespoon sugar
¼ cup Minute Tapioca
1 can French-fried onions

Preheat oven to 325 degrees. Boil and drain beans. Combine with all remaining ingredients except French-fried onions. Place in a casserole dish. Cover and bake for 1½ hours; uncover and stir well, then bake for another hour. Top with onions and bake for 5 more minutes. *Tip:* Vegetables may be prepared in advance and refrigerated in covered containers. Serves 10 generously.

Rose Sutherland
ChurchLIFE, IL

Vegetable Medley

10 ounces frozen broccoli
10 ounces frozen brussels sprouts
10 ounces frozen cauliflower
1 cup sliced carrots
1 can cream of mushroom soup

salt to taste
thyme to taste
pepper to taste
buttered bread crumbs (optional)

Preheat oven to 350 degrees. Partially cook all vegetables; do not over cook. Mix with soup and season to taste; top with buttered crumbs. Bake for 30 minutes or until bubbly.

Lisa Master
Worldwide Challenge, FL

Vegetable Nests

leftover mashed potatoes
favorite vegetables
favorite seasonings (salt-free preferred)

Molly McButter
freshly grated Parmesan or
    Asiogo cheese

Preheat oven to 425 degrees. Place potatoes in a greased casserole dish, forming a well or nest in the center. Bake for 20 minutes or until lightly browned. Meanwhile, steam vegetables until tender but crisp. Season as desired. Fill nest with vegetables and sprinkle with Molly McButter (sour cream flavor is great). Lightly coat with Parmesan or Asiogo cheese.

Gayle Anne VanFulpen
NewLife Publications, FL

Vinaigrette Green Beans

3 tablespoons vinegar
½ cup olive oil
1 teaspoon salt
⅛ teaspoon freshly ground pepper
¼ teaspoon paprika
dash cayenne pepper
1 tablespoon finely chopped pimiento
1 tablespoon finely chopped pickles

2 teaspoons finely chopped
    green pepper
1½ teaspoons finely chopped
    parsley
1 teaspoon finely chopped chives
    or onion
2 15-ounce cans green beans,
    drained

To make dressing, slowly add vinegar and oil to salt, pepper, paprika, and cayenne. Beat thoroughly. Add all vegetables except green beans to dressing. Pour dressing over green beans; cook slowly over low heat until heated through. *Tip:* Dressing may be made ahead and refrigerated. This makes about 1 cup dressing. *Variation:* Use dried pepper, parsley, and onion instead of fresh. This recipe was a gift from The Hitching Post in Austin, Texas.

Vonette Bright
Co-founder, Campus Crusade for Christ
Executive Director, Women Today International, FL

 A generous man will himself be blessed, for he shares his food with the poor (Prov. 22:9).

Yam and Apple Casserole

6–8 yams
5–6 apples, peeled
½ cup sugar
½ teaspoon salt

¼ cup butter
1 tablespoon cornstarch
1 cup water

Preheat oven to 350 degrees. Boil yams for 20 minutes; cool and peel. Alternately slice apples and yams into casserole, ending with apples on top. Mix remaining ingredients and pour over yams and apples. Bake for 1 hour.

Melissa Crabtree
Corporate Human Resources, FL

Yellow Squash Casserole

8–10 yellow squash, sliced
1 large Vidalia onion, chopped
½ cup light margarine
1 cup Pepperidge Farm herb
  dressing mix, *divided*

1 cup fat-free sour cream
1 can Campbell's Healthy Request
  cream of mushroom soup
8 ounces Chedarella cheese, grated

Preheat oven to 350 degrees. Steam squash and onion together for a couple minutes. Then mix with margarine, ¾ of the stuffing, sour cream, soup, and cheese just until moistened. Place in a baking dish and sprinkle remaining stuffing on top. Bake for 25–30 minutes. Even people who don't like squash will eat this!

Holly Weber/Laura Callaway
World Changers Radio, FL/International Finance, FL

Yullee Beans

2 packages frozen baby lima beans
2 pounds ground sausage
2 onions, sliced

1 cup sour cream
Monterey Jack cheese with
  jalapeños (optional)

Cook beans and drain. Fry sausage; drain and crumble. Sauté onions. Place beans, sausage, and onions into a crockpot. Stir in sour cream and mix well.

Top with Monterey Jack cheese if desired. Heat until bubbly. Serve as a main dish, or as a side dish with *Garlic and Rosemary Leg of Lamb* and *Broccoli Raisin Salad*. Serves 12 as a side dish or 6–8 as a main dish.

Mary Jane Morgan
Crusade Family

Yummy Broccoli and Fresh Dill Sauce

1 large bunch broccoli or 1 16-ounce package frozen broccoli
1 cup water
3 tablespoons cornstarch
1 tablespoon mustard

⅓ cup non-fat dry milk
3 tablespoons fresh chopped dill or ½ teaspoon dill seed
fresh dill (optional)

Cut florets and stem pieces; steam. Do not over cook. Beat remaining ingredients except fresh dill with a mixer. If using dill seed, blend with sauce. Cook over medium heat, stirring constantly until sauce thickens. Stir in fresh dill. Serve immediately over freshly steamed vegetables. Sprinkle with additional fresh dill if desired.

Gayle Anne VanFulpen
NewLife Publications, FL

Yummy Zucchini Bake

8–10 small zucchini
½ cup chopped onion
½ cup butter
1 cup grated cheddar cheese
½ cup grated Gruyère cheese

1 cup sour cream
1 teaspoon salt
½ teaspoon paprika
1 cup bread crumbs
grated Parmesan cheese

Preheat oven to 350 degrees. Boil whole zucchini for about 10 minutes or until slightly tender. Cut off ends and cut in half lengthwise. Arrange in a shallow buttered casserole. Sauté onion in butter. Add cheeses, sour cream, salt, and paprika. Pour over zucchini. Sprinkle with bread crumbs and Parmesan cheese. Bake for 30 minutes. Serves 6.

Linda Painton
Travel Department, FL

Pasta, Rice, & Beans

Pasta

Artichoke Linguini

5 tablespoons butter or margarine, *divided*
6 tablespoons olive oil, *divided*
1 tablespoon flour
1 cup chicken broth
1 clove garlic, crushed
1 tablespoon fresh parsley, minced
2–3 teaspoons fresh lemon juice
¼ teaspoon salt plus salt to taste

white pepper to taste
1 14-ounce can artichoke hearts, sliced and drained
3 tablespoons freshly grated Parmesan cheese, *divided*
2 teaspoons capers, rinsed and drained
1 pound linguini, cooked al dente and drained
2 ounces ham, chopped (optional)

Heat 4 tablespoons butter and 4 tablespoons oil in a small saucepan over medium heat. Add flour and stir until smooth (about 3 minutes). Blend in broth, stirring until thickened (about 1 minute). Reduce heat to low. Add garlic, parsley, lemon juice, and salt and white pepper to taste. Cool about 5 minutes, stirring constantly. Blend in artichokes, 2 tablespoons cheese, and capers. Cover mixture and simmer about 8 minutes. Melt 1 tablespoon butter in a large skillet over medium heat. Stir in 2 tablespoons oil, 1 tablespoon cheese, and ¼ teaspoon salt. Add cooked linguini and toss lightly. Arrange pasta on a platter and pour sauce over. Garnish with ham if desired.

Pat Billings
Crusade Family

 Nobody should seek his own good, but the good of others (1 Cor. 10:24).

Austrian Schinkenfleckerin

8 ounces broad noodles, broken
1 pound cooked ham, diced
1½ cups grated Parmesan or
    cheddar cheese, *divided*
1 cup light cream

2 eggs, beaten
¾ teaspoon salt (optional)
½ teaspoon pepper
2 tablespoons butter, melted

Preheat oven to 350 degrees. Cook and drain noodles. Combine with ham and ½ cup grated cheese. Place in a buttered shallow baking dish. Beat cream and eggs together; add salt (if the ham is not salty) and pepper. Pour over ham and noodles. Sprinkle with 1 cup grated cheese and butter. Bake for 45 minutes.

Lois Mackey
JESUS Film Project, CA

Baked Ziti

spaghetti noodles
ricotta cheese
jar spaghetti sauce

mozzarella cheese slices
grated Parmesan cheese

Preheat oven to 350 degrees. Boil noodles and put them into a baking pan. Spread ricotta cheese over and top with spaghetti sauce. Place mozzarella slices over sauce and sprinkle with Parmesan cheese. Bake for 25 minutes.

Jeff King
JESUS Film Project, FL

Black Pasta With Lobster

6 tablespoons butter
6 tablespoons flour
1 shallot, minced
1 cup fish stock or clam juice
3 tablespoons whipping cream

meat from 2 lobsters (or 1 pound)
1 large package frozen peas,
    cooked and drained
2 8-ounce packages black pasta,
    cooked

Melt butter in a saucepan; stir in flour and shallot to make roux. Add stock, stirring until smooth. Remove from heat. Blend in cream; add lobster and

peas. Heat gently, being careful not to boil. Serve over black pasta. Serves 6.
Tip: This can also be served in small portions as an appetizer.

Ingrid Bunner
Board of Director's Wife

Carriloni Bolognese

1 pound ground beef
¾ cup chopped onion, *divided*
1 clove garlic, minced
1 10-ounce package frozen chopped
    spinach, thawed
⅓ cup grated Parmesan cheese
¼ cup dry bread crumbs
2 eggs, beaten
½ teaspoon oregano
½ teaspoon salt
¼ teaspoon pepper

1 25-ounce package manicotti shells
1 package Kraft white sauce mix
2 tablespoons margarine
2 packages Kraft Italian-style
    spaghetti sauce mix
2 16-ounce cans tomatoes
1 16-ounce can tomato paste
2 cups water
1 16-ounce package sliced low-
    moisture, part-skim mozzarella
    cheese (optional)

Preheat oven to 350 degrees. Brown meat. Add ¼ cup onion and garlic; cook until tender. Stir in spinach, Parmesan cheese, bread crumbs, eggs, and seasonings. Fill manicotti shells. Prepare white sauce mix as directed on package. Stir in margarine. Combine spaghetti sauce mix, tomatoes, tomato paste, water, and ¼ cup onion; simmer for 10 minutes. Pour a small amount of tomato sauce into 2 greased 8×12-inch baking dishes. Layer ½ of pasta shells, white sauce, and tomato sauce in each dish, using ½ of each mixture at a time. Sprinkle with additional Parmesan cheese. Cover with aluminum foil and bake for 1¼ hours. Top with mozzarella cheese if desired, and return to oven until cheese melts.

Barbara Ball
ChurchLIFE, FL

I am firmly convinced that if Christians would open their homes and practice hospitality as defined in Scripture, we could significantly alter the fabric of society. — Karen Burton Mains

Chicken Lasagna

8 ounces lasagna noodles
½ cup chopped onion
½ cup chopped celery
3 tablespoons butter
1 can cream of chicken soup
⅓ cup milk

½ teaspoon dried basil, crushed
1½ cups cottage cheese
2 cups diced cooked chicken
2 cups shredded cheddar cheese
½ cup grated Parmesan cheese
¾ cup herb-seasoned bread crumbs

Preheat oven to 350 degrees. Cook noodles in boiling water; drain. Sauté onion and celery in butter until tender. Stir in soup, milk, and basil. Spread a little sauce in the bottom of a 9×13-inch baking dish. Layer ½ of the noodles in the dish. Top with ½ of sauce, cottage cheese, chicken, cheddar, and Parmesan cheese. Repeat layers and top with bread crumbs. Bake for 45 minutes.

Melissa Crabtree
Corporate Human Resources, FL

Cippino

1 32-ounce jar marinara sauce
1 8-ounce can tomato sauce
1 can chopped baby clams
1 teaspoon oregano
¼ cup grated Parmesan cheese
1 teaspoon minced garlic
Louisiana hot sauce to taste
½ pound boneless, skinless chicken
    breast, cooked and cut up

½ pound mild or hot ground
    sausage, browned and drained
1 pound cod fish
½ pound raw peeled shrimp
½ pound scallops
1 dozen clams in shell
linguini

Cook sauces, chopped clams, and seasonings in a large saucepan. Add chicken and sausage; cover and simmer for 35–40 minutes. Place scallops and cod in oven, and bake for 15 minutes. Peel shrimp. Twenty minutes before sauce mixture is done, add the cod, shrimp, scallops, and clams in their shells. Cook until clam shells open. Serve on linguini. Makes 4 large servings. *Variation:* Substitute your own tomato spaghetti sauce recipe for marinara sauce.

Ginni Christopher
Executive Ministry, FL

Easy Lasagna

1 pound ground beef
5 cups Ragu spaghetti sauce
8 ounces lasagna noodles, uncooked

1 pound Ricotta cheese
1 cup grated Parmesan cheese
8 ounces mozzarella cheese

Preheat oven to 350 degrees. Sauté ground beef; drain and mix with spaghetti sauce. Spread 1 cup sauce in a 9×13-inch pan. Place a layer of uncooked noodles in the pan. Top with ½ of the remaining sauce and layer ½ of each cheese. Add another layer of noodles and the rest of the sauce and cheeses. Bake covered for 30 minutes; uncover and bake for another 15–25 minutes.

Sherry Cumpstone
Worldwide Challenge, FL

Fettucine Alfredo With Mushrooms

2–3 heaping tablespoons butter, *divided*
1 clove garlic, minced
1½ cups sliced fresh mushrooms
1 cup whipping cream

1 tablespoon flour
1 tablespoon minced parsley
¾ cup grated Parmesan cheese
12 ounces spinach fettucine

Melt 2 tablespoons butter in a skillet; cool to room temperature. Stir-fry garlic and mushrooms in remaining butter until tender; set aside. Whisk cream into cooled butter; stir in flour, parsley, and cheese. Cook fettucine according to package directions. When fettucine is almost done, heat cream mixture gently until thickened over medium to medium-low heat; *do not boil*. Drain liquid from mushrooms and garlic; add to alfredo sauce. Pour sauce over fettucine and serve immediately. Serves 3 as a main dish; serves 6 as a side dish.

Aimee Fookes
Family Life, AR

Fettuccine San Clemente

12 ounces fettucine
½ pound broccoli, chopped
¼ pound mushrooms, sliced
2 small zucchini, sliced
2 cloves garlic, minced

½ cup butter
1 cup half & half
½ cup Parmesan cheese
1 teaspoon salt
¼ teaspoon white pepper

Cook fettucine according to package directions, and keep warm. Sauté vegetables and garlic in butter until crisp and tender. Add remaining ingredients and heat through, but don't boil. Serve over hot noodles. If you like a thicker sauce, mix cornstarch and milk into sauce before heating, and cook until thickened.

Kari Maggard
U.S. Ministry, FL

Fettucine With Sautéed Eggplant and Feta Cheese

1 pound fettucine
¼ cup extra virgin olive oil
1 medium eggplant, cubed

3 cups chunky spaghetti sauce
½ pound feta cheese, cubed

Cook fettucine in a large pot of boiling water until tender but firm. Heat oil in a large, heavy frying pan. Add eggplant; cook, stirring frequently until eggplant softens and begins to brown (about 5 minutes). Stir in spaghetti sauce and feta cheese; heat through. Drain the pasta. Toss gently with the sauce. Makes 4 servings.

Cindy Schmatjan
International Ministry, FL

Filled Noodles

2 cups flour
2 teaspoons baking powder
¼ teaspoon salt
3 eggs, *divided*
¼ cup water
1 pound lean ground beef

½ cup finely chopped onion
pinch of salt and pepper
1 teaspoon thyme
2 cans beef broth or consommé
1 large can V-8 juice

To make noodle dough, mix flour, baking powder, and salt in a bowl. Make a well, and add 2 eggs and water. Mix together until dough-like. Add a little flour or water if necessary to make into a ball of dough. Roll out dough on a floured board to about ⅛-inch thickness. To make filling, mix ground beef, 1 egg, onion, salt and pepper, and thyme in a bowl. Spread filling over the dough. Roll up dough like a jelly roll, and seal all the edges with cold water. Slice into 1½-inch wide pieces. To make cooking broth, heat the beef broth and V-8 juice in a very large pan. Carefully place spiral noodles in the broth, laying each one flat on the bottom of the pan. Do not layer because spirals will expand. If necessary, use two pans. Cook for about 25 minutes, making sure the liquid covers each noodle.

Michelle Treiber
NewLife Publications, FL

The Lord will guide you always; ...you will be like a well-watered garden, like a spring whose waters never fail (Isaiah 58:11).

Garden Lasagna

3 tablespoons oil
4 medium zucchini, coarsely chopped
1 large onion, chopped
1 medium green pepper, chopped
1 medium carrot, peeled and diced
½ cup chopped celery
1 clove garlic, minced
2 16-ounce cans stewed tomatoes, undrained
1 8-ounce can tomato sauce
1 6-ounce can tomato paste
2 tablespoons chopped fresh parsley
2 teaspoons Italian seasoning
1 teaspoon dried basil
¼ teaspoon ground pepper
9 lasagna noodles, cooked
1 pint ricotta cheese
2 cups (8 ounces) shredded Swiss cheese
1 cup grated Parmesan cheese

Preheat oven to 350 degrees. Heat oil in a large pot; add zucchini, onion, green pepper, carrot, celery, and garlic. Sauté over medium heat for 15 minutes. Stir in the next 7 ingredients and bring to a boil. Cover and reduce heat; simmer for 30 minutes. Uncover and simmer another 45 minutes until thick, stirring occasionally. Spread ¼ of sauce in a greased 9×13-inch baking dish. Top with 3 noodles, ⅓ of ricotta cheese, ¼ of Swiss, and ¼ of Parmesan. Repeat layers twice. Top with remaining sauce, Swiss, and Parmesan. Bake uncovered for 35–40 minutes. Let stand 5 minutes before serving.

Wendy Hill
National Ministry, FL

Italian Jumbo Shells

1 box jumbo shells	1 tablespoon chopped parsley
1 quart ricotta cheese	½ teaspoon salt
8 ounces mozzarella cheese, shredded	¼ teaspoon pepper
	⅛ teaspoon nutmeg
½ cup grated Parmesan cheese	1 28-ounce jar spaghetti sauce
2 eggs	

Preheat oven to 350 degrees. Boil shells according to instructions on box. Mix remaining ingredients except sauce, and stuff each shell with 1 tablespoon mixture. Then spread ¼ of the sauce on the bottom of a 9×13-inch pan. Lay shells in sauce and pour remaining spaghetti sauce over shells. Bake for 30 minutes. Serves 4–6. This dish looks very elegant for a dinner party.

Debbie Giancaspro Floyd
International School of Theology, PA

Cheerfully share your home with those who need a meal or a place to stay for the night (1 Peter 4:9).

Italian Spaghetti and Meatballs

4 slices dry bread, cubed	1 teaspoon crushed oregano
water	1 teaspoon salt or onion salt
1 pound ground beef	dash pepper
2 eggs	*Italian Spaghetti Sauce*
½ cup grated cheese	12 ounces spaghetti, cooked
2 tablespoons chopped parsley	

Soak bread in a little water; combine with remaining ingredients, mixing well. Form into small balls and brown in skillet. Add to *Italian Spaghetti Sauce* and cook together. Serve over spaghetti. Serves 6.

Italian Spaghetti Sauce:

¾ cup chopped onion	1 teaspoon sugar
1 clove garlic, minced	1½ teaspoons salt
1 tablespoon olive oil	½ teaspoon pepper
2 16-ounce cans tomatoes	2 teaspoons crushed oregano
2 6-ounce cans tomato paste	½ cup sliced mushrooms
1 cup water	

Cook onion and garlic in hot oil until tender, but not brown; stir in remaining ingredients. Simmer uncovered for 30 minutes; add meatballs, cover and cook 45 minutes to 2 hours longer.

Lois Mackey
CoMission, CA

Lasagna

1 pound ground beef
1 clove garlic, chopped
1 6-ounce can tomato paste
1 28-ounce can tomatoes
1 teaspoon salt
12 ounces cottage cheese

1 tablespoon parsley
1 teaspoon oregano
6 ounces lasagna noodles
1 pound cheddar cheese, grated
1 pound mozzarella cheese, grated
grated Parmesan cheese (optional)

Preheat oven to 350 degrees. Brown beef and garlic; drain. Add tomato paste, tomatoes, and salt. Simmer for 20 minutes. Mix in cottage cheese, parsley, and oregano. Let set for flavors to absorb. Cook lasagna noodles. In a very large 2-inch-deep pan, layer ingredients in order, using ½ of each ingredient: beef-tomato sauce, cooked noodles, cottage cheese mixture, cheddar and mozzarella cheeses. Repeat layers and sprinkle Parmesan cheese on top, if desired. Bake for 30 minutes. Serve with tossed green salad and hot rolls.

Jerri Younkman
International School of Theology, CA

Lasagna Alla Bolognese

¾ cup butter, *divided*
2 onions, finely chopped
½ cup finely chopped celery
2 small carrots, chopped
3 teaspoons salt, *divided*
¾ teaspoon pepper, *divided*
1 teaspoon oregano
1 pound lean ground beef

1 pound ground loin of pork
¼ cup water
6 tablespoons tomato sauce
½ cup flour
12 lasagna noodles, cooked
1 quart milk, heated
1 cup cream
1 cup grated Parmesan cheese, *divided*

Preheat oven to 350 degrees. To make meat sauce, heat ¼ cup butter in a skillet. Sauté onions, celery, and carrots for 10 minutes or until onion is lightly browned. Season with 2 teaspoons salt, ½ teaspoon pepper, and oregano. Add beef, pork, water, and tomato sauce. Simmer for 15 minutes, stirring frequently. To make cream sauce, melt ½ cup butter in a saucepan. Stir in flour, 1 teaspoon salt, and ¼ teaspoon pepper. Add hot milk and cook, stirring, until sauce is smooth and thick. Cover and cook over low heat for 5 minutes, stirring occasionally. Stir in cream. In a buttered 9×13-inch baking dish, arrange a layer of lasagna. Spread with ½ of the meat sauce; sprinkle with ¼ of the Parmesan cheese; and top with ½ of the remaining lasagna. Spread with ½ of the cream sauce and sprinkle with Parmesan. Repeat layers, ending with remaining cream sauce and Parmesan cheese. Bake for 15 minutes and serve in baking dish. *Tip:* This dish may be prepared ahead, then frozen; bake at 350 degrees for 30–45 minutes or until heated through.

Rita Ruzzi
Executive Ministry, FL

Lasagna Roll-Ups

2 bunches spinach, Swiss chard, or turnip greens, finely chopped
2 tablespoons grated Parmesan cheese
1 cup cottage cheese
½ teaspoon nutmeg
10 lasagna noodles, cooked
1 cup sliced onions

2 cups grated Muenster or Monterey Jack cheese
1 quart tomato sauce
2 cloves garlic, minced or crushed
½ teaspoon basil
½ teaspoon oregano
½ teaspoon marjoram

Preheat oven to 350 degrees. To make filling, steam greens until limp. Add Parmesan, cottage cheese, and nutmeg; mix well. Spread individual noodles with filling; roll up and lay sideways in a greased 9×13-inch baking pan. Sprinkle onions and Muenster cheese on top. To make sauce, combine the remaining ingredients in a bowl. Pour sauce over roll-ups. Bake for 1 hour. Serves 7–8.

Karen Horsey
International Ministry, FL

Meat and Noodle Casserole

1 pound ground meat
¼ cup chopped onion
4 ounces tomato sauce
1 teaspoon salt
½ teaspoon pepper
¼ teaspoon garlic powder

1 cup cottage cheese
1 cup sour cream
8 ounces egg noodles, cooked
   and drained
1 cup shredded cheddar cheese

Preheat oven to 350 degrees. Brown meat with onion, and drain. Add tomato sauce and seasonings, then cover and simmer for 5 minutes. Mix cottage cheese and sour cream with noodles. Layer casserole dish with ½ of the meat mixture, then ½ of the noodles. Repeat layers, then add cheese. Bake for 30 minutes.

Stephanie Ramirez
Student Venture, FL

Offer hospitality to one another without grumbling (1 Peter 4:9).

Mediterranean Pasta

1 pound ground sausage (low-fat
   works best)
2 medium onions, thinly sliced
1 teaspoon fresh minced garlic
1 tablespoon olive oil
2 medium zucchini, sliced
½ teaspoon dried oregano

½ teaspoon dried basil
dash black pepper
¼ teaspoon salt (optional)
2 large tomatoes, seeded and
   chopped
cooked spaghetti
grated Parmesan cheese

In a large skillet, brown sausage, breaking it up into small pieces. Drain fat and set sausage aside. In the same skillet, sauté onions, garlic, and olive oil over medium heat, stirring until onions are very soft and lightly browned. Add zucchini, oregano, basil, pepper, and salt. Cook 5 minutes more. Add tomatoes; cover and simmer for 10 minutes, stirring occasionally. Add sausage to mixture and heat through. Serve over spaghetti and top with Parmesan cheese. Serves 4. *Variation:* For a more colorful dish, use 1 zucchini and 1 yellow squash.

Cherie Allen
CoMission, FL

Mega Hamburger Noodle Bake

4 pounds lean ground beef
3 large onions, chopped
16 ounces noodles, cooked
1 pound sharp American cheese,
   shredded
3 cans tomato soup
3 cups water
¾ cup chopped green pepper

½ cup chili sauce
¼ cup chopped pimiento
1½ teaspoons salt
dash pepper
3 cups fresh bread crumbs
6 tablespoons butter, melted
green pepper rings (optional)

Preheat oven to 350 degrees. Divide beef and onion between 2 large skillets. Brown meat; drain fat. Combine meat and onion with noodles, cheese, soup, water, green pepper, chili sauce, pimiento, salt, and pepper. Mix, then place into 2 9×13-inch baking dishes. Combine butter and crumbs; sprinkle over casseroles. Bake uncovered for 40–45 minutes or until hot. Trim with green pepper rings, if desired. Serves 25–30.

Laurie Killingsworth
New Life Center, FL

Mexican Macaroni

¾ cup macaroni
½ cup chopped green pepper
½ cup chopped red pepper
1½ tablespoons butter, *divided*
1 tablespoon flour
½ cup milk

½ cup plain yogurt
¼ teaspoon dry mustard
½ cup grated Monterey Jack cheese
salt and pepper to taste
bread crumbs

Preheat oven to 350 degrees. Cook macaroni as directed on package; drain well. Place green and red peppers and ½ tablespoon butter in the microwave and cook 30 seconds until barely soft. In a pan, melt 1 tablespoon butter; blend in flour. Add milk, yogurt, and mustard. Cook, stirring constantly until thick. Add cheese; toss in the cooked peppers and salt and pepper to taste. Stir in macaroni; pour into a casserole and top with bread crumbs. Bake for 20–30 minutes. Serves 4–6.

Nina Locke
Crusade Family

Mom's Spaghetti

4–5 carrots, diced
3–4 stalks celery including tops, diced
1 small onion, diced
olive oil
½ pound ground beef
garlic powder to taste
1–2 large cans tomato sauce
1 cup sliced mushrooms (optional)
1–2 small zucchini, chopped
chili powder

1 teaspoon or more salt (or substitute dry mustard)
1 teaspoon sugar or more
1 teaspoon oregano or more
1 teaspoon parsley or more
2–3 bay leaves
1 teaspoon cinnamon (optional)
spaghetti
squirt of lemon juice
grated Parmesan cheese

In a large skillet, sauté carrots, celery, and onion in olive oil (add a little water occasionally to help it cook faster). In a separate pan, cook hamburger that has been lightly seasoned with garlic; drain grease. Lightly stir the hamburger into the vegetables. Add 1–2 cans of tomato sauce, depending on whether you like sauce thick or thin. If desired, add mushrooms and zucchini. Stir in seasonings to taste. Add cinnamon sparingly; a little bit gives sauce a different flavor. Simmer for at least 1 hour on lowest setting of skillet, stirring occasionally to prevent scorching. When sauce is nearly done, boil noodles with a small squirt of lemon juice for flavoring and a drop of oil to prevent sticking. When done, drain; rinse with hot water if desired. Pour sauce over noodles and top with Parmesan cheese. Serve with sourdough French bread. Makes 4–6 servings. This one-dish meal is filling, nutritious, low-cost, and freezes well. The longer it simmers, the better it is. *Variation:* Omit the hamburger for a vegetarian dish.

Sue Renard Robinson
Crusade Family

More Than Spaghetti

1 tablespoon fat
2 onions, chopped (1 cup)
1 green pepper, chopped
3 cloves garlic, slivered, or
 ¾ teaspoon garlic purée
1 pound ground meat
1 15¼-ounce can solid-packed
 tomatoes
3 tablespoons chili powder

1 cup water
1 4-ounce can sliced mushrooms
1 10-ounce package frozen green
 peas, cooked
1 can whole kernel corn
salt and pepper
8 ounces spaghetti, cooked
2 cups grated sharp cheddar cheese

Preheat oven to 350 degrees. Melt fat and sauté onions, pepper, and garlic, but do not brown. Add ground meat and cook until brown. Add tomatoes, chili powder, and water; cover and cook over low heat for 30 minutes. Add mushrooms, peas, corn, salt, and pepper. Then add cooked spaghetti to the sauce and blend well. Pour ½ of the spaghetti mixture into a large greased baking dish and cover with ½ of the cheese. Add remaining spaghetti mixture and cover with remaining cheese. Bake for 20–30 minutes. Serves 8–12.

Carol Williams
Crusade Family

Pasta and Picante
With Black Bean Sauce

1 medium onion, chopped
1 clove garlic, chopped
1 tablespoon vegetable oil
1 15-ounce can black or pinto beans
1 24-ounce can stewed tomatoes
½ cup picante sauce
1 teaspoon chili powder

1 teaspoon ground cumin
¼ teaspoon oregano
shredded Monterey Jack or
 cheddar cheese
4 cups hot, cooked pasta
chopped fresh cilantro

Cook onion and garlic in oil in a large skillet. Stir in remaining ingredients except pasta and cilantro. Bring to a boil. Reduce heat; cover and simmer 15 minutes, stirring occasionally. Uncover and cook over high heat until it reaches desired consistency. Serve bean mixture over pasta. Sprinkle with cheese and cilantro, and serve with additional picante sauce. This simple recipe is from my mother and is very good!

Barbara Ball
ChurchLIFE, FL

Pasta Pizza

2 cups pizza sauce
1 pound shredded mozzarella cheese
1 pound Italian sausage, cooked
  and drained
chopped onion as desired

chopped green pepper as desired
chopped black olives as desired
any other pizza toppings as desired
9 lasagna noodles, cooked

Preheat oven to 350 degrees. Spread a little pizza sauce on the bottom of a
9×13-inch baking dish. Starting with 3 noodles, layer the ingredients, placing some cheese and sauce in each of the 3 layers. Top with cheese and bake
for 30 minutes.

Sharon Scroggins
ChurchLIFE, FL

Pasta Primavera

4 ounces linguini
½ cup butter
1 cup chopped fresh broccoli
1 cup thinly sliced carrots
½ cup sliced green onion
1 clove garlic, minced
1 teaspoon basil

½ teaspoon salt
¼ teaspoon pepper
1½ cups sliced fresh mushrooms
16 ounces frozen pea pods
¼ cup water
grated Parmesan cheese
chicken (optional)

Cook linguini in boiling, salted water until tender. Drain and keep warm.
Meanwhile, melt butter in skillet. Stir in broccoli, carrots, onion, garlic,
basil, salt, and pepper. Cook for 6–7 minutes or until broccoli is tender. Add
mushrooms and cook for 2 minutes. Add pea pods and water; cover and
simmer for 2 minutes or until vegetables are crisp and tender. Stir in linguini
and toss. Place mixture in a serving bowl; sprinkle with Parmesan and toss.
Serves 4.

Kari Maggard
U.S. Ministry, FL

We loved you so much that we were delighted to share with you not only the
gospel of God but our lives as well, because you had become so dear to us
(1 Thes. 2:8).

Pasta With Red Pepper Pesto

12-ounce jar roasted red bell peppers or pimientos in water, drained

1 cup firmly packed fresh basil leaves, plus a few basil sprigs

1 clove garlic, minced

⅓ cup freshly grated Parmesan plus ⅓ cup thin shavings (2 ounces total)

¼ cup water

¾ pound Asian eggplant, sliced crosswise ¾-inch thick

1 pound yellow squash and zucchini, sliced diagonally ½-inch thick

2 teaspoons olive oil

2 cups coarsely chopped tomatoes

¾ pound dried fusilli or penne pasta

salt and freshly ground pepper

In a blender, process red peppers, basil leaves, garlic, and grated Parmesan until basil is finely chopped. Place water and eggplant in a 10-inch non-stick frying pan. Cover tightly and bring to a boil over high heat. Reduce heat; simmer until eggplant is tender when pierced (about 5 minutes). Add ½ of the zucchini and ½ of the oil. Cook uncovered over high heat, turning vegetables often until well browned (8–10 minutes). Remove from pan. Brown remaining zucchini in remaining oil. Remove from heat and combine with reserved vegetables and tomatoes.

Fill a 6-quart pan ¾ full of water; bring to a boil. Add pasta and boil until barely tender (8–12 minutes). Drain and return to pan; mix in pesto. Mound pasta and vegetables in a dish. Garnish with basil sprigs; top with cheese shavings. Mix at table. Add salt and pepper. Serves 4. This recipe is from my daughter, Robbyn.

Barbara Ball
ChurchLIFE, FL

 If you wait for perfect conditions, you will never get anything done (Eccl. 11:4).

Peanut Noodles

1 cup plain or hot and spicy V-8 juice

½ cup chopped green onions

½ cup chopped sweet red bell pepper

⅓ cup creamy peanut butter

1 clove garlic, minced, or ¼ teaspoon garlic powder

1 tablespoon brown or white sugar

½ teaspoon grated fresh ginger or ¼ teaspoon ginger powder

1 tablespoon soy sauce

dash red pepper or Tabasco sauce

8 ounces spaghetti, cooked

In a small or medium saucepan, combine all ingredients except spaghetti. Cook over medium heat, stirring until smooth and hot. In a large bowl, combine sauce and spaghetti. Toss until noodles are well-coated. Makes 4 servings.

Cherie Allen
CoMission, FL

Penne All' Arrabbiata
(Italian Penne With Firey Sauce)

¼ cup extra virgin olive oil
¼ cup butter
2 cloves garlic, minced
8 large ripe tomatoes, skinned and
    chopped
¼ teaspoon basil

salt and pepper to taste
½ teaspoon dried red chili peppers
    or 1 small cayenne pepper,
    finely minced
1 pound penne, cooked
freshly grated Parmesan cheese

Heat olive oil and butter in a large skillet over low heat. Sauté garlic for 3–5 minutes. Add tomatoes and seasonings. (Adjust the amount of chili pepper depending on how spicy you like the sauce.) Cover with a splatter screen, and cook over medium-high heat for about 1 hour, or until tomatoes are cooked down and most of the juice is evaporated. Mix some of the sauce with cooked pasta so every noodle is covered. Serve over penne and sprinkle with Parmesan cheese. Serve with salad and breadsticks or hot, crust bread. Serves 4.

Susie Klenk
Athletes in Action, IN

Penne Di Pollo

¼ cup julienned carrots
¼ cup julienned zucchini
¼ cup julienned yellow squash
¼ cup water
¼ cup broccoli florets
1 medium tomato, chopped
¼ cup chicken broth

¼ teaspoon basil
¼ teaspoon thyme
salt and pepper to taste
2 chicken breasts, cooked and
    cut into strips
8 ounces penne, cooked
grated Parmesan cheese

Spray a large, deep skillet with cooking spray. Cook carrots over medium heat for 5 minutes until softened. Add zucchini, squash, and water; cook for 5 minutes. Stir in broccoli, tomato, chicken broth, and seasonings. Cook for 5 minutes. Add chicken strips and heat through. Mix with penne in a large bowl. Top with Parmesan cheese.

Gretchen Pappas
Campus Ministry, CA

Penne With Gorgonzola and Tomatoes

3 tablespoons olive oil
1 medium onion, chopped
4 cloves garlic, chopped
1 14½-ounce can Italian plum
    tomatoes, drained and chopped
½ cup fresh chopped or 1 tablespoon
    dried crumbled basil

½ cup butter, at room temperature
6 ounces Gorgonzola cheese
1 pound penne
pepper to taste
1 cup freshly grated Romano
    or Parmesan cheese

Heat oil in a heavy skillet over medium heat. Add onion and garlic; sauté until translucent (about 8 minutes). Stir in tomatoes and basil. Cook until mixture thickens, stirring occasionally (about 20 minutes). Meanwhile, using a spoon, beat butter with Gorgonzola until blended. Cook pasta in a large pot of boiling, salted water until tender but still firm, stirring occasionally; drain well. Return pasta to pot. Whisk Gorgonzola mixture into tomato sauce. Add sauce to pasta and stir to coat. Season with pepper to taste. Sprinkle Romano cheese on top. This is our family favorite!

Barbara Ball
ChurchLIFE, FL

Pesto Pasta

1 8-ounce package any pasta
2¼ cups salt-free chicken broth, *divided*
2 teaspoons cornstarch
⅛ teaspoon pepper
¼ cup butter sprinkles
2 cloves garlic, chopped (2 teaspoons)

½ cup chopped fresh basil
¼ cup chopped fresh parsley
sliced mushrooms (optional)
meat (optional)
4 teaspoons grated Parmesan or Romano cheese

Cook pasta according to package directions without adding oil and salt. Drain and keep warm. In a non-stick skillet over medium heat, boil 2 cups chicken broth for 2 minutes. In a small bowl, combine ¼ cup chicken broth, cornstarch, and pepper; stir into broth. Cook until thickened, stirring constantly. In a small bowl, combine butter sprinkles, garlic, basil, and parsley; stir into broth mixture. Add mushrooms and meat if desired. When heated through, pour over pasta and top with cheese.

Stacie Unruh
Headquarters Development Office, FL

The poor shall eat and be satisfied; all who seek the Lord shall find him and shall praise his name (Psalm 22:26).

Pizza Casserole

3½-ounce package sliced pepperoni
6 ounces fettucine, broken and cooked
1 15½-ounce jar pizza sauce

1 cup mozzarella cheese, *divided*
1 4-ounce can sliced mushrooms
1 2¼-ounce can sliced pitted olives
1 tablespoon grated Parmesan cheese

Preheat oven to 400 degrees. Slice pepperoni in half; combine with pasta. Stir in pizza sauce, ¾ cup mozzarella cheese, mushrooms, olives, and Parmesan cheese. Transfer to a 12×7½×2-inch baking dish. Top with remaining mozzarella and bake for about 15 minutes until bubbling. Serves 6.

Crystal Keller
Computer Services, FL

Prego Spaghetti Pie

6 ounces spaghetti, cooked
¼ cup butter
⅔ cup grated Parmesan cheese
2 eggs, beaten

2 cups cottage cheese, *divided*
2 pounds hamburger, browned
1 large jar Prego spaghetti sauce
shredded mozzarella cheese

Preheat oven to 350 degrees. Combine spaghetti, butter, Parmesan cheese, and eggs. Arrange in 2 pie plates to form 2 crusts. Bake for 10–12 minutes; let cool. Spoon in 1 cup cottage cheese per pie. Top with cooked hamburger mixed with sauce. Bake for 30–40 minutes. Cover with mozzarella and bake until melted. Let cool 10–15 minutes before serving.

Anne Lawrence
World Changers Radio, FL

Salmon or Tuna Noodles Romanoff

8 ounces medium noodles, cooked
1½ cups creamed cottage cheese
1½ cups sour cream
½ cup chopped onion, sautéed
1 clove garlic, minced
1½ teaspoons Worcestershire sauce

dash red pepper sauce or
   cayenne pepper
½ teaspoon salt
1 16-ounce can salmon or
   2 6½-ounce cans tuna, drained
½ cup grated sharp cheddar cheese

Preheat oven to 325 degrees. Mix all ingredients except cheddar cheese. Place mixture in a casserole dish and top with grated cheese. Bake for 20–25 minutes. Serve with a tossed salad.

Cheryl Henderson
Contributions and Postal Services, FL

Seafood Lasagna

1 pound bay scallops
1 pound medium shrimp
16 ounces ricotta cheese
2 eggs
½ cup grated Parmesan cheese

16 ounces lasagna, cooked
1 pound Monterey Jack cheese,
   shredded
1 pound Velveeta cheese
1 pound crab meat

Preheat oven to 350 degrees. Parboil scallops and shrimp, and set aside. Mix ricotta cheese with eggs and Parmesan cheese. Place 1 layer of noodles in a lasagna pan and cover with ½ of the ricotta mixture. Sprinkle scallops over ricotta mixture and add ⅓ of Monterey Jack cheese. Cut Velveeta cheese into ¼-inch slices; arrange ⅓ of the slices over Monterey Jack cheese. Add another layer of noodles, remaining ricotta, crab, ⅓ of the Monterey Jack, and ⅓ of the Velveeta cheese. Then layer remaining noodles, shrimp, Monterey Jack, and Velveeta. Bake for 1 hour; let stand for 30 minutes before cutting. Serves 15.

Ingrid Bunner
Board of Director's Wife

Shrimp Capellini

1 box capellini (angel hair pasta)	1 teaspoon salt
2 bunches broccoli	1 teaspoon pepper
8 green onions, chopped	1 tablespoon dill weed
2 pounds shrimp, cooked and peeled	1 cup grated Parmesan cheese
1 12-ounce jar diced pimiento	2 cups olive oil
1 12-ounce can artichoke hearts, quartered	1 clove garlic, minced

Cook capellini al dente for 8–10 minutes. Drain and rinse in cold water. Cut broccoli into small florets and blanch in boiling water for 2 minutes. Drain and rinse in cold water. In a large bowl, toss all ingredients until well blended. Serve chilled or at room temperature.

Ann Wright
Women Today International, FL

Every house where love abides
And friendship is a guest,
Is surely home—and home, sweet home;
For there the heart can rest.
— Henry Van Dyke

Shrimp Noodle Supreme

8 ounces spinach noodles
1 3-ounce package cream cheese
1½ pounds medium shrimp,
    peeled and deveined
½ cup butter, softened
1 can cream of mushroom soup
1 cup sour cream
1 tablespoon chopped fresh
    or dried chives

½ cup half & half
½ cup mayonnaise
½ teaspoon Dijon mustard
¾ cup shredded cheddar cheese
1 tablespoon fresh chopped parsley
    (optional)
lemon slices or wedges (optional)
paprika
tomato wedges (optional)

Preheat oven to 325 degrees. Cook noodles as directed on package. Drain noodles and combine with cream cheese. Line a casserole with the noodle mixture. In a large frying pan, sauté the shrimp in butter until pink and tender (about 5 minutes). Place over the noodles. Combine soup, sour cream, chives, half & half, mayonnaise, and mustard. Stir until well blended; pour over shrimp. Sprinkle the top with cheddar cheese. Bake until heated through and cheese is melted. Garnish with fresh parsley and lemon or tomato wedges if desired. Sprinkle with paprika for added color. Makes 6 servings.

Frances Thomas
Crusade Family

 Rejoice with those who rejoice; mourn with those who mourn (Rom. 12:15).

Spaghetti Pie

6 ounces spaghetti
2 tablespoons butter or margarine
⅓ cup grated Parmesan cheese
2 eggs, well beaten
1 cup cottage cheese
1 pound ground beef or bulk
    pork sausage
½ cup chopped onion

¼ cup chopped green pepper
1 8-ounce can diced tomatoes
1 6-ounce can tomato paste
1 teaspoon sugar
1 teaspoon dried oregano, crushed
½ teaspoon garlic salt
½ cup shredded mozzarella cheese

Preheat oven to 350 degrees. Cook the spaghetti according to package directions; drain (should have about 3 cups spaghetti). Stir butter into hot spaghetti. Add Parmesan cheese and eggs. Form spaghetti mixture into a "crust" in a buttered 10-inch pie plate. Spread cottage cheese over the spaghetti crust. In a skillet, cook meat, onion, and green pepper until vegetables are tender and meat is browned. Drain excess fat. Stir in undrained tomatoes, tomato paste, sugar, oregano, and garlic salt; heat through. Place meat mixture in spaghetti crust. Bake uncovered for 20 minutes. Sprinkle mozzarella cheese on top; bake 5 minutes longer or until cheese melts. Serves 6.

Peggy Hawkins
JESUS Video Project, FL

Spanish Noodle Skillet

2 slices bacon, cut into 1-inch pieces (optional)
½ onion, chopped
½ green pepper, chopped
½ pound ground beef
1 teaspoon salt
dash pepper
¼ teaspoon oregano
2 cups puréed or stewed tomatoes
¾ cup water
1½ cups egg noodles

Fry bacon pieces until crisp; set aside. Sauté onion, green pepper, and ground beef in bacon fat; pour off excess fat. Add salt, pepper, oregano, tomatoes, and water. Cover and simmer for 10 minutes. Bring to a boil and add noodles a few at a time. Reduce heat; cover and simmer 10 more minutes, stirring occasionally. Top with bacon and serve. *Optional:* Stir in ¾ cup shredded cheese with noodles. Top with ¼ cup additional cheese just before serving.

Karen Horsey
International Ministry, FL

Stephanie's Southern Macaroni and Cheese

2½ cups uncooked macaroni
6 tablespoons butter or margarine
¼ cup flour
2¼ cups milk
½ teaspoon salt
dash pepper
3 cups shredded cheddar cheese, *divided*

Preheat oven to 400 degrees. Cook macaroni according to package instructions. Melt butter over low heat; add flour. Cook 1 minute until smooth.

Add milk, stirring constantly. Stir in salt and pepper. Place ½ of macaroni in a lightly greased 3-quart casserole. Top with 1 cup cheese. Repeat layers. Pour sauce over top and cover with remaining cheese. Bake for 35–40 minutes until lightly browned. Serves 6–8.

Stephanie Farris
Campus Ministry, KY

Stephen's Favorite Lasagna

1 pound lean ground beef
1 large Vidalia onion, chopped
garlic powder to taste
1 10-ounce package frozen chopped
  spinach, cooked and drained
16 ounces ricotta cheese
8 ounces Chedaralla cheese, grated
  and *divided*

3 packages Knorr 4-cheese pasta
  sauce mix
3½ cups low-fat milk
3 tablespoons light margarine
1 package lasagna noodles, cooked
grated Parmesan cheese

Preheat oven to 350 degrees. Brown ground beef with onion, seasoning with garlic powder. Combine beef mixture, spinach, ricotta cheese, and ¾ of Chedaralla cheese in a large bowl. Prepare sauce mix according to package directions using 3½ cups milk. Add margarine; continue to stir until thick and mixture starts to boil. Remove from heat. In a large rectangular pan, place ⅓ of sauce, ½ of noodles, then ½ of spinach mixture. Pour ⅓ of sauce and sprinkle with Parmesan cheese. Repeat layers of noodles, spinach, and sauce, then top with grated cheese. Bake for 45–60 minutes.

Holly Weber
World Changers Radio, FL

As far as God is concerned there is a sweet, wholesome fragrance in our lives. It is the fragrance of Christ within us, an aroma to both the saved and the unsaved all around us (2 Cor. 2:15).

Susie's Spaghetti

¼ cup extra virgin olive oil	1½ quarts cold water
2 cloves garlic, minced	½ cup grated Parmesan cheese, *divided*
1 28-ounce can tomato purée	1 pound lean ground beef
2 6-ounce cans tomato paste	1 egg
2 teaspoons salt	¼ cup Italian bread crumbs
2 teaspoons sugar	¼ cup vegetable oil
¼ teaspoon basil	1 pound rigatoni, spaghetti, or
¼ teaspoon black pepper	penne, cooked
2 medium onions, finely chopped	2–3 hard-boiled eggs, peeled
and *divided*	(optional)

To make the sauce, heat olive oil in a large kettle and sauté garlic on low heat for 3–5 minutes (*do not burn garlic*). Add tomato purée and paste; stir well. Add spices, 1 chopped onion, water, and ¼ cup Parmesan. Cook on medium-high heat until slightly bubbling. Cook for 2 hours. To make the meatballs, combine beef, remaining chopped onion, egg, bread crumbs, ¼ cup Parmesan, and salt and pepper to taste in a medium-sized bowl. Form into 2- or 3-inch meatballs. In a skillet, lightly brown meatballs in vegetable oil. Turn with tongs until all sides are lightly browned. *Do not cook through.* Drain meatballs and drop into sauce to cook for the remainder of the 2 hours. Stir every 15 minutes. If desired, drop eggs into sauce with meatballs. Toss some sauce with cooked pasta so every noodle is covered. Serve sauce and meatballs over pasta; sprinkle with additional freshly grated Parmesan cheese. Serve with lettuce salad tossed with extra virgin olive oil and balsamic vinegar and a loaf of warm, crusty bread. Serves 4 generously. *Tip:* Sauce can also be used for lasagna, pizza, and meatball/egg sandwiches.

Susie Klenk
Athletes in Action, IN

Tetrazzini

2 tablespoons chopped onions	1 cup diced cooked chicken, turkey,
1 tablespoon butter	or ham
1 can cream of mushroom soup	2 tablespoons chopped pimiento
½ cup water	1 tablespoon chopped parsley
½ cup shredded sharp Cheddar cheese	2 cups cooked angel hair pasta

In a saucepan, sauté onion in butter until tender. Blend in soup, water, and cheese. Heat until cheese melts, stirring occasionally. Add meat, pimiento, parsley, and pasta. Heat. Serves 3.

Laurie Killingsworth
New Life Center, FL

Tony's Pasta

2 yellow peppers
2 red peppers
1 large onion
3 cloves garlic, finely chopped
2 tablespoons olive oil
5–6 yellow tomatoes, chopped
1 red tomato, chopped (optional)

1 pound mushrooms (portabella, shiitake, or oyster), chopped
basil to taste
fresh parsley, finely chopped
1 pound perciatelli pasta, cooked
grated Parmesan cheese

Finely chop ½ of the peppers; cut the other ½ into strips. Finely chop ½ of the onion; cut the other ½ into thin strips. Sauté the chopped peppers and onion with garlic in olive oil until golden (about 10–15 minutes). Add yellow tomatoes, strips of pepper and onion, mushrooms, red tomato if desired, basil, and parsley. Simmer for about 5 minutes. Mix some sauce into the pasta; spoon the rest on top and sprinkle with Parmesan cheese. Serves 4. *Variation:* Substitute your favorite pasta if desired. This recipe is from Tony Capello.

Barbara Ball
ChurchLIFE, FL

Tortellini Salad With Italian Sausage

5 tablespoons olive oil, *divided*
1 pound sweet Italian or turkey sausage
9 ounces cheese-filled tortellini
1 6½-ounce jar marinated artichoke
    hearts
½ cup sliced ripe olives
½ cup crumbled feta cheese

¼ cup sliced green onion
½ cup chopped tomatoes
2 tablespoons white wine vinegar
1 teaspoon minced garlic
1 teaspoon dried basil
¼ teaspoon dried dill
2 cups torn fresh spinach leaves

Heat 1 tablespoon oil in a large skillet over medium heat. Add sausage and brown 8–10 minutes, turning occasionally. Reduce heat to low; cover and continue cooking 8–10 minutes more, turning once. When cool, cut sausage into ¼-inch slices. Cook tortellini according to package directions. Drain, rinse well, and toss with 1 tablespoon oil. Drain artichoke hearts, reserving marinade. Combine tortellini, sausage, artichoke hearts, olives, feta cheese, green onion, and tomatoes in a large bowl. In a small bowl, whisk together the reserved marinade (about ¼ cup), the remaining 3 tablespoons oil, vinegar, garlic, basil, and dill. Pour dressing over sausage-tortellini mixture. Refrigerate several hours. To serve, stir in spinach and let stand at room temperature 30 minutes. Serves 6 as an entree.

Anita Evans
Campus Ministry, FL

Trenette Al Pesto

18 fresh basil leaves (1 teaspoon
    dried basil)
1 clove garlic
5 ounces pine nuts or almonds
1¼ cups freshly grated Parmesan

3 tablespoons olive oil
salt and pepper
1 pound trenette linguini
12 ounces fresh green beans

In food processor, grind basil leaves and garlic. Gradually add the nuts, then cheese and olive oil. Add salt and pepper. Cook the pasta and green beans separately. Add 2–3 tablespoons of the pasta water to the pesto sauce. Stir sauce thoroughly into pasta. Serve pasta on a large plate surrounded by the green beans.

Rita Johnson
International Ministry, FL

He has not left you without testimony: He has shown kindness by giving you rain from heaven and crops in their seasons; he provides you with plenty of food and fills your hearts with joy (Acts 14:17).

Very Different Pasta With Pineapple

1½ cups chopped zucchini
1 cup chopped yellow squash
½ cup chopped onion
½ cup chopped green pepper
2 cups frozen Italian vegetables,
    thawed
3 cloves garlic, diced

dash oregano
1 jar spaghetti sauce
1 8-ounce can pineapple tidbits,
    drained
½ box tricolor pasta, cooked
2 cups shredded Monterey Jack or
    cheddar cheese

In a medium saucepan sprayed with Pam, sauté all vegetables together until soft. Add garlic and oregano. Pour in spaghetti sauce and pineapple; heat to a slow boil. Spoon pasta onto plates and sprinkle with shredded cheese. Top with desired amount of sauce. *Variation:* For extra protein and flavor, add crab meat or cooked chicken.

Kelly Hall
Corporate Human Resources, FL

Rice

Broccoli Rice ○

½ cup uncooked rice
    (1½–2 cups cooked rice)
1 onion, chopped
¼ cup margarine

2 cups chopped broccoli, cooked
    and drained
½ cup milk
⅔ cup grated cheese

Preheat oven to 350 degrees. Cook rice, if necessary. Sauté onion in margarine. Add remaining ingredients and bake in a covered casserole for 45 minutes. Serves 4.

Karen Horsey
International Ministry, FL

Flavorful Rice

1 cup uncooked rice
½ package Lipton's French onion
   soup mix

butter or gravy (optional)

Prepare rice as directed on package, adding French onion soup to the water while cooking. Rice may be buttered or served with gravy.

Vonette Bright
Co-founder, Campus Crusade for Christ
Executive Director, Women Today International, FL

French Rice

1 can onion soup, undiluted
½ cup butter or margarine, melted
1 4½-ounce jar sliced mushrooms

1 8-ounce can sliced water chestnuts
water
1 cup uncooked rice

Preheat oven to 350 degrees. Combine soup and butter. Drain mushrooms and water chestnuts, reserving liquid. Add enough water to reserved liquid to equal 1⅓ cups. Add mushrooms, water chestnuts, liquid, and rice to soup mixture; stir well. Pour into a lightly greased 10×6×2-inch baking dish. Cover and bake for 1 hour. Serves 6.

Juli Emory
Military Ministry, VA

Fried Rice

2 cups rice
½ cup oil
1 quart water
1 large onion, chopped
2 cans sliced mushrooms, drained

1 can bean sprouts, drained
¼ cup soy sauce
1 cup cooked meat
6 eggs

Fry the rice in oil until golden brown. Add water and onion. Simmer until rice is tender (about 20 minutes). Mix in the mushrooms, bean sprouts, soy sauce, and meat. In a separate skillet, scramble the six eggs, then add to rice mixture. When ready to serve, press rice mixture into individual cups and sprinkle with soy sauce.

Joette Whims
NewLife Publications, CA

Gourmet Brown and Wild Rice

2½ cups water
1 cup brown rice
¼ cup wild rice

¼ cup slivered almonds
¼ cup chopped green onion
1 tablespoon butter

Bring water to a full boil; add rice and stir once. Reduce heat to lowest setting and cook until all the water is absorbed (about 40 minutes). Sauté almonds and green onion in butter; add to cooked rice.

Jennie Mitchell
Josh McDowell Ministry, CA

Mushroom Rice Casserole

1 cup Uncle Ben's long-grain
   white rice
1 can beef broth or consommé
1 can French onion soup

¼ cup butter or margarine
½–¾ cup sliced fresh or
   canned mushrooms

Preheat oven to 350 degrees. Combine all ingredients in a 2½-quart casserole. If you use fresh mushrooms, make sure they are not at the top or bottom of the dish so they won't burn. Cover and bake for 45 minutes to 1 hour, or until liquid has been absorbed. *Variations:* If you don't like French onion soup, use 2 cans beef broth instead. To make this casserole a main dish, add ½–¾ cup diced raw chicken or beef and cook about 15–20 minutes longer.

Suzanne Davis
Finance, FL

Rice Supreme

¼ cup butter or margarine
1 can mushrooms, drained
½ small onion, minced

1 cup uncooked rice (not instant)
2 cans beef consommé

Preheat oven to 350 degrees. Melt butter in a 2- or 3-quart saucepan. Add onion and mushrooms; stir constantly and cook until onions are clear. Add consommé and rice. Pour into a casserole dish that has been sprayed with non-stick spray and bake for 35–40 minutes. To double recipe, use 3 cans consommé and 2 cups rice.

Cheryl Greenwald
Finance, FL

"When you give a luncheon or dinner, do not invite your friends, your brothers or relatives, or your rich neighbors; if you do, they may invite you back and so you will be repaid" (Luke 14:12).

Vietnamese Fried Rice

¼ cup cooking oil
¼–½ pound any cooked or raw meat, cut into thin strips
1 large onion, coarsely chopped
3 cloves garlic, minced
1 teaspoon salt
1 teaspoon pepper

1 teaspoon sugar
1 tablespoon soy sauce
3 cups cooked rice
1 cup vegetables such as peas, green beans, or carrots
2 eggs, beaten

Heat oil in a large skillet. Add meat, onion, and seasonings. Stir-fry until meat is tender and hot, about 1–2 minutes. Add rice and stir-fry 5 minutes. Add vegetables and stir well into rice-meat mixture. Just before serving, add eggs. Over medium heat, stir carefully through rice until eggs are cooked. Serve hot with a salad of leaf lettuce, cucumbers, fresh mint, and parsley. Serves 4.

Karen Horsey
International Ministry, FL

Yummy Wild Rice

1 cup brown rice
½ cup wild rice
½ cup fresh small pineapple chunks
  (optional)

1½ tablespoons lemon juice
2 large Granny Smith apples,
  chopped
⅛ teaspoon cardamon

Cook rices according to package directions. Combine remaining ingredients.
Stir into rice and cover 5 minutes to steam and set.

Gayle Anne VanFulpen
NewLife Publications, FL

Zucchini Rice Casserole

1½ cups water, *divided*
½ teaspoon salt, *divided*
½ cup rice
1 onion, chopped
1 pound zucchini (3–4 medium)

½ green pepper
1 8-ounce can tomato sauce
⅔ cup shredded cheese
¼ cup grated Parmesan cheese

Preheat oven to 325 degrees. Boil 1 cup water with ¼ teaspoon salt. Add
rice and onion. Reduce heat; cover and simmer until rice is tender (about
20 minutes). Scrub zucchini and cut into ½-inch slices. Boil ½ cup water
with remaining salt; add zucchini and green pepper. Cook about 5 minutes
or until zucchini is tender; drain. Add tomato sauce and zucchini mixture to
rice, and mix lightly. Place in a 1½-quart casserole and top with mixed
cheeses. Bake uncovered for about 20 minutes. For a complete meal, add
½–1 pound browned, drained ground beef. Serves 6.

Dorothy Brooks
Here's Life America, MA

Beans

Big Bean Pot

¾ pound (18 slices) bacon
3 medium onions, chopped
1 teaspoon garlic powder
½ teaspoon dry mustard
¾ cup brown sugar

¼ cup ketchup
½ cup cider vinegar
1 15½-ounce can kidney beans
1 15½-ounce can lima beans
2 21-ounce cans pork and beans

Preheat oven to 350 degrees. Sauté bacon and onions; drain. Add remaining ingredients and mix. Bake uncovered for 60–70 minutes. Makes 16 ½-cup servings.

Debbie McGoldrick
Student Venture, GA

Calico Beans

½ pound bacon, diced
1 pound ground beef
1 medium onion, chopped
1 can kidney beans, drained
1 can pork and beans
1 can lima beans, drained

¾ cup ketchup
1 teaspoon salt
⅓–1 cup brown sugar
2 teaspoons mustard
2 teaspoons vinegar

Preheat oven to 350 degrees. Fry bacon pieces until crisp. Remove from skillet, leaving about 2 tablespoons bacon drippings. Brown ground beef; add onion and cook slightly. Mix all the beans and the bacon. In a small bowl, combine the remaining ingredients, and add to the meat and beans. Bake uncovered for 45 minutes.

Joette Whims
NewLife Publications, CA

Easy Baked Beans

2 16-ounce cans navy beans
¾ cup brown sugar
1 teaspoon dry mustard

6 slices bacon, fried and crumbled
½ cup ketchup

Preheat oven to 325 degrees. Empty beans into a heavy pan. Add sugar, mustard, bacon (including drippings), and ketchup. Bake uncovered for 2½ hours. Makes 8 servings.

Ginny Purdy
Military Ministry, VA

 The righteous eat to their hearts' content, but the stomach of the wicked goes hungry (Prov. 13:25).

Mom's BBQ Bean Casserole

2 strips bacon, chopped
1 medium onion, chopped
2 1-pound cans pork and beans
salt to taste
½ cup molasses

dash of Worcestershire sauce
½ cup ketchup
dash of liquid smoke (optional)
½ teaspoon dry mustard

Sauté bacon and onion. Add remaining ingredients. Cook over low heat for 15 minutes, or pour into a casserole dish and bake at 350 degrees for about 30 minutes. These beans are great alongside potato salad at picnics.

Joanne Austin
International Ministry, FL

Monterey Beans

½ medium onion, diced
½ green pepper, diced
2 tablespoons olive oil
2 cups cooked kidney beans
2 ripe tomatoes, diced, or
 ¾ cup tomato sauce or V-8 juice

¼ cup beef bouillon
1 teaspoon chili powder
½ teaspoon salt
dash freshly ground pepper
¼ pound grated cheddar or
 Monterey Jack cheese

Sauté onion and green pepper in olive oil. Add remaining ingredients and cook slowly, stirring often until ingredients are blended and cheese is smooth (5–10 minutes). Serve over steamed brown or white rice.

Sandra Auer
International Ministry, FL

Southern Baked Beans

½ pound bacon
1 medium onion, chopped
½ cup brown sugar
¼ cup molasses

¼ cup ketchup
1 tablespoon prepared mustard
2 tablespoons Worcestershire sauce
1 large can pork and beans

Preheat oven to 350 degrees. Fry bacon until crisp, then crumble and set aside. Reserve 2 tablespoons bacon grease in pan and sauté onion until soft. Add all ingredients to pork and beans. Mix well. Bake for 1 hour.

Linda Crone
Josh McDowell Ministry, CA

Sweets

Cakes

Addie's Coconut Buttermilk Cake

1 teaspoon vanilla
1 teaspoon butter flavoring
1 tablespoon plus 1 cup buttermilk,
   divided
1 can flaked coconut
1 cup Crisco (no substitutes)

3 cups sugar
5 eggs, separated
¼ teaspoon baking soda
1 tablespoon hot water
3 cups flour

Preheat oven to 350 degrees. Combine vanilla, butter flavoring, 1 table-spoon buttermilk, and coconut; let stand while mixing cake. Cream Crisco and sugar. Add 1 egg yolk at a time and beat well. Dissolve soda in hot water; add to 1 cup buttermilk. Add flour and buttermilk alternately to sugar mixture. Beat egg whites until stiff, and fold in. Fold in the coconut mixture. Bake for 20 minutes, then reduce temperature to 325 degrees and bake for 45 minutes.

Ney Bailey
International Ministry, FL

Applesauce Cake

2 cups sugar
1 cup butter
dash salt
2½ cups applesauce
4 teaspoons baking soda
2 teaspoons cinnamon

1 teaspoon cloves
1 teaspoon allspice
9 ounces raisins or 2 pounds mixed
   dried fruit, chopped
1 cup chopped walnuts
5 cups flour

Preheat oven to 350 degrees. Cream sugar and butter; add salt. Heat apple-sauce and soda; add to creamed mixture along with the spices, raisins, and nuts. Add flour one cup at a time and mix thoroughly. Pour into a greased and floured 9×13-inch pan or 3 loaf pans, and bake for 1½ hours.

Barbara Ball
ChurchLIFE, FL

Bright's Favorite Cheesecake

6 ounces vanilla wafers, crushed
½ cup butter, melted
6 8-ounce packages cream cheese
1½ cups sugar
3 eggs

½ tablespoon vanilla
grated rind of ½ a lemon
1 cup heavy cream
Topping

Preheat oven to 300 degrees. Mix wafers and butter, and place on the bottom of a 10-inch springform pan. Soften cream cheese in a bowl. Add sugar and 1 egg at a time; then mix in vanilla, lemon rind, and cream. Bake for 2–2½ hours. Pour *Topping* over cheesecake and bake for 10 more minutes. *Variation:* If using an 11-inch springform pan, bake for 1½ hours.

Topping:
1 cup sour cream
2 tablespoons powdered sugar

½ teaspoon vanilla

Mix ingredients. Double the recipe if you prefer a thicker topping.

Vonette Bright
Co-founder, Campus Crusade for Christ
Executive Director, Women Today International, FL

Carrot Cake

2 cups flour
2 teaspoons baking soda
1 teaspoon salt
2 cups sugar
2 teaspoons cinnamon

4 eggs
1½ cups salad oil
3 cups shredded carrots
½ cup chopped pecans
Icing

Preheat oven to 350 degrees. Sift together the flour, soda, salt, sugar, and cinnamon. Add eggs and oil, and beat well. Stir in carrots and pecans. Pour into 3 greased and floured 8-inch cake pans or a 9×13-inch pan. Bake for 30 minutes. Cool in pans for 5 minutes. Ice cake as desired. This recipe is from my mother, Margaret Zachary.

Icing:

1 8-ounce package cream cheese
1 box powdered sugar
½ cup margarine

2 teaspoons vanilla
1 cup chopped pecans

Cream the cream cheese, then blend all ingredients until smooth.

Vonette Bright
Co-founder, Campus Crusade for Christ
Executive Director, Women Today International, FL

Cheesecake

¼ cup butter or margarine
1 cup graham cracker crumbs
¼ cup sugar
2 8-ounce packages cream cheese, softened

1 14-ounce can condensed milk
3 eggs
¼ teaspoon salt
¼ cup lemon juice

Preheat oven to 300 degrees. Combine margarine, crumbs, and sugar. Pat mixture firmly onto the bottom of a buttered 9-inch springform pan. In a large bowl, beat cream cheese until fluffy. Beat in milk, eggs, and salt until smooth. Stir in lemon juice and pour into pan. Bake for 50–55 minutes or until cake springs back when lightly touched. Don't over bake! Cool to room temperature, then chill.

Cindy Bibb
Church Dynamics International, CA

God's laws are pure, eternal, just. They are more desirable than gold. They are sweeter than honey dripping from a honeycomb (Psalm 19:9,10).

Cherry Cheesecake

⅓ pound graham crackers
½ cup butter, melted
1 cup sugar, *divided*
2 envelopes whipped cream mix

1 11-ounce package cream cheese, softened
2 cans cherry pie filling

Roll crackers until fine; mix crumbs, butter, and ¼ cup sugar. Line the bottom of an oblong glass baking dish. Prepare whipped cream mix according to package directions. Combine cream cheese and ¾ cup sugar; beat well. Fold into whipped cream. Pour over cracker crust and chill until firm. Top with cherry pie filling. Refrigerate until served.

Laurie Killingsworth
New Life Center, FL

Cherry Streusel Cake

1 cup plus 2 tablespoons butter,
    divided
1¼ cups sugar, *divided*
2 eggs

2¼ cups flour, *divided*
2 teaspoons baking powder
½ teaspoon salt
1 can cherry pie filling

Preheat oven to 350 degrees. Cream 1 cup butter and 1 cup sugar until light and fluffy. Add eggs and beat thoroughly. Sift together 2 cups flour, baking powder, and salt; add to sugar mixture, stirring well. (Batter will be very heavy.) Spread about ¾ of batter into a 9×13-inch pan. Pour pie filling down the center of batter, and gently spread over batter using a spatula. With a spoon, drop remaining batter over filling. Spread gently and swirl. Combine 2 tablespoons butter, ¼ cup sugar, and ¼ cup flour, and sprinkle on top. Bake for 45 minutes. Serves 12–16.

Barbara Ball
ChurchLIFE, FL

We are Christ's ambassadors. God is using us to speak to you: we beg you, as though Christ himself were here pleading with you, receive the love he offers you—be reconciled to God (2 Cor. 5:20).

Chocolate Cake

2 cups flour
1 teaspoon baking soda
½ teaspoon baking powder
1 teaspoon salt
1¾ cups sugar

¾ cup cocoa
¾ cup oil
1¼ cup water, *divided*
1 teaspoon vanilla
3 eggs

Preheat oven to 350 degrees. Beat together the first 7 ingredients with ¾ cup water. Add vanilla, eggs, and ½ cup water to mixture; beat another two minutes. Pour into cake pans; bake for 30–40 minutes, depending on pan size. This recipe is from Betty Scott and was served at our wedding. Everyone asks for it!

Joanne Austin
International Ministry, FL

CAKES

Chocolate Sponge Cake Roll

4 eggs, separated
2 tablespoons water
⅔ cup plus 2 tablespoons sugar,
    divided
¼ cup cocoa

⅓ cup flour
1½ teaspoons vanilla, *divided*
¼ teaspoon salt
½ teaspoon baking powder
1 cup whipping cream

Preheat oven to 375 degrees. Beat egg yolks with water. Gradually add ⅔ cup sugar, cocoa, flour, and 1 teaspoon vanilla. Beat egg whites with salt. When almost stiff, add baking powder. Fold into egg yolk mixture. Pour onto a greased cookie sheet lined with wax paper. Bake for 12 minutes. Turn cake onto a damp cloth and cool. Whip cream with 2 tablespoons sugar and ½ teaspoon vanilla. Spread over cake. Roll and wrap in waxed paper. Refrigerate.

Carrie Machiela
Executive Ministry, FL

Coconut Pound Cake

1½ cups butter
3 cups sugar
6 eggs
3 cups flour
1 teaspoon baking powder

¼ teaspoon salt
1 cup evaporated milk
1 tablespoon lemon flavoring
1 can flaked coconut
Frosting (optional)

Preheat oven to 325 degrees. Cream together butter and sugar. Add eggs 1 at a time and mix well. Sift together the flour, baking powder, and salt. Combine milk and lemon flavoring. Alternately add dry and liquid ingredients to creamed mixture, ending with dry ingredients. Add coconut and pour into a large tube pan that has been greased and floured and the bottom lined with brown paper. Bake for 1 hour and 15 minutes. Let cool in pan for about 15 minutes, then frost. *Variation:* If using cake flour, add another 6 tablespoons flour.

Frosting:

1½ cups powdered sugar
2 tablespoons butter, melted

3 tablespoons orange juice
1 teaspoon lemon juice

Mix all ingredients together.

Vonette Bright
Co-founder, Campus Crusade for Christ
Executive Director, Women Today International, FL

Donna Lynn's Date Cake

1½ cups boiling water
1 cup chopped dates
1¾ teaspoons baking soda, *divided*
½ cup margarine
1¼ cups sugar
2 eggs

1 cup whole wheat flour
1 cup white flour
¾ teaspoon salt
1 cup chocolate chips
½ cup brown sugar
½ cup chopped nuts

Preheat oven to 325 degrees. Pour boiling water over dates and 1 teaspoon baking soda. Allow mixture to cool to room temperature. Cream together margarine and sugar. Add eggs, then add date mixture. Stir in flour, ¾ teaspoon baking soda, and salt. Beat well until smooth. Pour into a greased oblong cake pan. Combine chocolate chips, brown sugar, and nuts, and spoon over the top of the cake batter. If you prefer it less sweet, use half the amount for topping. Bake for 45 minutes. This cake ices itself and is marvelous even a couple of days later. We've even eaten a piece with coffee as a Sunday morning breakfast!

Bob and Sandra Auer
International Ministry, FL

CAKES

He gave a loaf of bread, a cake of dates and a cake of raisins to each Israelite man and woman (1 Chron. 16:3).

Dump Cake

1 15¼-ounce can crushed pineapple   ½ cup margarine, melted
1 15-ounce can cherries   ½ cup crushed walnuts
1 box yellow cake mix

Preheat oven to 350 degrees. Layer ingredients in a 9×13-inch baking pan in the order listed. Bake for 1 hour.

Cathy Hertzler
Computer Services, FL

Dump Pumpkin Cake

1 29-ounce can solid pack pumpkin   1 box yellow cake mix
1 cup white sugar   ½ cup margarine, melted
1 13-ounce can evaporated milk   ¾ cup chopped nuts
3 large eggs   whipped cream
4 teaspoons pumpkin pie spice   brown sugar (optional)
¼ teaspoon salt   dash nutmeg (optional)

Preheat oven to 350 degrees. Mix pumpkin, sugar, milk, eggs, spice, and salt. Pour into a greased 9×13-inch pan. Sprinkle dry cake mix evenly over pumpkin mixture. Drizzle margarine on top and sprinkle nuts over all. Bake for 60–70 minutes or until a knife inserted in the center comes out clean. Serve with whipped cream, sweetened with brown sugar and nutmeg if desired.

Cheryl Henderson
CAPS, FL

Everyday Fruitcake

1 cup whole wheat flour
½ cup brown sugar
1 teaspoon baking powder
½ teaspoon salt
2 cups dried fruit assortment,
  coarsely chopped

¾ cup chopped walnuts or pecans
3 eggs, beaten
¼ cup honey
½ teaspoon vanilla
2 tablespoons frozen orange
  juice concentrate

Preheat oven to 325 degrees. In a bowl, combine wheat flour, brown sugar, baking powder, and salt. Combine ¼ of this mixture with dried fruit and nuts; set aside. Stir together eggs, honey, vanilla, and orange juice. Add dry ingredients and mix well. Fold in fruit mixture. Spoon into 2 3×6-inch or 1 4×8-inch loaf pan that has been well greased and the bottom lined with waxed paper. Bake for 1 hour or until well browned. Cool on rack 10 minutes, then turn out loaves and remove waxed paper.

Karen Horsey
International Ministry, FL

Fancy Fruit Cheesecake

purchased cheese cake
assortment of fruits

apricot jelly
warm water

Buy an inexpensive cheesecake and decorate it with fresh fruit. Arrange fruit by attractively overlapping on top of cheesecake. You can use slices of kiwi, peaches, strawberries, blueberries, raspberries, mandarin oranges, and grapes. Dilute apricot jelly with warm water, and drizzle over fruit to glaze. Refrigerate until ready to serve.

Linda Painton
Travel Department, FL

Forgotten Cake

5 eggs whites
½ teaspoon cream of tartar
⅛ teaspoon salt
1½ cups sugar

1 teaspoon vanilla
1½ cups whipping cream
fresh or frozen fruit

Preheat oven to 450 degrees. Beat egg whites, cream of tartar, and salt until whites hold peaks. Gradually add sugar, then vanilla. Pour into a greased and floured 8-inch glass baking dish. Place meringue in oven, turn oven off, and leave overnight. About 4 hours before serving, whip the cream and spread over meringue. Refrigerate. Serve topped with fresh or frozen fruit.

Vonette Bright
Co-founder, Campus Crusade for Christ
Executive Director, Women Today International, FL

> Produce fruit in keeping with repentance
> (Matt. 3:8).

Fruitcake

7 ounces Kelloggs All-Bran
   or Bran Buds
7 ounces caster sugar

7 ounces mixed dried fruit, chopped
¾ cup milk
7 ounces self-rising flour

Preheat oven to 350 degrees. In a bowl, mix All-Bran, sugar, dried fruits, and milk, and allow to stand for about 15 minutes. Mix flour with All-Bran mixture. Pour into a well-greased loaf pan. Bake for about 1½ hours or until a knife inserted in the center comes out clean. Slice and serve plain or buttered. *Variation:* In place of self-rising flour, you can use all-purpose flour mixed with 2 teaspoons baking powder.

Betty Hill
International Ministry, Nigeria

Fruit Cocktail Cake

2 eggs
1½ cups sugar
2 cups fruit cocktail with juice
2 cups flour
½ teaspoon salt

1 teaspoon cinnamon
2 teaspoons baking soda
1 cup chopped nuts
½ cup brown sugar
Icing

Preheat oven to 350 degrees. Combine eggs, sugar, and fruit cocktail with juice. Stir in dry ingredients and mix thoroughly. Pour into a large greased cake pan. Combine nuts and brown sugar, and sprinkle over cake. Bake for 40 minutes. Immediately top cake with hot *Icing*.

Icing:

1½ cups sugar
1 cup evaporated milk

⅔ cup butter or margarine
1 teaspoon vanilla

Place sugar, milk, and butter in a saucepan and bring to a boil. Boil for 2 minutes, stirring constantly. Remove from heat and add vanilla.

Jerry Younkman
International School of Theology, CA

Georgia Apple Cake

2 cups sugar
1½ cups cooking oil
2 eggs, beaten
2 teaspoons vanilla
juice from ½ lemon

3 cups flour
1¼ teaspoons baking soda
1 teaspoon salt
3 cups chopped apples
1 cup chopped nuts

Preheat oven to 325 degrees. Mix sugar, oil, eggs, vanilla, and lemon juice. Add flour, soda, and salt, then fold in apples and nuts. Pour into a greased bundt pan and bake for 1½ hours. Pour *Topping* over hot cake and let stand at least overnight. Delicious.

Topping:

1 cup brown sugar
¼ cup milk

½ cup butter
2 teaspoons vanilla

Mix ingredients and bring to a boil. Boil for 2½ minutes.

Belva Lee
JESUS Video Project, CA

Gooey Butter Cake ⏱

1 box yellow or other flavor cake mix
½ cup butter, melted
3 eggs

1 8-ounce package cream cheese
1 box powdered sugar

Preheat oven to 350 degrees. With a fork, combine cake mix, butter, and 1 egg, slightly beaten. Press into the bottom of a greased 9×13-inch pan.

CAKES

Beat together cream cheese, powdered sugar, and 2 eggs. Spread over cake mixture and bake for 30–40 minutes.

Cheryl Hile
Computer Services, FL

Grandma's Chocolate Cake

1 cup sugar	1 cup warm water
2 cups flour	1 teaspoon vanilla
¼ cup cocoa	1 cup mayonnaise or salad dressing
2 teaspoons baking soda	few drops red food coloring
¼ teaspoon salt	1 6-ounce package chocolate bits

Preheat oven to 350 degrees. Combine sugar, flour, cocoa, baking soda, and salt in a mixing bowl. Add the remaining ingredients except chocolate bits. Pour into a greased and floured 9-inch square pan. Bake for 35–40 minutes or until done. Sprinkle chocolate bits over hot cake to make a frosting. Cover for about a minute, then spread chocolate evenly over cake.

Marilyn Ehle
International Ministry, CO

Store up for yourselves treasures in heaven, where moth and rust do not destroy, and where thieves do not break in and steal. For where your treasure is, there your heart will be also (Matt. 6:20).

Heavenly Cake
(Contains no fat)

1 large angel food cake	peaches, kiwi, strawberries, bananas,
16 ounces non-fat vanilla yogurt	or raspberries (any combination)

Cut cake into three layers. Spread each layer with yogurt and top with sliced fruit. Put layers together and top with more yogurt. (Use as much yogurt as you want.) Refrigerate for 4–6 hours. This recipe is from my daughter, Robbyn.

Barbara Ball
ChurchLIFE, FL

Ice Cream Cake

1 cup graham cracker crumbs	2 cups milk
1 cup crushed unsalted saltines	1 quart butter pecan ice cream
½ cup margarine, melted	1 carton Cool Whip
2 small packages instant vanilla pudding	4–5 Heath bars, chopped

Mix crumbs, saltines, and margarine; pat into a 9×13-inch pan. Set aside.
Beat together pudding mixes, milk, and ice cream, and pour over crust. Place
in freezer. About 1 hour before serving, spread with Cool Whip and sprinkle
Heath bars on top. This dessert is *great* the second day!

Liz Lazarian
Women Today International, FL

Jewish Apple Cake

5 tablespoons sugar	4 eggs
1 tablespoon cinnamon	3 cups flour
3½ cups chopped apples	1 tablespoon baking powder
1 cup oil	½ teaspoon salt
2 cups sugar	¼ cup freshly squeezed orange juice

Preheat oven to 350 degrees. Mix sugar and cinnamon; toss with apples and
set aside. In a large bowl, beat oil, sugar, and eggs. In a separate bowl, mix
flour, baking powder, and salt. Alternately add flour mixture and orange
juice to creamed mixture. Generously grease a bundt pan with shortening.
Pour ⅓ of batter into pan, then ½ of apples; repeat layers, then top with
remaining batter. Bake for 1 hour and 20 minutes. Serve with Cool Whip or
with orange glaze made with powdered sugar and orange juice. Freezes well.

Doris Frageler
Leadership Ministries, Canada

*Keep my commands and you will live; guard my teachings
as the apple of your eye (Prov. 7:2).*

Marzipan Cake

1²/₃ cups flour
1 teaspoon baking powder
⅓ cup sugar
½ cup butter, softened

1 egg
¼ cup raspberry or apricot preserves
Filling

Preheat oven to 325 degrees. To prepare short pastry, sift flour and baking powder into a bowl; stir in sugar, butter, and egg, in order, until it's a smooth paste. Set aside while preparing *Filling*. Divide short pastry in half and use fingers to press each half into a 9-inch tart pan, lining it completely. Spread half of the preserves over each short pastry, and evenly divide *Filling* between them. Bake for 1 hour or until centers are well puffed. Serve in small wedges. Freezes very well.

Filling:

2 cups grated almonds or walnuts
2 cups sugar
1 cup butter

4 eggs
2 teaspoons almond extract

Combine nuts, sugar, and butter by hand, then beat in eggs with a wooden spoon. Beat in almond extract.

Rita Ruzzi
Executive Ministry, FL

Mississippi Mud Cake

1 cup margarine
½ cup cocoa
4 eggs, well beaten
1½ cups unsifted flour
2 cups sugar

dash salt
1½ cups chopped pecans
1 6¼-ounce bag miniature
    marshmallows

Preheat oven to 350 degrees. Melt margarine; add cocoa and eggs. Stir in flour, sugar, salt, and pecans; mix well. Grease and flour a 9×13-inch pan. Spread mixture into pan and bake for 30–35 minutes. Cake is done when sides pull away from pan. While baking, prepare *Frosting*. Immediately after removing cake from oven, pour marshmallows over the top. Spread *Frosting* over cake. Allow to cool completely, then cut into 2-inch squares. Yields 58 squares.

Frosting:

½ cup margarine, melted   ½ teaspoon vanilla
½ cup milk   ½ cup cocoa
1 pound powdered sugar

Combine all ingredients and mix well. Spread over cake.

Susan Conner
Campus Ministry, SC

Muzzy's Pound Cake

1½ cups sugar   1 teaspoon vanilla
5 eggs   ½ teaspoon baking powder
1½ cups plus 1 tablespoon flour,   1 teaspoon almond extract
   divided   (optional)
1 cup margarine or butter   chopped nuts (optional)

Preheat oven to 350 degrees. Beat together the sugar and eggs, then beat
together 1½ cups flour and butter. Combine the 2 mixtures and add vanilla.
Blend 1 tablespoon flour and baking powder into cake mixture just enough
to mix. Bake in a buttered tube pan or loaf pans for 1 hour. Check at
50 minutes to see if it is firm. Frost with *Lemon Glaze* or rub powdered
sugar on the cake while it's still hot.

Lemon Glaze:

1 cup sifted powdered sugar   2 tablespoons lemon juice

Stir together until blended. Add a little more powdered sugar or lemon juice
if necessary to make glaze the right consistency for drizzling.

Rosemary Priest
Associate Staff, AZ

Oatmeal Cake with Baked-On Topping

1½ cups boiling water   1½ cups flour
1 cup rolled oats   1 tablespoon baking powder
½ cup margarine   1 teaspoon salt
1 cup brown sugar   1 teaspoon cinnamon
1 cup white sugar   ½ teaspoon nutmeg
2 eggs

Preheat oven to 350 degrees. Pour the boiling water over the oats. In a separate bowl, mix remaining ingredients. Add the oatmeal mixture. Place into a greased 9×13-inch pan and bake for 35–40 minutes. Spread *Topping* on the cake and bake for 10 more minutes.

Topping:

1 cup coconut
¾ cup brown sugar
¼ cup evaporated milk

6 tablespoons margarine
1 teaspoon vanilla
½ cup chopped nuts

Combine all ingredients and cook until the sugar and margarine are melted.

Conda DeVries
International Ministry, FL

Piña Colada Cake

1 box Duncan Hines extra-rich
   yellow cake mix
1 can condensed milk

1 cup non-alcoholic Piña Colada mix
1 8-ounce carton Cool Whip
1 small can flaked coconut

Bake cake mix according to package directions. Immediately after removing from oven, pierce with a toothpick. Pour condensed milk evenly over the top; let cake cool. Pour Piña Colada mix over cake and allow time for mix to be absorbed. Refrigerate if desired. Spread Cool Whip on top and sprinkle with coconut. This recipe is from my mother, Margaret Zachary.

Vonette Bright
Co-founder, Campus Crusade for Christ
Executive Director, Women Today International, FL

Plain Pound Cake

1½ cups butter
3 cups sugar
6 eggs

3½ cups flour, sifted at least 3 times
¼ cup milk
1 tablespoon vanilla

Preheat oven to 300 degrees. Cream butter and sugar. Add eggs once at a time, blending thoroughly. Add flour, milk, and vanilla; mix well. Bake for 1 hour and 20 minutes. This recipe is from Aunt Esther Assef.

Becky and Susan McPherson
ChurchLIFE, AL

Prize Cheesecake

1 cup graham cracker crumbs (about 12 crackers)	2 large eggs, separated
¼ cup sugar	⅓ cup sour cream
¼ cup butter or margarine, melted	2 teaspoons powdered sugar
4 3-ounce packages cream cheese, softened	½ teaspoon vanilla
⅔ cup condensed milk	½ teaspoon grated lemon rind
	½ teaspoon lemon juice
	¼ teaspoon salt

Preheat oven to 300 degrees. In a medium bowl, combine crumbs, sugar, and butter; blend well. Reserve ¼ crumb mixture. Press remaining mixture firmly and evenly onto bottom and 1 inch up the side of a 9-inch springform pan. In a large bowl, beat egg yolks, sour cream, powdered sugar, vanilla, lemon rind, and lemon juice. In a small bowl, beat egg whites with salt until stiff but not dry. Gently fold into cheese mixture. Pour into pan and sprinkle reserved crumbs on top. Bake for 30 minutes. Cool in pan away from drafts. Refrigerate.

Cindy Bogan
JESUS Film Project, FL

All Scripture is God-breathed and is useful for teaching, rebuking, correcting and training in righteousness, so that the man of God may be thoroughly equipped for every good work (2 Tim. 3:16,17).

Scripture Cake

½ cup Judges 5:25, last clause	a pinch of Leviticus 2:13
2 cups Jeremiah 6:20	2 Chronicles 9:9 as desired
2 tablespoons 1 Samuel 14:25	½ cup Judges 5:25, first clause
6 of Jeremiah 17:11, separated	2 cups each 1 Samuel 30:12, chopped
1½ cups 1 Kings 4:22, first clause	
2 teaspoons Amos 4:5, first clause	2 cups Numbers 17:8, chopped

(All Bible verses are from the King James Version.) Preheat oven to 300 degrees. Cream butter, sugar, and honey. Add eggs yolks. In a separate bowl, mix flour, baking powder, and salt. Add desired spices, such as cinnamon, ginger, cloves, and nutmeg. Add dry ingredients to the creamed mixture, alternating with the milk. Coat the chopped figs, raisins, and almonds with flour to keep them from sinking to the bottom, and stir them into the mixture. Beat egg whites until stiff and fold into the batter. Bake in a well-greased 10-inch tube pan for 2 hours.

Carol Wunder
New Life Center, FL

Sour Cream Cake

1 cup sugar	1 teaspoon baking soda
1 cup flour	1 teaspoon vanilla
¼ teaspoon salt	1 egg
3 tablespoons cocoa	1 cup sour cream

Preheat oven to 325 degrees. Mix all ingredients at once; bake in a greased 8-inch pan for 40 minutes.

Vonette Bright
Co-founder, Campus Crusade for Christ
Executive Director, Women Today International, FL

Sour Cream Chocolate Pound Cake

1 cup butter	1 cup sour cream
2 cups sugar	2 teaspoons baking soda
2 eggs	2½ cups flour
2 squares unsweetened chocolate, melted	¼ teaspoon salt
	1 cup boiling water
2 teaspoons vanilla	*Icing*

Preheat oven to 325 degrees. Cream butter and sugar; add eggs one at a time, beating well after each. Stir in chocolate and vanilla. Mix sour cream and baking soda; add to chocolate mixture. Combine flour and salt. Add boiling water alternately with flour mixture. Pour into a tube pan that has been greased and dusted with cocoa. Bake for 1½ hours. Prepare *Icing* and spread on cake. Yields 20 servings.

Icing:

2 tablespoons butter	3 tablespoons warm water
2 squares unsweetened chocolate	2 cups powdered sugar

Melt butter with chocolate; blend in water. Add sugar and beat until the right consistency for spreading.

Linda Crone
Josh McDowell Ministry, CA

Squash Cake

3 cups grated zucchini	2 teaspoons baking powder
3 cups flour	4 eggs
3 cups sugar	1½ teaspoons cinnamon
1½ cups cooking oil	1 cup chopped nuts
1 teaspoon baking soda	*Frosting*

Preheat oven to 300 degrees. Combine all ingredients; place in a 9×13-inch pan and bake for 1½ hours. Cool cake and frost.

Frosting:

1 3-ounce package cream cheese, softened	1 teaspoon vanilla
½ cup margarine	2 cups powdered sugar

Blend ingredients together.

Marlyse Milburn
Milburn Projects, CA

The wisdom that comes from heaven is first of all pure; then peace loving, considerate, submissive, full of mercy and good fruit... (James 3:17).

Strawberry Heaven

1 10-inch angel food cake	1 pint strawberries, sliced
1 pint strawberries, mashed	strawberry halves
1 tablespoon milk	fresh mint leaves
12 ounces Cool Whip Lite, *divided*	

Cut cake horizontally into 3 layers. Place 1 cake layer on a serving plate. In a large bowl, stir mashed strawberries and milk into 1½ cups of the whipped topping. Spread ½ of the strawberry mixture on the cake layer. Arrange ½ of the sliced strawberries on top of the strawberry mixture. Repeat layers, ending with cake. Frost top and sides of cake with remaining whipped topping. Refrigerate 1 hour or until ready to serve. Decorate top and sides of cake with strawberry halves and mint leaves. Makes 12 servings.

Debra Brady
Staff & Ministry Opportunities, FL

Swedish Tarta

2 eggs
⅔ cup sugar plus extra for topping
⅔ cup flour

any fruit, such as apples, peaches, or blueberries, *divided*
½ cup melted butter

Preheat oven to 350 degrees. Cream eggs, sugar, and flour until fluffy, and pour into a greased 9-inch round cake pan. Add fruit in a circular fashion, reserving a little for topping. Over fruit, pour melted butter, and sprinkle with sugar to form a thin top crust as it bakes. (Use cinnamon-sugar mixture for apples.) Bake for 40 minutes. Top with fresh fruit. Serve plain or à la mode. Use this as a cake base for any fruit.

Shirley Heinmets
International Ministry, Europe

Texas Sheet Cake

1 cup water
1 cup margarine
¼ cup cocoa
2 cups flour
2 cups sugar

¼ teaspoon salt
1 teaspoon baking soda
2 eggs
1 cup sour cream
Chocolate Icing

Preheat oven to 325 degrees. In a saucepan, boil water, margarine, and cocoa for 2 minutes. Remove from heat and add flour, sugar, salt, and baking soda. Mix well, then stir in eggs and sour cream. Beat well. Pour into a greased and floured jelly roll pan. Bake for 40 minutes. Prepare *Icing* and ice cake while warm.

Chocolate Icing:

6 tablespoons milk   1 box powdered sugar
¼ cup cocoa   1 teaspoon vanilla
½ cup margarine   chopped nuts (optional)

Boil milk, cocoa, and margarine for 1 minute. Removed from heat and add remaining ingredients. Beat with a spoon until smooth.

Joette Whims
NewLife Publications, CA

Triple Chocolate and Vanilla Cheesecake

1½ cups finely crushed Oreos   4 eggs
  (18 cookies)   ⅓ cup unsifted flour
3 tablespoons margarine or butter,   1 tablespoon vanilla
  melted   2 squares semi-sweet chocolate,
4 8-ounce packages cream cheese,   melted
  softened   *Chocolate Glaze*
1 can sweetened condensed milk

Preheat oven to 325 degrees. Combine crumbs and margarine; press firmly onto the bottom of a 9-inch springform pan. In a large mixing bowl, beat cheese until fluffy. Gradually beat in sweetened condensed milk until smooth. Add eggs, flour, and vanilla; mix well. Divide batter in half. Add chocolate to ½ of the batter; mix well and pour into the pan. Top evenly with remaining vanilla batter. Bake 40–50 minutes or until cake springs back when lightly touched. Cool, then top with *Chocolate Glaze* and chill thoroughly.

Chocolate Glaze:

2 squares semi-sweet chocolate   ¼ cup whipping cream

In a small saucepan over low heat, melt chocolate with whipping cream. Cook and stir until thickened and smooth. Remove from heat.

Carolyn Justice
Single Life Resources, NC

 See how my eyes brightened when I tasted a little of this honey (1 Sam. 14:29).

Cookies & Bars

Apricot Balls

2 boxes dried apricots, finely ground
2 cans flaked coconut

1 can sweetened condensed milk
powdered sugar or Tang

Combine apricots and coconut; add milk. Shape into balls and roll in powdered sugar or Tang. Let stand until firm. Makes about 7 dozen balls the size of a quarter. They freeze beautifully.

Nancy Scott
JESUS Film Project, NC

Apricot Bars

1½ cups flour
1 teaspoon baking powder
¼ teaspoon salt
1½ cups rolled oats

1 cup brown sugar
¾ cup margarine
¾ cup apricot preserves

Preheat oven to 375 degrees. Sift together flour, baking powder, and salt; stir in oats and brown sugar. Cut in margarine until crumbly. Pat ⅔ of the crumb mixture into a 7×11-inch pan. Spread with preserves and cover with remaining crumb mixture. Bake for 35 minutes or until browned. Cool before cutting. Makes about 3 dozen bars or 6 dozen 1-inch squares.

Lois Mackey
CoMission, CA

Aunt Irma's Apple Bars

1 cup sugar
½ cup shortening or light margarine
1 cup unsweetened applesauce
1 teaspoon vanilla
2 cups flour
1 teaspoon baking soda

½ teaspoon salt
¼ teaspoon nutmeg
½ teaspoon cinnamon
½ cup raisins
powdered sugar
milk

Preheat oven to 350 degrees. Cream sugar and shortening. Add remaining ingredients except raisins, powdered sugar, and milk; mix well. And raisins and pour mixture into a greased 9×13-inch pan. Bake for about 20 minutes or until toothpick inserted in center comes out clean. Combine powdered sugar with a little milk and drizzle icing over cake.

Iris Cutshall
International Ministry, FL

Shine out among them like beacon lights,
holding out to them the Word of Life (Phil. 2:15).

Beacon Hill Cookies

1 cup chocolate chips ½ cup sugar
2 egg whites ½ teaspoon vanilla
dash salt ¾ cup finely chopped nuts

Preheat oven to 350 degrees. Melt chocolate chips, then set aside to cool. Beat egg whites until stiff and add salt. Gradually add sugar while beating until the mixture forms stiff peaks. Fold vanilla and eggs whites into the melted chocolate; add nuts. With a teaspoon, drop cookie dough onto a cookie sheet lined with waxed paper. Bake for 10 minutes. Slide wax paper with the cookies onto a cooling rack. Cool, then peel off carefully.

Carrie Machiela
Executive Ministry, FL

Brownies

½ cup butter 4 eggs
½ cup margarine 2 cups sifted cake flour
2 cups sugar ½ cup milk
½ cup cocoa 1 teaspoon vanilla
½ cup boiling water 1 cup nuts

Preheat oven to 350 degrees. Cream butter and margarine; add sugar and beat well. Mix cocoa and boiling water to form a smooth paste. Add cocoa to creamed mixture and beat well. Add eggs all at once and beat for 3 minutes. Mix in flour alternately with milk, then add vanilla. Fold in nuts and pour into a greased jelly roll pan. Bake for 40–50 minutes. Top with *Chocolate Lemon Frosting*.

Chocolate Lemon Frosting:

1½ squares unsweetened chocolate	1 teaspoon vanilla
¼ cup butter	2 teaspoons lemon juice
¼ teaspoon salt	1⅓ cups powdered sugar
1 egg, beaten	½ cup finely chopped nuts

Melt unsweetened chocolate with butter. Add salt and cool. Mix in egg, vanilla, lemon juice, and powdered sugar. Fold in nuts.

Barbara Ball
ChurchLIFE, FL

Brownies to Die For

8 ounces unsweetened chocolate	4 teaspoons vanilla
1 cup margarine	½ teaspoon salt
4 cups sugar	8 eggs
2 cups flour	1 package chopped walnuts (optional)

Preheat oven to 325 degrees. Melt chocolate and margarine in a large saucepan. Remove from heat; add sugar, flour, vanilla, salt, and eggs. Mix in nuts if desired. Pour into a deep pan that has been greased and floured. Bake for 35 minutes or until toothpick comes out clean. Then just fight off the crowd!

Sharon Ast
Board of Director's Wife

Caramel Chocolate Chip Bars

32 caramels	¼ teaspoon salt
5 tablespoons cream or milk	¾ cup brown sugar
1 cup flour	¾ cup butter, melted
½ teaspoon baking soda	6 ounces chocolate chips
1 cup rolled oats	

Preheat oven to 350 degrees. In a double boiler, melt caramels and cream then set aside. Mix dry ingredients with butter and place in a greased 9×13-

inch pan. Bake for 8–10 minutes. Sprinkle chocolate chips on top, then cover with caramel mixture. Bake for 15 more minutes. Cut while warm.

Conda DeVries
International Ministry, FL

Chocolate Cheerio Bars

¼ cup butter, melted
10 ounces marshmallows

1 cup chocolate chips
5½ cups Cheerios

Heat butter, marshmallows, and chips in a microwave oven for 1 minute or until melted. Stir in Cheerios. Pour into a greased 9×13-inch pan and let set for 30 minutes. Cut into bars.

Becky Leppard
International Ministry, FL

Chocolate Chip Cookies

2 cups butter or margarine, melted
2 cups packed brown sugar
1½ cups white sugar
3 eggs
2 teaspoons vanilla

6 cups flour
1½ teaspoons salt
1½ teaspoons baking soda
1 package semi-sweet chocolate
    chips

Preheat oven to 350 degrees. Mix butter and sugars by hand (no beaters) until smooth. Add eggs and vanilla. In separate bowl, combine flour, salt, and baking soda. Stir into sugar mixture then add chocolate chips. Drop dough by teaspoonful onto an ungreased cookie sheet and bake for about 10 minutes. Makes approximately 5 dozen cookies. *Tip:* To halve this recipe, use only 1 egg. This is a great cookie dough!

Liz Lazarian
Women Today International, FL

How sweet are your promises to my taste, sweeter than honey to my mouth! (Psalm 119:103)

COOKIES & BARS

Chocolate Chip Toasted Coconut Cookies

1 cup margarine
1 cup sugar
1 egg
1 teaspoon vanilla
1¾ cups flour
¾ teaspoon baking powder

⅛ teaspoon salt
¼ teaspoon cinnamon
⅛ teaspoon nutmeg
2 cups flaked coconut
6 ounces chocolate chips

Preheat oven to 375 degrees. Cream margarine; add sugar and cream until fluffy. Beat in egg and vanilla. Sift dry ingredients and add to sugar mixture. Mix in coconut and chocolate chips. Drop dough by teaspoonful onto an ungreased cookie sheet and bake for approximately 8 minutes. Makes 3 dozen cookies.

Cheryl Henderson
CAPS, FL

Chocolate Oatmeal Cookies

½ cup margarine
½ cup Crisco
2 cups sugar
2 eggs
½ cup cocoa
2 cups flour

2 teaspoons baking powder
½ teaspoon salt
3 cups rolled oats
1 cup chopped nuts or chocolate
chips, or ½ cup each

Preheat oven to 350 degrees. Cream margarine, Crisco, and sugar. Add eggs; beat until light and creamy. Sift the next 4 ingredients and add to sugar mixture. Mix in oats, nuts, and/or chocolate chips. Roll into balls and press on cookie sheet. Bake for 12 minutes.

Joanne Austin
International Ministry, FL

Chocolate Walnut Cookies

½ cup margarine
¼ teaspoon salt
1 cup sugar
1 egg
1 teaspoon vanilla

2 squares semi-sweet chocolate,
melted
¾ cup flour
½ cup finely chopped walnuts

Preheat oven to 325 degrees. Cream butter with salt until smooth and fluffy. Gradually add sugar. Add egg and beat well. Blend in vanilla and chocolate. Mix in flour, then walnuts until well blended. Drop dough by level table-spoonful 2 inches apart on a greased cookie sheet. Flatten slightly using a flat-bottomed glass covered with a damp cloth. If desired, sprinkle a few nuts on top of each cookie. Bake for about 15 minutes. Makes 3 dozen.

Sandy Davis
Campus Ministry, FL

Christmas Cookies
(Yugoslavia)

1 cup butter	4 egg whites
1½ cups sugar, *divided*	¾ cup finely ground walnuts
1 egg yolk	1 teaspoon lemon extract
¼–½ teaspoon salt	1 cup blackberry or current jelly
2½ cups flour	1 cup chopped walnuts

Preheat oven to 350 degrees. Cream butter with ½ cup sugar; beat until fluffy. Add egg yolk and salt. Stir in flour. Pat dough into a thin layer in the bottom of a 10×15-inch cookie sheet or 9×13-inch pan. Beat egg whites until stiff; gradually add remaining sugar. Continue beating until it is the consistency of meringue. Fold in the ground walnuts and lemon extract. Spread jelly over dough. Swirl meringue over jelly and sprinkle with chopped walnuts. Bake for 40–45 minutes. Cut into squares. Makes 3–4 dozen.

Linda Crone
Josh McDowell Ministry, CA

His intent was that now, through the church, the manifold wisdom of God should be made known to the rulers and authorities in the heavenly realms (Eph. 3:10).

Church Window Cookies

1 package semi-sweet chocolate chips	1 package multi-colored miniature
½ cup butter or margarine	marshmallows
1 cup chopped nuts	shredded coconut

Melt chips and butter; cool. Add nuts and marshmallows, stirring to blend. Divide in half and make 2 rolls or logs. Roll in coconut. Refrigerate overnight, then slice crosswise. *Variation:* For people who don't like coconut (like my husband), I roll the log in nuts instead of coconut. These look great and taste good, too!

Debra Brady
Staff & Ministry Opportunities, FL

Cocoa Brownies

6 heaping tablespoons cocoa
1½ teaspoons vanilla or
    creme de menthe extract
1⅓ cups butter
2¼ cups flour

2 cups sugar
1½ teaspoons salt
6 eggs
1 cup chopped nuts

Preheat oven to 350 degrees. Mix all ingredients and pour into a 9×13-inch greased pan. Bake for 35 minutes. *Variation:* I often substitute freshly ground whole wheat flour for the white flour, and no one knows the difference.

Shirley Heinmets
International Ministry, Europe

Cream Cheese Brownies

4 ounces Baker's German Sweet
    Chocolate
5 tablespoons butter or margarine,
    divided
1 3-ounce package cream cheese,
    softened
1 cup sugar, *divided*

3 eggs, *divided*
1 tablespoon plus ½ cup flour,
    divided
1½ teaspoons vanilla, *divided*
½ teaspoon baking powder
¼ teaspoon salt
½ cup coarsely chopped nuts

Preheat oven to 350 degrees. Melt chocolate and 3 tablespoons margarine in a small saucepan over very low heat, stirring constantly; cool. Blend remaining margarine and cream cheese until softened. Gradually add ¼ cup sugar, beating well. Blend in 1 egg, 1 tablespoon flour, and ½ teaspoon vanilla. Set aside. Beat remaining 2 eggs until thin and light in color. Gradually add ¾ cup sugar, beating until thickened. Add baking powder, salt, and ½ cup flour. Blend in cooled chocolate mixture, nuts, and 1 teaspoon vanilla. Spread about ½ of the chocolate batter in a greased 8- or 9-inch square pan. Add cheese mixture, spreading evenly. Drop remaining chocolate batter by tablespoonful over the top. Zigzag a spatula through the batter to marble it. Bake for 35–40 minutes or until top springs back when lightly pressed in center. Cool. Cut into bars or squares. Makes 16–20.

Cheryl Henderson
CAPS, FL

DB's Molasses Ovals

½ cup sugar	¾ teaspoon ground cloves
½ cup shortening	½ teaspoon baking soda
½ cup molasses	½ teaspoon salt
¼ cup water	1½ teaspoons ginger
1½ teaspoons cinnamon	1 egg
1 teaspoon baking powder	2½ cups flour

Place all ingredients except flour in a large bowl. Beat with mixer at low speed. Use a rubber spatula to stir in the flour. Cover dough with plastic and refrigerate for 1–2 hours. Preheat oven to 350 degrees. Roll teaspoonfuls of dough into oval shapes (approximately 2½ inches), and place 1 inch apart on ungreased cookie sheets. Bake for 10–12 minutes. With a spatula, remove cookies and place them on racks to cool. Store cookies in an air-tight container. Makes 3 dozen cookies.

Dave and Betsy Garrison
Finance, FL

Different Peanut Butter Cookies

1 cup flour	½ cup packed light brown sugar
½ teaspoon salt	½ cup white sugar
1 teaspoon cinnamon	½ cup creamy peanut butter
½ cup margarine, at room temperature	1 large egg
	1 teaspoon vanilla

Preheat oven to 350 degrees. Mix flour, salt, and cinnamon in a small bowl. Place remaining ingredients in a large bowl and mix with a spoon or mixer until well blended. Gradually add flour mixture, beating just until combined.

Drop by heaping teaspoonfuls 1½ inches apart on an ungreased cookie sheet. Bake for 10–12 minutes or until lightly golden. Do not overbake. Remove to a wire rack to cool. Makes 4 dozen cookies.

Shawnlei Breeding
Corporate Human Resources, FL

Dorothy Allen's Chocolate Chip Cookies

1 cup light or dark brown sugar
1 cup white sugar
1 cup butter-flavored Crisco
1 teaspoon vanilla
2 medium eggs, beaten
2 cups flour

½ teaspoon baking powder
½ teaspoon salt
1 teaspoon baking soda
6 ounces Nestle's chocolate chips
2 cups rolled oats

Preheat oven to 325 degrees. In a large bowl, cream together the sugars, Crisco, vanilla, and eggs. In another bowl, mix flour, baking powder, salt, and baking soda, and blend into the creamed mixture. Add chocolate chips and oats. You might want to mix with your hands because dough is very dry. Roll into balls, then flatten with your hand or a glass bottom. Bake for 15 minutes or until cookies are lightly brown or they will fall.

Philip Allen
JESUS Film Project, FL

 It is not good to eat too much honey, nor is it honorable to seek one's own honor (Prov. 25:27).

Favorite Brownies

1½ cups sugar
¾ cup margarine
1½ teaspoons vanilla
3 eggs (or egg substitute)
¾ cup flour

½ cup cocoa
½ teaspoon baking powder
½ teaspoon salt
1 cup chocolate chips
1 cup chopped nuts (optional)

Preheat oven to 350 degrees. Mix sugar, margarine, and vanilla; add eggs. Combine dry ingredients, then add to sugar mixture. Stir in chocolate chips and nuts. Spread in an 8-inch square pan. Bake for 35 minutes.

Adrien Webb
Finance, FL

COOKIES & BARS

Frosted Creams

1 rounded teaspoon cinnamon
1 teaspoon ginger
pinch salt
1 teaspoon baking soda
3 cups flour
1 cup shortening
1 cup sugar

3 eggs, separated
1 teaspoon vanilla
1 cup light molasses
1 cup hot water
2 cups powdered sugar
milk

Preheat oven to 350 degrees. Sift together the first 5 ingredients. Cream shortening and sugar. Add egg yolks, vanilla, and molasses to sugar mixture. Gradually add dry ingredients alternately with hot water. Fold in egg whites that have been beaten until stiff. Place in a 12×16-inch pan and bake for 30 minutes. Blend powdered sugar with enough milk to make the right consistency for spreading; frost when completely cool. Cut into squares.

Barbara Ball
ChurchLIFE, FL

Good-For-You Cookies

2 eggs, beaten
1 cup oil
1 cup raisins
6 ounces butterscotch chips
1 cup wheat germ
2 cups rolled oats
1 teaspoon baking soda
½ teaspoon vanilla

2 cups brown sugar
¼ cup buttermilk
½ cup chopped almonds
1 cup white flour
1 cup whole wheat or graham flour
¾ teaspoon salt
½ teaspoon baking powder

Preheat oven to 350 degrees. Combine ingredients in the order listed. Drop by teaspoonful onto a greased baking sheet. Bake for about 10 minutes or until light brown. Makes 4–5 dozen.

Nan Green
International Ministry, Africa

> *Food gained by fraud tastes sweet to a man, but he ends up with a mouth full of gravel (Prov. 20:17).*

Gravel

1 cup corn syrup
1 cup sugar
1 cup peanut butter

6 cups corn flakes
1 cup chocolate chips

Bring corn syrup and sugar to a boil. Add peanut butter. Mix in corn flakes and stir well. Press into a buttered 9×13-inch pan. Melt chocolate chips in microwave and spread over corn flake mixture. Cut into squares and cool.

Joette Whims
NewLife Publications, CA

James Blonde Brownies

⅔ cup butter
2 cups brown sugar
2 eggs
2 cups flour
1 teaspoon baking powder

¼ teaspoon baking soda
2 teaspoons vanilla
½ teaspoon salt
12 ounces chocolate chips

Preheat oven to 325 degrees. Melt butter and add sugar and eggs. Add flour, baking powder, baking soda, vanilla, and salt. Spread mixture into a greased and floured 9×13-inch pan. Sprinkle chocolate chips on top and bake for 30 minutes. Cool and cut.

Stacy James
Campus Staff, OH

Jen's Favorite Lemon Bars

2¼ cups flour, *divided*
1½ cups powdered sugar, *divided*
1 cup margarine, softened
4 eggs, slightly beaten

2 cups sugar
1 teaspoon baking powder
¼ cup plus 3 tablespoons lemon juice, *divided*

Preheat oven to 350 degrees. In a large bowl, mix 2 cups flour, ½ cup powdered sugar, and margarine. Press mixture into the bottom of an ungreased 9×13-inch pan. Bake for 20–30 minutes. Meanwhile, blend eggs, sugar, ¼ cup flour, and baking powder. After mixture is well blended, add ¼ cup

lemon juice. Pour mixture over warm crust. Return to oven and bake
25–30 minutes or until top is light golden brown. Cool completely.
Combine 1 cup powdered sugar and 3 tablespoons lemon juice; blend well.
Spread over cooled bars and cut. Makes 36 bars.

Patsy Morley
Board of Director's Wife

Krom Kakar
(Norwegian "Crumb Cake" Cookie)

1 cup sugar
3 eggs
3 egg yolks, well beaten
1 cup cream (not half & half)
½ cup butter, melted

1 cup flour
about ½ teaspoon vanilla
about ½ teaspoon lemon
powdered sugar (optional)

Mix sugar, eggs, and egg yolks; beat well. Heat both sides of a Krom Kakar
iron (purchase in a Scandinavian cookware shop). Add remaining ingredients except powdered sugar; beat well. Very lightly oil or grease the iron (it's
not necessary to grease the iron more than once). Pour on a small amount of
batter, about the size of a walnut. Close iron to bake on both sides at once.
Check after 1–2 minutes; cookies burn easily. When done, open the iron and
use a fork to pick off the flat cookie; roll it quickly on the metal tube. Store
in an airtight container. If desired, sprinkle with powdered sugar before serving. Makes 20 cookies.

Joan Tungseth
Computer Services, FL

Lemon Cookies

½ cup butter
1 cup flour
½ cup powdered sugar

pinch salt
Topping

Preheat oven to 350 degrees. With your hands, mix all ingredients except
Topping and press into a 9×13-inch glass pan. Bake for 5 minutes. Place baking dish on a cookie sheet to keep the bottom from scorching, and bake for
10 more minutes. Prepare *Topping* and pour over cookies. Bake for 25 minutes or until done.

Topping:

1 cup sugar

2 eggs

2 tablespoons lemon juice

½ teaspoon baking powder

2 tablespoons flour

Beat ingredients together.

Barbara Ball
ChurchLIFE, FL

COOKIES & BARS

Luscious Apricot Bars

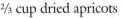

⅔ cup dried apricots

½ cup butter or margarine

¼ cup white sugar

1⅓ cups flour, *divided*

½ teaspoon baking powder

¼ teaspoon salt

1 cup brown sugar

2 eggs, well beaten

½ teaspoon vanilla

½ cup chopped nuts

powdered sugar

Preheat oven to 350 degrees. Rinse apricots; cover with water and boil for 10 minutes. Drain, cool, and chop. Combine butter, white sugar, and 1 cup flour until crumbly. Press into a greased 8-inch square pan. Bake for 25 minutes or until lightly browned. Sift together ⅓ cup flour, baking powder, and salt. Gradually beat brown sugar into eggs. Add flour mixture. Combine vanilla, apricots, and nuts. Spread over baked layer and bake for 30 more minutes. Cool in pan. Cut into bars and roll in powdered sugar. Makes 2½ dozen.

Barbara Ball
ChurchLIFE, FL

Marzipan Cookies

1½ cups flour

½ cup sugar

½ cup butter, softened

¼ cup brown sugar

½ teaspoon baking soda

½ teaspoon vanilla

¼ teaspoon salt

1 egg

¼ cup almond paste

½ cup chocolate chips

Preheat oven to 375 degrees. Mix all ingredients except the almond paste and chocolate chips. On an ungreased cookie sheet, put teaspoonfuls of dough about 2 inches apart and flatten into rounds. Top with ¼–½ teaspoon of almond paste on each, then top with another flattened round of dough, pressing together at edges. Bake about 8 minutes or until lightly browned. Melt the chocolate chips, then drizzle over cooled cookies.

Wendy Hill
National Ministry, FL

Mint Chocolate Chip Cookies

2 cups butter
1¾ cups brown sugar
4 eggs
2 teaspoons vanilla
5 cups rolled oats
4 cups flour

1 teaspoon salt
2 teaspoons baking powder
2 teaspoons baking soda
12 ounces chocolate chips
1 7-ounce bar Hershey's Cookies-N-Mint Chocolate, grated

Preheat oven to 375 degrees. Cream butter and brown sugar. Add eggs and vanilla, then set aside. Grind oats in a blender or food processor to make into a powder. Add to flour, salt, baking powder, and baking soda. Combine flour mixture and creamed mixture. Stir in chocolate chips and grated chocolate bar. Form into golf-ball-size balls and bake for 8–10 minutes. Makes 8 dozen delicious cookies.

Haydee Fuerte
Corporate Human Resources, FL

Mississippi Big Babies

1 cup margarine
1 cup Crisco
1 cup brown sugar
2 cups white sugar
4 eggs
2 teaspoons vanilla
4 cups flour
2 teaspoons baking soda
2 teaspoons baking powder

1 teaspoon salt
2 cups rolled oats
2 cups cereal of your choice
6 ounces chocolate chips
6 ounces peanut butter chips
1 cup coconut
1 cup chopped pecans
1 cup raisins

Preheat oven to 350 degrees. Using the largest mixing bowl available, cream margarine and Crisco. Add brown sugar, white sugar, eggs, and vanilla. Add flour, baking soda, baking powder, and salt; mix well. Stir in remaining ingredients. Using an ice cream scoop or ¼-cup measure, drop dough onto a cookie sheet. Bake for 15 minutes.

Debby Thompson
International Ministry, Eastern Europe

Mom's Peanut Butter Fingers

½ cup margarine
½ cup white sugar
½ cup brown sugar
1 egg, unbeaten
⅓ cup plus 4 tablespoons peanut butter, *divided*
½ teaspoon baking soda
¼ teaspoon salt
½ teaspoon vanilla
1 cup flour
1 cup quick oats
1 cup chocolate chips
½ cup powdered sugar
2–4 tablespoons milk

Preheat oven to 350 degrees. Cream margarine, white sugar, and brown sugar. Blend in egg, ⅓ cup peanut butter, baking soda, salt, and vanilla. Stir in flour and oats and spread in a greased 9×13-inch pan. Bake for 20–25 minutes. Remove from oven and sprinkle chocolate chips onto hot bars. Let stand 5 minutes, then spread evenly. Combine powdered sugar, 4 tablespoons peanut butter, and milk to icing consistency. Drizzle over bars and cool before cutting.

Kathy LaGambina
CoMission, FL

 Eat honey, my son, for it is good; honey from the comb is sweet to your taste (Prov. 24:13).

Oatmeal Honey Cookies

¾ cup canola oil
1 cup honey
1 large egg
1 teaspoon vanilla
1½ cups whole wheat flour
1 teaspoon salt
½ teaspoon baking soda
3 cups uncooked rolled oats
½–1 cup chopped walnuts, raisins, or coconut (optional)

Preheat oven to 300 degrees. Mix all ingredients. Drop by teaspoonfuls onto a greased cookie sheet. Bake for 15 minutes. Let set for a few minutes before removing from the baking sheet, but not too long or they will stick to the pan. Cool on cooling racks. Store in an airtight cookie jar (the honey will attract moisture and soften the cookies). Makes 5 dozen.

René Brygger
JusticeLINC, WI

One-Bowl Brownies

½ cup cocoa
¾ cup butter
2 cups sugar
3 eggs
1 teaspoon vanilla

1 cup flour
1 cup chopped nuts
½ teaspoon salt
½ teaspoon baking soda

Preheat oven to 350 degrees. Microwave cocoa and butter for 2 minutes or until melted. Stir in sugar, then beat in eggs and vanilla. Add remaining ingredients; stir well. Spread into a greased 9×13-inch pan. Bake for 30–35 minutes. Makes 24 brownies.

Becky Leppard
International Ministry, FL

Pam's Surprise Cookies

½ cup butter or applesauce
¾ cup packed brown sugar
1 egg
2 tablespoons vanilla
¾ cup coarsely chopped dates
      (optional)
1 cup flour

½ teaspoon salt
1 teaspoon baking soda
1 teaspoon baking powder
½ cup flaked coconut
½ cup granola
¾ cup chopped walnuts
1¾ cups semi-sweet chocolate chips

Preheat oven to 350 degrees. In a large bowl, cream butter and brown sugar until smooth. Add egg and vanilla; beat well. Stir in dates and let mixture set for 5 minutes. Beat at high speed for 3 minutes until very light brown and creamy. Combine flour, salt, baking soda, and baking powder in a small bowl, breaking up the lumps. Stir into creamed mixture. Add coconut, granola, walnuts, and chocolate chips. Drop by spoonful on a lightly greased cookie sheet. Bake for 10–15 minutes.

Jackie Jackson
Finance, FL

PVM Brownies
(Protein, Vitamin, Mineral)

4 cups water
½ cup sunflower seeds
1 cup soy granules
2 envelopes unflavored gelatin
cold water
sweetener equal to 1 cup sugar
    or ¾ cup honey

¼ cup dietetic cocoa (carob flour)
½ cup wheat germ
½ cup lecithin
1 teaspoon vanilla
pinch salt
dash cinnamon

These will take a trip to the health-food store for most of the ingredients. Boil water; add sunflower seeds to soften. Gradually add soy granules. Dissolve gelatin in a little cold water; add to mixture. Boil for 10 minutes. Remove from heat and add remaining ingredients. Beat well. Pour into a flat pan and refrigerate. When cool, cut into small squares.

Judy Anderson
Christian Embassy, CO

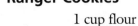

Ranger Cookies

1 cup brown sugar
⅔ cup shortening
1 egg, well beaten
1 teaspoon vanilla
¾ cup rolled oats

1 cup flour
¼ teaspoon baking powder
½ teaspoon baking soda
½ teaspoon salt
½ cup chopped pecans

Preheat oven to 350 degrees. Cream sugar and shortening; add egg, vanilla, and oats. Sift together flour, baking powder, baking soda, and salt. Add to creamed mixture, then stir in nuts. Drop by spoonful onto a greased cookie sheet and bake for 10–12 minutes.

Vonette Bright
Co-founder, Campus Crusade for Christ
Executive Director, Women Today International, FL

Ranger Macaroons

1 cup butter
1 cup white sugar
1 cup brown sugar
2 eggs
1 teaspoon vanilla
2 cups flour
1 teaspoon salt

1 teaspoon baking powder
1 teaspoon baking soda
2 cups corn flakes
1 cup chopped pecans
2 cups rolled oats
1 cup coconut

Preheat oven to 375 degrees. Mix butter, sugars, eggs, and vanilla until creamy. Sift dry ingredients and add to creamed mixture. Thoroughly mix in remaining ingredients. Drop by teaspoonfuls onto ungreased baking sheets. Bake for 12–14 minutes.

Jacquie Tanner
Campus, WI

Seven-Layer Bars

½ cup butter
1 cup graham cracker crumbs
1 cup flaked coconut
6 ounces butterscotch chips

6 ounces chocolate chips
1 cup chopped nuts
1 can Eagle Brand sweetened
   condensed milk

Preheat oven to 325 degrees. Melt butter in a 9×13-inch pan. Add the next 5 ingredients in layers and carefully pour milk on top. Bake for 25–30 minutes or until slightly brown.

Marlyse Milburn
Milburn Projects, CA

Skillet Cookies

2 eggs
1 cup sugar
1 cup chopped dates

½ cup margarine
3 cups Rice Krispies
¾ cup chopped nuts

Place the first 4 ingredients in a skillet. Cook for 15 minutes over low heat, stirring constantly. Remove from heat and stir in Rice Krispies and nuts.

When cool, form into balls. *Variation:* Shape balls like strawberries and roll in red colored sugar. Use a green icing decorator to make a stem and leaf on the end.

Nancy Scott
JESUS Film Project, NC

Snickerdoodles

1 cup shortening
2 eggs
1½ cups plus 2 tablespoons sugar, *divided*
½ teaspoon salt

2¾ cups flour
2 teaspoons cream of tartar
1 teaspoon baking soda
2 tablespoons cinnamon

Preheat oven to 375 degrees. Mix shortening, eggs, 1½ cups sugar, and salt. Sift together flour, cream of tartar, and baking soda. Stir mixtures together and chill dough for at least 1 hour. When ready to bake, combine cinnamon and 2 tablespoons sugar. Form dough into walnut-size balls and roll in cinnamon mixture. Place 2 inches apart on an ungreased cookie sheet. Bake for 8–10 minutes. Cookies puff up and then flatten out. Makes 3–4 dozen.

Mary Canada
President's Office, FL

So Easy Cookies

2 cups margarine
2 cups sugar
3 eggs

1 teaspoon vanilla
½ teaspoon salt
4 cups flour

Preheat oven to 350 degrees. Mix all ingredients thoroughly. Drop by teaspoonful onto a cookie sheet or put through a cookie press. Bake for 12 minutes.

Jane Prall
Crusade Family

This is my command: Love each other (John 15:17).

Sour Cream Raisin Bars

2 cups raisins	3 egg yolks
1 cup brown sugar	1½ cups sour cream
1 cup butter or margarine	1 cup sugar
1¾ cups rolled oats	2½ tablespoons cornstarch
1 teaspoon baking soda	1 teaspoon vanilla
1¾ cups flour	

Preheat oven to 350 degrees. Cook raisins in a little water for 10 minutes; drain and let cool while mixing rest of bars. Cream together brown sugar and butter. Add oats, baking soda, and flour; mix well. Pat ½ of mixture into a 9×13-inch pan. Press down and bake for 7 minutes. In a heavy saucepan, combine egg yolks, sour cream, sugar, and cornstarch. Mix well and cook, stirring constantly until mixture is thickened and comes to a boil; do not undercook. Add raisins and vanilla. Pour over crust; top with remaining crumbs. Bake for 30 minutes.

Conda DeVries
International Ministry, FL

Spritz

2 cups butter (no substitutes)	1 teaspoon vanilla
1 cup sugar	1 teaspoon almond extract
1 egg, well beaten	4 cups flour

Preheat oven to 400 degrees. Mix ingredients in order; chill dough for at least 1 hour. Put into a cookie press, and press onto an ungreased cookie sheet. Decorate with sprinkles as desired. Bake for about 10 minutes or until slightly browned. Cookies burn easily, so watch carefully.

Joette Whims
NewLife Publications, CA

If you really keep the royal law found in Scripture, "Love your neighbor as yourself," you are doing right (James 2:8).

Tea and Comfort Cookies

1 cup margarine	½ cup white sugar
2 tablespoons milk	1½ cups flour
2 teaspoons vanilla	2½ cups rolled oats
½ teaspoon salt	2 cups flaked coconut
1 teaspoon baking soda	1 12-ounce package chocolate chips
1¼ cups brown sugar	1 package chopped nuts (optional)

Preheat oven to 350 degrees. Place the first 7 ingredients in a mixing bowl; blend well. Add flour and blend again. Add remaining ingredients and combine thoroughly. Drop by teaspoonful onto a cookie sheet and bake for 12–15 minutes.

Sharon Ast
Board of Director's Wife

When others are troubled, needing our sympathy and encouragement, we can pass on to them this same help and comfort God has given us (2 Cor. 1:4).

Ultimate Brownies

1⅓ cups flour	4 eggs
1 teaspoon baking powder	¼ cup milk
½ teaspoon salt	1½ teaspoons vanilla
1 cup butter	1 cup chopped walnuts (optional)
1 cup cocoa	6 ounces chocolate chips (optional)
2 cups sugar	powdered sugar

Preheat oven to 350 degrees. In a small bowl, mix flour, baking powder, and salt; set aside. Melt butter in a medium saucepan or microwave. Stir in cocoa and pour into a large bowl. With a mixer, blend in sugar. Add eggs and blend in; add flour until entire mixture is smooth. Blend in milk, vanilla, walnuts, and chocolate chips. Pour into a greased and floured 9×13-inch pan. Bake for 25–30 minutes. Brownies are done when toothpick inserted into center comes out clean. Cool in pan. Sprinkle with powdered sugar and cut into 2- to 3-inch pieces. Serves 18.

Aimee Fooke
Family Life, AK

Unbaked Chocolate Cookies

2 cups sugar
½ cup milk
3 tablespoons cocoa
½ cup butter

½ cup peanut butter
1 teaspoon vanilla
3 cups rolled oats

Put sugar, milk, cocoa, and butter into a saucepan and boil. Stir in peanut butter and vanilla. Pour mixture over oatmeal; combine thoroughly. Drop by teaspoonful onto wax paper. Cool.

Marlyse Milburn
Milburn Projects, CA

Whole Wheat Chocolate Chip Cookies

1 cup brown sugar
1 cup sugar
½ cup plus ⅓ cup margarine, melted
2 eggs
⅓ cup canola oil
1–2 teaspoons vanilla

3 cups wheat flour
1 teaspoon baking soda
1 teaspoon salt
12 ounces semi-sweet chocolate chips
1–2 cups chopped pecans or walnuts

Mix sugars well. Combine margarine, eggs, oil, and vanilla. Add to sugars and stir until well blended. Add flour, baking soda, and salt; mix well. Stir in chips and nuts. Chill for about 1 hour before baking. Bake at 375 degrees for 8–10 minutes, depending on whether you prefer chewy or crunchy cookies. Makes 3–4 dozen.

Jennifer Waddell
Campus Ministry, LA

Yum-Yums

½ cup butter
1 cup white sugar
2 eggs, well beaten
1½ cups flour
1 teaspoon baking powder

½ teaspoon salt
1 teaspoon vanilla
1 cup chopped nuts
1 egg white
1 cup brown sugar

Preheat oven to 350 degrees. Cream butter; add white sugar, then the eggs. Mix in flour, baking powder, and salt. Add vanilla. Spread dough on a baking sheet. Sprinkle nuts over batter. Beat egg white until stiff; gradually add brown sugar and spread over nuts. Bake for 30 minutes. Cut into bars.

Nancy Scott
JESUS Film Project, NC

> *Pleasant words are a honeycomb, sweet to the soul and healing to the bones (Prov. 16:24).*

Zucchini Cookies

2 cups grated zucchini
2 cups sugar
1 cup oil or margarine
2 eggs
4 cups flour
1 teaspoon cinnamon

1 teaspoon baking soda
1 teaspoon nutmeg
1 teaspoon cloves
1 teaspoon salt
2 cups raisins
2 cups chopped nuts

Preheat oven to 350 degrees. Mix all ingredients. Drop by spoonful onto a greased baking sheet. Bake for 10–12 minutes or until browned.

Marlyse Milburn
Milburn Projects, CA

Other Sweets

Almond Praline Sauce

3 tablespoons butter, *divided*
2 tablespoons slivered almonds
1 cup brown sugar

¼ cup light corn syrup
dash salt
½ cup evaporated milk

Melt 1 tablespoon butter in a saucepan; add almonds and sauté until lightly browned. Add 2 tablespoons butter, brown sugar, corn syrup, and salt. Cook over low heat, stirring constantly until sugar is thoroughly dissolved. Slowly blend in evaporated milk; cool. Serve over coffee ice cream or orange sherbet.

Judy Anderson
Christian Embassy, CO

Brown Sugar Candy

1½ cups brown sugar
1½ cups white sugar
1 cup half & half
1 tablespoon Karo white syrup

1 teaspoon vanilla
3–4 tablespoons butter
1 cup chopped nuts

Mix the first 4 ingredients in a saucepan and cook to the soft-ball stage. Add vanilla and butter. Beat until the color changes and it can be poured easily. Add nuts and pour onto a greased platter.

Bailey Marks
International Ministry, FL

Wherever we go he uses us to tell others about the Lord and to spread the Gospel like a sweet perfume (2 Cor. 2:14).

Candied Nuts

1 pound raw peanuts
1 cup sugar

½ cup water
dash salt

Preheat oven to 300 degrees. Cook ingredients in a saucepan until water is evaporated. Pour onto a lightly greased cookie sheet and sprinkle with a little salt. Bake for 15 minutes. Stir, then bake for another 15 minutes.

Debbie McGoldrick
Student Venture, GA

Cathy Pugh's Peanut Brittle

1 cup sugar
½ cup light corn syrup
1 cup roasted peanuts

1 tablespoon margarine
1 teaspoon vanilla
1 teaspoon baking soda

Mix sugar and syrup; cook for 4 minutes. Add peanuts, margarine, and vanilla, and cook for 1½ minutes. Add baking soda; stir very quickly and pour onto a greased pan. Do not try to spread it out.

Philip Allen
JESUS Film Project, FL

Chocolate Covered Strawberries

12 ounces semi-sweet chocolate
paraffin wax, melted

1 pint strawberries

Melt chocolate in a double boiler. Add a small amount of melted wax. Dip washed strawberries into chocolate mixture and place on wax paper to dry. Chill until ready to serve.

Donelle Tison
International School of Theology, CA

Chocolate Fondue

1 14-ounce can Eagle brand
    condensed milk
6 ounces chocolate chips

1 12-ounce jar caramel ice cream
    topping
¼ cup strong coffee

Mix all ingredients in a saucepan. Heat, then pour into a fondue pot or small crockpot to keep warm. For dipping, use angel food or pound cake, ginger cookies, nuts, or fruit such as grilled pineapple, strawberries, bananas, or apples.

Belva Lee
JESUS Video Project, CA

Chocolate Frosting

2 tablespoons sweet butter
¾ cup semi-sweet chocolate chips
6 tablespoons heavy cream

1¼ cups powdered sugar
1 teaspoon vanilla

Place all ingredients in a saucepan over low heat. Whisk until smooth. Cool slightly. Add more powdered sugar if necessary to reach the right consistency for spreading. Spread on cake while frosting is still warm.

Barbara Ball
ChurchLIFE, FL

Chocolate Glaze

10 ounces semi-sweet chocolate,   3 tablespoons vegetable shortening
   cut into pieces

Melt chocolate and shortening, whisking until smooth. Cool slightly before
using as glaze on cake or other desserts.

Barbara Ball
ChurchLIFE, FL

Chocolate Ice Cream

6 eggs, beaten   1 teaspoon vanilla
2 cups sugar   pinch of salt
3 12-ounce cans evaporated milk   whole milk
1 large can Hershey's chocolate syrup

Mix eggs and sugar, then add evaporated milk and chocolate syrup. Blend
vanilla and salt; stir well. Pour into a 1-gallon ice cream freezer. Add whole
milk to make a full gallon; stir. Place in an ice cream freezer container. Add
rock salt and freeze until ready.

Brenda Morrow
ChurchLIFE, NC

Cocoa Frosting

3½ cups powdered sugar   ⅓ cup butter
½ teaspoon salt   ⅓ cup hot milk
⅓ cup cocoa   ½ teaspoon vanilla

Sift sugar, salt, and cocoa together. Cream butter with ½ of the sugar mixture. Add remaining sugar mixture alternately with milk; beat until smooth.
Add vanilla.

Dorothy Brooks
Here's Life America, MA

Dream Frosting

1 package instant vanilla pudding 1½ cups milk
1 package Dream Whip

Mix pudding and Dream Whip with milk. Beat at high speed for 5–7 minutes. Makes enough to cover a large cake.

Grace Frick
Crusade Family

Easy Caramel Icing

1½ cups packed brown sugar 2 tablespoons butter
¼ cup cream 1 teaspoon vanilla

Mix brown sugar, cream, and butter in a saucepan. Bring to a boil and cook for 3 minutes, stirring constantly. Remove from heat. Add vanilla and cool to lukewarm. Beat until creamy and thick enough to spread. Spread quickly on cake because icing hardens fast. Add a little cream if necessary to thin.

Midge Piedot
Crusade Family

Easy Penuche Frosting

½ cup butter ¼ cup milk
1 cup packed brown sugar 1¾–2 cups sifted powdered sugar

Melt butter; add brown sugar. Boil and stir over low heat for 2 minutes. Add milk; bring to a boil, stirring constantly. Cool to lukewarm. Gradually add powdered sugar. Beat until thick enough to spread. If too thick, add hot water. Good on spice or white cake.

Dorothy Brooks
Here's Life America, MA

 See how my eyes brightened when I tasted a little of this honey (1 Samuel 14:29).

OTHER SWEETS

Fluffy Frosting

2 tablespoons flour
½ cup milk
¼ cup shortening

¼ cup butter
½ cup powdered sugar
1 teaspoon vanilla

Cook flour and milk together until thick. Cool slightly. Beat remaining ingredients until very light. Add flour mixture and beat thoroughly.

Midge Piedot
Crusade Family

A fool thinks he needs no advice, but a wise man listens to others (Prov. 12:15).

Foolproof Fudge

3 cups chocolate or peanut
   butter chips
1 14-ounce can condensed milk

dash salt
1 cup chopped nuts
1½ teaspoons vanilla

In a heavy saucepan over low heat, melt chips with condensed milk and salt. Remove from heat; stir in nuts and vanilla. Spread evenly into an 8- or 9-inch square pan lined with waxed paper. Chill for 2 hours or until firm. Turn fudge onto cutting board. Peel off paper and cut into squares. Store loosely covered at room temperature.

Ethel Opie
Church Dynamics International, CA

French Cream Frosting

½ cup butter or margarine
2¼–2½ cups powdered sugar
1 egg

3 squares unsweetened chocolate,
   melted and cooled
1 teaspoon vanilla

Cream butter and sugar. Add egg; mix thoroughly. Blend in chocolate and vanilla. Beat to spreading consistency; thin with milk if necessary. This recipe frosts 2 8- or 9-inch layers.

Nancy Schurle and Kerry Fix
Crusade Family

Granny Hawks's Chocolate Gravy

2½ cups milk
⅓ cup flour
1 cup sugar

pinch salt
3 scant tablespoons cocoa
1 teaspoon vanilla

Pour milk into a heavy saucepan and warm over medium-high heat. Mix dry ingredients in a bowl until well blended and lumps are minimal. Add to milk; stir constantly to remove lumps and keep from sticking. Heat until sauce is smooth and bubbling slowly. Remove from heat and add vanilla. Let sauce set until it is the consistency of gravy. Serve over warm biscuits with butter. Serves 4–6.

Teresa Belew
Family Life, AR

Guiltless Cream Bars

8 ounces nonfat lemon yogurt
¼ cup frozen orange juice concentrate

2 packages Equal
½ teaspoon vanilla

Combine all ingredients, mixing well. Freeze in popsicle trays or a large bowl.

Gayle Anne VanFulpen
NewLife Publications, FL

Hard Candy

3¾ cups sugar
1½ cups light corn syrup
1 cup water

1 teaspoon any flavoring
food coloring
powdered sugar

Mix sugar, syrup, and water in a large saucepan. Stir over medium heat until sugar dissolves. Boil without stirring until drops of syrup form hard brittle threads in cold water. Remove from heat. After boiling has ceased, stir in flavoring and food color. Pour onto powdered foil. Cool; break into pieces.

Liesl Buck
International Ministry, FL

Hot Fudge Sauce

¼ cup butter
1½ squares bitter chocolate
¾ cup sugar
pinch salt

¼ cup cocoa
½ cup light cream
1 teaspoon vanilla

Melt butter and chocolate. Mix together sugar, salt, and cocoa, then add to butter and chocolate. Stir until smooth. Slowly add cream and bring to a boil, stirring constantly. Remove from heat, then add vanilla. Store in a jar in the refrigerator until ready to use, then reheat. *Tip:* This makes a nice gift in a small jar topped with ribbon.

Nina Locke
Crusade Family

Microwave Peanut Brittle

1 cup raw peanuts
1 cup sugar
½ cup light corn syrup
⅛ teaspoon salt

1 teaspoon butter
1 teaspoon vanilla
½ teaspoon baking soda

Mix peanuts, sugar, syrup, and salt in a 1½-quart glass casserole dish. Microwave on high for 8 minutes, stirring after 4 minutes. Stir in butter and vanilla, then cook for 2 more minutes. Stir in baking soda. Pour onto a greased baking sheet. Using two forks, stretch until thin. Cool, then break into pieces.

Becky Rivera
Student LINC, FL

No-Cook Marshmallow Frosting

½ teaspoon salt
2 egg whites
¼ cup sugar

¾ cup Karo syrup
1¾ teaspoon vanilla

Add salt to egg whites and beat until mixture forms soft peaks. Gradually add sugar and syrup, beating thoroughly after each addition until mixture firmly peaks. Fold in vanilla.

Midge Piedot
Crusade Family

Parksu's Fudge

4 ½ cups sugar
1 12-ounce can evaporated milk
½ cup butter
18 ounces chocolate chips

1 7-ounce jar marshmallow cream
1 teaspoon vanilla
1 cup coarsely chopped nuts

Mix sugar, milk, and butter in a saucepan; heat and bring to a boil. Boil for 6 minutes, then remove from heat. Add chocolate chips and stir until melted. Stir in marshmallow cream until smooth. Add vanilla and nuts. Pour into a 9×13-inch buttered pan. Refrigerate. Makes 5 pounds.

Becky Leppard
International Ministry, FL

Smooth Hot Fudge Topping

1 cup whipping cream
1 cup sugar

2 tablespoons cocoa
dash salt

Mix ingredients in a saucepan and bring to a rolling boil. Boil 1 minute. Beat while cooling to serving temperature. Drizzle over ice cream while still warm. This recipe is easy and never fails to produce creamy topping.

Joette Whims
NewLife Publications, CA

Spiced Nuts

2 teaspoons cold water
1 egg, slightly beaten
½ cup sugar
½ teaspoon salt

¼ teaspoon cinnamon
¼ teaspoon ground cloves
¼ teaspoon ground allspice
2 cups pecan halves

Preheat oven to 250 degrees. Mix all ingredients together. Spread on a cookie sheet and bake for 1 hour, stirring occasionally.

Debbie McGoldrick
Student Venture, GA

Pies

Aunt Hettie's Pecan Pie

3 eggs, beaten
⅔ cup sugar
1 cup light Karo syrup
¼ teaspoon salt

1 teaspoon vanilla
¼ cup butter or margarine, melted
1 cup pecans
1 9-inch pie crust, unbaked

Preheat oven to 350 degrees. Mix all ingredients except crust, and pour into pie crust. Bake for 50 minutes or until knife comes out clean.

Carolyn Justice
Single Life Resources, NC

*"Go and enjoy choice food and sweet drinks, and send some
to those who have nothing prepared" (Neh. 8:10).*

Bimini Key Lime Pie

6 tablespoons margarine, melted
1½ cups graham cracker crumbs
3 tablespoons sugar
1 8-ounce package regular or
    light cream cheese

1 can sweetened condensed milk
⅓ cup key lime juice
½ teaspoon vanilla
1 carton regular or Cool Whip Lite

Preheat oven to 350 degrees. Mix margarine, crumbs, and sugar. Press into a 9-inch pie plate. Bake for 10 minutes; cool. Combine cream cheese, milk, lime juice, and vanilla in a large mixing bowl. Blend until smooth. Pour into cooled crust; chill. Top with Cool Whip. *Variations:* You may want to substitute a purchased graham cracker crust, or serve pie frozen. *Tip:* Eagle Brand sweetened condensed milk makes a thicker pie than Carnation.

Laura Staudt
Women Today International, FL

PIES

Chess Pie

⅓ cup milk
1 cup plus 6 tablespoons sugar,
  divided
3 egg yolks
½ cup butter

1 cup raisins
¾ cup coarsely chopped nuts
1 teaspoon vanilla
1 9-inch pie shell, baked
3 egg whites

Preheat oven to 300 degrees. Put milk, 1 cup sugar, and egg yolks into a blender and process. Combine with butter, raisins, nuts, and vanilla in a saucepan. Cook slowly until thickened. Pour into baked pie shell. Beat egg whites until stiff. Add 6 tablespoons sugar and continue beating until whites stand in peaks. Place on top of pie mixture and bake for 15 minutes. This was my mother's recipe that I use for holiday entertaining. It's not a pie, but a confection.

Vonette Bright
Co-founder, Campus Crusade for Christ
Executive Director, Women Today International, FL

Chocolate Dream Pie

3 eggs whites
¼ teaspoon cream of tartar
1 cup sugar
16 saltine crackers, crushed

½ cup chopped nuts
1 teaspoon vanilla
Filling
whipped cream

Preheat oven to 350 degrees. To make the crust, beat eggs whites until fluffy. Add cream of tartar and sugar; beat until stiff. Stir in crushed crackers, nuts, and vanilla. Press into a pie plate and bake for 30 minutes. Let cool and then refrigerate until chilled. Prepare *Filling* and pour into chilled crust. Top with whipped cream. The ladies love this dessert—it's showy and delicious!

Filling:

½ cup margarine
¾ cup sugar
1 square unsweetened chocolate, melted

½ teaspoon vanilla
2 eggs, chilled

Cream margarine and sugar; add melted chocolate, vanilla, and 1 egg. Beat for 2 minutes, then add second egg and beat for 2 more minutes.

Judy Anderson
Christian Embassy, CO

Chocolate Mousse Pie

3 cups chocolate wafer crumbs
½ cup sweet butter, melted
16 ounces semi-sweet chocolate
6 eggs, *divided*

2 cups whipping cream plus more
  for topping
6 tablespoons powdered sugar
Chocolate Leaves

To make crust, combine crumbs and butter. Press onto the bottom and up the sides of a 9- or 10-inch springform pan. Chill for 30 minutes. To make filling, melt chocolate in a double boiler or in a microwave oven. Cool to lukewarm. Add 2 eggs; mix well. Separate the remaining 4 eggs. Add yolks and mix well. Whip the cream with powdered sugar. With egg whites at room temperature, beat until stiff but not dry. Stir a little of the cream into the chocolate mixture; then add remaining cream to the egg whites. Gently blend both mixtures, then pour into the crust and chill for at least 6 hours or overnight. Decorate top of pie with additional sweetened whipped cream and *Chocolate Leaves*.

Chocolate Leaves:

2 scant tablespoons vegetable
  shortening

8 ounces semi-sweet chocolate
camellia or other waxy leaves

Melt shortening and chocolate. Using a spoon, generously coat underside of leaves. Chill or freeze until firm. Peel away each leaf, starting at the stem end. Refrigerate.

Barbara Ball
ChurchLIFE, FL

Chocolate Swirl Chiffon Pie

1 envelope gelatin
1 cup plus 2 teaspoons sugar, *divided*
¼ teaspoon salt
1½ cups milk
2 squares unsweetened chocolate

3 eggs, separated
1 teaspoon vanilla
¼ cup whipping cream
1 pie shell, baked

Mix gelatin, ½ cup sugar, salt, and milk in a double boiler. Add chocolate squares. Cook over hot water until melted, then beat with egg beater until smooth. Beat egg whites slightly, then slowly stir into chocolate mixture. Cook 3 more minutes, stirring constantly. Add vanilla and chill until slightly thickened. Beat egg whites until foamy; gradually add ½ cup sugar and beat until stiff. Gradually fold in chocolate mixture. Whip cream with 2 teaspoons sugar. Pour ½ of the chocolate mixture into the pie shell. Spoon ½ of the whipped cream on top, and cut through filling with a spatula to form a swirl. Layer the remaining chocolate and whipped cream, and swirl. Chill.

Cheryl Henderson
Contributions and Postal Services, FL

Cousin Ina's Pumpkin Pie

1¾ cups canned pumpkin
½ cup brown sugar
½ cup white sugar
¼ cup plus 2 tablespoons orange honey, *divided*
1 teaspoon cinnamon
⅛ teaspoon ground cloves

⅛ teaspoon ground ginger
½ teaspoon salt
1 cup whole milk
½ cup evaporated milk
2 eggs, slightly beaten
1 tablespoon grated orange peel
1 10-inch pie shell, unbaked

Preheat oven to 425 degrees. Combine pumpkin, sugars, ¼ cup honey, spices, and salt; blend thoroughly. Stir in the whole milk, evaporated milk, and eggs. (At this point, you may set in the refrigerator overnight.) Fill crust with pumpkin mix. Dribble 2 tablespoons honey on top and sprinkle with orange peel. Bake for 35–40 minutes or until filling is almost firm in the center. Remove from oven and cool.

Vonette Bright
Co-founder, Campus Crusade for Christ
Executive Director, Women Today International, FL

Cranberry Mince Pie

⅔ cup sugar
2 tablespoons cornstarch
⅔ cup plus 2 tablespoons water, *divided*
1½ cups fresh cranberries, rinsed and drained

1 pint homemade or purchased mincemeat
pastry for 2-crust pie
1 egg yolk
whipped cream

Preheat oven to 425 degrees. In a saucepan, combine sugar and cornstarch; add ⅔ cup water. Cook and stir over high heat to boiling. Add berries; bring to a boil. Reduce heat and simmer for 5–10 minutes, stirring occasionally. Pour mincemeat into pie crust and top with berries. Cover with vented crust. Mix egg yolk with 2 tablespoons water; brush egg wash over top of crust. Bake in lower half of oven for 30 minutes. Cool; serve with real whipped cream. For those who think regular mincemeat pie is too strong, this is a great variation. It's a traditional Christmas dessert.

Kit Coons
Family Life, SC

Eggnog Pie

½ box gingersnaps, crushed
½ cup butter or margarine
1 cup sugar, *divided*
1 envelope unflavored gelatin
½ teaspoon salt
3 eggs, separated

1¼ cups milk
¼ teaspoon cream of tartar
½ cup whipping cream, chilled
2 drops yellow food coloring
nutmeg to taste

Preheat oven to 350 degrees. To make crust, mix gingersnaps and butter. Press mixture firmly and evenly against sides and bottom of a 9-inch pie pan. Bake for 10 minutes; cool. To make filling, mix ½ cup sugar, gelatin, and salt in a saucepan. Mix egg yolks and milk; stir into sugar mixture. Heat over medium heat, stirring constantly until boiling. Cover and refrigerate several hours until thick. Beat egg whites and cream of tartar until foamy. Beat in remaining ½ cup sugar, 1 tablespoon at a time. Beat until stiff and glossy; do not overbeat! Fold cooled egg mixture into meringue. Beat cream in a chilled bowl until stiff. Fold into egg mixture. Pour filling into cooled pie shell and sprinkle with nutmeg. Refrigerate until set (at least 3 hours).

Judy Douglass
U.S. Ministries

French Chocolate Silk Cream Pie

¾ cup margarine
1 cup plus 2 teaspoons sugar
2 squares semi-sweet chocolate
    (or equivalent chocolate chips)

1½ teaspoons vanilla
3 eggs
1 pie shell, baked
whipped topping

Cream margarine; gradually add sugar. Blend in chocolate and vanilla. Add 1 egg at a time, beating for 3–4 minutes after each. Pour into cool pie shell; spread with topping.

John Cannon
President's Office, FL

PIES

Fresh Peach-Blueberry Pie

2–3 sliced ripe peaches
1 pint fresh blueberries
1 cup sugar
dash salt

juice of 1 lemon
2 rounded tablespoons tapioca
pastry for 2-crust pie

Preheat oven to 375 degrees. Mix peaches and blueberries. Combine sugar and salt. Add sugar mixture, lemon juice, and tapioca to fruit, and mix until fruit is coated. Allow mixture to set for 20 minutes or until juice is absorbed. Pour into pie shell. Top with pie crust and cuts slits in crust. Bake for 30–40 minutes or until golden brown.

Fay Hendley
Contributions and Postal Services, FL

Frozen Almond Chocolate Mousse

⅔ cup whole almonds
½ cup graham cracker crumbs
3 tablespoons sugar, *divided*
3 tablespoons butter, melted
1 pint butter brickle or coffee
    ice cream

6 ounces chocolate chips
2 large eggs, separated
1 cup whipping cream, *divided*
3 tablespoons imitation rum
    flavoring

Preheat oven to 300 degrees. Spread almonds in a single layer on a baking sheet and toast in oven for 15–20 minutes until lightly browned. Chop fine while warm. Combine ⅓ cup almonds with cracker crumbs, 1 tablespoon sugar, and butter. Press into an oiled springform or cake pan. Bake at 350 degrees for 10 minutes. Cool, then chill in freezer. Spoon ice cream onto crust and freeze. Melt chocolate over hot water. In a small bowl, beat egg whites to soft peaks. Beat in 2 tablespoons sugar, 1 at a time. Beat ½ cup cream to soft peaks. Combine warm chocolate and rum flavoring. Fold in egg whites, then beaten cream. Reserving 2 tablespoons almonds for garnish, fold almonds into chocolate mixture and pour over ice cream. Beat remaining ½ cup cream and place dollops around the edge. Sprinkle reserved almonds on top. Freeze for at least 3 hours.

Lynn Copeland
NewLife Publications, OK

Frozen Key Lime Pie

2 cans low-fat sweetened
    condensed milk
1 cup key lime juice

1 tablespoon vanilla
1 graham cracker crust
Cool Whip

Thoroughly combine milk, lime juice, and vanilla. Pour into the crust and freeze overnight. Serve with dollops of Cool Whip. This is a crowd-pleaser. Serves 6–8.

Patsy Morley
Board of Director's Wife

Frozen Strawberry Pie

½ cup Grape Nuts cereal
¼ cup brown sugar
1 cup flour
¼ cup margarine
2 egg whites

1 cup sugar
16 ounces frozen whole
    strawberries, thawed
1 teaspoon lemon juice
2 cups Cool Whip

Preheat oven to 275 degrees. To make crumb mixture, mix Grape Nuts, brown sugar, and flour. Cut in margarine and stir until crumbly. Spoon crumbs into a 9×13-inch pan and bake, stirring occasionally until brown. Set aside ¼ of the crumb mixture. Whip egg whites until stiff. Add sugar, strawberries, and lemon juice, then fold in Cool Whip. Place in pan and top with remaining crumb mixture. Freeze overnight. Serve immediately after taking from freezer because pie softens quickly.

Angela Rosa
Sunport Ministry Office, FL

Fudge Pie

1 cup butter or margarine
1–2 squares unsweetened chocolate
2 cups sugar
4 eggs

1 cup flour
½ teaspoon cinnamon
1 teaspoon vanilla
¼ cup chopped walnuts

Preheat oven to 350 degrees. Melt butter and chocolate in a heavy saucepan over low heat, then add sugar and eggs 1 at a time. Add remaining ingredients, stirring only until flour is blended; do not over mix. Pour into an ungreased 10-inch pie plate. Bake for 25–30 minutes or until toothpick comes out clean. Cool for 20 minutes.

Arlyne Lockard
History's Handful, CA

PIES

> Green tomato pie. Oh my! It's green tomato pie.
> I thought the fall would never come
> With green tomato pie.
> I loved it when I was a kid and I'll love it till I die—
> That death-defyin', tantalizin' green tomato pie!
>
> — Delores Kagi

Green Tomato Pie

1 cup sugar
2 tablespoons flour
1 teaspoon salt
½ teaspoon cinnamon
½ teaspoon nutmeg

6 medium green tomatoes
1 teaspoon grated lemon rind
3 tablespoons lemon juice
pastry for 8-inch 2-crust pie
1 tablespoon margarine

Preheat oven to 425 degrees. Mix sugar, flour, salt, and spices. Core and slice tomatoes; cut slices into quarters. Toss tomatoes with sugar mixture. Add lemon rind and juice. Let stand for about 20 minutes. Spoon tomato mixture into pie crust and dot with margarine. Cover with top crust; slit to allow steam to escape. Bake for 40–45 minutes. Makes 6 servings.

Delores Kagi
International Ministry, FL

Hershey Bar Pie

1 4-ounce Hershey chocolate bar   1 graham cracker crust
1 12-ounce carton Cool Whip   chocolate shavings

Melt chocolate bar and stir in half of Cool Whip. Chill for 1 hour. Top with remaining Cool Whip and sprinkle with chocolate shavings.

Jennifer Kautsch
New Staff, Texas

Holiday Pies

⅓ cup brown sugar   ½ teaspoon cinnamon
⅔ cup currants or raisins   ⅛ teaspoon nutmeg
⅓ cup golden raisins   ⅛ teaspoon ginger
½ cup diced citron or candied fruit   ⅛ teaspoon ground cloves
¼ cup chopped almonds   1 teaspoon vanilla
¼ cup apple juice   pastry for 2 10-inch 2-crust pies
grated rind and juice of 1 lemon   butter
1 orange, peeled and chopped   milk
2 small pears, peeled and chopped   white sugar
2 large tart apples, peeled and chopped

Combine the first 14 ingredients about 2 weeks ahead of time. Store in a large tupperware bowl in refrigerator, stirring occasionally. When ready to bake, spoon half the mince into pie crust; dot with butter. Cover with top crust; seal and make a few slits. Moisten top with milk and sprinkle with sugar. Repeat with second pie. Bake at 425 degrees for 30–40 minutes. Makes 2 pies.

Wendy Hill
National Ministry, FL

Pecan Pie

2 tablespoons butter   2 eggs, well beaten
½ cup sugar   ¼ teaspoon salt
2 tablespoons flour   ½ cup chopped pecans
1 cup light Karo syrup   1 9-inch pie shell, unbaked
½ teaspoon vanilla

Preheat oven to 350 degrees. Cream butter and sugar. Add remaining ingredients in the order listed. Pour into pie shell. Bake for 40–45 minutes or until center is firm. This is an economical, but expensive-tasting pie.

Gwen Martin
International School of Theology, CA

PIES

Rhubarb-Orange Cream Pie

3 eggs, separated
1¼ cups sugar, *divided*
¼ cup butter, softened
3 tablespoons frozen orange
  juice concentrate

¼ cup flour
¼ teaspoon salt
2½ cups chopped rhubarb
⅓ cup chopped pecans
1 9-inch pie shell, unbaked

Preheat oven to 375 degrees. To make meringue, beat egg whites until stiff. Gradually add ¼ cup sugar while beating. Add butter and orange juice to egg yolks; beat. Add remaining sugar, flour, and salt; beat well. Add rhubarb to yolk mixture and stir well. Gently fold in meringue. Pour into pie shell and sprinkle with nuts. Bake on bottom rack of oven for 15 minutes. Reduce heat to 325 degrees and bake for 45–50 more minutes.

Joette Whims
NewLife Publications, CA

 Because your love is better than life, my lips will glorify you (Psalm 63:3).

Savannah Mud Pie

1 bag chocolate cookies (not cream-
  filled), crushed in food processor
½ cup margarine, melted
1 gallon coffee ice cream, softened

Sauce
1 cup toasted pecans
1 large carton Cool Whip
chocolate curls

Mix crushed cookies and margarine. Press into a 9×13-inch pan. Spread softened ice cream on top and freeze until firm. Prepare *Sauce*; when cooled, layer on top of ice cream. Sprinkle nuts over fudge layer and top with Cool Whip. Freeze until ready to serve. Garnish with chocolate curls. Yields 16–24 servings.

Sauce:

2 small cans evaporated milk
¾ cup margarine
2 teaspoons vanilla

2 cups sugar
8 squares semi-sweet baking
  chocolate

Mix all ingredients and boil for 1 minute; cool.

Susan Conner
Campus Ministry, SC

Sour Cream Lime Pie

1½ cups graham cracker crumbs
1¾ cups sugar, *divided*
10 tablespoons butter, *divided*
3 tablespoons cornstarch
1 tablespoon grated lime or lemon rind

2 cups whipping cream, *divided*
⅓ cup fresh lime juice
1¾ cups sour cream, *divided*
1½ teaspoons vanilla

Preheat oven to 350 degrees. Melt 6 tablespoons butter. Combine with crumbs and ½ cup sugar; stir well. Firmly press crumb mixture evenly on the bottom and sides of a 9-inch pie plate. Bake for 10–12 minutes or until lightly browned. Remove from oven and let cool. Combine 1 cup sugar, cornstarch, and lime rind in a medium saucepan. Gradually add 1 cup whipping cream, stirring until smooth. Add lime juice and 4 tablespoons butter; cook over medium heat, stirring constantly until butter melts and mixture thickens and comes to a boil. Remove from heat and let cool. Add 1 cup sour cream, stirring well. Pour lime mixture into prepared crust. Beat 1 cup whipping cream at high speed until foamy; gradually add ¼ cup sugar, beating until soft peaks form. Fold in ¾ cup sour cream and vanilla. Spread whipped cream mixture over filling. Chill for at least 4 hours.

Helen Koopman
JESUS Film Project, CA

Sour Cream Peach Pie

¾ cup sugar
2 tablespoons flour
¼ teaspoon salt
1 cup sour cream
1 egg, slightly beaten

1 teaspoon vanilla
2 cups sliced canned peaches
1 pie shell, unbaked
Topping

Preheat oven to 400 degrees. Combine sugar, flour, and salt. Beat in sour cream, egg, and vanilla. Add peaches and pour into pie shell. Bake for 15 minutes, then reduce temperature to 350 degrees and bake for 30 more minutes. Add *Topping* and bake at 400 degrees for 10 minutes.

Topping:
¼ cup sugar
⅓ cup flour

¼ cup butter, softened
1 teaspoon cinnamon

Combine all ingredients.

Conda DeVries
International Ministry, FL

Sweet Potato Pie

3 medium sweet potatoes
2 cups sugar
½ cup butter or margarine,
 softened or melted
4 tablespoons vanilla
4 tablespoons cinnamon

2 tablespoons nutmeg
1 tablespoon ground cloves
2–3 eggs, beaten
½ cup condensed milk
2 8- or 9-inch pie crusts

Preheat oven to 350 degrees. Boil sweet potatoes with skins until tender. Drain water; cool potatoes. Peel potatoes and put in a bowl; mash. Add sugar, butter, vanilla, cinnamon, nutmeg, and cloves. Beat together. Add eggs and milk to mixture. Add more milk if batter is too thick. Batter should not be lumpy or runny. Fill pie crusts ¾ full. Bake for 35–40 minutes or until top is lightly browned. Cool before serving.

Melvita Chisholm
Intercultural Resources, NY

The Best Chocolate Pie

1 4-ounce Hershey's chocolate bar
    with almonds

1 small carton Cool Whip
1 graham cracker pie crust

Carefully melt the chocolate. Reserving enough Cool Whip for garnish, mix the Cool Whip into the chocolate. Pour into crust and refrigerate. Serve with a dollop of Cool Whip.

Mary Jane Morgan
Crusade Family

Toasted Coconut Pie

3 eggs, beaten
½ cup margarine, melted
1 teaspoon vanilla
1½ cups sugar

4 teaspoons lemon juice
1⅓ cups flaked coconut
1 9-inch pie crust, unbaked

Preheat oven to 350 degrees. Mix eggs, margarine, vanilla, sugar, and lemon juice. Stir in coconut. Pour into pie crust and bake for 40–45 minutes. Serve warm or cool.

Cheryl Henderson
Contributions and Postal Services, FL

Tropicana Pie

1 13¼-ounce can crushed
    pineapple, drained
1½ cups seedless raisins
1 tablespoon lemon juice
1 envelope unflavored gelatin

¼ cup cold water
1 small box vanilla instant pudding
1 cup sour cream
1 9-inch pie crust, baked

Combine pineapple, raisins, and lemon juice in a saucepan. Soften gelatin in water and stir into pineapple mixture. Simmer for 5 minutes, stirring often; refrigerate until cool. Prepare pudding according to package directions; fold in sour cream. Add to pineapple mixture and spoon into pie crust. Chill thoroughly.

Nan Green
International Ministry, Africa

Wonder Pie Crust

2 cups flour
1 teaspoon salt

1 scant cup shortening or lard
½ cup ice cold water

Sift together flour and salt. Cut shortening into flour with a pastry cutter. Add water a little at a time just until dough sticks together. Use as little flour as possible to roll out dough. Line pastry tins. Makes 1 double crust or 2 single crusts.

Joette Whims
NewLife Publications, CA

> *You have done so much for me, O Lord.*
> *No wonder I am glad! (Psalm 92:4)*

Desserts

Almond Strawberry Crepes

Filling:

2 cups cottage cheese
1 teaspoon grated lemon rind
½ teaspoon salt

3 tablespoons honey
½ teaspoon vanilla

Crepes:

3 eggs
¾ cup flour
2 tablespoons sugar

½ teaspoon salt
1 cup milk
1 tablespoon butter, melted

Sauce:

¼ cup sugar
1 tablespoon cornstarch
1 cup water

2 10-ounce packages frozen sliced
  strawberries, slightly thawed
slivered almonds

Preheat oven to 250 degrees. Combine all ingredients for *Filling* in a bowl and mix well; set aside. For *Crepes*, beat eggs until thick. Sift dry ingredients together over eggs; beat just until smooth, then stir in milk and butter. Heat a 6-inch heavy frying pan over low heat. Test temperature with a few drops of water; when drops bounce, temperature is right. Lightly grease pan with butter. Pour in a scant ¼ cup batter at a time; fry until crepe top appears dry and underside is golden. Turn; brown other side. Repeat, lightly greasing pan before frying each crepe.

Spoon about 2 tablespoons *Filling* into center of each crepe; roll up and place seam-side down in a shallow baking pan. Keep warm in oven. To make *Sauce*, combine sugar, cornstarch, and water in a pan; cook, stirring constantly, until sauce thickens and boils for 3 minutes. Stir in strawberries and heat just to boiling. Arrange crepes on a serving dish; spoon sauce over the top and sprinkle with almonds. Makes 12 crepes. *Tip:* Crepes may be made ahead, filled, and refrigerated; reheat at 350 degrees for 10 minutes just before serving.

Lois Mackey
CoMission, CA

Baked Pineapple

1 medium can crushed pineapple	2 tablespoons flour
1 egg, beaten	½ cup margarine, melted
¼ cup sugar	3–4 bread slices, cubed

Preheat oven to 375 degrees. Thoroughly mix pineapple, egg, sugar, and flour; pour into a baking dish. Combine bread slices and margarine; place on top of pineapple and bake for 45–60 minutes.

Doris Jones/Evelyn English
Prayer Ministry, FL

Blueberry Cheese Squares

1 roll prepared cookie dough (lemon, butterscotch, or other flavor)	¼ cup sugar
	1 egg
1 8-ounce package cream cheese	½ teaspoon vanilla
1 cup sour cream	1 can blueberry pie filling

Preheat oven to 375 degrees. Slice dough in ¼-inch slices. Overlap in an ungreased 9×13-inch pan. Bake for 12–15 minutes, then allow to cool a few minutes. Meanwhile, combine cream cheese, sour cream, sugar, egg, and vanilla. Beat until smooth. Pour pie filling over cookie crust. Top with cream mixture and bake for 25–30 minutes. Serves 12.

Lois Mackey
CoMission, CA

Blueberry Torte Dessert

½ pound vanilla wafers
(about 56), crushed
½ cup butter. melted
40 large marshmallows

½ cup milk
½ pint whipping cream
1 can blueberry pie filling

Combine wafers and butter; press ½ of mixture into a buttered 9-inch square pan. Melt marshmallows in milk over low heat, then allow to cool. Whip cream and add to marshmallows. Spoon ½ of marshmallow mixture over wafers, then spread the blueberry pie filling. Layer remaining marshmallow mix, then remaining wafer mixture. Refrigerate for several hours or overnight.

Conda DeVries
International Ministry, FL

Cherries in the Snow

1 box graham cracker crust mix
1 package Dream Whip or 1 cup
whipping cream, whipped
1 8-ounce package cream cheese
2 cans tart red cherries with juice

4 tablespoons cornstarch
½ cup sugar
½ teaspoon cinnamon
6 drops red food coloring

Prepare crust mix as directed on package and spread in a 9×13-inch cake pan. Combine whipped cream and cream cheese. Thicken the cherries and juice with cornstarch; add sugar, cinnamon, and food coloring. Pour ½ of the cherry filling on the crust; spread on cream mixture, then top with remaining cherries. Freeze for 2 hours. Set out 30 minutes before serving. Serves 15.

Nan Green
International Ministry, Africa

Cherry Delight

½ pound vanilla wafers, crushed
½ cup butter or margarine
1½ cups powdered sugar
1 egg
1 teaspoon vanilla

1 cup whipping cream
1 small can crushed pineapple, drained
1 small bottle maraschino cherries,
    chopped
½ cup chopped nuts

Place ⅓ of wafers in a buttered, shallow pan. Cream butter and sugar; add egg and vanilla, and beat until fluffy. Spread over crumbs. Cover with ½ of the remaining crumbs. Whip cream; add pineapple, cherries, and nuts. Spread over the layer of crumbs and top with remaining crumbs. Refrigerate for 24 hours.

Marilyn Klein
U.S. Ministry, CA

Cherry Kuchen

1⅓ cups flour
¼ teaspoon baking powder
½ teaspoon salt
2 tablespoons plus ¼ cup sugar,
    divided
⅓ cup margarine

1 can cherries, drained
1 teaspoon cinnamon
1 egg, beaten
1 cup sour cream, sour milk, yogurt,
    or combination

Preheat oven to 400 degrees. Combine flour, baking powder, salt, and 2 tablespoons sugar in a bowl. Cut in margarine. Pat mixture on bottom and sides of a 9-inch pie pan. Arrange cherries in crust. Combine ¼ cup sugar with cinnamon; sprinkle over cherries. Bake for 15 minutes. While baking, combine egg and sour cream. Pour over cherries and bake for 30 more minutes. Serves 6.

Karen Horsey
International Ministry, FL

Cherry Pudding

1 cup sugar
1 cup flour
1 teaspoon baking soda

1 egg, beaten
1 can unsweetened pie cherries
  with juice

Preheat oven to 325 degrees. Combine all ingredients. Bake in an ungreased 8-inch square pan for 45 minutes. This is a simple dessert for everyday.

Barbara Ball
ChurchLIFE, FL

Chin Chin
(Yoruba dish from Nigeria)

1 cup flour
2 rounded teaspoons baking powder
nutmeg or cinnamon
8 teaspoons sugar

⅓ cup margarine or vegetable oil
2 eggs
½ cup milk or more

Sift flour and baking powder; add spices and sugar. Rub in margarine. Beat together eggs and ½ cup milk, and combine with flour mixture. Add enough milk to make dough workable. Keeping dough stiff, roll evenly on a flat surface. Let dough rest for approximately 2 hours, then cut into thin strips or shapes. Deep fry in hot oil until brown.

Leona Mason
Crusade Family

Chocolate Bags

12 ounces Swiss dark chocolate,
  coarsely chopped
4 small paper bags, with 4×2-inch
  bases and coated lining

softened ice cream or mousse
  (white chocolate works well)
Raspberry Sauce
fresh raspberries or strawberries

(Bags used for fresh ground coffee or popcorn work well; trim down to 3 inches high. If bags are not coated, line them with wax paper.) Melt the chocolate in a double boiler over hot but not simmering water. Open bags so that the top forms a rectangle, and stand them upright on a flat surface or baking sheet. Divide the chocolate among the bags. With a small pastry brush, brush the chocolate up 2 inches from the bottom with long, swift strokes until the inside of each bag is evenly coated, with a little extra chocolate in the corners. To create the bag effect, tap the bags lightly near the bottom of the narrow sides so sides will be slightly indented. Freeze the bags for 10 minutes or until the chocolate is set. Fill the bags with softened ice cream or a mousse and freeze.

When ready to use, remove from the freezer one at a time, and turn upside down. Gently peel away the paper starting at the bottom. (The bags must be filled or they will break as you are peeling.) Cover the bags with plastic wrap and return to freezer. Remove bags from freezer about 1 hour before serving. Spoon an equal amount of *Raspberry Sauce* onto 4 dessert plates, and swirl on plate. Place an upright chocolate bag in the middle of each plate. Place fresh raspberries or strawberries in each bag on top of ice cream or mousse until the bag overflows. This makes a pretty presentation.

Raspberry Sauce:
10 ounces fresh or frozen raspberries   ¼ cup sugar

In a 1-quart saucepan, combine the raspberries and sugar. Bring to a boil and remove. Purée in a food processor or blender. Strain and refrigerate.

Ingrid Bunner
Board of Director's Wife

Chocolate Biscotti

¾ cup almonds   ½ teaspoon salt
1 egg white, slightly beaten   3 eggs
2½ cups flour   ¼ cup light corn syrup
½ cup sugar   1 teaspoon almond extract
⅓ cup cocoa   2 squares semi-sweet chocolate
1½ teaspoons baking soda   2 teaspoons shortening

Preheat oven to 325 degrees. Toast almonds by baking in a pan for 10 minutes; cool. Coarsely chop ⅓ cup nuts. In a blender at medium speed, blend remaining nuts until finely ground. In a large bowl, combine ground nuts, flour, sugar, cocoa, baking soda, and salt. Reserving 1 tablespoon egg white, add remaining egg white, eggs, corn syrup, and almond extract. Mix to a stiff dough, then add chopped nuts.

With floured hands, roll dough into 3 6-inch logs. Place 3 inches apart on a greased and floured cookie sheet. Flatten logs until ½-inch thick. Brush with reserved 1 tablespoon egg white. Bake for 25 minutes. Cool on a wire rack for about 10 minutes. With a serrated knife, carefully cut into diagonal ½-inch slices. Return to cookie sheet and bake for another 10–15 minutes, turning halfway through. Cool on wire rack. Melt together the chocolate and shortening. Using a plastic bag with a small corner snipped off, pipe chocolate over cookies.

Wendy Hill
National Ministry, FL

Chocolate Delight

1 cup flour	2 8-ounce tubs Cool Whip, *divided*
½ cup butter	2 small boxes chocolate pudding
½ cup walnuts, finely chopped	2½ cups milk
1 8-ounce package cream cheese	¾ cup nuts (optional)
1 cup powdered sugar	1 Hershey bar, grated

Preheat oven to 375 degrees. Mix flour, butter, and walnuts; press into the bottom of a greased 9×13-inch pan. Bake for 15 minutes and cool. Mix cream cheese, sugar, and 8 ounces Cool Whip; spread over crust (it's not easy to spread). Combine pudding, milk, and ½ cup nuts. Spread over Cool Whip layer. Place remaining Cool Whip over chocolate pudding layer. Sprinkle the Hershey bar, then ¼ cup nuts on top. Chill for at least 2 hours; best if refrigerated 24 hours.

Becky Leppard
International Ministry, FL

Chocolate Dessert

½ cup butter	3 egg whites, stiffly beaten
2 cups powdered sugar	1 box vanilla wafers, crushed
1 teaspoon vanilla	½ gallon vanilla ice cream, softened
2 squares chocolate, melted	½ cup chopped pecans
3 egg yolks, beaten	

Cream butter and sugar; add vanilla. Mix in chocolate, then add egg yolks. Fold in egg whites. Line a 9×13-inch pan with ½ of the crushed wafers. Pour in chocolate mixture and spread ice cream on top. Sprinkle dessert with crumbs and pecans. Cover with foil and freeze.

Barbara Ball
ChurchLIFE, FL

Chocolate Mint Dessert

1 cup flour
1 cup sugar
½ cup margarine, softened

4 eggs
1½ cups Hershey syrup

Preheat oven to 350 degrees. In a large bowl, combine all ingredients until smooth. Pour into a greased 9×13-inch pan. Bake for 25–30 minutes; cool completely. Spread *Mint Cream Center* on cake; cover and chill. Pour *Chocolate Topping* over. Cover and chill for 1 hour before serving.

Mint Cream Center:

2 cups powdered sugar
½ cup margarine, softened
1 tablespoon water

¾ teaspoon mint extract
8 drops green food coloring

Combine all ingredients. Beat until smooth.

Chocolate Topping:

6 tablespoons margarine

1 cup semi-sweet chocolate chips

Melt margarine and chips together. Cool slightly.

Carolyn Kirby
International Ministry, Hungary

Chocolate Sundae Dessert

40 Oreo cookies, crushed
½ cup butter, melted
1 cup sugar
1 5⅓-ounce can evaporated milk

2 ounces unsweetened chocolate
1 quart vanilla ice cream, softened
1½ cups Cool Whip
½ cup chopped nuts

Combine cookie crumbs and butter; blend well. Reserve ½ cup for topping, and press remaining crumbs into a 9×13-inch pan and freeze. Combine sugar, milk, and chocolate; boil, stirring constantly. Set aside to cool. Layer ice cream over frozen crust. Top with chocolate mixture and refreeze. Spread Cool Whip over dessert, and sprinkle reserved crumbs and nuts on top. Cover pan and keep frozen until 15 minutes before serving.

Becky Rivera
Student LINC, FL

Chocolate Truffle Loaf
With Raspberry Sauce

16 ounces semi-sweet chocolate	¼ cup powdered sugar
½ cup light corn syrup	1 teaspoon vanilla
½ cup butter	*Raspberry Sauce*
2 cups heavy cream, *divided*	mint leaves
3 egg yolks, slightly beaten	

Line an 8½×4½×2½-inch loaf pan with plastic wrap. In a 3-quart pan, stir chocolate, syrup, and butter over medium heat until melted. Mix ½ cup cream with egg yolks. Add to chocolate mixture; stir constantly and cook for 3 minutes. Cool to room temperature. Beat remaining cream, powdered sugar, and vanilla until soft peaks form. Fold into pan. Refrigerate overnight or chill in freezer for 3 hours. Before serving, garnish with *Raspberry Sauce* and fresh mint leaves. Serves 12. *Tip:* This can be kept in the freezer and used when needed for guests.

Raspberry Sauce:

fresh or frozen raspberries	sugar to taste

Either purée, strain, or leave berries whole. Add sugar and let set for at least 30 minutes.

Kit Coons
Family Life, SC

Cranberry Apple Crisp

5 cups peeled sliced apples   2 tablespoons flour
  (5 medium)   1 teaspoon cinnamon
1½ cups fresh or frozen cranberries   *Topping*
1 cup sugar

Preheat oven to 375 degrees. Grease an 8×12-inch, 2-quart baking dish. In a large bowl, combine all ingredients except *Topping*. Toss to coat fruit. Spoon into a baking dish. Sprinkle *Topping* evenly over fruit mixture. Bake for 30–40 minutes, or until golden brown and apples are tender. Serve with ice cream or whipped topping.

Topping:

1 cup rolled oats   ⅓ cup butter
½ cup firmly packed brown sugar   ½ cup chopped nuts (optional)
⅓ cup flour

In a small bowl, combine rolled oats, brown sugar, and flour. Using a pastry blender or fork, cut in butter until crumbly. Stir in nuts.

Kari Maggard
U.S. Ministry, FL

Cream Puff Dessert

1 cup water   4 cups milk, *divided*
½ cup margarine   2 small packages instant vanilla
1 cup flour   pudding
4 eggs   12 ounces Cool Whip
1 8-ounce package cream cheese   hot fudge sauce

Preheat oven to 400 degrees. For crust, bring water and margarine to a boil. Add flour all at once; beat in and remove from heat. Beat in eggs 1 at a time. Spray an 11×14-inch pan with non-stick spray. Spread crust in pan and bake for 35 minutes; cool for 30 minutes. To make filling, mix cream cheese with ¼ cup milk; blend until smooth. Add remaining milk and vanilla pudding mix. Spread over cooked crust and cool for 30 more minutes. Spread Cool Whip over pudding and drizzle with hot fudge sauce.

Carrie Machiela
Executive Ministry, FL

DESSERTS

Creamy Apricot Mousse

1 17-ounce can California apricot
   halves with juice
water
2 small packages apricot Jell-O

1½ cups boiling water
1 cup plain yogurt
2 cups Reddi-Whip plus more
   for garnish

Drain apricots, reserving syrup. If necessary, add water to syrup to measure 1 cup; set aside. Reserve 6 apricots halves for garnish; purée remainder in blender or food processor; set aside. Dissolve Jell-O in boiling water. Add apricot syrup and chill until consistency of thick egg whites (about 45–60 minutes). Stir in puréed apricots and yogurt until well blended. Gently fold in Reddi-Whip. Pour into a lightly oiled 6-cup mold; chill until firm. Unmold, then garnish with Reddi-Whip and reserved apricot halves cut into quarters. Makes 10–12 servings.

Sherry Cumpstone
Worldwide Challenge, FL

Date and Nut Torte

1 cup sugar
4 eggs, well beaten
1 cup fine, dry bread crumbs
1 teaspoon baking powder

2 cups cut-up dates
1 cup chopped walnuts
whipped cream or ice cream
   (optional)

Preheat oven to 350 degrees. Beat sugar gradually into eggs. Mix together the bread crumbs and baking powder, then stir into egg mixture. Add dates and nuts, and spread in a well-greased 8-inch square pan. Bake for 35 minutes until set. Serve with whipped cream or ice cream.

Vonette Bright
Co-founder, Campus Crusade for Christ
Executive Director, Women Today International, FL

Hospitality is more than entertaining. It is expecting God to do great things through you as you reach out to touch the lives of others.
— Vonette Bright

Flan Dessert

¼ cup sugar
3 eggs
3 egg yolks
2 teaspoons vanilla

1 14-ounce can sweetened
    condensed milk
1¼ cups milk
2 ounces cream cheese, softened

Preheat oven to 350 degrees. Place sugar in a small skillet over medium-high heat and stir while it liquifies. Allow the sugar to boil and turn walnut brown, stirring occasionally. Watch carefully so that it does not burn. Pour the caramel into the bottom of a 9-inch flan pan or souffle dish, and quickly spread caramel evenly with a rubber spatula over bottom of pan. Blend all other ingredients in a food processor and pour into flan pan. Place in a baking pan in center of oven, pour boiling water halfway up sides of baking pan. Bake for 1 hour and 10 minutes or until knife comes out clean. Let cool, then refrigerate. *Tip:* Can be prepared 3 days ahead.

Barbara Ball
ChurchLIFE, FL

Frosted Fruit Cocktail

3 ripe bananas, mashed
1 cup sugar
1 15¼-ounce can crushed pineapple
    with juice

2 lemons, juiced and strained
2 cups orange juice
2 cups ginger ale

Mix ingredients in the order given. Freeze in a clean ½ gallon milk carton. Scoop out desired portion about 30 minutes before serving. When mushy, serve in sherbet dishes or at a pot-luck in small Dixie cups. Serves 24. Keep in freezer to have on hand for company. This is great served with Mexican food.

Gwen Martin
International School of Theology, CA

 The fruit of the righteous is a tree of life, and he
who wins souls is wise (Prov. 11:30).

Frozen Macaroon Delight

1 package coconut macaroons,
   crumbled
1 pint whipping cream, whipped
1 cup chopped nuts

1 teaspoon vanilla
¼ cup powdered sugar
2 pints lime sherbet
2 pints raspberry sherbet

Combine crumbled macaroons, whipped cream, nuts, vanilla, and sugar. Put ½ of the macaroon mixture in a 9×13-inch cake pan. Place spoonfuls of sherbets over crumbs, alternating colors. Spread remaining crumb mixture over sherbet. Freeze at least 24 hours. Serves 16.

Suzie Brenneman
International Ministry, Central Asia

Frozen Strawberry Mousse

2 cups heavy cream
1 cup sugar
½ teaspoon salt
1 quart strawberries, crushed

½ cup chopped almonds, toasted
whole strawberries (optional)
mint sprigs (optional)

Whip cream until it begins to thicken. Gradually add sugar, beating constantly. Add salt; beat until cream is stiff. Fold in crushed strawberries and almonds. Turn into a 2-quart mold and freeze until firm. Unmold onto a serving plate. Garnish with whole strawberries and mint sprigs, if desired. Makes 6–8 servings.

Ginni Christopher
Executive Ministry, FL

Fruit and Cookie Pizza

1 package chocolate chip cookie
   dough
1 15¼-ounce can sliced pineapple
1 8-ounce package light cream
   cheese, softened

⅓ cup sugar
1 teaspoon vanilla
1 banana, sliced
2 kiwi, peeled and sliced
½ cup strawberries, sliced

Preheat oven to 350 degrees. Press cookie dough onto a 14-inch pizza pan. Bake until browned and puffed. Cool completely in pan on wire rack. Drain

DESSERTS

pineapple and reserve juice. Beat cream cheese, sugar, reserved juice, and vanilla in a medium bowl until smooth. Spread over cooled cookie crust. Arrange pineapple slices over outer edge of cream cheese. Arrange bananas, kiwi, and strawberries in a pattern over pizza.

Yvonne Bibby
International Ministry, FL

I am the vine; you are the branches. If a man remains in me and I in him, he will bear much fruit (John 15:5).

Fruit Stew

1 can sliced pears
1 can pineapple chunks
maraschino cherries (optional)
1 can sliced peaches
1 can apricot halves

6 tablespoons butter or margarine
1 cup brown sugar
2 tablespoons cinnamon
1 tablespoon nutmeg

Preheat oven to 350 degrees. Drain fruit. Melt butter with brown sugar. Mix all ingredients together. Bake for 1 hour.

Jeanette Entz
Campus Ministry, TX

Hello Dollies

¼ cup butter
1 cup graham cracker crumbs
1 cup unsweetened flaked coconut
12 ounces semi-sweet chocolate chips

1 cup nuts, chopped
1 can Eagle Brand sweetened
 condensed milk

Preheat oven to 325 degrees. In a 9×13-inch pan, melt butter so that it coats the bottom. Sprinkle crumbs on butter, then coconut, chips, and nuts. Pour milk evenly over nuts. Bake for 30 minutes; do not overbake. Cut into squares when cool.

Sabrina Genasci
World Changers Radio, FL

Instant Pudding Dessert

1 cup flour
½ cup butter
½ cup chopped nuts, *divided*
1 8-ounce package cream cheese

1 cup powdered sugar
1 large container Cool Whip, *divided*
2½ cups milk
1 5-ounce box chocolate pudding

Preheat oven to 350 degrees. Reserving ⅔ tablespoon nuts for topping, crumble together flour, butter, and nuts. Pat into the bottom of a 9×13-inch pan and bake for 15 minutes; cool. Blend cream cheese and powdered sugar. Fold in ½ of the Cool Whip. Spread on crust. Combine milk and pudding mix; spread onto cream cheese mixture. Top with remaining Cool Whip and reserved nuts; chill. *Variation:* Substitute any flavor of pudding for the chocolate.

Helen Koopman
JESUS Film Project, CA

Peach Melba

frozen raspberries, thawed
1 tablespoon cornstarch

canned or fresh peach halves
ice cream

To make sauce, combine raspberries and cornstarch, and heat until thickened. Cool and chill. For each serving, use 2 peach halves; add a scoop of ice cream and pour raspberry sauce on top. Serve immediately.

Barbara Ball
ChurchLIFE, FL

Peach Pizza

1½ cups plus 1 tablespoon flour, *divided*
2 tablespoons plus ½ cup sugar, *divided*
¼ teaspoon baking powder

½ cup butter
6 fresh peaches, peeled and sliced
cinnamon to taste
1 cup sour cream
2 egg yolks

Preheat oven to 400 degrees. To make crust, mix 1½ cups flour, 2 tablespoons sugar, and baking powder. Cut in butter and pat onto a 12-inch pizza pan. Arrange peaches on crust. Sprinkle with cinnamon, ½ cup sugar, and 1 tablespoon flour, dotting with additional butter. Bake for 20 minutes. Mix sour cream and egg yolks. Pour over dessert and bake for 20 more minutes.

Arlyne Lockard
History's Handful, CA

Pecan Torte With Raspberry and Lemon Glaze

5 eggs
1½ cups pecans
1 cup sugar
1 teaspoon vanilla
¼ cup flour

1 teaspoon baking powder
½ cup seedless red raspberry jam,
  heated
1 tablespoon lemon juice
½ cup powdered sugar

Preheat oven to 350 degrees. Place the first 6 ingredients in a food processor and blend for 1 minute or until pecans are finely ground. Pour batter into a greased 10-inch springform pan. Bake for about 30 minutes or until top is lightly browned and a toothpick inserted in center comes out clean; do not overbake! Allow to cool in pan. When cool, spread with raspberry jam. Combine lemon juice and powdered sugar, and drizzle over torte in a lacy pattern so some of the jam is visible.

Barbara Ball
ChurchLIFE, FL

Poppy Seed Custard Torte

1 cup plus 1 teaspoon butter, *divided*
2 cups flour
½ teaspoon salt
1 tablespoon plus 1½ cups sugar,
  divided
1 package Knox unflavored gelatin
⅓ cup cold water

1½ cups milk
5 eggs, separated
2 teaspoons cornstarch
¼ cup poppy seeds
1 teaspoon vanilla
½ teaspoon cream of tartar
1 8-ounce container Cool Whip

Preheat oven to 350 degrees. To make crust, mix 1 cup butter, flour, salt, and 1 tablespoon sugar. Press into an ungreased 9×13-inch pan. Bake for 25 minutes, then cool. To make filling, soften gelatin in cold water, and set aside. Beat the egg yolks well; combine with milk and 1 cup sugar, and cook over water. Stir with a wire whisk. Add cornstarch and stir until thick; remove from heat. Mix in poppy seeds, 1 teaspoon butter, and vanilla. Add softened gelatin and mix together; set aside until cool. Beat egg whites with ½ cup sugar and cream of tartar until stiff. Fold into poppy seed mixture. Pour into cooled crust; top with Cool Whip and refrigerate overnight.

Barbara Nigh
Contributions and Postal Services, FL

Pumpkin Dip

1 can pumpkin pie filling
2 8-ounce packages light cream
   cheese
2 teaspoons nutmeg

2 teaspoons cinnamon
ginger snaps, sliced apples, or
   sliced pears
orange juice

In a large mixing bowl, blend all ingredients until smooth. Pour into a covered plastic container and chill for at least 2 hours or overnight. Serve with ginger snaps, apples, or pears (dip fruit in orange juice to keep from turning brown).

Laura Staudt
Women Today International, FL

> *In my inner being I delight in God's law*
> *(Rom. 7:22).*

Raspberry Delight

1 cup vanilla wafer crumbs
1 cup butter
1½ cups powdered sugar
2 eggs
1 cup whipping cream, whipped

1 package frozen raspberries
   (do not thaw)
½ cup nuts
¼ teaspoon vanilla

Line a 9-inch square pan with crumbs. Cream butter and sugar, then add eggs 1 at a time. Spread over crumbs. Reserving a few nuts for garnish, fold in raspberries, nuts, and vanilla. Spread over butter mixture, and sprinkle remaining nuts on top. Chill overnight. Serves 9.

Jeanne Lawrence
Crusade Family

Rhubarb Kugan

1½ cups flour
1 tablespoon sugar
½ teaspoon baking powder
½ cup butter or shortening
1 egg, beaten

2 tablespoons milk
5 cups sliced rhubarb
1 3-ounce package raspberry or
 other red Jell-O
Streusel Topping

Preheat oven to 350 degrees. Mix dry ingredients, then cut in butter. Add egg and milk. Dip fingers into flour, and pat crust into a square pan, bringing crust over halfway up sides of pan. Place rhubarb in crust and sprinkle with Jell-O. Cover with *Streusel Topping*. Bake for 40–50 minutes.

Streusel Topping:
½ cup flour
1 cup sugar

¼ cup butter, melted

Mix all ingredients together.

Barbara Nigh
Contributions and Postal Services, FL

Rhubarb Pudding

½ cup sugar
1 large egg
1 cup sour cream
1½ cups flour

⅛ teaspoon salt
1 teaspoon baking soda
3 cups chopped rhubarb

Preheat oven to 350 degrees. Mix sugar, egg, and sour cream; beat until light. Add flour, salt, and baking soda. Stir in rhubarb. Pour mixture into a greased and floured 9×13-inch pan. Bake for 40 minutes. To serve, spoon pudding into small dessert glasses and pour heavy cream over.

Joette Whims
NewLife Publications, CA

No mere man has ever seen, heard, or even imagined what wonderful things God has ready for those who love the Lord (1 Cor. 2:9).

Rhubarb Torte

2¼ cups flour, *divided*
½ teaspoon salt
2¾ cups sugar, *divided*
1 cup butter

4½ cups chopped rhubarb
6 egg yolks
1 cup cream
Meringue

Preheat oven to 325 degrees. Mix 2 cups flour, salt, 2½ cups sugar, and butter; pat into a 9×13-inch cake pan. Bake for 20 minutes. In a saucepan, heat ¼ cup sugar, rhubarb, egg yolks, cream, and ¼ cup flour. Cook until thick and clear, stirring often since it burns easily. Pour over baked crust and top with *Meringue*. Bake for about 5–8 minutes or until top is slightly browned.

Meringue:

6 egg whites
¾ cup sugar

½ teaspoon cream of tartar
½ teaspoon vanilla (optional)

Whip egg whites. Gradually add sugar and cream of tartar while beating until stiff peaks form. Add vanilla if desired.

Conda DeVries
International Ministry, FL

Russian Cream 🌐

1 cup half & half
¾ cup sugar
1½ teaspoons plain gelatin
2 tablespoons cold water

1 cup sour cream
1 teaspoon vanilla
light cookies
strawberries

Heat half & half and sugar until lukewarm. Soak gelatin in cold water; add to the sugar mixture. When gelatin and sugar are dissolved, remove from heat and cool. When the mixture begins to thicken, stir in slightly whipped sour cream. Add vanilla. Pour into a ring or individual molds. Serve with fresh strawberries and a light cookie, or put slices of Russian Cream on a cookie and top with a strawberry. This makes a delightful ladies' lunch dessert.

Barbara Ball
ChurchLIFE, FL

Spiced Peaches

2 large cans cling peach halves
  or slices with juice
1⅓ cups sugar

1 cup cider vinegar
4 cinnamon sticks
2 teaspoons whole cloves

Drain peaches, reserving syrup. Combine peach syrup, sugar, vinegar, cinnamon sticks, and cloves in a saucepan. Bring mixture to a boil, then lower heat and simmer for 10 minutes. Pour hot syrup over peaches and let cool. Chill.

Vonette Bright
Co-founder, Campus Crusade for Christ
Executive Director, Women Today International, FL

Strawberry Blintzes

1¼ cups Bisquick
3 eggs
2 cups milk
¼ cup butter, melted
Filling

1 package frozen strawberries,
  thawed
1 tablespoon lemon juice
¼ teaspoon almond flavoring
sour cream (optional)

Preheat oven to 400 degrees. Beat Bisquick, eggs, milk, and butter with a rotary beater until smooth. For each pancake, spoon 2–3 tablespoons batter onto a lightly greased griddle. Spread with back of spoon. Bake until small bubbles appear, then loosen edges gently; turn and brown the other side. Place ¼ cup *Filling* on each pancake; roll up and place in a 7×11-inch baking dish. Bake for 10 minutes. Heat strawberries with lemon juice and almond flavoring. Serve over rolled pancakes and top with a dollop of sour cream if desired. Makes 15–20.

Filling:

1 cup cottage cheese
1 3-ounce package cream cheese
3 tablespoons lemon juice

1½ tablespoon grated lemon rind
¼ cup sugar

Whip cheeses, lemon juice and rind, and sugar until creamy.

Lois Mackey
CoMission, CA

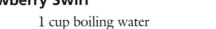

Strawberry Swirl

1 cup graham cracker crumbs
3 tablespoons sugar, *divided*
¼ cup butter, melted
2 cups fresh strawberries, sliced
1 small package strawberry Jell-O

1 cup boiling water
½ pound marshmallows
½ cup milk
1 cup whipping cream, whipped

Mix crumbs, 1 tablespoon sugar, and butter. Press firmly on the bottom of a 9-inch-square baking dish. Chill until set. Sprinkle 2 tablespoons sugar over fresh berries; let stand for 30 minutes. Dissolve Jell-O in boiling water. Drain berries, reserving juice. Add water to juice to make 1 cup, then add to Jell-O. Chill until partially set. Meanwhile, heat marshmallows and milk, stirring until marshmallows melt. Cool thoroughly, then fold in whipped cream. Add berries to Jell-O, then swirl in marshmallow mixture to marble. Pour into crust and chill until set.

Pearl Bancroft
Crusade Family

Swedish Rice Pudding

2–3 eggs
3 cups warmed milk
1 teaspoon vanilla
1 cup cooked rice

1 tablespoon butter
scant ½ cup sugar
cinnamon

Preheat oven to 300–325 degrees. Whip eggs; add warmed milk and vanilla. Combine cooked rice, butter, and sugar. Let stand for 5 minutes. Pour milk mixture into rice and blend well. Pour into a buttered casserole dish and sprinkle with cinnamon. Place casserole in a pan of water 1 inch high; bake for 45 minutes. Do not allow pudding to boil; eggs will separate if oven is too hot. Pudding is done when a knife inserted comes out clean.

Joan Tungseth
Computer Services, FL

 Every branch that does bear fruit he trims clean so that it will be even more fruitful (John 15:2).

Trifle

1 8-inch pound cake
2 packages lady fingers, *divided*
1 cup raspberry jam, *divided*
2 10-ounce packages frozen
   raspberries with juice
1 cup pineapple juice

4 cups custard, *divided*
2–3 cups fresh or frozen sliced peaches
2 cups diced pineapple
2 bananas, sliced
2 cups whipped cream
walnuts, chocolate, or almonds

Cut pound cake into 4 layers. Put 1 layer of cake in a punch bowl, large glass bowl, or large trifle dish. Place ¼ of lady fingers around edge of bowl. Spread a thin layer of raspberry jam over the cake and lady fingers. Drain juice from raspberries; reserve ¼ cup and discard the rest. Combine raspberry and pineapple juices. Pour ½ cup of juice mixture over the cake. Spread 1 cup custard, and cover with peaches. Add a second layer of cake and place ¼ of lady fingers around edge of bowl; spread with raspberry jam. Sprinkle ¼ cup juice over cake, spread 1 cup custard, and cover with pineapple. Lay the third cake layer and lady fingers, spread with jam, and sprinkle with ¼ cup juice. Add 1 cup custard and top with bananas. For fourth layer, repeat cake, lady fingers, jam, and juice. Add custard and raspberries; top with whipped cream. Garnish with walnuts, shaved chocolate, or sliced almonds. Cover with plastic wrap. Serves 20–25. *Tip:* This can be prepared 4–6 hours in advance, but add the whipped cream just before serving. Trifle always looks elegant, and is great for a Christmas party or a cool summer dessert.

Barbara Ball
ChurchLIFE, FL

Let us consider how we may spur one another on toward love and good deeds. Let us not give up meeting together, as some are in the habit of doing, but let us encourage one another (Heb. 10:24,25).

Accompaniments

Sauces

Barbecue Sauce

¾ cup ketchup
¾ cup water
2 medium onions, chopped
2 tablespoons vinegar
2 tablespoons Worcestershire sauce
1½ teaspoons salt

½ teaspoon pepper
1 teaspoon chili powder
1 teaspoon paprika
1 clove garlic, minced
1 teaspoon liquid smoke
1 tablespoon brown sugar

Combine all ingredients in a saucepan and simmer for 5 minutes. This sauce keeps indefinitely in refrigerator and has a delicious pit-barbecue taste. For oven-barbecued spareribs, cut ribs into pieces, place into baking pan, and cover with sauce. Bake at 350 degrees for 45–60 minutes.

Lee Etta Dickerson
Women Today International, FL

Basic White Sauce

Thin (like coffee cream—for creamed vegetables, soups, etc.)
1 tablespoon butter
½–1 tablespoon flour
¼ teaspoon salt

⅛ teaspoon pepper
1 cup milk

Medium (like thick cream—for creamed and scalloped dishes)
2 tablespoons butter
2 tablespoons flour
¼ teaspoon salt

⅛ teaspoon pepper
1 cup milk

Thick (like batter—for croquettes, souffles, etc.)

¼ cup butter   ⅛ teaspoon pepper
¼ cup flour   1 cup milk
¼ teaspoon salt

Melt butter over low heat in a heavy saucepan. Blend in flour and seasonings. Cook over low heat, stirring until mixture is smooth and bubbly. Remove from heat; stir in milk. Bring to a boil, stirring constantly. Boil for 1 minute. Makes 1 cup.

Variations:

Cheese Sauce—Make 1 cup medium white sauce. Add ¼ teaspoon dry mustard to seasonings. When white sauce is finished boiling, blend in ½ cup shredded sharp cheddar cheese. Stir until cheese is melted. Use for vegetables, rice, macaroni, and egg dishes.

Rich Cheese Sauce—Make 2 cups medium white sauce. Add 2 teaspoons dry mustard and 1 teaspoon Worcestershire sauce to seasonings. After boiling, add 2 cups shredded sharp cheddar cheese. Stir until cheese is melted.

Mushroom Sauce—Make 1 cup medium white sauce. Add 1 cup sliced mushrooms and 1 teaspoon grated onion to the butter and sauté on low for 5 minutes before adding flour.

Egg Sauce—Make 1 cup medium white sauce. Carefully stir in 2 diced, hard-boiled eggs. Season as desired with white pepper, tarragon, or paprika. Good with salmon or other fish.

Curry Sauce—Make 1 cup medium white sauce. Combine ½ teaspoon curry powder with the butter before adding flour and other seasonings. Goes perfectly with chicken, lamb, shrimp, and rice.

Barbara Ball
ChurchLIFE, FL

Chattanooga Horseradish Sauce

1 16-ounce jar pineapple preserves   1 8-ounce jar horseradish
2–3 teaspoons Coleman's dry mustard   1 16-ounce jar apple jelly

Mix ingredients in a blender; keep in the refrigerator. This innocent-looking mixture has enormous punch. It is great served with ham, beef, and sandwiches. *Tip:* Put it in pretty little jars to give as gifts.

Nina Locke
Crusade Family

ACCOMPANIMENTS

Chicken Barbecue Sauce

1 cup olive oil
¾ cup lemon or lime juice
2 teaspoons garlic salt
2 tablespoons paprika

2 teaspoons oregano
1 teaspoon salt
lots of fresh ground pepper

Mix all ingredients with a fork or whip. Pour over cut-up, uncooked chicken pieces; cover and marinate for several hours. Grill over charcoal, being careful not to burn. This light and savory sauce is delicious on chicken.

Sandra Auer
International Ministry, FL

No mere man has ever seen, heard, or even imagined what wonderful things God has ready for those who love the Lord (1 Cor. 2:9).

Chili Sauce for Hot Dogs or Hamburgers

½ cup chopped onion
1½ cups finely chopped celery
oil
1 pound ground beef
1 pound dark brown sugar
2 bottles Open Pit barbecue sauce
2 15-ounce cans tomato sauce

juice of ½ lemon
¼ cup white vinegar
1 teaspoon dry mustard
2 heaping teaspoons chili powder
1 teaspoon Tabasco sauce
2 heaping teaspoons paprika
2 cans kidney beans

Brown onion and celery in oil. Add ground beef and sauté slightly. Add remaining ingredients and blend thoroughly. Simmer until thick (1½–2 hours). May be canned in jars or frozen for future use. Heat and serve over hot dogs or hamburgers on buns. Makes about 2 quarts.

Charlotte Day
Crusade Family

Chinese Brown Sauce

2 tablespoons butter
1 cup water
4 teaspoons cornstarch

2 teaspoons sugar
3 tablespoons soy sauce

Melt butter in a saucepan. Mix remaining ingredients and add to butter.
Cook, stirring constantly, until thick and clear.

Liesl Buck
International Ministry, FL

Coach's Barbecue Sauce

1 cup butter
2 large onions, diced
1 pint ReaLemon juice
2¾ cups vinegar

½ cup Worcestershire sauce
3 ounces lemon pepper marinade
3 tablespoons garlic salt
black pepper to taste

Sauté butter and onions for 10–15 minutes. Add remaining ingredients;
bring to a boil, then simmer for 30–45 minutes. This delicious barbecue
sauce is not only good for marinating, but can be used to baste meat regularly
during cooking because the sauce will not burn.

Dick Madison
ChurchLIFE, AL

Coney Island Sauce

2 pounds ground beef
4 medium onions, chopped
¼ cup chopped green pepper
2 quarts tomato sauce
4 teaspoons chili powder

6 cloves garlic, chopped
1 tablespoon pepper
2 teaspoons cumin
5 teaspoons sugar

Brown ground beef, then add onion and green pepper; simmer. Add tomato
sauce and seasonings, then simmer for about 20 minutes. Pour over hot
dogs on buns.

Karen Langerveld
Campus Ministry, WA

Gramma's Barbecue Sauce

3 cups chopped onion
4 cups sugar
4 cups ketchup

3 cups vinegar
2 teaspoons Tabasco sauce
5 tablespoons Worcestershire sauce

Put all ingredients in a large pot and simmer for 1 hour. Sauce can be made ahead and frozen in smaller containers. Great on all kinds of meat and it keeps well.

Alison Druckemiller
Keynote Communications, IN

Let us not become weary in doing good, for at the proper time we will reap a harvest if we do not give up (Gal. 6:9).

Hard Sauce

⅓ cup butter
1 cup powdered sugar

¼ teaspoon lemon extract
¾ teaspoon vanilla

Cream butter while adding sugar gradually. Add flavorings and mix well. Pile lightly on a serving dish; chill but do not harden. Serve with hot puddings. *Variations:* Add a dash of cinnamon for flavor; add 1 tablespoon cream as the last ingredient and beat until fluffy; or beat in ½–⅔ cup crushed berries or bananas.

Vonette Bright
Co-founder, Campus Crusade for Christ
Executive Director, Women Today International, FL

Italian Spaghetti Sauce

1¼ pounds ground beef
2 large onions, chopped
1 tablespoon shortening
1 8-ounce can tomato sauce
2 6-ounce cans tomato paste
2 puree cans water

2 bay leaves
2 whole red peppers
4 cloves garlic, minced
salt and pepper to taste
4 teaspoons sugar
dash chili powder

Brown ground beef and onions in shortening. Add remaining ingredients and simmer. This is an old recipe from my mother, Lena Lee.

Barbara Ball
ChurchLIFE, FL

Mushroom Sauce

½ cup chopped onion
½ cup diced green pepper
¼ cup diced red pepper
3 tablespoons butter

3 cups medium *Basic White Sauce*
1 cup canned sliced mushrooms
1 teaspoon dried basil

Sauté onion and peppers in butter. Stir in *Basic White Sauce*, mushrooms, and basil. Simmer for 5 minutes. Makes 4 cups. *Variation:* In place of *Basic White Sauce*, substitute 2 cans cream of chicken soup and ⅔ cup milk.

Carolyn Houska
Arrowhead Conferences and Events, CA

To travel through the desert with others, to suffer thirst, to find a spring, to drink of it, and not to tell others is exactly the same as enjoying Christ and not telling others about Him. — Corrie ten Boom

---

Pesto Sauce

2 cups fresh basil leaves
¼–½ cup freshly grated Parmesan
  cheese
2–4 cloves garlic

¼–½ cup olive oil
¼ cup pine nuts
salt to taste

Combine the first 3 ingredients in a food processor or blender. Blend until smooth; add a little of the oil if needed. When ingredients are blended, add the remaining olive oil, pine nuts, and salt. Blend briefly. Adjust amounts of Parmesan, garlic, olive oil, and pine nuts according to your tastes. Serve 1 or 2 tablespoons pesto per serving of cooked pasta. Pesto will keep in refrigerator for several weeks.

Sue McDaniel
International Ministry, FL

Sour Cream Cucumber Sauce

1 cup sour cream
1 tablespoon vinegar
1½ tablespoons lemon juice
1 teaspoon sugar

dash pepper
1 teaspoon grated onion
1 cucumber, peeled, seeded,
 and chopped

Blend and chill. Serve on seafood or salads.

Joette Whims
NewLife Publications, CA

ACCOMPANIMENTS

Spaghetti Sauce

1 pound ground beef or turkey
4 cups chopped onion
4 cloves garlic, minced
2–2½ quarts tomato sauce
3 tablespoons basil
3 tablespoons wine vinegar

1 cup grated carrots (optional)
1 cup grated zucchini (optional)
2 cups chopped bell peppers
 (optional)
2 cups chopped mushrooms
 (optional)

Brown meat, onions, and garlic in a 5-quart Dutch oven until the meat is brown. Add remaining ingredients and simmer for 1–3 hours. *Tip:* For chunkier sauce, chop instead of grate vegetables and substitute 1 quart stewed or chopped tomatoes for a quart of tomato sauce. Freeze extra for future meals.

Dianne Webb
Finance, FL

Teriyaki Sauce

12 ounces Kikkoman soy sauce
1 cup sugar

freshly grated ginger root to taste

Cook soy sauce down to half the amount by boiling in an open kettle for about 20 minutes. Add sugar and ginger root; cook for 10 more minutes. Strain mixture; refrigerate. Use sauce to marinate steaks for at least 2 hours. Also good on pork chops cooked at 400 degrees for 45 minutes.

Vonette Bright
Co-founder, Campus Crusade for Christ
Executive Director, Women Today International, FL

West African Peanut Sauce

5 cups water
4 medium tomatoes, chopped
1 tablespoon vegetable oil
1 onion, chopped
1 teaspoon salt

¼ cup peanut butter
2 tablespoons tomato paste
2 beef bouillon cubes
1 large okra, chopped (optional)

Put water, tomatoes, oil, and beef in a Dutch oven. Cover and boil for 10 minutes. Add onion, salt, peanut butter, tomato paste, and bouillon cubes. If desired, add okra. Reduce heat and simmer for 20 minutes. Goes well with beef or chicken, served over rice.

Mark Austin
JESUS Video Master Studio, FL

Side Dishes

Applesauce

6 large apples, peeled, cored,
    and cut up
½ cup apple cider

¼ cup sugar
cinnamon to taste

Bring apples and cider to a boil; turn down to simmer. Cook for 20 minutes, then add sugar and cinnamon; stir. Cover and refrigerate.

Anne Lawrence
World Changers Radio, FL

Baked Apples and Bananas

apples, peeled and sliced
bananas, peeled and sliced
4 tablespoons butter, *divided*

brown sugar
2 tablespoons flour
2 tablespoons white sugar

Preheat oven to 325 degrees. Using the desired number of apples and bananas, place a layer each of apples and bananas in a buttered casserole; dot with 2 tablespoons butter and brown sugar. Repeat layers, using as many as possible because the fruit will shrink. Crumble together flour, white sugar, and 2 tablespoons butter; sprinkle on top. Bake for 1½–2 hours. Excellent accompaniment with meat or poultry.

Elizabeth Marks
International Ministry, FL

Curried Fruit

1 16-ounce can peach halves
1 20-ounce can pineapple slices
1 16-ounce can pear halves
¾ cup light brown sugar

½ cup butter, melted
2 or more teaspoons curry powder
5 or more maraschino cherries
with stems

Preheat oven to 350 degrees. Drain fruit on paper towels; place in a baking dish. Mix brown sugar, butter, and curry, and pour over fruit. Bake uncovered for 1 hour. Top with cherries and serve. *Variation:* May be refrigerated overnight. Heat at 350 degrees for 30 minutes, then place into a chafing dish and top with cherries.

Juli Emory
Military Ministry, VA

 Tell the righteous it will be well with them, for they will enjoy the fruit of their deeds (Psalm 3:10).

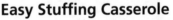

Easy Stuffing Casserole

4 cups prepared stuffing
3 eggs, slightly beaten
1 cup cottage cheese, *divided*

1 pint sour cream
2 cans cream of mushroom soup

Preheat oven to 350 degrees. Mix stuffing, eggs, and ½ cup cottage cheese, and place in a casserole dish. Mix sour cream and soup, and pour over stuffing mixture. Cover and bake for 30 minutes. Uncover and top with remaining cottage cheese; bake for 10 more minutes.

Sus Schmitt
Computer Services, FL

Scalloped Oysters

1 cup cracker crumbs
½ cup butter, melted
1 tablespoon salt
1 tablespoon Worcestershire sauce

1 cup whipping cream
1 28-ounce can oysters, drained,
   or fresh oysters

Preheat oven to 350 degrees. Combine crumbs, butter, salt, and Worcestershire sauce. Place ½ of the crumb mixture into a 1-quart baking dish or in shells. Combine ½ of the cream and ½ of the oysters, and place over crumbs. Make a second layer. Bake for 15–20 minutes.

Barbara Ball
ChurchLIFE, FL

Be devoted to one another in brotherly love. Honor one another above yourselves (Rom. 12:10).

Sweet Cranberry Applesauce

1½ cups honey
2 unpared apples, chopped
1 pound whole cranberries
½ teaspoon salt

1 teaspoon ground cloves
1 teaspoon ground cinnamon
½ teaspoon ground ginger

Combine ingredients in a 3-quart pot. Cook over medium heat for 20–30 minutes. Serve warm or cold. This is wonderful for holidays.

Debbie McGoldrick
Student Venture, GA

Zucchini Stuffing

4 zucchini, cubed
1 large yellow onion, chopped
2 cups chicken bouillon

2 boxes chicken-flavored Stove Top stuffing
1 cup sour cream (low-fat, if desired)
1 can cream of chicken soup

Preheat oven to 350 degrees. Cook zucchini and onion in a little water until tender; drain. Heat bouillon; mix with dressing and seasoning packets. Set aside. Combine sour cream, soup, zucchini, and onions. In a lightly greased 9×13-inch pan, layer ½ of dressing, all of zucchini mix, then remaining dressing. Bake for 30 minutes. This is my husband's all-time favorite.

Angela Rosa
Sunport Ministry Office, FL

Et Cetera

Aunt Veronica's Gypsy Pickles

1 quart large kosher dill pickles, drained
¾ cup white vinegar

1¾ cups sugar
1 teaspoon celery seed
2 teaspoons garlic powder

Cover pickles with ice cold water. Let stand for 1 hour, then drain and slice. Combine remaining ingredients; pour over pickles. Roll jar to mix. Place in refrigerator and shake periodically for a week.

Liesl Buck
International Ministry, FL

Crystal Chip Pickles

14 large dill-size cucumbers
1 quart vinegar
8 cups sugar

1 tablespoon salt
2 tablespoons mixed whole spices

Wash cucumbers; cover with boiling water and let stand 24 hours. For the next 3 mornings, pour off water and cover with fresh boiling water. On the fourth morning, slice cucumbers ½-inch thick. Heat vinegar, sugar, salt, and spices; pour over sliced cucumbers. For the next 3 mornings, pour off syrup, heat, and pour back over sliced cucumbers. On the fourth morning, heat pickles and syrup together; pour into canning jars and seal.

Joette Whims
NewLife Publications, CA

Pilaf Seasoning

2 chicken bouillon cubes
½ teaspoon rosemary

½ teaspoon thyme
½ teaspoon marjoram

Mix all ingredients together. Add to cooked rice.

Dorothy Gregory
Here's Life America, MA

Sweet Corn Relish

2 cups finely chopped celery
1 cup finely chopped onion
1 cup finely chopped green pepper
1 cup finely chopped red pepper
    (optional)
1 can French-style green beans,
    rinsed and drained

1 large can tiny peas, rinsed
2 cans tiny white corn, rinsed and
    drained
1 cup sugar
½ cup vinegar
½ cup oil
½ cup water

Mix the first 7 ingredients. To make dressing, boil sugar, vinegar, oil, and water for 1 minute to dissolve sugar. Cool, then pour over vegetables. Let stand for 24 hours.

Sus Schmitt
Computer Services, FL

Taco Seasoning

2 teaspoons onion powder
½ teaspoon red pepper
1 teaspoon salt
½ teaspoon garlic powder

1 teaspoon chili powder
¼ teaspoon oregano
½ teaspoon cornstarch
½ teaspoon cumin

Mix all ingredients. To make tacos, add 1½ tablespoons mixture to 1 pound browned ground beef and ½ cup water. *Optional:* Add 1–2 tablespoons tomato paste or ketchup to the taco mixture; simmer for 10 minutes. Make 4–5 times as much and store. You'll never need to buy mixes again.

Joanne Austin
International Resources Ministry, FL

Children's Recipes

Bunny Salad ⏰

4 lettuce leaves
4 canned pear halves
8 sliced almonds

8 raisins
4 red cinnamon candies
8 tablespoons cottage cheese

Wash and dry lettuce leaves. Shred one leaf on each plate to form a bed. Place a pear half, sliced-side down, on each plate. On the narrow end of each pear half, arrange the following to form the bunny's face: 1 red cinnamon candy on the tip for the nose; about ½ inch away, place 2 raisins for eyes; about ½ inch behind the eyes, make ears by inserting 2 sliced almonds into the pear at an angle. Place 2 tablespoons cottage cheese at the wide end of each pear half to make a tail. Makes four servings.

Ruth and Amanda Leppard
Crusade Kids

Candy Cookies

1 12-ounce package butterscotch
   chips
½ cup creamy peanut butter

½ cup shelled and halved
   cocktail peanuts
5 cups corn flakes

Melt butterscotch chips and peanut butter in a double boiler. Add peanuts. Stir in corn flakes and drop by spoonful onto wax paper. Chill.

Sus Schmitt
Computer Services, FL

Children's Torte

1 box graham crackers   1 can chocolate frosting

Do not separate crackers. Layer 5–10 graham crackers, topping each layer with chocolate frosting. Frost sides and top of cracker layers. Refrigerate overnight to soften; cut into thin slices to serve. *Tip:* This dessert looks so nice that it can be served to adults also. This recipe is from my daughter, Robbyn.

Barbara Ball
ChurchLIFE, FL

Chocolate-Chocolate Ice Cream Sandwiches

1 pint chocolate ice cream,   2 tablespoons shortening
  slightly softened   30 chocolate chip cookies
6 ounces semi-sweet chocolate chips

For each sandwich, press 1 slightly rounded tablespoon ice cream between 2 cookies; place in a jelly roll pan. Freeze until firm. Melt chips and shortening, stirring occasionally. Let stand for 2 minutes. Dip half of each sandwich into chocolate. Place in pan and freeze until firm. Wrap in plastic to store. Makes 15 sandwiches.

Joette Whims
NewLife Publications, CA

Christmas Ornaments

2 cups baking soda   1¼ cups water
1 cup cornstarch   2 tablespoons ground cloves

Mix ingredients and bring to a low boil over medium heat, stirring until mixture has the consistency of dough. Put in a bowl and cover with a damp cloth; refrigerate for 30 minutes. Knead for 3–4 minutes. Flour the working area and rolling pin. Roll out dough to ¼-inch thickness. Cut with cookie cutters into desired shapes. With a straw, make a hole in the top of each ornament. Preheat oven to 350 degrees. Put ornaments in oven and *turn oven off.* Turn over when tops are hard. When completely hard and dry, sand lightly with fine sandpaper. Paint as desired on both sides. When dry, spray with clear enamel or varnish.

Gayle Anne VanFulpen
NewLife Publications, FL

> *It is good to be children sometimes, and never better than at Christmas.* — Charles Dickens

Christmas Tree Bread

1 tablespoon cinnamon
½ cup sugar
¾ cup chopped nuts
3 cans refrigerated biscuits
½ cup melted butter
1 cup powdered sugar

about 2 tablespoons milk
1 teaspoon vanilla
green food coloring
red hots
silver shots

Preheat oven to 475 degrees. Mix cinnamon, sugar, and chopped nuts. Dip each biscuit in melted butter, then in the cinnamon mixture. Arrange biscuits in a tree pattern on a cookie sheet. Bake for 10–15 minutes or until lightly browned. Combine powdered sugar with a small amount of milk and a few drops of green food coloring; drizzle over tree. Sprinkle with a few red hots and silver shots. *Tip:* Easy and unique for a girls' Christmas brunch.

Carol Williams
Crusade Family

Coconut Kisses

1 can sweetened condensed milk
3 cups shredded coconut

1 teaspoon vanilla
⅛ teaspoon salt

Preheat oven to 375 degrees. Mix ingredients together and drop by spoonful onto a greased baking sheet. Bake for 8 minutes.

Gayle Anne VanFulpen
NewLife Publications, FL

CHILDREN'S

Crispy Peanut Butter Brownies

1 package brownie mix
7 ounces marshmallow creme
6 ounces chocolate chips

½ cup peanut butter
2 cups Rice Krispies

Prepare brownie mix and bake in a 9×13-inch pan according to package directions. Warm marshmallow creme a little so that it's easier to spread, then spread over warm brownies. Melt together chocolate chips and peanut butter; combine with Rice Krispies. Spread on top, then cool before cutting. This recipe is from Mary Strauss.

Lynn Copeland
NewLife Publications, OK

Desiree's World's Best "Nachos"

1 cup butter, softened
¾ cup white sugar
¾ cup firmly packed brown sugar
1 teaspoon vanilla
2¼ cups flour

1 teaspoon baking soda
1 teaspoon salt
12 ounces Nestle semi-sweet
    chocolate chips
1 cup chopped nuts

Combine butter, sugars, and vanilla; beat until creamy. In a separate bowl, mix flour, baking soda, and salt. Add to mixture. Stir in chocolate chips and nuts. Serve with tortilla or corn chips as dessert or a sweet treat.

Desiree and Michael Heckman
Crusade Kids

Dirt Cake

½ cup butter
1 8-ounce package cream cheese
½ cup powdered sugar
2 3¼-ounce packages instant
    chocolate pudding
3½ cups milk

1 large clay pot
1 package Oreo cookies, with
    middles removed, crushed
1 trowel
1 package gummy worms

Combine butter, cream cheese, and sugar. In another bowl, combine pudding mixes and milk. Place a layer of foil on the bottom of the clean clay pot to cover the hole. Combine the contents of both bowls. In the clay pot, alternate layers of Oreos and pudding, ending with the Oreos. Insert gummy worms throughout. Serve with a clean trowel.

Donna Knopf
International Ministry, FL

Edible "Play Dough"

1 3-ounce package vanilla pudding
1 cup whole milk

½ cup peanut butter
1 cup dry powdered milk

Combine the pudding and whole milk; add peanut butter. Mix in powdered milk until the texture is like play dough. Break off a portion about the size of a golf ball. Mold it like play dough, then shape a batch of "cookies" to share with family or friends. No baking required.

Rebecca, Jason, and Rachael Burns
Crusade Kids

Fingerpaint Recipe
(non-edible)

1 cup cold water, *divided*
½ cup cornstarch
1 envelope unflavored gelatin

2 cups hot water
½ cup powdered detergent
various food colors

Mix ¾ cup cold water with cornstarch. Mix ¼ cup cold water with gelatin. Slowly stir hot water into cornstarch mixture. Stir over medium heat until it boils and becomes clear. Remove from heat and add gelatin mixture. Stir in detergent until dissolved. Cool and divide into separate jars for the different colors. Add food coloring to make the desired shades.

Gayle Anne VanFulpen
NewLife Publications, FL

Fool's Toffee

1 box saltine crackers
1 cup butter

1 cup dark brown sugar
14 ounces chocolate chips

Preheat oven to 375 degrees. Butter a foil-covered cookie sheet, and cover with a single layer of crackers. In a saucepan, melt butter and sugar. Boil for 4 minutes. Pour mixture over crackers and spread evenly. Bake for 5 minutes. Sprinkle chocolate chips over the crackers. When chips soften, spread them to cover the crackers. Let cool in refrigerator, then break into pieces.

Stacie Unruh
Headquarters Development Office, FL

A fool's fun is being bad; a wise man's fun is being wise! (Prov. 10:23)

Frozen Apricot Salad

1 6-ounce can frozen orange juice
   concentrate, thawed
1 cup sugar
1 tablespoon lemon juice
3 bananas, diced

1 8-ounce can crushed pineapple
   with juice
1 orange juice can of water
1 17-ounce can apricots, drained
   and chopped

Mix all ingredients. Spoon into muffin tins lined with paper cups; freeze until firm. Store in plastic containers after set. These make a good children's snack.

Juli Emory
Military Ministry, VA

Fudgy Banana Pops
(frozen bananas)

8 bananas
lemon juice
¼ cup butter
¼ cup light corn syrup
2 tablespoons water

6 ounces semi-sweet chocolate chips
6 ounces sweet chocolate pieces
chopped nuts, shredded coconut,
   or small candies

Dip peeled bananas in lemon juice. Insert wooden skewers and freeze. Combine butter, corn syrup, and water in a saucepan. Bring to a boil, then removed from heat. Add chocolate and stir until smooth. Dip frozen bananas into chocolate mixture. Spread evenly over bananas and scrape off excess with a small spatula. (If chocolate mixture becomes too thick, place pan in very hot water.) Sprinkle with nuts, coconut, or candies. Place on a lightly greased shallow pan. Return to freezer immediately; do not allow bananas to soften. Serve frozen.

Dorothy Gregory
Crusade Family

Grandma Lawrence's Thumbprint Cookies

½ cup soft shortening
¼ cup brown sugar
1 egg, separated
½ teaspoon vanilla
1 cup flour

¼ teaspoon salt
finely chopped nuts
chopped candied fruit, jelly, or
    tinted frosting

Preheat oven to 375 degrees. Mix shortening, brown sugar, egg yolk, and vanilla. Sift together flour and salt, and stir into mixture. Roll into 1-inch balls. Dip into the slightly beaten egg white, then roll in nuts. Place 1 inch apart on an ungreased cookie sheet, and have kids gently press thumb into center of each cookie. Bake for 10–12 minutes; cool. Fill thumbprint with candied fruit, jelly, or tinted frosting.

Jessica, Natalie, and Angela LaGambina
Crusade Kids

Hide-and-Seek Muffins

1½ cups flour
2 teaspoons baking powder
½ teaspoon baking soda
½ teaspoon salt
7 tablespoons sugar, *divided*

2 eggs
1 cup milk
½ teaspoon vanilla
4 tablespoons butter, melted
12 medium strawberries

Preheat oven to 375 degrees. Combine dry ingredients except 3 tablespoons sugar. In a separate bowl, combine eggs, milk, vanilla, and butter. Whisk about 20 times. Pour into dry mixture and stir until moist. Place cupcake liners in a muffin tin and fill about halfway. Roll strawberries in the remaining sugar and place one in the center of each muffin, pushing it down with your finger. Bake for 15–20 minutes. Remove from the pan to cool; cool at least 10 minutes before eating (centers can be very hot).

Jessica, Natalie, and Angela LaGambina
Crusade Kids

Homespun Peanut Butter

8 cups toasted salted peanuts   1 cup honey
2 tablespoons canola or olive oil

Put ingredients in a blender and purée until smooth.

Lori Burns
U.S. Recruiting Office, FL

Instant Treat

any flavor sugar-free pudding,   cinnamon
   prepared   graham crackers

Sprinkle cinnamon over crackers, and spread pudding on top.

Gayle Anne VanFulpen
NewLife Publications, FL

Less Mess Cake

1½ cups flour   ⅓ cup oil
1 cup sugar   1 tablespoon white vinegar
3 tablespoons cocoa   1 teaspoon vanilla
1 teaspoon baking soda   1 cup cold water
½ teaspoon salt

Preheat oven to 350 degrees. Measure dry ingredients into a cake pan; mix well with a fork. Make 3 holes in the dry mixture. Pour oil into 1 hole, vinegar into another, and vanilla into the last. Pour water over all; mix carefully. Bake for 35–40 minutes. Cool before cutting.

Amanda Leppard
Crusade Kid

Microwave Apple Crisp

4 cups sliced apples
½ cup sugar
¾ cup flour, *divided*
¼ teaspoon cinnamon

½ cup oatmeal
½ cup brown sugar
¼ cup soft margarine

Place apples in an 8-inch square glass pan, and sprinkle sugar, ¼ cup flour, and cinnamon over apples. Mix ½ cup flour with remaining ingredients, and sprinkle over apple mixture. Microwave on high for 10–12 minutes. Turn after 5 minutes cooking time.

Becky Rivera
Student LINC, FL

Mini Sweet Hamburgers

vanilla wafers
chocolate cookies (such as Keebler
    Grasshoppers)

green icing
sesame seeds
honey

Use vanilla wafers as buns. Stick chocolate cookies to vanilla wafers with green icing. Let icing ooze out to look like lettuce. Stick sesame seeds to top of bun with honey.

Sus Schmitt
Computer Services, FL

Mom's Special Occasion Fruit Dip

1 tub strawberry cream cheese
1 small carton whipped topping
grapes
mandarin or fresh oranges

pineapple chunks
apple slices
banana chunks

Mix cream cheese and whipped topping in a blender until smooth. Serve with a platter of fruit.

Jessica, Natalie, and Angela LaGambina
Crusade Kids

Monster Cookies

½ cup butter or margarine, softened
1 cup white sugar
1 cup plus 2 teaspoons brown sugar, firmly packed
3 eggs
2 cups peanut butter
¼ teaspoon vanilla

¾ teaspoon light corn syrup
4½ cups uncooked oats
2 teaspoons baking soda
¼ teaspoon salt
1 cup M&Ms
6 ounces chocolate chips

Preheat oven to 350 degrees. Cream butter and gradually add sugars, beating well. Add eggs, peanut butter, vanilla, and corn syrup; beat well. Mix in oats, baking soda, and salt, stirring well. Stir in remaining ingredients. Drop dough by ¼ cupful 4 inches apart on a lightly greased cookie sheet. Bake for 12–15 minutes. Center of cookies will be slightly soft. Cool slightly on sheets; remove to wire racks and cool completely.

Debbie McGoldrick
Student Venture, GA

Only a fool despises his father's advice; a wise son considers each suggestion (Prov. 15:5).

Muddy Buddies

1 cup semi-sweet chocolate chips
½ cup butter
1 teaspoon vanilla

9 cups Rice Chex
1½ cups powdered sugar

Microwave chocolate chips and butter for 1 minute or until smooth. Stir in vanilla. Place Rice Chex in a bowl. Pour melted chocolate over cereal and stir until evenly coated. Place cereal mixture into ziplock bags with the powdered sugar. Seal and shake until all pieces are well coated. Spread on waxed paper to cool.

Ruth and Amanda Leppard
Crusade Kids

One Two Three Quesadillas

refried beans
flour tortillas

shredded cheese
salsa (optional)

Spread beans lightly on 1 tortilla shell. Sprinkle with cheese and top with a second tortilla. Microwave for 50 seconds; cut into wedges to cool. Enjoy with salsa if you like.

Jessica, Natalie, and Angela LaGambina
Crusade Kids

CHILDREN'S

Oreo Ice Cream Pie

1 package Oreos, *divided*
½ gallon ice cream, softened

1 8-ounce carton Cool Whip,
softened

Crush 12 cookies and press into a pie pan to make a crust. Crush the remaining cookies. Mix ice cream, Cool Whip, and crushed cookies, reserving a few crumbs for topping. Spoon mixture into crust and sprinkle with reserved crumbs. Freeze.

Carolyn Freshour
International Ministry, Africa

Peanut Butter Bars

1 cup peanut butter
1 cup butter
2 cups powdered sugar

1½ cups finely crushed graham crackers
2 4-ounce dark chocolate bars
1 4-ounce milk chocolate bar

Mix the first 4 ingredients and press into a 9×13-inch pan. Melt chocolate bars and spread on top. Chill thoroughly before cutting into pieces.

Joanne Austin
International Ministry, FL

Play Clay

1 cup flour
2 teaspoons cream of tartar
1 cup water

½ cup salt
1 tablespoon oil
food coloring as desired

Mix ingredients well, and cook over medium heat until water evaporates, stirring constantly. Store in an air-tight container.

Maggie Bruehl
National Ministry, FL

Pocketful of Pizza

1 can refrigerated pizza dough
1 tablespoon vegetable oil
¼ cup pizza sauce
1 cup shredded mozzarella cheese,
   divided

½ cup cooked Italian sausage
1 tablespoon finely chopped onion
⅛–¼ teaspoon garlic powder
¼ of a 3-ounce package sliced
   pepperoni

Preheat oven to 425 degrees. Roll pizza dough into a 12-inch circle. Fold loosely in half; place on a lightly greased cookie sheet and unfold. Brush with oil. Layer pizza sauce, ½ cup mozzarella cheese, sausage, onion, garlic powder, and pepperoni on half the circle. Top with remaining mozzarella. Fold dough over filling. Turn edge of lower dough over edge of upper dough; pinch edge to seal. Prick top with a fork. Bake about 10 minutes or until golden brown.

Joette Whims
NewLife Publications, CA

Quick Cobbler

1 can cherry pie filling	2 cups Bisquick
½ cup milk	2 tablespoons sugar

Preheat oven to 450 degrees. Empty cherry pie filling into a 9×9-inch pan. Combine milk, Bisquick, and sugar to a paste, and drop by spoonful over cherry filling. Bake for 20–25 minutes.

Gayle Anne VanFulpen
NewLife Publications, FL

Everyone should be quick to listen, slow to speak and slow to become angry (James 1:19).

Rice Krispie Candy

⅔ cup dark corn syrup	½ cup butter
⅓ cup water	6 cups Rice Krispies
1 cup sugar	1 cup chopped walnuts

Mix syrup, water, sugar, and butter, and cook to a soft boil. Pour over Rice Krispies and nuts. Stir and place in a buttered 9×13-inch pan. Cool and cut into 40 pieces.

Lila Kremer
ChurchLIFE, NE

Simple Sloppy Joes

1 pound ground beef	2 tablespoons ketchup
1 onion, chopped	½ teaspoon salt
1 can chicken gumbo soup	½ teaspoon pepper
2 tablespoons prepared mustard	hamburger buns

Brown beef with onion over medium heat; drain. Add remaining ingredients at lower heat, cooking for 20–30 minutes. Serve on hamburger buns.

Shawnlei Breeding
Corporate Human Resources, FL

CHILDREN'S

Snow Cream Cones

2 cups milk
2 eggs, beaten
1½ cups sugar
½ teaspoon salt

3 teaspoons vanilla
clean fresh snow
syrups or fresh fruit (optional)

Mix all ingredients except snow and syrup. Add clean fresh snow until mixture is the texture of ice cream. Add syrups or fresh fruits to taste. Store in freezer.

Gayle Anne VanFulpen
NewLife Publications, FL

Springtime Flower Pots

1 scoop ice cream
1 lollipop

green frosting

Place ice cream in a small dish. Push lollipop stick down into the center of the ice cream scoop for a flower. Use decorator tube frosting to make grass on top of the ice cream hill.

Gayle Anne VanFulpen
NewLife Publications, FL

Squish 'n Squeeze Frosting

1 cup powdered sugar
4½ teaspoons milk

¼ teaspoon vanilla

Place sugar in a 1-quart ziplock bag. Pour the milk and vanilla into the bag, and seal. Squish the bag with your hands for about 2 minutes until frosting is smooth. Squeeze frosting down to the corner of the bag. Cut the tip with scissors. Squeeze frosting over cake.

Ruth Leppard
Crusade Kid

Holiday Entertaining & Menus

As Christians, we have the joy of using our homes, especially our kitchens, to touch our families, friends, neighbors, and even strangers. Whether we prepare a meal for a special occasion or invite others in to experience Christian hospitality just for fun, food becomes one way we express our love and joy.

In this section of the cookbook, we offer menus and traditions that Campus Crusade staff members use to "cook up" a good time. They range from elaborate holiday activities to get-togethers that can be planned in a short time. Whenever you see an italicized recipe title, the complete directions for making the dish will be included in the appropriate section of the cookbook.

We hope that these suggestions will help you form traditions of your own or add to the ones you have, and that you will experience more of the joy that comes from using your kitchen to encourage others and introduce people to our Lord Jesus Christ.

Bright's Christmas Traditions

Bill and Vonette Bright

Christmas Eve Supper

Bright's Traditional Chili
cornbread with butter

tossed green salad
Chess Pie

Christmas Morning Breakfast

Swedish strudel

juice and coffee

449

Christmas Dinner

Martinelli's Spiced Cider or	persimmon salad
sparkling cider	mashed potatoes with giblet gravy
roast turkey with cornbread stuffing	*Jan's Hominy Grits*
whole cranberry sauce	*Scalloped Corn*
Sweet Potato Casserole	*Spiced Peaches*
Vinaigrette Green Beans	pumpkin and pecan pies with
Angel Biscuits	whipped cream

The traditional Christmas celebration for our family begins on Christmas Eve with an early chili supper. Years ago, I made the chili with ground beef, but now I use ground turkey or ground chicken breast to cut down on fat. I serve *Bright's Traditional Chili* in a soup tureen at the table with hot cornbread and butter, a tossed green salad with a choice of dressings, and *Chess Pie*. After dinner, we attend the Christmas Eve service at our church. Later in the evening, we often let our grandchildren open one gift if they can't wait until morning.

On Christmas Day, we open gifts as early as we can pull ourselves out of bed. We open each gift separately, recording who receives what, and enjoying the expressions on the little ones' faces. Then we usually have a breakfast of Swedish strudel that I have purchased at a bakery, along with juice and coffee. We want to save calories for our traditional Christmas dinner.

For the Christmas dinner, I purchase a turkey. Before Christmas Eve, I make *Sweet Potato Casserole*, *Vinaigrette Green Beans*, and *Angel Biscuits*, and freeze them in bags. Either the night before or Christmas morning, I stuff the bird with cornbread stuffing prepared with a base of Mrs. McCobin prepared mix, chopped celery, onion, turkey broth or melted butter (or both), parsley, and more sage for added flavor.

We also have mashed potatoes and gravy made with giblet broth. To make the gravy richer, I process cooked giblet meat in a blender to liquefy, then add it to the turkey drippings. I thicken the gravy with broth mixed with flour, salt, pepper, and other seasonings.

Just before meal time, I set out the food buffet-style. To decorate the table, I pour the cider into stemmed dessert dishes and spoon the cranberries into small stem glasses. I place the persimmon salad in an attractive bowl

and use it as a centerpiece. After we have the blessing, we toast each other with cider.

Everyone begins the meal by eating their salad, then they help themselves to the buffet dishes. As the family finishes the main course, I serve coffee and pie. When everyone has finished eating, we clear the table except for silverware, water glasses, cranberry sauce, and cider glasses. Later, we return to the table for round two, when I put out special bread for turkey sandwiches and make the other dishes available.

Our New Christmas Tradition

Howard and Barbara Ball

Martinelli cider	*Scalloped Oysters*
Caviar Crown appetizer with crackers	Jackson salad
parsnip acorn squash soup	*Trifle*
Crown Roast of Pork with Savory Stuffing	Swedish Egg Coffee

Several years ago, our daughter, Robbyn, invited my husband, Howard, and me to spend Christmas in her new cabin in Truckee, California. Christmas in the snow—what fun! Robbyn, who is a gourmet cook par excellence, suggested replacing the traditional turkey dinner (which we still have on Thanksgiving) with something different. This wasn't easy for me to accept at first, but now I'm delighted. This menu has become a new tradition, and although some years we are separated by many miles (our son, Bob, his wife, Jill, and our grandsons Carson and Max live in Boise, Idaho; Robbyn and our grandson Tobyn live in Vacaville, California), we all serve the same main dishes.

One of our traditions started thirty years ago when we moved to a four-room bungalow in California. En route, the moving company lost all of our Christmas decorations. At Christmas, we purchased inexpensive decorations and also decided to make some of the decorations for the tree. Robbyn chose cranberries, which are easy to string, and Bob chose popcorn, which is more difficult because the popcorn breaks easily. A loud argument broke out between Robbyn and Bob over who had the hardest job. After tears, the job was finished. I kept those strings, and since then have put them on the tree each year. We laugh as we look at the cranberries and popcorn, remembering those days gone by.

I always decorate our dinner table with two large wooden angels given to us by Robbyn. I also add greens, a variety of candles, and family pictures of different sizes. The pictures bring a family closeness even though Howard and I may have other guests who become like our family.

Before the meal, we greet each other with a cider toast and enjoy the *Caviar Crown* appetizer and crackers. I begin the meal by serving the soup, followed by the roast, salad, and oysters. When we finish eating, we sit around the table and enjoy our *Swedish Egg Coffee*. (Howard got the recipe forty-four years ago in a gift shop with the purchase of a coffee pot. He says the coffee saved our marriage.)

Later, we bring out the bowl of *Trifle*, which makes a beautiful presentation. Howard always serves the dessert. To stimulate conversation, we each write a question for every person at the table on the inside of our place cards and read them aloud. This has given our new Christmas traditions a special closeness.

Douglass Holiday Traditions

Judy and Steve Douglass

Steve and I believe that establishing traditions is one of the most important elements of a strong family life. Many of our traditions relate to food and holidays. The first weekend in December, I serve our traditional *Eggnog Pie*. This helps me get our house decorated early, and we can enjoy the holiday feeling for the entire month. Just before Christmas, Steve and I host a festive dessert for the people with whom we work.

Since Steve comes from a Swedish background, every Christmas morning I serve a brunch that includes Swedish pancakes and lingonberries. I grew up in Texas so when we spend the holidays with my family, we eat tamales and chili on Christmas Eve. When we stay at home, I fix split pea soup on Christmas Eve. For the main dinner on Christmas and Thanksgiving, we have the traditional turkey with an old family recipe for cornbread dressing.

We celebrate many holidays with our good friends Ken and Susan Heckman and their children. Our group invariably grows to include singles, neighbors, and family friends who do not have plans for the holiday meal. We bring favorite recipes to share. One of my favorite dishes is corn pudding. One of Susan's best Christmas treats is peaches and cream. For the meal, we set out the good china and silver so our children experience more formal and elegant dining.

Another wonderful part of these meals is the table talk. Each person is asked to share something appropriate for the season. At Thanksgiving, we each share one or two things for which we are thankful. At Christmas, we tell about a highlight from the past year or a meaningful gift from God that we have received. For Easter, we tell about an opportunity we have had to share Christ with someone.

The Twelve Days of Christmas

Lana Jones and the Hawaii Kai Christian Church

To reach out to people with physical or emotional needs during the holidays, the Hawaii Kai Christian Church delivers gifts anonymously for twelve days. These gifts are "from the heart and not the pocketbook." The givers work around the schedules of those they want to surprise. The givers place gifts in plastic bags and, when no one is home, hang them from gates, back doors, or whatever is most convenient.

Here's how the process works. On December 13, deliver the first gift with a card that says something like this:

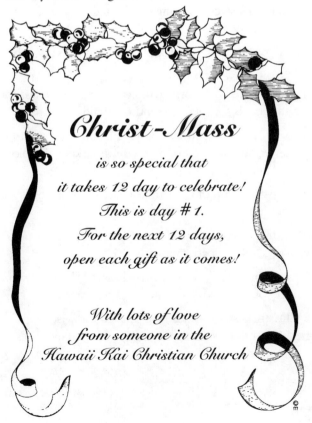

Christ-Mass

*is so special that
it takes 12 day to celebrate!
This is day # 1.
For the next 12 days,
open each gift as it comes!*

*With lots of love
from someone in the
Hawaii Kai Christian Church*

The remaining gifts do not need a card, unless you include a poem or Bible verse. On the 12th day—Christmas Eve—deliver the gift in person with a hug. Invite the person for Christmas dinner if appropriate.

The following list contains suggestions on what to give. On the third day, try to give something that represents the Trinity. If you are giving to a family, on the day that corresponds to the number of children, give each child a bottle of bubbles or other small toy.

Day 1:   One angel ornament (an angel speaks to Mary) or a pineapple, banana bread, small canned ham, devotional book, small poinsettia

Day 2:   1 sheep and 1 donkey miniatures (present at Christ's birth; reveals His role as a lowly shepherd) or one pair of socks, two pot holders, a set of dish towels

Day 3:   Ornaments depicting the Trinity, or 3 candles labeled with Father, Son, and Holy Spirit

Day 4:   4 red candles (to signify Christ's love and His blood) or 4 pieces of fruit, small toys, favorite verses, mugs

Day 5:   Christmas spices of cinnamon, cloves, allspice, nutmeg, and ginger (to give Him a sweet offering) or 5 small tablets, 5 comic strips cut from newspaper

Day 6:   6 sprigs of holly or a six-pack of soda, box of Kudos, bouquet of 6 flowers

Day 7:   7 jingle bells (Jesus is born! Ring out the good news), or unused Christmas cards for them to send to friends

Day 8:   8 bows in bright Christmas colors (His birth brought brightness into our world) or a box of 8 crayons, markers, or colored pencils, tree ornaments

Day 9:   9 tea bags for a cup of Christmas tea or popcorn balls, candy canes, paper doilies

Day 10:   10 muffins or cookies (the sweet love of Jesus) or pieces of decorative soap, holiday paper napkins

Day 11:   11 pieces of straw in a Christmas basket (He was born in a manger) or candy kisses, pencils, paper stars

Day 12:   12 Christmas star cookies (the star led the wise men) or a dozen eggs, doughnuts, stationery with matching envelopes

Take Christ out of Christmas, and December becomes the bleakest and most colorless month of the year. — A. F. Wells

Simple Holiday Entertainment

Ken and Susan Heckman

Entertaining as a family during holiday times is a tradition in our home. We decorate our house for the holiday, birthday, or graduation; set the theme; and use familiar menus. Also, we often make food for a couple of parties at once and freeze the extra. Our priority is to reach out to others by sharing Christ's love, and the food facilitates our goal.

Serving simple meals allows us to spend more time with the guests. We invite a small group so the event doesn't get "wild," and plan kid-friendly meals such as barbecues, hamburgers, hot dogs, grilled chicken, or pizza. We provide multi-generational activities such as board games, foosball, basketball, or Legos. For special holiday times we try to purchase after-season table decorations for 75–90% off, then use them for family fun nights. We also buy inexpensive favors for each guest or let our children make the favors.

We do a lot of "build it at the table" and "cook it at the table" meals. The interaction as you work together is fun for all and encourages the development of relationships. For a "make it at the table" meal, use a large dish with several compartments placed on a lazy susan to hold the various components. We serve individual pizzas or several large ones and set out cheeses, olives, pineapple, cashews, browned hamburger, pepperoni, pizza sauce, onions, olive oil, fresh or dried herbs, even hot dogs. Or we serve a nachos meal by placing chips on cookie sheets or in individual pie plates, then let our guests stack chips with goodies such as cheese, olives, browned hamburger, salsa, chopped cooked chicken. We broil them, then top with sour cream, sliced green onions, olives, salsa, and guacamole.

Some of our favorite "build it at the table" meals are tacos; burritos; taco, chef, or Chinese chicken salads; *Javanese Dinner*; sub sandwiches; and topped baked potatoes. We add warmed rolls or garlic sticks along with a simple fruit salad, green salad, or finger salad of bite-size raw vegetables with salad dressing as a dip.

Our favorite "cook it at the table" meal is Mickey Mouse pancakes (1 large circle with 2 small circles connected as ears) with bacon, ham, or sausage. Others are grilled sandwiches, quesadillas, and of course fondue (chicken, beef, shrimp, or chocolate). We also enjoy a dessert made of wonton skins with a ½-inch slit cut lengthwise in the middle of each. Pull one end through the slit, then deep fry at the table in a fondue pot until light golden color. Drain, then drip honey over or dust with powdered sugar.

To host a Quilting Bee, invite a group of adult single and married friends or a family or two to enjoy a "work, visit, eat evening." During the Christmas season, ask guests to bring cards to address, gifts to wrap, catalogs to order from, or just a nail file to fix their nails. Provide something light to eat, usually dessert and munchies. *Peach Melba* from London is a long-time favorite. Other get-togethers may feature a craft time or framing a picture, a "bring your photos and albums and catch-up time," or bring your mending. This is a fun time to try new recipes or even cook together. One time we asked everyone to bring a new appetizer and the recipe to share.

Lepine Family Thanksgiving
Bob and Mary Ann Lepine

As a family, we follow a tradition of eating *Hardtack* during our Thanksgiving meal. As an unleavened bread, hardtack lasts for months without spoiling. The Pilgrims brought hardtack during the voyages across the Atlantic Ocean.

As our family eats our traditional *Hardtack*, we remind each other of the hardships the Pilgrims endured to come to our country. I ask, "Who else can you think of who needed bread to sustain them on a long trip?" The answer, "The Israelites, who ate the daily manna that God provided after He brought them out of slavery in Egypt." Asking and answering this question gives family members the opportunity to remember how God sustains us and provides for our needs.

Rainey's Thanksgiving Brunch
Dennis and Barbara Rainey

Before we leave for a traditional Thanksgiving meal at Barbara's parents' home, we and our kids enjoy a special brunch. Everyone dresses in their Sunday clothes. The children make lace cards, decorate the table, and set it with our finest plates and glasses. They place five kernels of corn on each plate and set a place card at each setting. We make *Rainey's Thanksgiving French Toast*, which takes 45 minutes to bake. While the meal is in the oven, we gather around the table and read sections of *The Light and the Glory*, by Peter Marshall and David Manuel, which tells of the strong Christian faith of many original American settlers, including the Pilgrims.

Then we pass a basket around the table, and each person places one kernel of corn into it and mentions one thing for which he or she is thankful. Once the basket has gone around five times, we write what we have said on our place cards. We save the cards to look over in future years.

Significant Celebrations

Ney Bailey and Mary Graham

Mary Graham's Thanksgiving

strawberry-banana Jell-O with
    cream cheese
fresh spinach salad
turkey with dressing
Sweet Potato and Carrot Purée

fresh vegetables
mashed potatoes with gravy
homemade rolls
pumpkin and pecan pies

Many years ago, I invited my entire office staff and their families for Thanksgiving dinner. I set large, round tables for the adults and low coffee tables for the children. But I forgot one small detail—I'd never stuffed and cooked a turkey! The morning of the party, I wondered what on earth to do with it.

I share a home with Ney Bailey, but she was away for the holiday. I remembered that her father, who lived in Shreveport, was a gourmet cook. I called him and he talked me through the process, from washing the bird to seasoning the stuffing to stirring the gravy. ("You have to stir it like the devil!") When I hung up the telephone, I was as confident as Julia Childs. That was the best turkey I've ever tasted—before or since. And the Thanksgiving meal is now my favorite one to prepare.

Although we're single, Ney and I enjoy inviting families to our home on Thanksgiving. Children add a dimension that is incomparable. Ney finds

Bible verses about giving thanks that children can read. Before the meal, we ask them to read the verses, then ask everyone what they are especially thankful for. One secret Ney and I have learned is to ask our guests to limit themselves to one conversation at the table so everyone can participate.

If we invite a large crowd, we seat the children at another table. We take extra care to make their table just as lovely as the adult one. We provide a centerpiece (sometimes with sweet, edible touches), linens, pretty dishes (even if they're paper), and lovely glasses that little hands can hold. We use name cards and put little items beside the plates such as stickers or small toys.

Roast Turkey a la Ney's Daddy

Preheat oven to 325 degrees. Wash the 18–22 pound turkey, inspecting well for pin feathers. Dry the turkey inside and out. Rub the skin of the turkey with 1½ sticks softened butter. Cover the turkey with salt and pepper (yes, cover!). Place the turkey breast-side-down on a turkey rack with water in the pan up to the bottom of the rack. (It's not as pretty when you cook it with the breast side down but the white meat is much juicier.) "Tent" the turkey with foil placed loosely over the bird. While baking, baste with natural juices in the pan every 30–45 minutes. Roast for 3½–4 hours, until the thigh juices run clear and the legs open slightly. Let the turkey set for at least 30 minutes before carving.

"Why do you look for the living among the dead?
He is not here; he has risen!" (Luke 24:5)

Easter Party

biggest punch bowl you can make	chips
take-out chicken	veggies and dip
salads of every imaginable variety	deviled eggs
that can be made the day before	Easter cake (see directions below)
baked beans	fresh strawberries dipped in chocolate

For Christians, Easter Sunday is the most significant celebration. Yet for many families, Easter has fewer traditions than any other major holiday of the year. Unlike Thanksgiving, Christmas, and birthdays, the question is often asked, "What should we do on Easter?" Once the Sunday morning service ends, what can a person do to make the day more memorable?

One year, Ney Bailey and I planned a party for some of our dearest friends and their families. What began as a little party grew into a tradition that we have honored for the past few years.

The day of the party, we have a huge punch bowl ready when our guests walk in the door and replenish it as often as necessary. As they arrive, we assign our guests to teams, making sure that family members are on the same team. The rule is, if you are old enough to walk, you are old enough to play.

Then we have an egg hunt with 500 plastic eggs filled with M&Ms. After the egg hunt, relay races, and contests, we ask each team to act out skits or stories expressing the real meaning of Easter. We offer prizes to make winning worth the effort. The children are thrilled to be on teams with their parents, and everyone performs their very best.

While the teams huddle to plan their part of the program (which will be performed after dinner), Ney and I and volunteers slip into the kitchen to prepare a simple picnic-style meal that we serve on paper plates. We allow our guests to eat inside or outside, setting their plates on tables or their laps. After everyone finishes eating, we clear away the mess.

Then we enjoy the "performances." Scores are tallied and prizes presented. By then, we are ready to thank the Lord, acknowledge the joy of being together for such wonderful fellowship, and say goodnight.

Easter Cake

Make two round layer cakes. Cut one as shown to make bow tie and ears. Arrange uncut cake on cake tray. Add bow tie and ears. Frost with white icing and sprinkle with coconut. Use jelly beans for eyes and licorice laces for whiskers and mouth.

Special Dinner for Entertaining

Ingrid Bunner

variously colored peppers filled
with a favorite soup
red potatoes on rosemary stalks
baked fish fillets

colorful vegetable
Mandarin Orange Salad
Chocolate Bags

Find peppers of different colors such as green, orange, red, and yellow. Peppers are usually pointed on the bottom, so make sure they can stand before you buy them. Cut off the top, clean out the inside, and rinse. Fill with a soup and put the top back on. (The peppers don't hold very much, but they can be refilled.) Place each pepper on a paper doily on a small plate.

Plan a whole fish fillet for each person you are serving. Also buy the smallest red potatoes you can find. Purchase rosemary in stalks, and remove the leaves at the bottom of the stalks. Leave some leaves at the top.

Bake the fish fillets at 450 degrees for about 40 minutes for 4 pounds of fish. Parboil the potatoes and thread 3 potatoes on each stalk of rosemary like skewers. Put on a pan and drizzle olive oil over them and sprinkle over any rosemary you have taken off the stalks. Bake at 350 degrees for 20 minutes or until potatoes are done. Serve each guest 1–2 stalks. The potatoes you don't thread onto the stalks can be baked in a pan with olive oil and rosemary, and served in a bowl for second helpings.

To round out the meal, serve *Mandarin Orange Salad* with dressing and a colorful vegetable. Then finish the meal by serving *Chocolate Bags*.

Index

𝒟

2

R

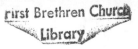
W

Y

Z